An exciting study of ancient slavery in Greece and Rome

This book provides an introduction to pivotal issues in the study of classical (Greek and Roman) slavery. The span of topics is broad – ranging from everyday resistance to slavery to philosophical justifications of slavery, and from the process of enslavement to the decline of slavery after the fall of the Western Roman Empire. The book uses a wide spectrum of types of evidence, and relies on concrete and vivid examples whenever possible.

Introductory chapters provide historical context and a clear and concise discussion of the methodological difficulties of studying ancient slavery. The following chapters are organized around central topics in slave studies: enslavement, economics, politics, culture, sex and family life, manumission and ex-slaves, everyday conflict, revolts, representations, philosophy and law, and decline and legacy. Chapters open with general discussions of important scholarly controversies and the challenges of our ancient evidence, and case studies from the classical Greek, Hellenistic, and Roman periods provide detailed and concrete explorations of the issues.

- Organized by key themes in slave studies with in-depth classical case studies
- Emphasizes Greek/Roman comparisons and contrasts
- Features helpful customized maps
- Topics range from demography to philosophy, from Linear B through the fall of the empire in the west
- Features myriad types of evidence: literary, historical, legal and philosophical texts, the bible, papyri, epitaphs, lead letters, curse tablets, art, manumission inscriptions, and more

Ancient Greek and Roman Slavery provides a general survey of classical slavery and is particularly appropriate for college courses on Greek and Roman slavery, on comparative slave societies, and on ancient social history. It will also be of great interest to history enthusiasts and scholars, especially those interested in slavery in different periods and societies.

Peter Hunt is a professor at the University of Colorado where he teaches a wide variety of courses including Greek and Roman slavery. He has written two books: *Slaves, Warfare, and Ideology in the Greek Historians* and *War and Peace, and Alliance in Demosthenes' Athens*. His previous work on slavery includes chapters in the *Cambridge World History of Slavery* and the *Oxford Handbook of Greek and Roman Slaveries* as well as the slavery chapter in the *Cambridge World History, vol. 4*.

To Isabel and Julia

Ancient Greek and Roman Slavery

Peter Hunt

WILEY Blackwell

This edition first published 2018

© 2018 Peter Hunt

All rights reserved. No part of this publication may be reproduced, stored in a retrieval system, or transmitted, in any form or by any means, electronic, mechanical, photocopying, recording or otherwise, except as permitted by law. Advice on how to obtain permission to reuse material from this title is available at http://www.wiley.com/go/permissions.

The right of Peter Hunt to be identified as the author of this work has been asserted in accordance with law.

Registered Office
John Wiley & Sons, Inc., 111 River Street, Hoboken, NJ 07030, USA
John Wiley & Sons Ltd, The Atrium, Southern Gate, Chichester, West Sussex, PO19 8SQ, UK

Editorial Office
350 Main Street, Malden, MA 02148-5020, USA

For details of our global editorial offices, customer services, and more information about Wiley products visit us at www.wiley.com.

Wiley also publishes its books in a variety of electronic formats and by print-on-demand. Some content that appears in standard print versions of this book may not be available in other formats.

Limit of Liability/Disclaimer of Warranty
While the publisher and authors have used their best efforts in preparing this work, they make no representations or warranties with respect to the accuracy or completeness of the contents of this work and specifically disclaim all warranties, including without limitation any implied warranties of merchantability or fitness for a particular purpose. No warranty may be created or extended by sales representatives, written sales materials or promotional statements for this work. The fact that an organization, website, or product is referred to in this work as a citation and/or potential source of further information does not mean that the publisher and authors endorse the information or services the organization, website, or product may provide or recommendations it may make. This work is sold with the understanding that the publisher is not engaged in rendering professional services. The advice and strategies contained herein may not be suitable for your situation. You should consult with a specialist where appropriate. Further, readers should be aware that websites listed in this work may have changed or disappeared between when this work was written and when it is read. Neither the publisher nor authors shall be liable for any loss of profit or any other commercial damages, including but not limited to special, incidental, consequential, or other damages.

Library of Congress Cataloging-in-Publication Data

Names: Hunt, Peter, 1961- author.
Title: Ancient Greek and Roman slavery / Peter Hunt, University of Colorado,
  Boulder, Colorado.
Description: Hoboken, NJ : Wiley-Blackwell, 2018. | Includes bibliographical
  references and index. | Description based on print version record and CIP
  data provided by publisher; resource not viewed.
Identifiers: LCCN 2017013713 (print) | LCCN 2017017166 (ebook) | ISBN
  9781119421061 (epub) | ISBN 9781405188050 (hardback) | ISBN 9781405188067
  (paper)
Subjects: LCSH: Slavery—Greece—History. | Slavery—Rome—History. | BISAC:
  LITERARY CRITICISM / Ancient & Classical.
Classification: LCC HT863 (ebook) | LCC HT863 .H86 2018 (print) | DDC
  306.3/6209495—dc23
LC record available at https://lccn.loc.gov/2017013713

Cover image: World History Archive / Alamy Stock Photo
Cover design by Wiley

Set in 10/12 Warnock Pro by Aptara Inc., New Delhi, India

1 2018

Contents

List of Illustrations   *vii*
Preface   *ix*
Acknowledgments   *xi*
Modern and Ancient References: Abbreviations   *xiii*

1   Introduction and Historical Context   *1*

2   Definitions and Evidence   *17*

3   Enslavement   *31*

4   Economics   *49*

5   Politics   *67*

6   Culture   *83*

7   Sex and Family Life   *99*

8   Manumission and Ex-Slaves   *117*

9   Everyday Conflict   *137*

10   Revolts   *155*

11   Representations   *173*

12   Philosophy and Law   *191*

13   Decline and Legacy   *209*

References   *221*
Index   *239*

Illustrations

Figures

Figure 1.1 A tablet from Pylos, ca. 1200 BCE, written in Linear B syllabograms.
Figure 3.1 Epitaph of Timothea.
Figure 4.1 Slave auction scene.
Figure 7.1 Greek symposium scene depicted on a vase found in Campania.
Figure 7.2 Letter about rent for live-in *hetaira*.
Figure 8.1 Family tree of Pasion.
Figure 8.2 Columbaria 1 in the Codini Vineyard near Rome.
Figure 9.1 Slave holding chamber pot.
Figure 9.2 Egyptian WANTED poster for runaway slave.
Figure 10.1 Coin commemorating the suppression of the second Sicilian slave revolt.
Figure 10.2 Coin of the slave king Antiochus (originally Eunus).
Figure 11.1 Grave relief of Hegeso.
Figure 11.2 Terracotta of a comic slave mask.
Figure 11.3 *Lararium* in the House of the Vettii.
Figure 12.1 EID MAR Denarius, Roman silver coin (42 BCE).
Figure 12.2 Metal slave collar.

Maps

Map 1 Mainland Greece and the Aegean.
Map 2 The Roman Empire around 150 CE.
Map 3 The powers of the Mediterranean in 220 BCE.
Map 4 Origins of slaves at Athens in the fifth and fourth centuries BCE.
Map 5 Spartacus at large in Italy.
Map 6 After the disintegration of the Roman Empire: Europe and the Mediterranean in 530 CE.

Preface

I wrote this book with two audiences in mind. I hope it will be a useful resource for college courses on Greek and Roman slavery and a supplementary text for more general classes involving ancient social history. But it should also provide a general introduction for any other reader who wants or needs to know more about this fascinating topic, for example, those interested in comparative slave societies or in other aspects of ancient Greek or Roman culture or history. These two intended audiences have determined many aspects of this book.

In particular, within the main text I have preferred what I consider the clearest and most interesting presentations of a topic rather than the most recent. I have kept references to secondary scholarship sparse and unobtrusive, and I have confined myself to works in English whenever possible. Nevertheless, my citations and "Suggested Reading" sections include recent works and should provide a good start for further investigations of particular topics—for the purpose, for instance, of research papers. I have also not hesitated to cite my own scholarly publications when these provide more detailed treatments of topics or arguments I mention. I do not claim to be a particularly important scholar of ancient slavery, but I am the one with whom I most frequently agree.

The book is organized topically rather than having a Greek and then a Roman half. Each chapter sets out a major issue in the study of slavery and considers theoretical approaches, our ancient evidence, and key controversies. Contrasts and parallels between Greek and Roman slavery usually play a role in either the introduction or conclusion of each chapter. The bodies of most chapters are devoted to case studies from classical Greece and Rome – and Hellenistic examples play a role in several chapters. The focus on particular cases allows greater depth and I have been willing to forgo general coverage for the sake of this goal. For example, in Chapter 7, I focus on slave prostitutes in classical Athens but not at Rome and on slave families at Rome without attempting equal treatment for Greek cases. The quantity and richness of our evidence has often determined such choices. And even in the cases for which we seem to have the best evidence, I'll need to admit our ignorance regularly.

Despite this selectivity, this is not a short book. I begin with two introductory chapters: an overview of classical slavery within the context of Greek and Roman history and a chapter about the challenges historians face studying ancient slavery and the methods they use. The next three chapters (3–5) consider large-scale issues about the institution of slavery: the supply of slaves, the economics of slavery, and its political ramifications. The next three chapters (6–8) treat aspects of the lives of ancient slaves: their culture, sex and family lives; manumission from slavery and its consequences. Chapters 9 and 10 consider the antagonistic aspects of the relationships between slaves and masters: first slave resistance on an everyday and individual level and then open slave revolts. Two chapters (11 and 12) focus on the perspectives of slaveholders: how they represented slaves in literature and art and then the philosophical and legal justifications, critiques, and ameliorations of slavery. I conclude with a discussion of the decline of classical slavery and its legacy extending to the present.

Acknowledgments

In writing this book, I have benefitted greatly from the support of institutions, colleagues, friends, research assistants, editors, and family. I have been lucky to have such fine and supportive colleagues in the Department of Classics at the University of Colorado Boulder. I owe special thanks to Noel Lenski – now at Yale – and to John Gibert for their advice and conversation, and for sharing some of their work with me pre-publication – and to Cathy Cameron in the Department of Anthropology, who did the same. My treatment of Epictetus and slavery owes a great deal to an honors thesis that my student, Angela Funk, wrote on that topic. The University of Colorado has supported my research and my writing with a LEAP grant for associate professors, a sabbatical, a fellowship from the Center for the Humanities and the Arts, and a College Scholar Award. I am also most grateful for the hard work of several graduate research assistants: the meticulous efforts of Stephanie Krause and Wesley Wood contributed a great deal to tightening the manuscript up for publication; they also drafted the maps; David Kear's long experience as an editor greatly improved the first half of the manuscript. John Nebel generously allowed me to use a photo of his own EID MAR denarius and arranged the permission from Gorny & Mosch for the image of the Manius Aquillius denarius.

I also owe thanks to several skillful and meticulous editors from Wiley-Blackwell: Haze Humbert first suggested the idea for this book and supervised the project over the years; Deirdre Ilkson edited early drafts of several chapters; and Louise Spencely edited the final manuscript. The two anonymous readers provided constructive criticism as well as many helpful suggestions and improved the manuscript greatly. Sara Forsdyke and David Lewis generously shared some of their forthcoming work with me; I am also indebted to them for valuable discussions of ancient slavery on several occasions. I am immensely grateful to Susan Treggiari for her astute comments and suggestions on several chapters; and to my wife, Mitzi Lee, who read over the material related to her field of expertise, ancient philosophy, and saved me from several missteps there. Of course, I alone am responsible for the mistakes that remain.

Modern and Ancient References: Abbreviations

References to modern scholarship are by author and date – either in footnotes or parentheses – with the full citations in the References section.

I cite ancient authors, by line numbers in drama and poetry or by book, chapter, and subsections in most prose authors. You may be more used to page citations, but those are only correct for one particular edition or translation of an author, whereas the lines, books, chapters, and section are usually the same across all translations and editions – though some translations of plays and poetry do not follow the original line numbers. "Fr." stands for "fragment" and I refer to the collection of fragments by author and date, which you can look up in the bibliography – except for the *Fragmente der griechichen Historiker* listed in the abbreviations below.

I have followed the naming and numbering conventions of the Loeb Classical Library whenever possible. I cite the "Attic orators" – Aeschines, Antiphon, Demosthenes, Isaeus, Isocrates, and Lysias – by Loeb speech number alone. As is customary, I cite certain speeches that are probably by Apollodorus as by Pseudo-Demosthenes, [Demosthenes], where the square brackets indicate that the speeches are spurious, that is, falsely ascribed to Demosthenes. I cite other spurious speeches of Demosthenes with square brackets as well as the *Constitution of the Athenians*, falsely ascribed to Xenophon, [Xenophon], and the *Oeconomica*, falsely ascribed to Aristotle, [Aristotle]. I refer to Didorus Siculus, *Library of History*, Herodotus, *The Histories*, Livy, *History of Rome*, and Thucydides, *History of the Peloponnesian War* by the author's name alone.

Especially in epigraphy and papyrology there are standard modern collections, typically abbreviated. I use the following in this book:

BGU: Berliner griechische Urkunden, 1895–
https://www.degruyter.com/view/serial/119344

CIL: Corpus Inscriptionum Latinarum, 1853–
http://cil.bbaw.de/cil_en/index_en.html

FGrH: Fragmente der griechischen Historiker, 1923–
http://referenceworks.brillonline.com/browse/brill-s-new-jacoby IG

IG: Inscriptiones Graecae, 1860–
http://www.bbaw.de/en/research/ig
http://epigraphy.packhum.org/

P.Oxy.: Oxyrhynchus Papyri, 1898–
http://www.papyrology.ox.ac.uk/POxy/

SEG: Supplementum Epigraphicum Graecum, 1923–
http://www.brill.com/publications/online-resources/supplementum-epigraphicum-graecum-online

Some of these collections are complicated multi-volume collections with publication dates spanning a century and various publishers and editors. Online versions are sometimes available. There's no hiding the fact that these are not easy to use, especially for students getting started. Wikipedia has articles on each of these sources and is often a good place to start. I have also provided helpful web addresses either for online versions or for the current publisher.

For the sake of clarity and ease of use, I have otherwise avoided abbreviations.

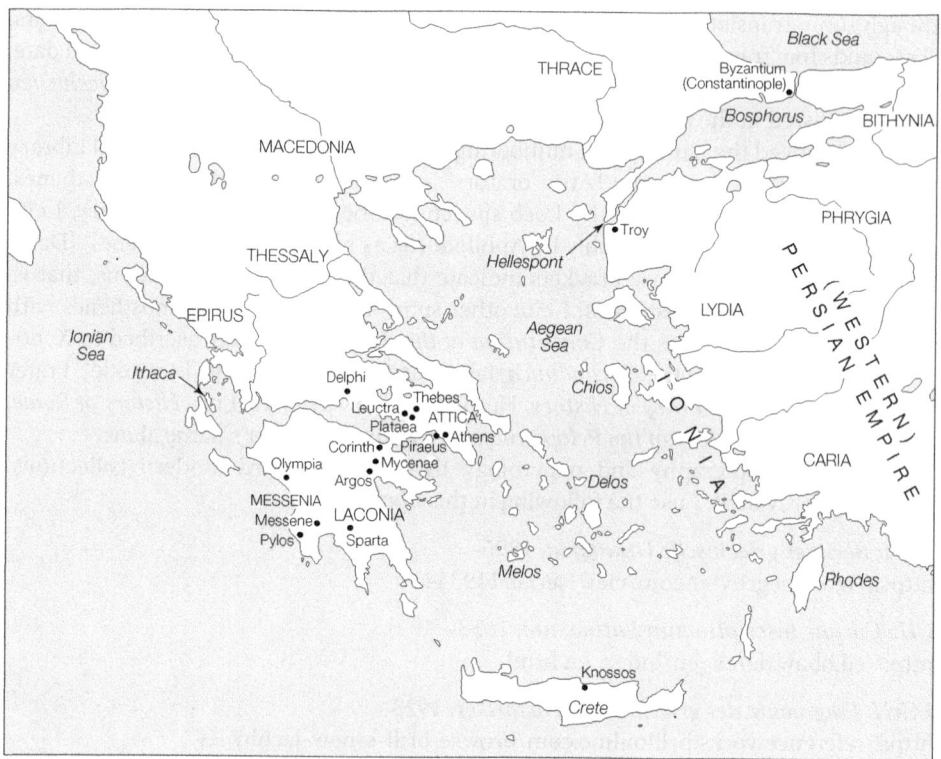

Map 1 Mainland Greece and the Aegean. *Source*: Courtesy of Stephanie Krause.

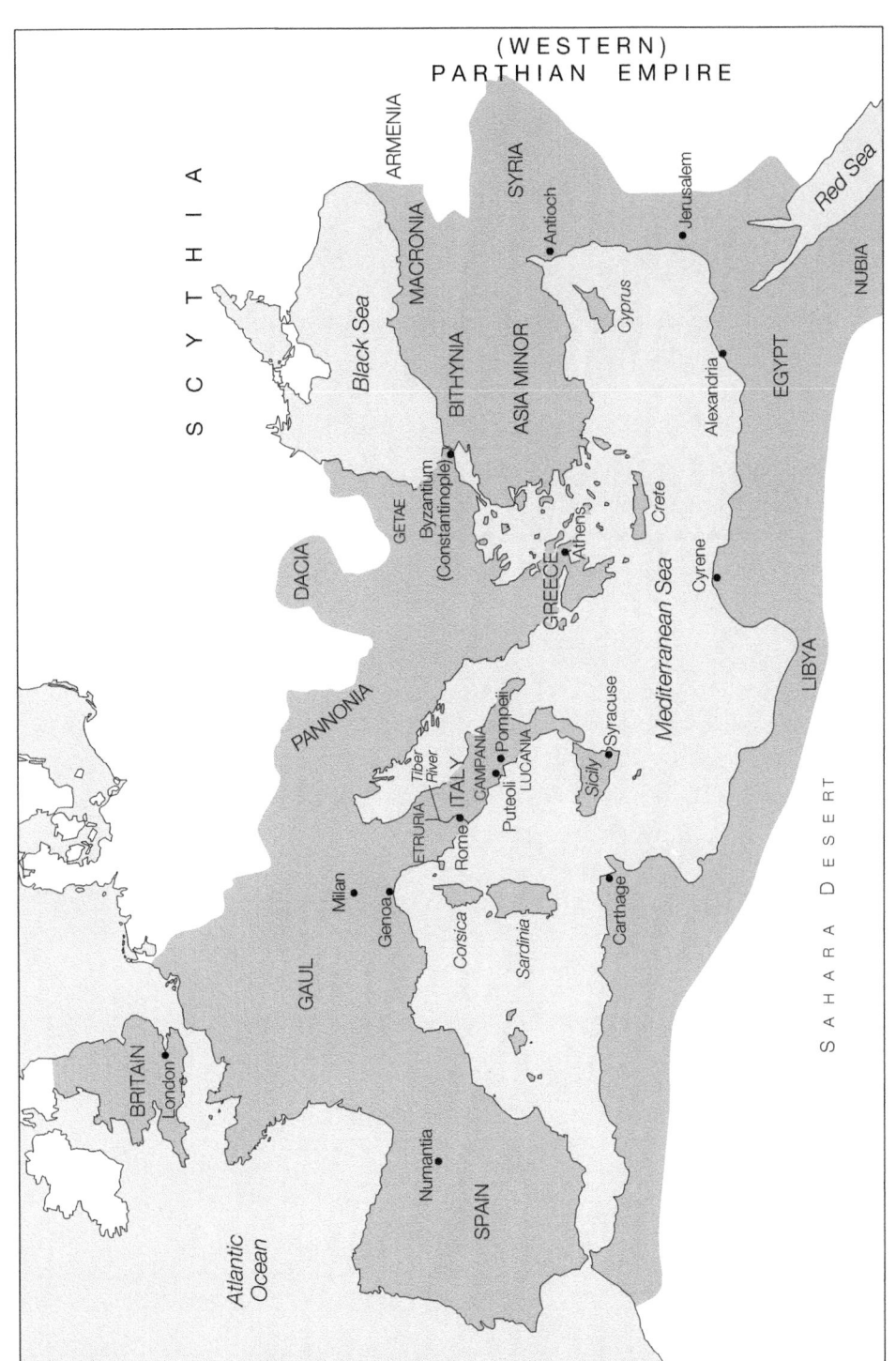

Map 2 The Roman Empire around 150 CE. *Source:* Courtesy of Stephanie Krause.

1

Introduction and Historical Context

Slaves who love the class of masters provoke a great war with the other slaves.
Euripides (Athenian playwright, ca. 480–406 BCE),
Alexander, fr. 50 in Nauck 1889

Slavery is a cruel institution, but it was central to ancient Greek and Roman civilization for around a thousand years. The prevalence of classical slavery justifies the claim that, during some periods, Greece and Rome were true "slave societies" just as surely as the pre-Civil War American South. But reconstructing and understanding Greek and Roman slavery has long presented a tricky and complex, but fascinating, challenge for historians, who have had to rely on elegant arguments, painstaking investigations, and bold inferences from evidence that is often sparse and difficult to interpret. That evidence is also biased since it is slaveholders rather than slaves who wrote almost every text that has survived from antiquity. For example, the Euripides quotation above is the only hint we have of what must have been a common dynamic among household slaves: conflicts between those slaves determined to resist their oppression in small ways or large and those hoping to get ahead by pleasing their masters. And even this single short quotation comes from a play written by a slave master.

Despite the paucity of evidence from slaves themselves, the issues involved have generated passionate debates. Historical interest has also been piqued by a general admiration for the sophistication and historical significance of classical culture and the inevitable question, "how could they have allowed and indeed approved of slavery?" So, instead of giving up, historians have devised ingenious methods to span the millennia between us and the classical world and to get the most out of our recalcitrant evidence. For example, slaves often paid to buy their own freedom. A long series of such payments was recorded on a stone retaining wall below the temple of Apollo at Delphi in Greece, in part to publicize the terms of the agreement and thus to prevent either party from reneging. The increase of the average price paid from the third to the first century BCE suggests that the demand for slaves in Roman Italy outpaced the number of people enslaved in Rome's almost constant wars in the second century BCE (Hopkins and Roscoe 1978, 134–71) – a surprising result we'll discuss in Chapter 4. Though not all such bold theories have withstood scrutiny, we would not understand Greek and Roman slavery nearly as well as we do were it not for historians willing to try new approaches and to push against the limits of our evidence.

Ancient Greek and Roman Slavery, First Edition. Peter Hunt.
© 2018 Peter Hunt. Published 2018 by John Wiley & Sons, Ltd.

An understanding of Greek and Roman slavery is important for several cultural and historical reasons. First, students interested in the culture of the classical world, ancient Greece and Rome, need to understand its system of slavery, one of its central institutions. In classical literature, for example, you find slaves wherever you turn. Their presence is often obvious: Achilles and Agamemnon quarrel over captive slave women in Homer's *Iliad*; near the beginning of Aristotle's *Politics*, we find his infamous doctrine of natural slavery; witty, scheming slaves often drive the action of Roman comedies; powerful ex-slave administrators play a large role in Tacitus' history of the reign of the emperor Claudius. Less obviously, slavery permeated Greek and Roman thinking, as evidenced by their frequent use of analogies to slavery. When the orator Demosthenes appealed to the Athenians not to submit to *slavery* to Macedonia, he was not saying that the Athenians were in imminent danger of actual slavery – being sold away from their families or whipped for refusing an order. Nevertheless, his metaphorical use of *slavery* evoked a concrete, everyday, and violent institution familiar to his audience.

Second, classical slavery has had profound effects on modern slave societies, not just in the American South, but also in Brazil, the Caribbean, and elsewhere – some of which we'll explore in the final chapter. From the seventeenth through the nineteenth century, the study of the Classics played a huge role in Western education and thus Greek and Roman models were constantly present in the minds of slaveholders in the New World. They were deeply influenced, for example, by the Roman law of slavery. George Fitzhugh, in his infamous defense of slavery in the US South, *A Sociology for the South* (1854), drew on Aristotle's doctrine of Natural Slavery to justify slavery based on race. Classical models often shaped the way that modern slaveholders conceived of and justified slavery.

Third, classical styles, ideas, and values have remained important to Western culture in general, so understanding the role of slavery in ancient Greece and Rome can yield insight into ideas and debates important to the modern period. In the nineteenth century, at the beginning of the *Communist Manifesto*, Karl Marx uses the opposition of slave and master in antiquity as his first example of the class struggle between oppressor and oppressed: "The history of all hitherto existing society is the history of class struggles: Freeman and slave, patrician and plebian, lord and serf..." (Marx and Engels 1955 [originally 1848], chapter 1). Following his lead, several modern communist groups have named themselves after Spartacus, the leader of a great slave revolt against the Romans. The philosopher Friedrich Nietzsche in *On the Genealogy of Morals, A Polemic* condemned Christianity as a slavish religion in contrast to Greek and Roman paganism (Nietzsche 1994 [originally 1887], I.8–10). Finally, the West's cherished ideal of political freedom had its origin in a slave society, classical Greece, where the opposite of freedom was a vivid and concrete reality: slavery.

So far, I have been treating Greek and Roman slavery as if they constituted a natural unit. This may at first appear arbitrary. Linking together ancient Greece and Rome as the "classical" civilizations is arguably an artifact of post-Renaissance Western cultural history and of the important role both Greek and Roman literature, art, and philosophy has played in that history. In fact, the culture and society of the thousand-odd Greek city-states of the classical period or of the later and larger Hellenistic kingdoms was quite different from that of Rome and the enormous empire it eventually controlled. Nevertheless, historical links and cultural similarities justify treating the slavery of Greece and Rome together. Even the contrasts between Greek and Roman slavery – of which there are many – often prove to be illuminating of both.

Over the course of the second and first centuries BCE (from 200–31 BCE) Rome conquered Greece itself and the Hellenistic kingdoms of the Eastern Mediterranean. Greece, however, did not disappear after its conquest. Rather, Greek-speaking elites continued to dominate the eastern half of the Roman Empire. Indeed, this Greek-speaking eastern half of the empire survived as the Byzantine Empire even after the dissolution of the Western Roman Empire in the fifth century CE. So, Greek history and the history of Greek slavery became part of Roman and then medieval history. For example, papyrus posters advertising rewards for the return of fugitive slaves survive, preserved in the desert. Most of these date from the period when Egypt was part of the Roman Empire and partially subject to its laws, but they are written in Greek, which remained the language and provided the cultural background of the elite in this former Hellenistic kingdom. It is simplistic to categorize slavery in Egypt in this period as purely Greek or Roman – not to mention the Egyptian context.

Although Rome conquered Greece, Greek art, literature, and thought had a profound influence on Roman culture. The embrace and imitation of Greek culture by the Romans has important consequences for the study of Roman slavery. For example, Roman philosophers were all adherents to one or another of the schools of philosophy founded by the Greeks. To understand the views on slavery of Seneca (c. 4 BCE–65 CE), a Roman aristocrat and advisor to the emperor Nero, we need to keep in mind that, as a Stoic, he was an adherent of a school of Hellenistic Philosophy. It is still possible to take these considerations into account and to treat either Greek or Roman slavery by itself. This book capitalizes on the benefits of covering the two subjects together and especially on the enlightening contrasts and parallels such an approach allows.

Greek History and Slavery: An Overview

It is not only the connections between Greek and Roman history that are important here; in general, a system of slavery can only be understood within its wider historical context. In the case of Greek and Roman slavery, this context extends over more than two thousand years and, largely because of the extent of the Roman Empire, comprises slavery from Spain to Iraq and from Britain to Egypt. So we are not talking about just a little historical context, but a lot. Here I can only provide a brief sketch of those aspects of Greek and Roman history most relevant to slavery. As I treat particular issues in later chapters, I'll provide more background. For now, it is just the big picture that we need.

The first speakers of Greek probably migrated to the area we now know as Greece around 2000 BCE. By 1600 BCE they had developed the high culture and bureaucratic states that scholars call Mycenaean civilization after the spectacular finds at the site of Mycenae in the Peloponnese. The Mycenaean states kept records on clay tablets in a script known as Linear B. Some tablets contain the Linear B version of the classical Greek word for slave: *doulos/doulē* (masculine/feminine). The people so described are usually unnamed, humble, and dependent on a more important person, often a religious figure. But they sometimes seem to own land and pay taxes, something we would not expect of slaves. Other tablets list groups of workers supported by state rations, including women and children but no men.[1] Some groups are described with ethnic adjectives

---

1 E.g., the Pylos Aa/Ab/Ad series with Shelmerdine 2008, 138–139 and Chadwick and Ventris 1973, 156.

1 Introduction and Historical Context

Table 1.1 The periods of Greek history.

Dates	Historical period	
1600–1150 BCE	Mycenaean Civilization	Bureaucratic palace governments, writing in Linear B
1150–750 BCE	Dark Age	Decline in population and material conditions, no writing during most of period
750–500 BCE	Archaic Period	Growth in population, alphabetic writing, formation of city-states, Panhellenism and colonization
500–323 BCE	Classical Period	Democracy in Athens, Persian and Peloponnesian Wars, most influential period of Greek culture, ends with Macedonian dominance of mainland Greece
323–30 BCE	Hellenistic Period	After Alexander's conquest of the Persian Empire, Greek and Macedonian elites ruled large areas of the Near East. Starting after 200 BCE, Rome defeats, dominates, and eventually annexes the Hellenistic Kingdoms
30 BCE–400 CE	Roman Period	Greece and Hellenistic kingdoms part of Roman Empire
400–1453 CE	Byzantine Empire	Eastern, Greek-speaking Roman Empire survives the fall of the western Empire, finally falls to the Ottomans

that indicate that they were foreigners and, according to one reconstruction, slave captives whose husbands had been killed in war. Thus slavery may well have existed in Greece as far back as we have textual evidence. Unfortunately, we do not know much more about Mycenaean slavery.

In the century or so after 1200 BCE, the Mycenaean palaces were destroyed, population plummeted, large-scale construction ceased, and literacy was entirely lost – thus this period is known as a Dark Age. Historians did not even know that the Mycenaeans were Greek speakers until Michael Ventris, a professional architect rather than a scholar, deciphered the writing system in 1952. Writing appears again in Greece in the

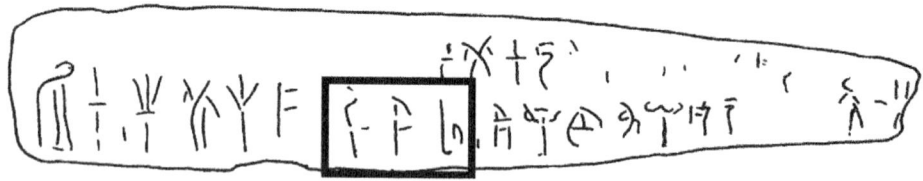

Figure 1.1 Slaves in the Linear B Tablets? A tablet from Pylos, ca. 1200 BCE, written in Linear B syllabograms: "At (?) Pylos, slaves of (?) the Priestess, on account (?) of sacred gold: 14 [ ]women" – or perhaps "in exchange for sacred gold." The word in the box, do-e-ra[i], is the antecedent for the classical Greek word for slave (feminine: *doulai*), but what the term implied in Linear B is not clear. "The Priestess" was an important, religious figure. *Source*: PY Ae 303 translated in Duhoux 2008, 295–296. Illustration from *The Pylos Tablets: Texts of the Inscriptions Found 1939–1954* by Emmett L. Bennett. Copyright © 1955, renewed 1983 by Princeton University Press. Reprinted by permission.

course of the eighth century, 800–700 BCE, after the adaptation of the Phoenician alphabet for writing Greek. This was only one of the many ways in which archaic Greece drew upon the older, larger, and more sophisticated civilizations in the Near East: Babylonia, Assyria, Lydia, and Egypt. All of these societies possessed slaves, who are mentioned already in the twenty-third century BCE and in the Code of Hammurabi, but none were slave societies (Turley 2000, 39). It is possible that archaic Greek aristocrats, in a newly prosperous society and enamored of other aspects of Eastern art, clothing, and technology, decided that a bought slave was another luxurious foreign status symbol they would like to acquire. But this is not the only scenario we can imagine. Slavery was common throughout the ancient world: in particular, the enslavement of the women of a defeated enemy was almost ubiquitous. Greeks probably did not need to learn about slavery from anybody.

The return of writing to Greece was far from the whole story. The eighth century also saw growth in population, wealth, and trade, as well as cultural changes. In particular, the Homeric *Iliad* and *Odyssey*, our best evidence for eighth-century culture and society, were first committed to writing at this time. Slaves play important roles in both epics. For example, upon his return home, the hero Odysseus, an exemplary master, reestablishes his relationship with the loyal slaves in his household and eventually punishes the disloyal ones. Since the suitors of Penelope, Odysseus' wife, have been cruel masters to the slaves in Odysseus' house in his absence, an anonymous slave woman curses them (*Odyssey* 20.116–19, trans. Lattimore 1967):

> On this day let the suitors take, for the last and latest
> time, their desirable feasting in the halls of Odysseus.
> For it is they who have broken my knees with heart-sore labour
> as I grind the meal for them. Let this be their final feasting.

We can easily imagine slaves in the classical period uttering similar prayers; both loyalty and resentment towards their masters are well attested. But in two interrelated ways, slavery as portrayed in Homer is different from what we find later. First off, although Odysseus captured some of his slaves himself and paid for others, Homer does not present slaves as essentially foreign. In contrast, slaves in the classical period were virtually never native to the city in which they worked; indeed, Greek-born slaves were relatively rare in Greece. Second, in Homer the distinction between slave and free often seems less important than the distinction between the heroic nobles and everybody else. By the classical period, the distinction between slave and free was of paramount importance.

We also see in Homer signs of the early development of the *polis*, the city-state, the form of political organization that was to dominate Greece until the supremacy of Macedonia in the late fourth century. Greece was not a single nation state, but rather each city – eventually most cities were walled – along with the countryside around it was an independent political entity. The extent of ancient Greece was also different, larger than modern Greece: in addition to the whole coast of the Aegean, there were Greek *poleis* (the plural of *polis*) in Sicily, in southern Italy and France, and on the coasts of the Black Sea, as well as a few on the northern coast of Africa. Some of these city-states raided their non-Greek neighbors for slaves or at least traded slaves, both practices we'll discuss in Chapter 3.

The growth and development of Greek society and culture continued in the seventh and sixth centuries. Our sources of information, however, are not good since no contemporary histories survive and we are left to interpret short poems or the writings of later historians, who had to base their accounts on unreliable oral traditions. Two important events during this period affect our understanding of slavery. First, a later, fourth-century BCE historian, Theopompus, reports that the Chians were the first Greeks to use "bought barbarians [foreigners]" for slaves – we have little idea when.[2] According to Theompompus' model, cities had previously obtained slaves directly, by enslaving the people they captured in war, the most common practice in Homer's epics. Throughout the classical period, it was always possible to enslave war captives, but it was often financially more advantageous to ransom captured soldiers back to their native city – assuming that it had not been destroyed. As a result, most slaves in the classical period were probably non-Greeks imported and purchased rather than captured directly.

The second crucial development occurred in Athens, the most populous and best-known city-state in Greece. In the early part of the sixth century BCE, an Athenian politician named Solon abolished debt bondage and, perhaps, a certain type of share-cropping – a development we'll revisit in Chapter 5. He thus reduced the ability of the rich to exploit the poor among the citizens. If similar events and processes occurred in other cities – as did the development of democracy – this may have helped drive the market for foreign slaves, outsiders to whom no rights need be given and who could be exploited to whatever extent was practical. The evidence of Homer shows that slaves were used from the eighth century on; it's likely that they became more common during the sixth century.

Our sources of information become much better after the start of the classical period in 500 BCE, which roughly coincides with two of the Greeks' proudest accomplishments.[3] First, hostilities with Persia began in 499 BCE; the mainland Greeks repelled invasions by the vast Persian Empire in 490 and 480–79 BCE. In the aftermath of these defensive struggles, Athens led the counter-attack that freed the Greek cities of the Ionian coast from Persian control. Athens eventually turned its anti-Persian alliance of Greek city-states, the Delian League, into an empire, from which many of its "allies" tried to escape in vain. In the process, Athens became a wealthy and powerful state. This wealth supported its outstanding achievements in the arts and literature, many of which belong to this period. It is also likely that this period of wealth and population growth was also the time in which slaves at Athens were most numerous.

Second, Athens became a democracy following the reforms of Kleisthenes in 508 BCE. As opposed to oligarchies, which typically allowed only the wealthy to exercise political rights, Greek democracies gave such rights to the poor. This made it harder for the rich to subject the poor to subordinating economic relationships and contributed to the tendency, already encouraged by Solon's reforms, for the rich to buy slaves to fill their labor needs. In addition, although the rich did not really consider the poor their equals, an ideology emerged in which the main distinction among men was between the free citizens and the slaves. This was an egalitarian and democratic way of thinking as far as the male citizens were concerned, but it was not a generous worldview when it came to slaves, who lacked basic rights and were often despised as inferior foreigners.

---

2 Theopompus, Fr. 122 (a) in Shrimpton 1991.
3 Some historians prefer 510 or 479 BCE as the beginning of the classical period.

Despite amazing cultural accomplishments in medicine, art, tragedy, comedy, history, and philosophy, the fifth century was a period of frequent wars, at first against Persia but later mostly between Greek states. These culminated in the long, extremely bitter, and costly Peloponnesian War (431–404 BCE) between Athens and its empire on one side and the Peloponnesian League under Sparta on the other. During this struggle, Athens lost more than half of its citizen population in battle – and suffered a terrible plague to boot. In these wars, slaves too could be recruited to fight in the navy – sometimes with the promise of freedom as a reward. Other slaves took advantage of hostilities to flee slavery, since enemy cities could be as close as thirty miles from each other and did not, of course, return fugitive slaves to their masters in a hostile city. For example, the historian Thucydides reports in *The History of the Peloponnesian War* that more than twenty thousand slaves escaped from Athens when a Spartan fort was established nearby (7.27).

Warfare continued in the fourth century but was never as intense. Several states made bids to dominate the Greek world, but none succeeded until Macedonia finally achieved domination over almost the whole of mainland Greece. Although slavery was known in Macedonia, it played a smaller role in this society – dominated by aristocrats and mainly populated by dependent peasants – than it had in the city-states to the south. When Alexander of Macedon conquered the whole of the vast Persian Empire (335–323 BCE), he mainly left the economies and labor practices of the areas he conquered intact. Alexander died without an heir to the throne and eventually his generals fell to fighting over the huge empire he had created. The result of these wars, which lasted for fifty years, was the formation of a number of stable independent monarchies, called the Hellenistic Kingdoms.

Greeks and Macedonians who had emigrated from their homelands constituted the ruling class in these kingdoms. There they used domestic slaves just as in Greece. The mass of the population in the Hellenistic Kingdoms, however, was composed of natives, mainly peasants engaged in agriculture. Their status and way of life often predated even the expansion of the Persian Empire in the sixth century and did not change with the Macedonian conquest either. Slavery in the Hellenistic Kingdoms was therefore primarily an urban phenomenon practiced by the Greek and Macedonian ruling class. Nevertheless, we know more about some aspects of Hellenistic slavery than that of the classical period: the manumission records at Delphi back in mainland Greece and the papyri from Hellenistic Egypt provide particularly good evidence, which we'll use in several places.

Rome came into contact with the Hellenistic world in the third century. Shortly after 200 BCE, Rome decisively defeated Macedonia, and eventually it conquered all the Hellenistic kingdoms. Rome did not annex the last kingdom, Ptolemaic Egypt, until 30 BCE, but even before then, by the middle of the second century at the latest, Rome was the most powerful state in the Mediterranean. Even the proud kingdoms of Alexander's successors needed either to do as Rome wanted or to suffer the consequences. Nevertheless, slavery in Greece continued after its conquest by Rome and even after the fall of Rome. The eastern, Greek-speaking half of the Roman Empire, known as the Byzantine Empire, outlasted the fall of the western Empire by almost a millennium. Its people referred to themselves as the *Romaioi*, which is Greek for "the Romans" – yet another striking example of the eventual blending of Greek and Roman culture. These *Romaioi* owned slaves all the way up to the final fall of Constantinople in 1453 CE.

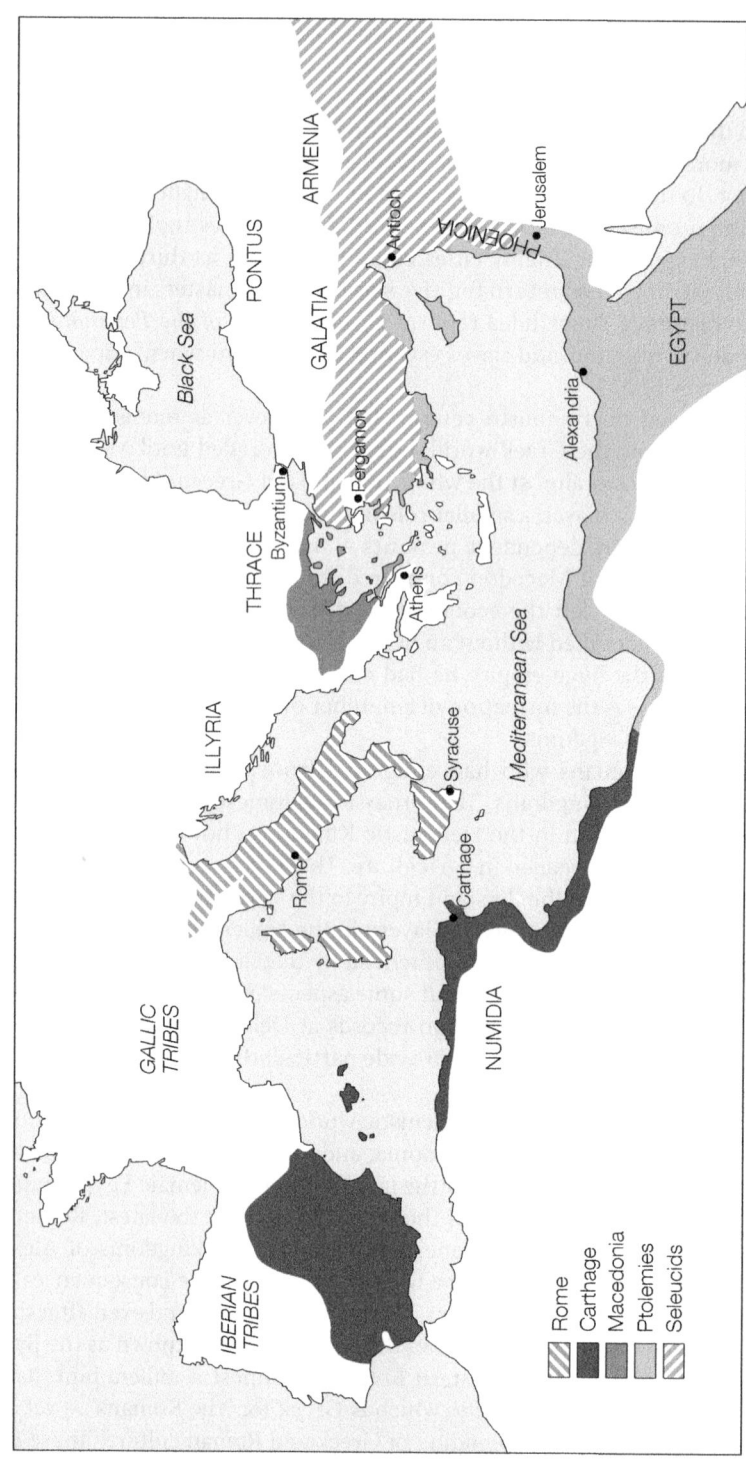

Map 3 The powers of the Mediterranean in 220 BCE. *Source:* Courtesy of Stephanie Krause.

Rome's Expansion

The traditional, but legendary, date for the founding of Rome on seven hills overlooking the river Tiber is 753 BCE; archaeology confirms that by the middle of the next century the city center, the *forum*, had been built between these hills. Already by the end of the sixth century BCE, the city of Rome was one of the largest in Italy. Unfortunately, most of our detailed information about the long early history of Rome (750–350 BCE) comes from sources written down centuries later, whose accuracy inspires little confidence. The oldest genuine document, parts of which survive, is the law code known as the Twelve Tables, which may have been enacted around 450 BCE. Among other topics, the Twelve Tables contain regulations about slaves, including several regarding manumission. As was the case with Greece, Roman slavery went back to the earliest period of its recorded history.

The basic theme of the first eight centuries of Roman history, from about 750 BCE to 50 CE, is the expansion of Roman territory and power through warfare. Rome's growth began with its control of a league of cities to its south, the Latin League, who spoke Latin just as the Romans did. Rome slowly grew to control more and more neighboring states in central Italy, either directly or as subordinate allies. After its final victory over the Samnites of south-central Italy (290 BCE), Rome controlled almost the whole of the Italian Peninsula. Two long and bloody wars against Carthage, a powerful Phoenician city in North Africa, left Rome at the end of the third century victorious and possessing overseas provinces including Sicily and parts of Spain. Rome's domination, defeat, and eventual annexation of the great Hellenistic kingdoms was an inevitable, if slow, process – as was the conquest of Spain. Hard inland campaigns brought Gaul – roughly modern France – under Roman rule (58–50 BCE). Rome eventually controlled all the territory west of the Rhine and south of the Danube. Rome's eastern conquests brought its frontiers to, and occasionally past, Armenia. In the north the Romans managed to conquer about half of the island of Britain. The emperor Claudius conducted this last campaign in the 40s CE, but the Romans acquired the vast majority of their empire during the Republic and during the reign of the first emperor, Augustus, who died in 14 CE. There were still wars and some emperors conducted important and successful campaigns, but not at the same constant and intense level as before. Since conquest provided large numbers of slaves, we'll consider in Chapter 3 whether the prevalence of slavery peaked and then began to decline as this source of slaves dried up.

As a result of this long process of expansion, Rome became one of the largest and most powerful empires in world history. Nevertheless, Rome suffered setbacks and pauses. For example, its wars against the Samnites and Carthaginians were marked by famous defeats. But for much of its history, starting in the fourth century BCE, Rome had a way of losing battles, sometimes disastrously, but eventually winning the wars. Historians focus on two basic factors in Rome's resilience and success.

First off, unlike the Greek city-states that jealously guarded their local citizenship, the Romans allowed conquered people to advance through various gradations of partial citizenship and eventually to become Roman citizens. This was not a quick or peaceful process: it often took many generations for a state to go from enmity and defeat – often repeated defeat – through subordinate status to full incorporation in the Roman Empire. Nevertheless, Roman power and territory grew in this way, slowly but surely. Rome could eventually draw on a much larger population than any of its rivals. In contrast, the Hellenistic monarchies never succeeded in winning over the populations that Alexander the Great and his army had conquered. The Greek and Macedonian ruling class remained a relatively small foreign elite, centered in the cities, and superimposed upon a much larger and often hostile native population.

Rome's ability to incorporate foreign states paralleled its treatment of former slaves. Rome was almost unique among slave-societies in that slaves formally freed by a Roman citizen became citizens themselves, a practice we'll consider in more detail in Chapter 8. Rome imported or directly captured large numbers of slaves in every generation for centuries; some proportion of these gained manumission. So some historians suspect that the citizen population of Rome, or even Italy as a whole, eventually included a large proportion of ex-slaves and their descendants.

The second basic factor behind Rome's military success was its social cohesion, which helped Rome to mobilize its strength effectively against external enemies. Up until the mid-fourth century BCE, social conflicts had occasionally hampered Rome; class tensions and political conflict plagued the late Republic (133–30 BCE). Nevertheless, for a long and crucial part of Rome's expansion, from the mid-fourth to the mid-second century BCE, Roman society was marked by remarkable unity, an ideology of inclusion, and an ethos of shared sacrifice for the community. Rome's eventual success in the Second Punic War (218–201 BCE) highlights these qualities. In 218 BCE Hannibal, the Carthaginian commander, crossed the Alps from Spain to invade Italy itself. He decimated large Roman armies in three battles and ranged up and down Italy with his army for years and didn't return to Carthage until 203 BCE. Nevertheless, few of Rome's Italian allies went over to the Carthaginians and the Romans themselves presented a united front. They continued to mobilize new armies to replace their losses and eventually won the war.

The inclusiveness of the Romans is revealed in a story set at the nadir of Roman fortunes after Rome's third and worst defeat by Hannibal, at Cannae. At this time, the Senate called for *volones*, slave volunteers, to replenish the army, and was able to form an entire legion from them. After fighting bravely for Rome, the *volones* gained their freedom as a reward. It is not that remarkable that the Romans out of dire necessity turned to arming and freeing slaves; the Greeks did that as well, as we'll see in Chapter 5. What sets Rome apart from Greece is that the Romans were not embarrassed about this expedient, but rather they celebrated the *volones* (e.g., Livy 23.35.8). In practice Roman slavery was often extremely brutal and violent, but one stream in Roman ideology stressed the ability of some people, even slaves, to rise to the status of Romans by their virtue and hard work.

Rome's wars of conquest directly supplied large numbers of slaves, starting in the third century BCE at the latest. By the second century, Rome's acquisition of slaves through war reached a remarkably high level. In addition, the wealth that empire brought allowed rich Romans to buy more slaves from beyond the borders of the realm. Many of these lived in cities and contributed to the ostentatious and luxurious lifestyle of the wealthy Romans. In Italy, the heartland of the empire, these slaves also constituted a large fraction of the agricultural work force. Some historians have estimated that the population of Italy in this period was more than 25 percent slaves, mostly first-generation slaves. We'll explore the repercussions of this in Chapters 3 and 5, and look at the theory that Italy was converted from a country of small independent farmers into a landscape dominated by large estates with slave workers. In many parts of the Roman Empire, however, slavery mainly remained primarily an urban phenomenon.

Table 1.2 Roman government and the periods of Roman history.

Date	Period	Political developments
753 (?)–ca. 500 BCE	Regal	Kings
ca. 500–133 BCE	Republic	Representative government dominated by an oligarchy of wealth and birth
133–30 BCE	Late Republic	Constitutional crises and eventually civil wars
30 BCE–235 CE	Empire	A series of hereditary monarchies
235–284 CE	Crisis of the Third Century	Many civil wars, assassinations, and foreign invasions
284–476 CE	Late Empire	More bureaucracy and militarization of society. Empire divided into western and eastern (Byzantine) halves

Roman history is traditionally divided into periods based on its system of government. We know very little about the earliest period, the Regal period, when Rome was ruled by kings: later Romans told many stories about these early monarchs, but historians disagree about how many of these, if any, are true. After the Romans expelled their kings, probably around 500 BCE, Rome became a republic. Each year the people elected powerful magistrates, headed by two consuls, to govern. The Roman system of government was a complex one with various branches – including a powerful senate, made up of former magistrates – and many of its features served to limit the power any one official possessed. On the whole, however, Rome's government was a representative republic whereas Greek democracy, as at Athens, was direct: in a Greek democratic city, the assembled people made most decisions themselves and delegated little power to magistrates.

Another contrast was that while Greek democracies tried to establish political equality among the citizens, the Roman Republic was deliberately set up to favor the rich citizens and the magistrates. Any citizen could address the Athenian assembly – the herald proclaimed, "who wishes to speak?" – while the convening officials, from the wealthiest classes, controlled the agenda and speakers at a Roman assembly. In Athens, every citizen's vote carried the same weight. But the Roman Centuriate Assembly, for example, elected high officials and decided issues of war and peace. Its voting units were called *centuries*. Citizens were allocated to these *centuries* based on their wealth class in such a way that most of the *centuries* were composed of wealthier citizens. The poor, despite their great numbers, were allocated to fewer *centuries*. To make the process even less democratic, units composed of the upper classes voted first, and the issue could be decided and the voting halted before the *centuries* for most of the population even had a chance to vote.

One crucial social reform during the second half of the fourth century BCE was the abolition of debt bondage for Roman citizens. The elimination of debt bondage sharpened the divide between Roman citizens, who from this point on were rarely faced with the prospect of servitude, and imported slaves, devoid of all rights. In this respect, the Roman situation resembled that at Athens after Solon's abolition of debt bondage. In other ways, however, the societies were different. As we'll explore in Chapter 5, Roman ideals still allowed for subordinating economic ties between rich and poor, those between a rich patron and his poorer clients for example. But for one Athenian citizen to be permanently employed by, or be subordinate to, another was thought disgraceful. Paradoxically, the ideal of equality among the citizens perhaps contributed to Athens' general refusal to allow slaves – or usually foreigners – to become citizens. That would be to concede too much to them. At Rome, in contrast, a hierarchical view of citizenship as including higher and lower ranks was one factor that made it easier for the Romans to accept ex-slaves as citizens – of low rank of course.

Roman conquests continued unabated throughout the late Republic (133–30 BCE), but an escalating spiral of social conflict, violent political strife, and finally a series of hard-fought civil wars also marked this period. Competition among aristocrats became increasingly bitter and eventually violent. Since successful politicians were often victorious generals, their competition eventually involved the clash of Roman armies more loyal to their commanders than to the Republic. Some historians hold that the displacement of Italian smallholders by slave-worked farms meant that the traditional recruiting ground of the Roman state – free Italian farmers – was being depleted. They argue that, in consequence, Roman legionaries were recruited from the poor and landless, who, without a livelihood to return to, were more dependent than ever on their generals (see the section Slave and Freedmen Administrators in the Early Roman Empire in Chapter 5). In times of political conflict they were likely to support their own generals, even when it meant marching against Rome itself.

The rapid expansion of Rome and the consequent acquisition of so many slaves also caused problems for Rome in a more direct way. In the period 140 to 70 BCE, slaves rose in open revolt on three separate occasions: twice in Sicily, Rome's first overseas province, and once in Italy itself (Chapter 10). It is only in rare circumstances that slaves are able to successfully revolt; the sheer number of new slaves in Sicily and Italy was a crucial factor in these uprisings, each of which lasted for years and required major military campaigns in order to suppress them. Evidence of slaves' hostility towards their owners appears throughout Roman history, either in the form of open violence or day-to-day resistance. Slave owners sometimes emphasized the hostility of their slaves with the aphorism, "You have as many enemies as you have slaves," a pithy four words in Latin: "Quot servi tot hostes" (Seneca, *Epistles* 47.5). The actual relations between slaves and masters were complex and could vary greatly from one case to another, as we'll explore more closely in Chapter 9. For example, slaveholders celebrated the outstanding loyalty of some slaves who were willing to die for their masters, especially during the civil wars that led to the fall of the Republic, a topic we'll revisit in Chapter 11.

The final result of these civil wars was the conversion of Rome into a monarchy, the Empire, which lasted into the fifth century CE. The first Roman emperor, Augustus, claimed that he was restoring the Republic and, in legal terms, he ruled by virtue of possessing a bundle of traditional powers, albeit previously divided among different officials and limited in duration. The Senate still sat and, for a while, assemblies elected officials – but only from those vetted by the emperor. Despite this legal façade, everybody knew that the emperor's real power lay in his control of the armies on the frontiers and the Praetorian Guard, detachments of troops stationed in Rome itself, contrary to Republican practice. Individual emperors varied in their relationships with the senatorial order, upon which they still depended to govern the vast empire and command its armies. As we'll see in Chapter 5, emperors also used their slaves and ex-slaves as a loyal bureaucracy and even the equivalent of a cabinet: such men were loyal only to the emperor, unlikely to take offense at being given frequent orders – as a blue-blooded senator would – and they often possessed the expertise needed to administer an empire of sixty million people.

Sometimes a tyrannical or insane emperor terrorized the Senate; most emperors enjoyed generally smooth relations and ruled without serious challenge or dispute. Despite two interludes of civil wars due to a disputed succession – both after an unpopular emperor's assassination without a viable heir – the basic imperial system continued into the third century CE. The "Crisis of the Third Century," 235–284 CE, involved a long series of civil wars, assassinations of emperors, and foreign invasions by Goths, Franks, Alemanni, and a resurgent Persia. These forces devastated large swaths of the empire, some of which had not seen a foreign army for centuries. Plagues also contributed to a decline in population. Amazingly, a series of brilliant military emperors, culminating with Diocletian (284–305 CE), restored Rome's fortunes and reestablished order. As a result, however, the late Roman Empire was more militarized and bureaucratic than before. The political division between the Eastern, Greek-speaking provinces and the Latin west was first officially instituted by Diocletian and reemerged for good at the end of the fourth century CE. Equally important to the development of the late Empire was the conversion of the emperor Constantine to Christianity. After a long history of sporadic Roman persecutions of Christians, Christianity became the dominant religion of the Roman Empire over the course of the fourth century CE.

Renewed invasions by the Goths, among others, led to the sacking of Rome in 410 CE and the fifth century saw the western Empire ravaged by invaders, while emperors became increasingly impotent until a Germanic king deposed the last emperor in the west in 476 CE. The eastern Empire, which historians refer to as the Byzantine Empire, was reduced by Persian and then Islamic conquests in the seventh century, but it lasted until the capture of Constantinople by the Ottomans in 1453 CE.

Most scholars agree that Italy, the heart of the Roman Empire, was a slave society during the late Republic and early Empire. Slaves were numerous in the cities: Roman aristocrats might have a couple of hundred slaves working just in their mansions in Rome. More important, slave-worked large farms dominated agriculture, the most important part of the economy. This period, perhaps from about 150 BCE to 150 CE, and this place, Italy and Rome in particular, provide a large proportion of our evidence. But we should not project the picture we get from these Italian sources onto the whole expanse of the Roman Empire. Although large slave-run farms existed in different provinces of the Empire, the domination of agricultural labor by slaves seems mainly to have been an Italian phenomenon.

In addition, the dependence on slaves in agriculture varied over time. Scholars used to paint a simple picture of the rise and fall of Roman slavery. The conquests of the Republic and early Empire drove the transition to the use of slave labor. When these conquests slowed and then ceased, so the argument goes, Roman aristocrats found substitutes for slave labor, in particular the *coloni*, whom some historians argue were precursors to medieval serfs. The actual situation is more complex, and we will consider critically both the rise (Chapters 3 and 4) and the fall of Roman slavery (Chapter 13) in more detail.

Contrasts and Comparisons

Both Greece and Rome had a long history of slave use, but the period during which we can describe them as slave societies – when slavery was prevalent, even in agriculture – was much shorter. These periods included the classical, "golden" ages of both civilizations. It is ironic that the greatest cultural accomplishments of Greece and Rome were the products of the periods when slavery was most prevalent.

The two slave societies were limited in space as well as time. For example, we can call Athens and similar city-states slave societies, but we could not describe Thessaly as such, with its serf-like lower classes and rare use of slaves in the classical period. Roman Italy was a slave society, but many provinces outside of Italy mainly retained their previous social structure, usually based on the labor of peasants or serf-like classes. In both cases, we must be careful not to extrapolate too boldly from evidence that is concentrated in time and place. We know vastly more about classical Athens than about any other Greek city. Similarly, Rome and Italy from the late Republic through the second century CE are better attested than earlier and later periods or the rest of the Empire, although the bias of our Roman sources is less severe than is the case with classical Athens versus the rest of Greece. Thus, while our evidence is better for the places and times when slavery was most important, that does not mean that slavery was as pervasive everywhere and in every era.

The direct democracy of Athens and other Greek cities and the Roman republican system make Greece and Rome stand out among many other societies throughout world history that displayed a similar technological, social, and economic complexity. The legal and political rights they accorded to every free man inspired the modern embrace of democracy and the rule of law. In a sharp and unhappy contrast, slaves were common in both societies and devoid of legal rights or social status. Both societies made a sharp distinction between the in-group of male citizens, who could rarely lose this status, and the "outsiders within," foreign slaves, who lacked rights.

Greek and Roman slavery were different in other ways. Although the dichotomy between slave and citizen was sharp in both cases, the line between the two was more permeable at Rome than in Greece. Greek cities jealously guarded their citizenship and rarely allowed any foreigners to become citizens. Thus ex-slaves remained in the category of *metics*, resident foreigners, with almost no hope of eventually attaining political rights in the cities where they lived. In contrast, Roman freedmen and freedwomen could join the ranks of the citizens. Consequently, Rome's system of slavery is sometimes classified as an "open" one, while Greek slavery was "closed." This does not imply that Roman slavery was milder than Greek slavery. We can't be sure what proportion of Greek or Roman slaves actually attained their freedom in the first place, nor can we gauge the average treatment a slave received in Greece versus Rome, as we'll examine in more depth in Chapters 8 and 9.

Another and more obvious contrast is the much larger scale of the Roman Empire and thus of Roman slavery. A high estimate for the population of the whole Greek world during the classical period is between seven and ten million inhabitants. The Roman Empire at its peak probably contained approximately fifty to sixty million people. This difference, almost a ten-fold one, still understates the difference in scale between the two societies: the classical Greek world was composed of perhaps a thousand city-states, a fair proportion of which were independent, while the entire Roman Empire was at many times a single political entity. The Hellenistic world occupies an intermediate position with a total population perhaps somewhat larger than that of the Roman Empire, but divided among different states. These differences of scale – especially between classical Greece and the Roman Empire – meant that total numbers of slaves, the scale of enslavement, and the slave trade differed greatly in each case.

There was also a difference in the distribution of slaves among free families. The social structure of classical Greek city-states was more egalitarian than at Rome. The rich in classical Greece were not as rich as the Roman elite and a broader proportion of families in Greece were somewhat affluent. These basic economic facts were reflected in the ownership of slaves. Roman aristocrats had hundreds of slaves, and holdings into the thousands were not rare. Although one Athenian supposedly owned a thousand mine slaves, other Greeks of the highest classes possessed only about ten to thirty slaves. On the other hand, even the seemingly average Athenians represented in Aristophanes' comedies owned from a couple to a dozen slaves. Such comic households were not average in the strict sense, but rather richer. Nevertheless, it is possible that half of the citizen households in Athens possessed at least one slave during the fat years of the Athenian Empire. Thus, to judge from Athens, Greek citizens were more likely than Roman citizens to possess slaves; classical Greek slaves were more apt to live in small households rather than among a large group of slaves owned by a noble.

A different distribution, however, characterizes the Hellenistic world. Hellenistic aristocrats were generally grander and richer than their classical antecedents, but their wealth in land consisted of farms with attached peasant workers, rather than with slaves, as had been common practice during the classical period. Their domestic establishments probably contained more slaves than one would have found at Athens, but total ownership was probably less than at Rome at the height of Roman slavery, since the Hellenistic world did not possess many equivalents to the large farms worked by slaves common in Italian agriculture at that time.

Suggested Reading

Pomeroy, Burstein, Donlan, and Roberts 2013 is a recent authoritative textbook on Greek history, clear and accessible. Boatwright, Gargola, Lenski, and Talbert 2013 provides the same for Roman history. Kolchin 1993 is a clear, judicious, and engaging introduction to slavery in the United States. There are a number of good general treatments of Greek and Roman slavery. Wiedemann 1988 collects important ancient sources for both slave systems and Andreau and Descat 2011 treats them both with frequent comparisons. Fisher 1993 is a short, balanced survey of Greek slavery whereas Garlan 1988 takes a French, Marxian approach to that topic. David Lewis (forthcoming) looks at Greek slavery in the context of the whole ancient Mediterranean and Near East. On Roman slavery, Bradley 1994 highlights its brutality and slave resistance; Joshel 2010 is a concrete and lively treatment with many excellent illustrations.

2

Definitions and Evidence

For anyone who, despite being human, is by nature not his own but someone else's is a natural slave. And he is someone else's when, despite being human, he is a piece of property . . .
Aristotle, *Politics* 1.1254a 14–16, trans. Reeve 1998

Slavery is the fact that one man is the property or possession of another.
Herman J. Nieboer, *Slavery as an Industrial System: Ethnological Researches* (2010, originally 1900), 7

Slavery is the permanent, violent domination of natally alienated and generally dishonored persons.
Orlando Patterson, *Slavery and Social Death: A Comparative Study* (1982), 13

What Is Slavery?

Greek slavery was plainly different from Roman slavery; both were very different from New World slavery on the one hand, and from the slavery attested in anthropologists' reports on less complex societies on the other hand. But what was the same? Why do we apply the same term, slavery, in such varied societies across such a large span of history and geography? What exactly is slavery?

Non-historians sometimes assume that any extreme system of oppression constitutes slavery. For example, somebody today might condemn a clothing manufacturer for using "slave labor" in its Third-World factories. If asked to explain the use of "slave labor," that person might point out that the workers are paid poorly, work long hours in appalling conditions, and may be fired if they get sick and cannot work for a couple of days. In this case, the use of "slave labor" expresses severe disapproval; we all deplore slavery, and so we ought to deplore the practice of this hypothetical clothing company.

Historians generally do not approve of oppression, and virtually all condemn slavery severely, but to understand how different societies and institutions work, more precise categories and criteria are needed: "nasty" and "nastier" are not the most helpful terms. Herman Nieboer, an early anthropologist of slavery, provides what has become the traditional historical definition in terms of property in the quotation above – a criterion

Ancient Greek and Roman Slavery, First Edition. Peter Hunt.
© 2018 Peter Hunt. Published 2018 by John Wiley & Sons, Ltd.

that goes back to Aristotle in fourth-century Greece. Such a definition does not necessarily imply bad treatment; people can take good care of things they own, and they can take good care of their slaves. Indeed, in most slave societies we can find slaves who, in material terms at least, are treated well. For example, some slaves in Athens managed banks for their masters, sometimes gained their freedom, and, in at least a couple of cases, ended up among the wealthiest men in the city. In the process they almost certainly also made their masters rich. These slaves were probably far too valuable for their owners to risk angering them, much less not feeding them enough or whipping them.

While some slaves were treated well, the majority were not. It is important, however, to look at the situation of slaves in the context of other members of society. For instance, the plight of the free poor in the ancient world was often extreme. They rarely starved to death, but malnutrition was common and the threat of starvation was a constant concern; they suffered through winters with inadequate clothing. In contrast to slaves, nobody else suffered a direct financial loss if a poor free person died. Dependent peasants and serf-like classes of various sorts, such as the Helots subject to Sparta, often lived lives as harsh in material terms as slaves. They were not fully free either: some owed much of their produce to their lords; others also owed days of personal service; and many were not allowed to leave their farms. Like slaves, such classes rarely had any outside power to turn to if they wanted to mitigate their oppression or curb egregious abuses.

While it is thus important to realize how harsh was the lot of most people throughout most of history, this grim context does not make slavery any better. A few key points will neutralize any temptation to underestimate the horrors of slavery. First of all, to treat a person like property is in itself to humiliate and dehumanize him or her. Plenty of evidence for this feeling in the ancient world exists: already a character in Homer's *Odyssey* bemoans that "Far-seeing Zeus takes away half of a man's worth when the day of enslavement comes upon him" (17.323). Second, most people do not buy expensive property, like slaves, just for the sake of treating it well, but rather to use their property and often to profit from its use. Calculating masters wanted their slaves to stay alive, but they also wanted them to work as hard as possible. In many cases they used punishment and the threat of punishment to make their slaves work hard. Third, not all masters were calculating or effective; many appear to have beaten or abused their slaves out of anger or cruelty despite the fact that they were damaging their own financial interests. Slaves had virtually no recourse against this sort of treatment.

Finally, we need to focus on what is typical and what is exceptional, and well-treated, elite slaves were exceptional. Athens was large enough to provide work for perhaps a couple of dozen slaves in bank management; in contrast, the Athenian silver mines may have employed over twenty thousand slaves. A Roman noble may have kept a couple of highly educated, well-treated Greek slaves as status symbols and tutors to his children. But over a thousand slaves may have spent their lives doing hard manual labor on his farms scattered across the Italian countryside. So, even though historians define slavery in terms of property rather than nastiness, classical slavery was still a deplorable, and usually a harsh, system of exploitation.

The definition of slavery in terms of the property relation between the master and the slave is useful because ownership is a familiar concept. Yet Orlando Patterson points out in *Slavery and Social Death* (1982) that ownership is more complex than it seems. For one thing, people in different societies possess all sorts of property rights in other people. For example, the marriage arrangement in which prospective grooms give "bride-price" to their bride's fathers implies that the bride was in some sense the property first of the father and then of her husband. This did not constitute anything like slavery: a wife was proud of her bride-price and would be ashamed if her family had not received one. In light of these counter-examples and other issues, Patterson proposed an influential alternative definition of slavery.

Patterson defines slavery as the "the permanent, violent domination of natally alienated and generally dishonored persons" (1982, 13). That slavery is permanent and heritable – the children of slaves typically become slaves – distinguishes it from debt bondage and indenture, both of which can be as harsh as slavery and can involve sale of a person, but are not necessarily permanent and often not heritable. Many systems of oppression ultimately depend on violence, but the violence of slavery is particularly prominent and open. For example, slaveholders at a wide variety of places and times used the whip to punish and intimidate slaves. And most slave systems required a supply of new slaves. Reducing free people to slavery generally requires violence – often war – or the open threat of violence. It is not surprising that the free members of a society think that slaves lack honor – although the slaves' own views may differ! By "generally dishonored" Patterson means that they are not dishonored on one occasion or in some particular way, but are fundamentally without honor, without respect, within a society.

The most enlightening part of Patterson's definition is the concept of natal alienation, which is related to the "social death" of his book's title. Slaves are *natally* alienated in that they lack all the rights that other people acquire with *birth*: their claims on their parents, their relations with siblings, and their links with and prestige deriving from their ancestors. In fact, slaves have parents and sometimes have siblings, children, and wives; they remain socially dead because they cannot acquire any such claims or establish any formally recognized relationship other than the one subordinating relationship with their masters. In the words of Brent Shaw, "Chattel slaves are normally denied a viable family life and tradition, and are thereby deliberately cut off from the rich and complex ways in which the identity of the person is attached through the family to community traditions and empowerments" (1998, 14). In the modern world, we are used to the idea that people are born with human rights, but in ancient societies a person's rights came from being somebody's son or somebody's wife or a member of a clan or a village or larger state. Slaves are shut out from any of these rights. Patterson believes that slaves are socially dead in this sense. That may be why they can be treated as things, as possessions, and why defining slavery in terms of ownership rarely leads you astray. It is, nevertheless, important to understand Patterson's viewpoint for the additional insights it yields.

Despite these satisfactory and illuminating definitions, it would be an oversimplification to imagine that ancient slaves constituted an homogenous category surrounded by a precise border. Some ancient slaves enjoyed perquisites that we would associate with freedom. For example, one group of slaves in classical Athens were called the *choris oikountes*, "those living apart" (Kamen 2011). They seem to have lived separately from their masters, sometimes in families. They paid their masters a set amount each month but were not regularly subject to their masters' commands. And, both in Greece and Rome, some slaves had *de facto* control of personal property – considerable wealth in some cases. Since masters could, at their discretion, reverse these arrangements and sell their slaves away to who knows what fate, both the *choris oikountes* and wealthy slaves still fit our definition of slaves. On the other side of the line, some groups do not fit the definitions of slavery, even though we would not regard them as fully free. For example, the Helots were a group subject to the Spartans – treated in detail in Chapter 10 on account of their rebelliousness. They were not allowed to leave their farms; they owed a proportion of their produce and, sometimes, personal service to the Spartans. As we'll see in Chapter 13, the *coloni adscripti* of the late Empire and eventually medieval serfs endured similar obligations and restrictions – and historians have found other cases throughout the classical world. Such persons could not be sold individually; they lived in their own families and villages. So we do not categorize them as slaves. Still it would be ridiculous to insist that they were completely free. The same is arguably true of many ex-slaves and certainly of those in Hellenistic Greece subject to *paramonē*, a sort of conditional or deferred freedom that we'll meet again in Chapter 7 (Zelnick-Abramovitz 2005; *contra* Sosin 2015).

Two considerations should keep these complexities from dismaying us too much. First, there were many unambiguous slaves and unambiguous free persons. Our definitions of slavery tell us something important about a large proportion of the people in the classical world – not everything about everybody, of course! Second, this same imprecision and complexity affects many other key concepts that historians rightly consider crucial to their craft: capitalism, industrialism, the market economy, democracy, imperialism, law, and others. These terms are all subject to debate, partial, and hard to delimit precisely. They are still valuable, virtually irreplaceable, for historians. We are also better off with a definition of slavery. Although my focus will be those people who fit this definition, unexpected privileges are an important part of their story. And those groups, like the Helots, "between slavery and freedom" will also figure in this book.

Historians of slavery use the expression "slave society," to indicate societies in which slavery was a central institution (Turley 2000, 62–100). Throughout history, many societies have allowed slavery, but slave societies are far fewer: ancient Greece and Rome and the three New World slave systems – in Brazil, the Caribbean, and United States South – are members of that short list. Historians use different criteria to determine whether slavery is central to a society or not (Bradley 1994, 12–30). These range from the numerical proportion of slaves in the population, to slavery's economic, cultural, or institutional impact on a society. Do slaves constitute more than, say, 20 percent of the population? Do slaves dominate key areas of the economy? Does the society's elite derive their wealth from slave labor? Did slavery play a dominant part in the culture and institutions of a society? In Chapter 4, I will use the economic definition of slave society, but the different criteria often go together: slaves become a large proportion of a population when their economic role is important, something that often translates into high visibility in a state's culture and institutions.

Ancient Evidence and Its Difficulties

Historians of ancient slavery have far less evidence to work with than do their counterparts who study modern slavery. Historians of slavery in the American South, for example, can draw on a variety of primary sources, some types of which exist in large quantities. They possess full law codes, records of legislative debates, political pamphlets, plantation records, newspapers with news and editorials, posters describing fugitive slaves, memoirs and letters by slave owners, both male and female, and books written by slave owners to justify the practice of slavery to an increasingly hostile world outside the South. All of this evidence comes from slave owners, and so has a particular bias, while accounts by writers visiting the South provide different perspectives.

But historians of modern slavery still have a difficult time reconstructing the slaves' side of the story. Contemporary narratives by escaped or freed slaves often had an openly abolitionist agenda; they aimed to present slavery in the worst possible light. Such accounts are not likely to dwell on any aspects of slavery that might make their condemnation of the institution at all ambiguous. Historians also worry that some slave autobiographies were in part ghost-written or heavily edited by white, highly educated abolitionists. Their perspective probably aligns closely with the ex-slaves' abhorrence of slavery, but it could distort the slaves' feelings, thoughts, and recollections in other ways. In the 1930s, the New Deal's Federal Writers Project conducted systematic and extensive interviews with living ex-slaves. These had the advantage of recording ex-slaves' exact words but had the disadvantage of asking people to recall events in the distant past; and most of the ex-slaves interviewed had been young at the time the Civil War brought an end to slavery. So even with a wealth of textual evidence and eye-witness accounts, historians of modern slavery still encounter problems interpreting their evidence, especially when it comes to the thoughts, feelings, and experiences of the slaves themselves.

These difficulties, however, are small indeed compared to those that face a historian attempting to reconstruct systems of slavery that existed between 3000 and 1500 years ago. Some of these challenges are the same as those that face any historian of the ancient world. The primary challenge is that writing, and thus textual evidence, was far less fundamental to classical Greece and Rome than it is in the modern world. Especially once we look beyond the elite, literacy was low and the culture essentially oral. One reason for this is that, in the absence of printing presses, writing something down was often expensive and time-consuming. So less was originally committed to writing, and spoken words, of course, leave no trace. Texts inscribed on stone, epigraphic evidence, often survive to the present, but most ancient writers employed perishable materials such as papyrus. For these to survive after the fall of Rome, through the Middle Ages, to the early modern age and the printing press, most texts needed to be recopied every few centuries. Papyrus texts preserved in the Egyptian desert constitute one exception, but overall only a tiny fraction, probably far less than 1 percent, of what was written down in classical times has survived to the present day. For example, Antisthenes was a disciple of Socrates and, reportedly, the son of a slave woman. We know that he wrote a treatise *On Freedom and Slavery*, but all that survives is one short quotation from this in a later source. If we had the whole of *On Freedom and Slavery*, we might know more about what Athenian intellectuals, and perhaps even slaves, thought about the institution of slavery, opinions that are otherwise poorly attested.

While less was written down and little of that survives, that is not all: what *has* survived is often not what historians of slavery would find most valuable. For example, we only occasionally have ancient statistics or enough evidence to allow us to derive our own statistics. As a rule, classical states did not even collect the sorts and amount of statistics that a modern nation does. Ancient Greek and Roman governments sometimes counted their people, usually when they wanted to know how many soldiers they could muster. Only very rarely do they seem to have (perhaps) counted the slaves. So historians need to make indirect arguments about the numbers of slaves and the proportion of the population that they constituted. For instance, starting in the sixth century BCE, Greek states sometimes taxed slave sales and manumission, the formal liberation of a slave (Zelnick-Abramovitz 2013, 21–27). The Romans too had exacted a 5 percent tax on manumissions starting in the fourth century BCE (Livy 7.16.7). Somebody must have known, and probably wrote down, slave prices in the process of collecting some of these taxes; such records did not need to last and, written on perishable materials such as papyrus, have disappeared long ago. We do possess several large collections of Greek inscriptions on stone commemorating manumissions, one set of which (from Hellenistic Delphi) even includes prices, invaluable evidence. Nevertheless, the big picture is that only rarely are ancient historians well informed even about basic issues such as slave prices and numbers.

Certainly, nobody sat down and wrote what they thought social historians from a different culture a couple of thousand years later might want to know. Rather, people usually wrote texts for their own immediate purposes. So ancient authors did not normally describe the way their world worked but simply assumed their readers knew. Just as a modern novelist would not bother explaining that most adults in the United States have jobs located someplace other than their homes and thus they "go to work," rich Romans rarely felt the need to specify where in the house their slaves slept; everybody knew. As in this case, the things that must have been most obvious at the time are often those that historians today have the most difficulty figuring out.

Because ancient Greek and Roman authors rarely felt the need to describe the institution of slavery, we usually have to learn about slavery when it comes up in passing in texts about something else entirely. On the one hand, we do possess a couple of books of advice for rich Greeks and Romans about how to manage their farms as more or less absentee owners. Such books needed to treat slavery directly since the management of slave workers was a large part of running a farm. These works are crucial for the historian. On the other hand, we need to use evidence from all sorts of sources with no particular focus on slavery: tragedies, epic poems, epitaphs (inscriptions on gravestones), the text of laws and ancient commentaries on them, law court speeches, novels, bureaucratic records on papyrus, and ancient historical narratives. Inscriptions on stone, for example, often record official information, such as lists of slaves among the property confiscated from some condemned men in Athens, while epitaphs may bring us closest to the actual words or sentiments of slaves themselves. Even here we cannot always be sure whether it was the slave, his or her surviving family, or the slaveholder who put up the monument and decided what words were to be inscribed. These types of sources can help us understand ancient slavery, but they all are difficult to interpret for one or more reasons – as we shall see when we investigate particular cases throughout this book.

One last problem is crucial. Ideally, scholars of ancient slavery would have copious evidence by masters and by slaves, both male and female, as well as by people who were neither masters nor slaves. The most obvious bias in our surviving evidence, however, is that wealthy men, slaveholders almost without exception, produced virtually all of it. In their writing, they occasionally reveal their thoughts about slavery in general and about their own slaves in particular. They sometimes even represent the lives and words of slaves: for example, slaves play important roles in Greek tragedies. But it was wealthy free men who wrote these plays.[1] Rarely do we hear directly from women and almost

---

1 The Roman comic playwright Terence (second century BCE) was an ex-slave as was the philosopher Epictetus (late-first and early-second century CE); many epitaphs of ex-slaves also survive. Evidence from ex-slaves is invaluable since they had experienced slavery. But they were rarely typical slaves to begin with and, upon gaining freedom, generally acquired slaves of their own if they could afford them. See Chapter 8.

never from slaves themselves. So historians are faced with the problem of figuring out how slaves actually spoke, thought, and acted based on how their masters depicted them – and slave masters were hardly disinterested and objective observers of their slaves. This bias in our sources makes it hard to avoid a top-down view of ancient slavery and limits our insight into slaves' perspectives or the active role slaves sometimes played in shaping their lives.[2] In this book, I have tried whenever possible to understand or at least imagine the slave's perspective, but these attempts must often remain speculative or superficial due to our one-sided evidence.

That wealthy men wrote the vast majority of classical literature sometimes introduces another distortion: slaves may be overrepresented, especially domestic slaves in comparison to the free poor. The lifestyle of the wealthy in both Greece and Rome depended on domestic slaves; their houses were teeming with them. Domestic slaves were a part of the everyday life of the rich and thus figure often in the literature they produced. In contrast, the free poor often played less of a role in the lives of the affluent. In some times and places we know less about them than about slaves: the free poor can disappear almost entirely from the world of our literary texts. For example, the theory of natural slavery in Aristotle's *Politics* seems to assume that people are divided in two classes: natural masters and natural slaves. But what about all the people who were neither, who were free but not masters? The dichotomy of slave versus master was one way that ancient writers understood and simplified their world, which was, in fact, more complicated.

The example of ancient comic plays illustrates all these points. Both Greek and Roman comedies usually took place within the context of prosperous households and therefore included slave characters. Free Athenians who were not rich enough to own slaves hardly figure at all. The purpose of comedy is to amuse and entertain, so we cannot assume that the slave characters and the way they acted were typical at all. Many modern comedies are far from realistic about life today – I'm sure you can think of examples. Ancient playwrights were just as imaginative and willing to be unrealistic in their quest for laughs. The plays of Aristophanes (ca. 446–386 BCE), for example, included fantastic elements: in *The Birds*, a city of birds controls the world by intercepting the smoke from religious sacrifices, which the gods need to live on; another is set in Hades, the underworld. Can we trust Aristophanes to present realistic slaves? Even later comic writers whose plays were set within more or less typical households probably never worried, "Am I being unrealistic here?" Plays were judged on how well they entertained the audience, not on their veracity.

Writers of comedy, who were free men, addressed themselves to an audience composed also of free men, many of whom were slave owners. In early Athenian comedies, we find simple jokes at the expense of slaves. These make it obvious that slaves are not the intended audience, since it's doubtful that slaves enjoyed jokes about terrified slaves getting beaten. But much of the humor and attraction of the presentation of slaves in comedy is more complex: for example, many comedies include a stereotypical character, the "clever slave," who is smarter than his master and often outwits him. The

---

[2] The argument that this tendency is the fault of modern historians or the result of adopting a certain definition of slavery (e.g., Vlassopoulos 2011a, 122–127; 2016a, 90–91) underestimates the difficulties of our evidence.

audience may even have identified with these slave characters, who were, nevertheless, base or trivial in their goals and mentality, a characterization that reassured audiences of slaves' inferiority.

We shall return to the complex and controversial clever slave character in Chapter 11. While it might be tempting to say that we learn nothing from such a problematic source as comedy, we can often make plausible guesses about what is a comic distortion and what is realistic. For example, that every family in Athenian comedy owns at least a couple of slaves does not mean that even poor Athenians owned slaves. Nevertheless, if we consider that even families depicted in comedy as poor or middle-class possess slaves, we can reasonably conclude that slave ownership was not confined to a small class of rich Athenians. Not just in the case of ancient comedy, but whenever we are trying to learn from an ancient text, we need to consider its original author, the audience it addressed, and why it was written.

So far we have been looking at textual evidence, but archaeologists study the ancient world by looking at material remains including sculpture, pottery, houses, farms, tombs and graves, temples and other public buildings, mines, and workshops. What material evidence can contribute to the study of ancient slavery and how easy it is to interpret varies greatly. Some material remains vividly confirm what we already know: many texts refer to the chaining and binding of slaves and, sure enough, archaeologists have found a variety of manacles and fetters from around the classical world (Thompson 1993). Sometimes archaeological evidence can shed light on issues that our texts do not illuminate. I've already mentioned the mystery of where slaves sleep. Excavations of large Roman houses sometimes suggest a separate, crudely finished area with tiny, low rooms in which slaves lived. We cannot, however, be sure whether all slaves lived there or whether personal attendants slept on the floors nearer to their masters. And most houses show no sign of designated slave quarters (George 2011, 387–390). Another case involves archaeological surveys of the remains of ancient walls, ditches, farms, and surface pottery fragments in the countryside. From this evidence scholars can try to estimate the average size of farms in different periods and places, crucial information for evaluating the role of slaves in agriculture. But material remains were not produced for the benefit of future archaeologists, and their interpretation can be as tricky as textual analysis.

Actual Practices Versus Ways of Thinking

Knowing what people thought about themselves, their world, and their place in it is just as important as knowing what people did, their actual practices, but it requires a different approach. Take, for example, a passage from the late Roman Empire in which Vegetius warns slaveholders against allowing slaves to ride their horses, because they may injure them.[3] We can infer from this that slaves sometimes rode horses and that sometimes the horses ended up injured. Why else would Vegetius bother to warn about it? But we would also like to know whether slaves were given permission to ride as a perk or had to ride the horses as part of their job, to exercise the horse when the master

---

3 *On Veterinary Medicine (Mulomedicina)* 1.56.12–13; cf. Xenophon, *Oeconomicus* 11.18.

didn't want to. And how much of a problem was the laming of horses? These are examples of the issue of determining practice, what people did.

But Vegetius also claims that slaves ride horses recklessly out of competitiveness when they race each other. And he adds that the slaves don't care about their masters' loss when a horse is injured; they are delighted when this happens. These statements describe the thinking and (hostile) feelings of slaves. They are probably more interesting and important for our understanding of ancient slavery than the likelihood that some slaves exercised their masters' horses. In this case – as often – we do not get the slave's perspective directly, but rather what a member of the slaveholding class imagined slaves felt. One reason to be suspicious is a significant oversimplification of the whole situation: a master might suffer the loss of a horse; the slave responsible was unlikely to escape harsh punishment and might not be delighted for long. Indeed, Vegetius urges masters to curb reckless riding with the utmost severity – and this in a society where slaves could be whipped for much less.

Last, but not least, Vegetius is likely to have harbored all sorts of prejudices against slaves. His generalization about their careless riding may reflect stereotypes rather than an accurate judgment. To take a modern example, comments about "women drivers" being worse than men persisted long after insurance statistics proved the opposite. One can easily imagine a skilled slave groom indignantly insisting that he is actually much better with the horses than his young master, who, for example, rides infrequently and, when he does, is always trying to show off to his friends.

When it comes to slaves, both kinds of questions, about practices and about ways of thinking, are hard to answer. In the absence of direct evidence from slaves, arguments about their thinking are necessarily speculative; they are worth attempting nonetheless. For instance, in Chapter 6, we'll see that slaves at Athens often retained a strong and proud sense of their original ethnic identity – many of them were from Thrace or from one of the western provinces of the Persian Empire. But the views of slave owners about slaves and slavery, the topic of Chapters 11 and 12, are better known thanks to the comparatively large volume of textual evidence they have left us.

What Is Typical? When and Where?

Even when we are able to draw convincing conclusions from a piece or a body of evidence, we encounter the problem of typicality. In the case of some basic facts, ancient historians may know that something holds true for all ancient slaves: for example, that they were legally treated as property. Occasionally, historians may know to which slaves, at what times and places, a certain statement applies. More often, however, our evidence allows us to draw a conclusion of limited scope, and we need to consider carefully how widely we can apply it. This is particularly true when our evidence consists of a story about something that happened on one occasion.

Such anecdotes sometimes provide our only evidence for a practice, but stories often seem interesting and worth recording because they are *not* usual. To use a well-known example: newspapers do not bother to report every time a dog bites a person, but if a person bites a dog, that gets news coverage. According to this whimsy, historians of the future might come to the completely wrong conclusion by counting newspaper references to person and dog bites. We definitely see this "man-bites-dog effect" in what gets reported by ancient historians. A startling case is that of the wealthy Roman Vedius Pollio, who, according to the story, would feed disobedient or incompetent slaves to the lamprey eels he kept in the fish-pond on his property (Seneca, *De Ira* 3.40). On the face of it, this seems like outlandish behavior, more like biting a dog than getting bit by one. We also learn about one reaction to his behavior: when Vedius was about to kill a slave whose only offense was to drop and break a glass, the emperor Augustus, who was present, prevented him, had all the glasses in the house broken, and the fish pond filled. On the one hand, all this suggests an egregious practice that evoked disapproval and punishment. On the other hand, even the loss of fine glassware and a fishpond seems like a light punishment for a person we would regard as a deranged serial murderer. The story ends up revealing the low value placed on the lives of slaves. More often, however, we lack the evidence to suggest how people judged an action, and it is far more difficult to make inferences from anecdotes.

Even when we have a substantial body of evidence about a practice at one time and place, it can be hard to decide whether things were similar for other contemporary slaves or for slaves living at other times. For example, classical Athenian references to slave families are rare. But manumission inscriptions from Hellenistic Delphi seem to reveal a world in which many slaves had familial ties of one sort or another, a topic we'll explore in Chapter 7. Did slaves have better prospects of family life in the Hellenistic period? Was slavery at Delphi somehow special or different? Or, does this mean that slaves throughout Greek history had family ties, but that we only find good evidence of them in this one time and place? In this case, some limited form of the last option is probably correct, but we also need to consider the possibility of selection bias in the evidence from Delphi. Only slaves who gained their freedom left manumission inscriptions, on which family members would sometimes be mentioned. The life experiences of such slaves were probably better in many ways than those slaves who never managed to obtain liberty. Such favored slaves may have been atypical in their ability to form and keep family ties just as they were atypical in their ability to buy their freedom.

To generalize from one time and place to another presents more obvious problems as well. Modern historians often emphasize local variations within the system of slavery: slavery in Virginia was not the same as slavery in the deep South; conditions on neighboring plantations varied greatly depending in part on the personalities involved. The experience of ancient Greek slaves is no more likely to have been the same at all times and places. The case for typicality is often worth making, especially if there is no evidence to the contrary. But one must remain cautious about what we really know and what we merely suspect might be the case: that similar practices took place at other times and places.

Common Sense and Comparative History

Historians often make inferences such as the following: if slaves ran away whenever they could, they must have hated slavery. The starting point for drawing such a conclusion seems to be common sense: people flee from what they hate and not from what they enjoy. Such reasoning is fine for some purposes; slave flight on the whole does indicate dissatisfaction with slavery. But an unstated assumption behind arguments from common sense is that all people think and act alike, and this is not the case. For example, most modern religions have a strong moral element that dictates how people should behave and treat one another: the Bible contains not only narratives of God and humans but also the Ten Commandments. It might therefore seem a matter of "common sense" to ask whether ancient Greek religion seemed to condemn or to justify slavery. But ancient Greek religion was more a matter of ritual and mythology – including stories in which gods behave badly – and less a matter of moral rules. Particular rituals and festivals might be open to slaves or not, but Greek religion had no position on slavery and we would be led astray by "common sense" if we tried to find one. For this reason, careful historians try to learn as much as possible about the practices, feelings, and thoughts of ancient Greeks and Romans and their slaves, so that their inferences are based on ancient habits of thought and action rather than imposing a "common sense" that may be modern and thus inappropriate. Our understanding will never be as intuitive or as dependable as our common sense about the times and milieu we actually live in, but it can allow plausible conclusions to be drawn.

One problem with this procedure is that we often do not have enough information about ancient habits of thought and action, especially when it comes to slaves, who were often foreigners and cannot be assumed to resemble closely their Greek or Roman masters. As a result, historians of ancient slavery sometimes turn to comparative history.[4] The basic assumption of this method is that slave societies are similar, and so what holds for one should hold for another. Comparative historians apply what we know about the better known slave societies of the modern world to the poorly known institutions of ancient slavery. For example, tens of thousands of epitaphs from Roman ex-slaves have survived. Historians used to infer from this that most Roman slaves gained their freedom. But nineteenth-century Brazil also possessed a vibrant and conspicuous urban population of ex-slaves. And, in the case of Brazil, historians have the actual statistics, which show that, while some skilled, urban, or household slaves had opportunities to obtain and save money and eventually buy their freedom, most agricultural or mine slaves, the vast majority of the slave population, had little chance of manumission (Garrigus 2011, 237). It is thus certain that conspicuous evidence of ex-slaves does not prove a high overall rate of manumission. Our evidence for ancient slaves regularly obtaining their freedom may only apply to a subset of the slave population.

The comparative method is far from foolproof, as you may have guessed from its dubious basic assumption. It may be more decisive in undermining than in establishing facts – as in the case of manumission rates. Often, when historians know something about both an ancient and a modern system of slavery, they find that the two are different: the existence of states without slaves and of abolitionists in the modern world provides an obvious contrast with the ancient world. Consequently, it is risky to fill in the blank areas in our map of ancient slavery by drawing on parallels from modern slavery.

But this is not the only way to use comparative history. Admittedly, it is difficult to *prove* something by the comparative method; the objection, "but ancient slavery might not have been like modern slavery in that respect," is always possible and often persuasive. But, after all, other historical methods do not always result in indisputable conclusions. And almost all scholars of ancient slavery find it worth their while also to learn

---

4 See Cartledge 2003, Webster 2005 and 2008 for Greek and Roman examples; see Skocpol and Summers 1980 for a theoretical analysis.

about other systems of slavery; often the benefit is simply to stimulate new ways of looking at things and new questions to ask. For instance, the retention of African identity by slaves has long been a focus of scholarship on New World slavery (Childs 2011, 171–173). Historians and archaeologists studying ancient Greek slavery, who knew that slaves in Athens were likewise imported from other cultures, were thus prompted to ask, "Can we tell whether slaves at Athens too retained any sense of their cultures of origins?" – a question we'll explore in Chapter 6. Even when comparative history does not provide a conclusive answer, it can suggest new questions to ask.

Finally, it is always better to make an explicit comparison than to let an unstated comparison sneak in – sometimes under the guise of "common sense." For example, one might unreflectively assume that Roman ex-slaves and their descendants would be subject to racial prejudice. This would be an unconscious use of the comparative method based on our knowledge that ex-slaves and their descendants in the United States were and are subject to racial prejudice. In fact, Roman attitudes towards ex-slaves, for example, could be hostile and were tinged with ethnic chauvinism. They were not linked to skin color nor were they as systematic as modern racism. As a result, ex-slaves and their children had a much easier time joining the mainstream of Roman society, especially in cities. And occasionally rich and powerful freedmen or their children and grandchildren were even able to join the Roman elite, as we'll see in Chapters 5 and 8.

Modern Politics and Ancient Slavery

Although parallels with modern slave societies can stimulate new areas of inquiry and new approaches to our ancient evidence, modern concerns sometimes distort the interpretation of ancient slavery. In part this is because the evidence about ancient slavery is often ambiguous; the choice of one from several possible interpretations of this evidence may depend on which is more appealing in a modern political or social context.

For example, the study of ancient slavery first became a focus of intense modern interest in the context of debates about the abolition of the slave trade in the early nineteenth century. Pro-slavery writers could point to the prestigious high culture of the classical world and argue that the development of this culture depended on slavery. Anti-slavery writers argued that the alienation of the elite from practical matters stunted technological innovation and led to the fall of Rome. Or they claimed that the moral corruption attendant on this brutal system of oppression weakened the Roman Empire and left it vulnerable to invasion from outside. The attitude of the Christian church to Roman slavery became a particular bone of contention. Some abolitionist scholars tried to claim that the conversion of Rome to Christianity necessarily meant the end of classical slavery and therefore that slavery was intrinsically un-Christian. Christians today feel strongly that this last statement is manifestly true and current sympathies are, of course, with the abolitionists. Unfortunately, their historical claim about Christianity is untenable: centuries of Christian accommodation with slavery need to be explained away, no Christian abolitionist movement in antiquity can be detected, and no evidence exists that the decline of classical slavery was due to anything other than economic and social factors, as we'll examine in Chapter 12 and 13. In fact, in parts of medieval Europe, "through the accumulation of power and real estate, the church found itself in possession of large numbers of slaves," which it had no intention of letting go (Phillips 1985, 49).

The admirable qualities of Greek and Roman culture and their importance to Western civilization led to another distortion. Classical culture is liable to the charge, mainly accurate, of being based on slavery. Rather than saying that we admire the cultures of ancient Greece and Rome, but we deplore their use of slaves, some scholars have tried to palliate ancient slavery by exaggerating the differences between ancient and modern slavery. As we shall see, ancient slavery was plenty brutal: there is little to choose between an Athenian silver mine and a Brazilian sugar plantation. And, though not racist in the modern sense, ancient slavery was often justified by a sense of ethnic superiority.

It is easier to see the flaws in older historians' viewpoints than your own biases, but historians today are also unlikely to be immune to the influence of politics and ideology. We probably also prefer topics or angles of argumentation that resonate with present political concerns. For example, historians today are acutely sensitive to multiculturalism and perhaps too eager to find it in the ancient world, an outgrowth of the topic's political relevance. It is not possible to attain perfect objectivity and to escape the various influences of your own political views, and your cultural and social milieu. Indeed, it can be hard enough just to notice them. Despite all this, careful historians strive to and often succeed in writing accounts of history that are accurate and convincing regardless of where, when, and by whom they are read.

Suggested Reading

In addition to his influential redefinition of slavery, Patterson 1982 draws on evidence from a wide range of societies to explore key issues in the sociology and even the philosophy of slavery. For contrasting appraisals of his impact on the study of ancient Greek slavery, see Hunt 2016b and Lewis 2016. Vlassopoulos 2016b argues against "essentialist" conceptions of slavery altogether. Lenski and Cameron 2018 collect essays evaluating or applying the concept of a slave society. Some contributors hold that the concept itself is flawed while others argue that it needs to be applied more widely, that there were more slave societies in world history than the canonical five. David Lewis presents strong arguments that in the ancient Mediterranean Carthage too was a slave society (forthcoming, Chapter 13). Hopkins 1993 and Webster 2008 examine methodological issues in the study of classical slavery. Scott 1990, a brilliant work of comparative history, explores the systematic biases in our evidence that complicate historians' understanding of slaves and other groups subject to intimidation and consequently unable to express their true opinions publicly and directly. McKeown 2007 focuses on several key controversies in the study of ancient slavery. He argues that the approach scholars take is determined in part by the traditions of the discipline of history in their countries and by varied ideological commitments.

3

Enslavement

> *[Odysseus wept] As a woman weeps, lying over the body*
> *of her dear husband, who fell fighting for her city and people*
> *as he tried to beat off the pitiless day from city and children;*
> *she sees him dying and gasping for breath, and winding her body*
> *about him she cries high and shrill, while the men behind her,*
> *hitting her with their spear butts on the back and the shoulders,*
> *force her up and lead her away into slavery, to have*
> *hard work and sorrow, and her cheeks are wracked with pitiful weeping.*
> Homer, *Odyssey* 8.523–30, trans. Lattimore 1965

Introduction

When students first hear about slavery in the ancient Greek and Roman worlds, they sometimes assume that only black Africans were slaves and wonder how the Greeks would have obtained slaves from the sub-Saharan regions. Students fall into this error because the predominant image of slavery today is of the enslavement of Africans in the New World. Although features of better known, modern slave systems sometimes help us understand, or at least imagine, aspects of ancient slavery about which we have little evidence, we cannot assume that just because something was true of New World slavery it was true in the ancient world. People of any race or ethnicity can be enslaved – and most have been at one point or another.

Most slaves in classical Greece came from Thrace, the Black Sea area, and the eastern coast of the Aegean (Map 1; cf. Map 4 below). Some came from Syria and Egypt. In fact, one typical slave name in comedy was Xanthias, which means "Blonde." This may reflect the northern provenance of many slaves. Greek comedy gives us additional evidence. Comic actors wore standard masks that stayed the same over the generations. Slave characters in comedy wore masks with red hair attached. This convention probably reflects a time when the stereotypical slave was imported from the north and had red hair – or, more probably, had red hair more often than the Greeks themselves did. Slaves in classical Greece were generally ethnically different from the Greeks, but they were rarely African.

Ancient Greek and Roman Slavery, First Edition. Peter Hunt.
© 2018 Peter Hunt. Published 2018 by John Wiley & Sons, Ltd.

In the Hellenistic period, dark-skinned African slaves were imported from Nubia, south of Egypt, into Ptolemaic Egypt. Several famous works of Hellenistic art depict such slaves, but they seem to have been a small minority of the slave population. Images of dark-skinned African slaves may be overrepresented in art, since they appealed to Hellenistic artists and patrons interested in exotic and unusual subjects. Most slaves, however, again came from other Hellenistic kingdoms and their borderlands and not from Africa.

Roman slaves came from a wide range of areas at different points in Rome's expansion and its empire. Many slaves would come from those areas where the Romans were currently fighting or where their wars and conquests had left lawless and chaotic conditions, but the slave population was always a mixed one, with some slaves coming from one area and others from another. The regions that supplied Rome with slaves included at one point or another virtually the whole of Europe, northern Africa, and the Near East.

The answer to the question of *where*, geographically, slaves came from is, thus, a complicated one with large variations over time. More important and just as complicated is the question of *how* previously free people ended up in slavery. Enslavement in the ancient world could come about in many ways, and it will help to outline these possibilities. First, however, let's address a red herring. Some historians describe *importation* as a source of slaves both in classical Greece – where slaves could be called "bought barbarians" – and at Rome. Importation is a source of slaves in one sense but not in another. Importation explains how a Roman senator, for example, obtained a particular male slave: he bought him from a merchant who had imported him from, say, Bithynia on the southern coast of the Black Sea. Importation does not, however, explain how this free inhabitant of Bithynia, to continue our example, became a slave in the first place. This question of *how* previously free people ended up in slavery can be particularly hard to answer since the original enslavement often took place on the fringes of the classical world, out of sight of the Roman senator in our example, and in a place for which our sources of information can be almost non-existent.

Importation does bring up an important distinction among ways that people became slaves: some types of enslavement involved people from a society becoming slaves in that same society; other types involved the forcible migration of people to another society, more or less at the same time as their enslavement. We'll consider first the ways that people could fall into slavery within their own society, a less common occurrence, and then the methods of enslavement that involved concurrent transfer between societies.

In many periods and places, people could fall into debt bondage. This occurred when people took out loans on the security of their labor or person – in the same way that a mortgage today is a loan taken out on the security of a house. In the event of default, it was the creditor who typically set the terms of this labor. So it is rare for people ever to escape debt bondage: their labor is often counted as merely offsetting the interest on their debt. In this way, a debtor can end up obligated to life-long, full-time, involuntary labor. Despite these grim prospects, people in debt bondage are not generally considered slaves, since they can't be sold, the status is not hereditary, and they can continue to live with their families. In some cases, however, a debt bondsman became the creditor's property and, in particular, could be sold away from his home and family. Some historians identify this last situation, when the debtor has become a chattel slave, as debt slavery instead of debt bondage. Debt bondage was common throughout the ancient world but only occasionally was it a major path to slavery.

In the ancient world, unwanted infants were left out to die, "exposed." It is surprising to modern expectations that even at places and times where abortion was considered immoral, the exposure of infants was accepted – by our male sources at least. One explanation is that abortion was censured as a woman's usurpation of a father's right to his offspring whereas it was traditionally the father who decided whether a child was exposed, and thus this practice was acceptable (Oldenziel 1987, 100). Exposure provided a source of slaves because, if somebody found and took care of an exposed child, they could raise him or her as their slave, since the reassertion of free status was legally possible, but unlikely in practice. Some people may have even made a living by regularly checking the places where babies were typically exposed and taking some of them to care for and raise as slaves. Both of these types of enslavement, through debt and through exposure, involved a person being enslaved within their own society, but once somebody was a slave they could be sold anywhere.

Turning to the other category, enslavement outside of a person's society, war captives were often enslaved. This was not an inevitable result of military defeat. For example, the defeated state would often accept peace terms, and victors often preferred a subject state to mass enslavement. Nevertheless, the evidence is overwhelming that Greek and Roman wars produced many slaves. Not only could soldiers be captured, but, when armies ravaged an enemy's countryside or sacked a city, they often captured and reduced to slavery many civilians. A similarly violent, but smaller scale, source of slaves was the activity of pirates and kidnappers. These thrived especially in places and periods lacking strong states with an interest in maintaining order – especially states with naval power. In the late Republic, tens of thousands of war captives were regularly imported to Italy; in addition, the chaos in the Eastern Mediterranean – where humbled and defeated states could no longer field strong navies to protect trade – also encouraged piracy and consequently enslavement on a grand scale. For example, an ancient source claims that one group of pirates was capable of mustering a thousand ships and that the slave market on the island of Delos was capable of handling the sale of ten thousand slaves each day, many of them the victims of pirates (Strabo, *Geography* 14.5.2).

Our discussion so far does not imply that all slaves were born free and then enslaved; many slaves were born into slavery. The general rule about the inheritance of status was that – in the absence of an official marriage, which slaves could not contract – a child had the same status as his or her mother. Thus, children born to slave women were slaves regardless of the status of the father – who was sometimes the woman's owner, as we shall see in Chapter 7. Later I'll consider the controversial topic of what proportion of Roman slaves were born in slavery in different periods.

The way an individual was enslaved was important to his or her life; the way most slaves became slaves affected the way the whole institution of slavery operated within a given society. Most obviously, if the slave population could not reproduce itself, then new people needed to be enslaved each generation, if slave numbers were to remain constant. The process of enslavement is usually a violent process, which was almost indescribably wrenching for the persons enslaved. In addition, the whole texture of relationships between masters and slaves was affected by whether few, some, or all of the slaves are born in slavery. To take just one example, relations between masters and slaves as well as among slaves are profoundly influenced by whether or not they all speak the same language. And, in Chapter 10, we'll see that a high proportion of new slaves was a factor that made slave rebellions more likely. In contrast, both Greek and Latin had special terms for slaves born in a master's household, probably reflecting a time when such slaves were relatively rare: both the Greek and the Latin term (*verna*) imply something like "home born" or "native born." And, in general, such slaves were considered well behaved and loyal: some of them had close ties with their masters, attested in epitaphs put up by Roman masters to their beloved *vernae*.

```
(Picture of open hands; in prayer?)
          D. M.
        TIMOTHEAE
         M ULPIUS
         NICANOR
          VERNAE
         SUAE F
    SOL TIBI COMMENDO
    QUI MANUS INTULIT EI
```

Figure 3.1 Epitaph of Timothea: "To the sacred spirits. For Timothea, his verna, Marcus Ulpius Nicanor made [this]. Sun, I give over to you [for punishment] whoever attacked her." The slaveholder Nicanor took a familial interest both in the commemoration of Timothea, his deceased *verna*, and in obtaining vengeance for her – through the Sun god – since she was apparently a victim of violence. Historians agree that there must have been far more home-born slaves in Rome than are identified as *vernae* on their epitaphs; presumably, the designation was confined to those home-born slaves who enjoyed some intimacy with their masters. The owner's name, Nicanor, is Greek, as was common among slaves, ex-slaves, and sometimes their descendants at Rome (see Chapter 8). His full name suggests that he may have been an ex-slave of the emperor Trajan (born Marcus Ulpius Traianus) or a descendant of such an ex-slave (see Chapter 5). *Source*: Palazzo Nuovo, Capitoline Museum, *CIL* 6.14099. Line drawing from VROMA: http://www.vroma.org/.

The source of slaves is closely related to the ratio of males and females among the slave population. In the New World, slave systems that depended mainly on new slaves, such as those of Brazil and the Caribbean, tended to depend mainly on male slaves, who were more capable of heavy labor and thus commanded a higher price after being transported across the Atlantic – conversely, women slaves were in high demand in Africa

(Lovejoy 2012, 14, 63–64). This unbalanced sex ratio in Brazil and the Caribbean limited natural reproduction among the slave population, since the birthrate depends on the number of fertile women. In the American South, however, by the time the importation of slaves ceased in the nineteenth century, a natural population containing approximately equal numbers of males and females had reasserted itself. This sex ratio, in turn, made it possible for the slave population to reproduce itself and even to grow without any new source of slaves. To understand how the institution of slavery worked in any place and period, it is crucial to determine whether it followed one of these patterns or something intermediate.

The ethnic origin of slaves also influenced the institution. It especially affected how masters thought about their slaves and justified slavery. Most notoriously, New World slavery was based on racist distinctions: according to most slaveholders, it was only black Africans who deserved to be in slavery. The peoples from whom the Greeks and Romans took their slaves could not be distinguished on the basis of skin color – which was not always easy even in the New World. Nevertheless, Greeks and Romans often expressed contempt for their slaves on the ground that they came from inferior cultures. When one Greek city enslaved the citizens of another, this way of justifying slavery was more difficult: Greeks generally felt they belonged to a single category in contrast to non-Greeks. As a result some strident critiques of slavery in the classical Greek world focused only on the enslavement of Greeks and not slavery in general (see Chapter 12).

During the second and first centuries BCE, many slaves at Rome were Greeks from mainland Greece and from the Hellenistic Kingdoms of the Eastern Mediterranean. The Romans held Greek culture in high esteem and, in Chapter 6, we'll revisit the issue of how the Romans dealt with slaves whom they in some respects considered culturally superior to themselves. In most cases, however, the Romans did not think highly of the people they enslaved. For example, Cicero complained that Caesar's invasion of Britain was not likely to be profitable: there was no plunder to be had other than captives and, he snidely remarks, "none of those are likely to be well trained in music or literature" (Cicero, *Letters to Atticus* 4.16.7). This was probably a pointed contrast to the slaves of Greek background that might be expected from wars in the Eastern Mediterranean.

Where and how people were enslaved is, consequently, not an isolated aspect of a slave system. Even when historians cannot come to agreement about the dominant source of slaves in one period or another of Greek and Roman history, their debates contribute to our understanding of important aspects of classical slavery. In this chapter, we consider two case studies. First, an enigma surrounds the role of warfare as a source of slaves in classical Greece, especially Athens: why do we find mostly foreign (non-Greek) male slaves when we might expect Greek female slaves? Second, historians have long assumed a change in the main sources of slaves between the Roman Republic and Empire, a shift from war captives to born slaves, but this conclusion has been challenged. Historical demography, the quantitative study of human populations, has recently made decisive contributions to this topic.

Warfare and the Sources of Athenian Slaves?

Most slaves at Athens in the classical period were not born into slavery. Striking evidence of this comes from lists, inscribed on stone, of the property confiscated from a number of wealthy Athenians who were condemned for sacrilege in 415 BCE. These lists are known as the Attic *Stelai*: Attica is the territory of Athens, and *stelai* denotes the thin, rectangular stones, shaped like tall gravestones, on which the lists were inscribed. The Attic *Stelai* list the confiscated property which the state put up for auction, and tell how much it sold for and how much tax was levied. Among this property were slaves belonging to the condemned. The lists identify those slaves born into slavery with the word *oikogenés*, home-born, but only a small fraction of the slaves listed have that designation (Pritchett and Pippin 1956, 280–281). More of the slaves are identified by their place of origin: for example, "Potainios, a Carian" (Stelai 2.77 in Pritchett 1953, 251). All these places of origin are non-Greek. An even larger set of slaves have names that consist of ethnic expressions, for example, Thrax (Thracian) as a name. Of these ethnic names on the Attic *Stelai*, seventeen out of eighteen are non-Greek. This leaves only eight slaves with Greek names. Even they are not necessarily Greek given that some of the slaves whose origins are both specified and foreign had Greek names. Thus, the vast majority of the slaves on the Attic *Stelai* seem to have been born outside of Athens and indeed outside of Greece.

About a hundred personal names are found on inscriptions in the mining area of Athens, mainly on epitaphs or simple religious dedications. Many of these must be the names of mine slaves. That so many of the names are not Greek suggests, again, that more than half of such slaves were of foreign, non-Greek descent (Lauffer 1979, Table 6 (124–128), 140). Foreign slaves also predominate in comedy (Ehrenberg 1974, 171–173). In a law court speech, Demosthenes mentions the "barbarians (non-Greeks) from whom we import slaves" (Demosthenes 21.48). Finally, a couple of passages suggest that masters could not assume that an Athenian slave could even speak or understand Greek.[1] Some of this evidence may not be dependable: for example, slave names may not reflect origins, and slave traders had incentives to misrepresent the origins of slaves belonging to less marketable ethnic groups (Braund and Tsetskhladze 1989, 119–121). Enslaving Greeks became an awkward and controversial practice – a topic we'll revisit in Chapter 12 – and may be under-represented in our evidence as a result; for we do indeed hear anecdotes about Athenians and other Greeks falling into slavery. On balance, however, I am convinced that most slaves in Athens were neither Athenian nor Greek. But, of course, our sources are not such that we could venture a percentage for the non-Greeks among the slave population at Athens: was it 65 percent or 95 percent?

The brutal practices of Greek warfare seem at first to suggest how foreigners ended up as slaves in Athens. The first text in Greek literature, Homer's *Iliad*, describes how, when a city is sacked, the men are killed and the women and children taken as slaves (e.g., *Iliad* 9.590–594). The tents of the Greek heroes outside Troy are filled with captive slave women, and a quarrel about one of them motivates the central conflict between Achilles and Agamemnon. In the simile with which we began the chapter, Homer pictures the scene of enslavement: a city's foes drag a woman into slavery after having killed her husband. Homer presents a heroic version of eighth-century warfare, but occasionally this picture is confirmed by evidence from the classical period. Most infamously, when the Athenians defeated the small island of Melos, they enslaved the women and children and killed the men (Thucydides 5.116). Their notorious general, Alcibiades, even acquired a Melian slave mistress in the process. So far the picture seems to make

---

1 Plato, *Meno* 82b; Xenophon, *On Hunting* 2.3, 6.18.

sense: enslavement in war was a longstanding practice in the Greek world and continued to provide most slaves in the classical period when Greece had become a slave society. There remains, however, a big problem with this model: direct evidence about the slave population at Athens, the Greek slave population about which we know the most, does not match what we would expect of a population captured in war.

First of all, if the Athenians captured their slaves in war, Homeric style, we would expect a slave population consisting mainly of women and children from the states that Athens fought against. The slave population at Athens, however, seems to have contained more men than women. The Attic *Stelai* recorded 37 men to nine females. Statistically, such a skewed sample is almost impossible, if the actual ratio was 50/50, and if the *Stelai* provide a random sample of the slave population.[2] I have a theory about one way that this sample may be biased: the wives of the condemned probably left their husbands and returned to their paternal homes taking with them some of their personal servants, predominantly female. So the property that remained to auction and be recorded on the *Stelai* contains fewer female slaves than were in the original households. There may be other ways in which the gender ratio on Attic *Stelai* is skewed, but it is striking that we also find predominantly male slaves in comedy, even though most comedies were set in the household: we expect female slaves to predominate among domestic slaves, but they are a minority even there.

By itself the unexpected sex ratio, more men than women, is perhaps explicable. Walled cities were rarely captured, so women were often safe inside, while men were the ones out fighting and thus at risk of capture. But difficulties remain. Athens fought wars against the Persian Empire during the first half of the fifth century, but for a generation before the Attic *Stelai* were inscribed, Athens' main enemies were other Greek cities. But we find no slaves from any of these places: no Thebans, no Corinthians, no Lacedaemonians, no Aeginetans, and no Megarians. Rather, as you can see from Map 4, based on different types of inscriptions, slaves at Athens seem to come from a large variety of non-Greek areas in the Eastern Mediterranean and Black Sea, with Thrace and the eastern coast of Asia Minor providing the largest groups. This data leaves us with two questions. First, why did warfare among the Greeks not provide more slaves? Second, how did non-Greeks end up as slaves in Athens if not as the result of capture in war?

I mentioned already that Greek walled cities were rarely taken by storm. Out of a thousand or so city-states, only a handful – such as Melos – would suffer this fate in a generation. This greatly reduced the potential for the enslavement of whole populations with women and children. Some soldiers could be captured and enslaved. In one exceptional case – the greatest defeat in known history according to Thucydides (7.87.5–6) – the Syracusans and their allies destroyed the entire army and navy sent against them from Athens and captured Athenians and subject-allies, in numbers in excess of ten thousand. Most of these ended up being sold into slavery (7.85.3; 7.87.3). Enslavement was not, however, the most common treatment of captured soldiers. Usually Greek armies kept such captives as prisoners of war. They might then return them to their cities for a ransom; for a captured soldier was usually worth much more to his own family, if they had the money, than on the slave market. In addition, city-states

---

2 Pritchett and Pippin 1956, 276 and Pritchett 1961, 26. Both male and female slaves were valuable (Pritchett and Pippin 1956, 276, 278) and ought to have been reported on these lists.

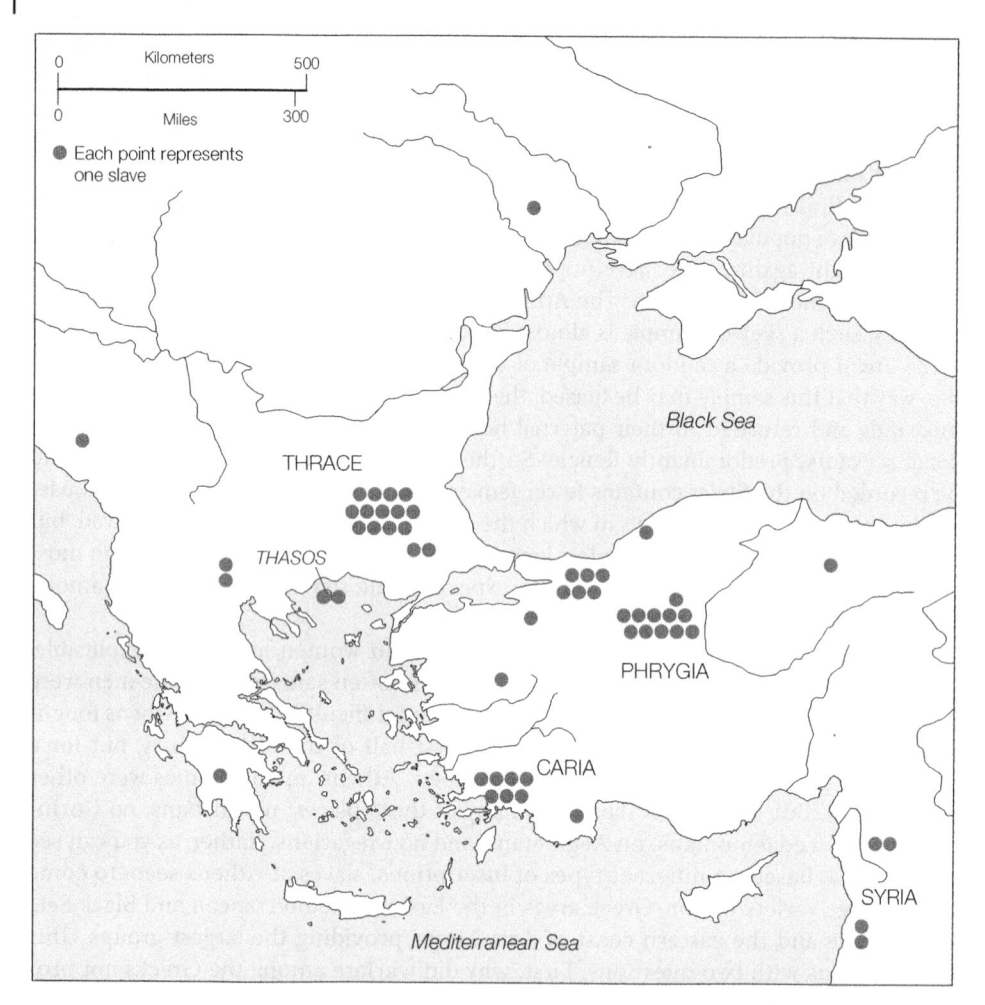

Map 4 Origins of slaves at Athens in the fifth and fourth centuries BCE. The slaves attested on inscriptions at Athens rarely seem to be Greek. Rather they come from areas like Thrace, on the outskirts of the Greek world, and from the western provinces of the Persian Empire, such as Phrygia and Caria. From *The Cambridge World History*, Volume 4, ed. Craig Benjamin. Cambridge: Cambridge University Press, p. 91, Map 4.1, based on Morris 1998, figures 12.2 and 12.3. *Source*: Morris 1998. Reproduced with permission of Cambridge University Press.

generally wanted to get their citizens back, so the peace treaties that ended most wars often required both sides to release the prisoners of war they had taken. Even though war was common and war captives were potentially liable to enslavement, warfare among the Greeks still could not provide a large proportion of the slaves at Athens.

The second question (how did so many non-Greeks end up in slavery?) is more complicated. The historian Theopompus wrote in the fourth century that the Chians were the first Greeks who used "bought barbarians" as slaves (Athenaeus, *The Learned Banqueters* 265 C). This statement suggests two things: first, it confirms our impression that most slaves were non-Greek, hence "barbarians"; second, it shows that Greeks thought of contemporary slavery as marked by import rather than direct capture – hence "bought" slaves. But, knowing that the Greeks bought their slaves only provokes other questions: how did so many non-Greeks end up on the slave market, and why was it the Greeks who bought them?

War may still be at the root of Greek slavery but at one remove. Many people may have been enslaved in war and then imported to the Greek world. The areas on the outskirts of the Greek world from which slaves were imported to Greece were not usually of much interest to Greek historians, and they did not produce their own historians. Nevertheless, we do occasionally hear about wars among non-Greeks, for example, the various revolts of Persian governors against the King of Persia and the resulting wars. During some periods, these conflicts explain how so many slaves came into Greece from the western areas of the Persian Empire in Asia Minor, a major source of slaves. Our sources sometimes report wars between rival principalities in Thrace.[3] It is safe to assume that other Thracian wars – especially those far inland – were not reported or even known by Greek historians. Such unattested wars could explain the many Thracian slaves at Athens.

The Greek demand for slaves may even have encouraged slaving in the hinterlands of Greek settlements on the coasts of Thrace and Asia Minor: as one historian puts it, "there seems every reason to suppose that the slave trade at the coast served to generate instability and conflict in the interior" (Braund 2011, 115). The sale of slaves to the Greeks was lucrative. Raids and wars became more profitable and perhaps more likely to occur once captives could be converted into cash or traded for desirable and otherwise unobtainable luxury goods from the Greeks. In eighteenth- and nineteenth-century Africa, this phenomenon was a well-known and devastating effect of the export of slaves to the New World. That it occurred also on the outskirts of the Greek world is likely enough.

Greek colonies, numbering in the hundreds, sometimes intervened directly and undertook slave raids against their non-Greek neighbors: for example, the Greek mercenary and philosopher Xenophon took part in such a raid, completely unprovoked, while on the northern coast of Asia Minor (Xenophon, *Anabasis* 6.3.2–3). Large numbers of these Greek cities lay in close proximity to non-Greek populations on the coasts of Thrace, Asia Minor, the Black Sea, Sicily, and Italy. Often the Greek city, a colony, was on the coast and had captured enough land from the natives for the settlers to farm but still faced a foreign hinterland. The sporadic raids or small wars of such cities with their neighbors may not make it into the historical record even if, in total, they resulted in the enslavement of many people.

A final possibility takes us away from war altogether. Recall that it was only with Solon's reforms that citizens of Athens were secure from ever falling into slavery for debt. The non-Greek states from which Greece obtained slaves did not develop democracies and may never have curbed debt bondage. Quite possibly, poor Thracians or Lydians possessed so few rights that they could fall into debt bondage and, in some cases, even be sold away from their homelands. And Herodotus claims that the Thracians – presumably poor Thracians – sold their children into slavery (5.6.1). Slavery and sale abroad might also have become a punishment for criminals or for political enemies. This type of punishment for crime or simply for poverty would have become more attractive given Greece's demand for slaves. Once there is a ready market for humans, some people will find ways to supply it and thus to profit from it.

---

3 E.g., Thucydides 2.98.1; Xenophon, *Anabasis* 7.22.2; Demosthenes 23.10.

So far we have treated the supply side of the slave trade; we'll defer discussing the demand for slaves in Greece until we get to the economics and politics of Greek slavery in the next two chapters. For now, let's turn to the Roman slave supply.

A Sea Change in the Roman Slave Supply?

In Roman law, "Slaves are either born or made" (Justinian, *Institutes* I.3). As we have already seen, people could be "made" into slaves in a variety of ways or they could be born into slavery. Historians have traditionally held that the many brutal wars of Rome's expansion supplied the vast majority of slaves, "made slaves," until the pace of conquest slowed during the reign of Augustus (31 BCE–14 CE). After this watershed, so the theory holds, the main external source of slaves was slowly shut off, the price of slaves increased, and Roman slaveholders turned increasingly to natural reproduction, "born slaves," to replenish their slave labor force. Despite this expedient, the number of slaves slowly declined. Some historians have even sought the beginnings of serfdom in the decline in slavery and in the binding of Roman peasants to their land in the late Empire, from the third to fifth centuries CE. We shall return to this last theory in Chapter 13, but for here it is enough to say that this grand scheme of a transition from slavery to serfdom is much too simple. Here we focus on the traditional view of the Roman slave supply (Table 3.1) and whether it is generally correct.

Before we get to the main issues, one implication of the dates I have chosen is worth stressing. In this chapter, we are not concerned with what happened after 200 CE. From the vantage point of modern historians, centuries sometimes shrink, like cities seen from an airplane, and we may (falsely) assume that there was only room for one big trend in the slave supply under the Roman Empire. But the third through fifth centuries CE were different from the first two. Warfare again became more frequent and more intense. This warfare was obviously less successful than that of the Republic – after all, the Roman Empire suffered many invasions and eventually Rome was sacked and the western Empire fell to invaders – but it is entirely possible that enslaved war captives became more numerous again in the violent late Empire. In any case, over the whole, vast course of Roman history, there may have been several shifts in the slave supply; we are focusing on just one possible shift, between the period of Roman expansion, c. 300–1 BCE, and the period of stability following it, 1 BCE–200 CE. And, indeed, smaller ups and downs within each of these periods are quite possible.

The traditional theory does not primarily rest on direct evidence about the slave population. It is mainly an inference from the military history of Rome and the growth in the number of slaves. Roman armies fought often and intensely even before the

Table 3.1 Traditional view of the Roman slave supply.

Dates	Intensity of warfare	Proportion of war captives	Proportion of born slaves
300–1 BCE	Higher	Higher	Lower
1 CE to 200 CE	Lower	Lower	Higher

beginning of the First Punic War in 264 BCE, and Italy's slave population may have been, very roughly, 300,000 already in 220 BCE. Rome continued to fight many wars in the second and first century BCE, and its empire grew immensely. The slave population of Roman Italy had perhaps grown to about 1.5 million by the reign of Augustus, about 25 percent of a total population of 5.7 million (De Ligt 2012, 72 (accepting Scheidel), 190, 341–342). The temple of Janus provides a memorable symbol of Rome's almost constant warfare during these centuries. The Romans closed the doors of this temple whenever they were at peace – after winning all their wars of course. Augustus states in his autobiographical *Res Gestae* that before his reign the Senate had closed the doors only two times in the whole long history of the city (Augustus, *Res Gestae* 13). This story dramatizes a key fact: the Roman Republic was almost always at war and often on two or three fronts at once.

Critics of the traditional picture of a switch in the main source of slaves can point to successful and large wars during the first two centuries CE, but nothing as constant and intense as the wars by which Rome obtained its vast empire. So the objection that the *Pax Romana*, the Roman Peace under the early Empire, was not that peaceful does not really get to the heart of the matter. There was in fact a contrast in the intensity of warfare between the last three centuries BCE and the first two centuries CE. The traditional view is not vulnerable to critique in the intensity-of-warfare column.

The primary difficulty in confirming the rest of the traditional theory is the almost complete lack of quantitative information about made and born slaves at any point in Roman history. We find evidence in both periods of the import of slaves, of their capture in war, and of slave families with children. None of this gives us much information about the proportion of slaves coming from one source or another. Some historians have detected a greater concern with slave families in Columella (writing around 50 CE) than in the two earlier agricultural writers, Cato (234–149 BCE) and Varro (116–27 BCE). Might this difference reflect the greater difficulty of importing slaves in the later period and a consequent emphasis on breeding? It may, but most historians are reluctant to put too much weight on this difference: you can't infer a trend from three authors, separated by two hundred years. For all we know, slave breeding was an individual and eccentric interest of Columella.

The lack of quantitative evidence leaves us in a quandary. On the one hand, nobody ever claimed that the source of slaves went from 100 percent war to 100 percent reproduction. So finding counter-examples will never be decisive. On the other hand, historians would like a statistical answer, for example, 30 percent of the slaves in 100 BCE were born in slavery while in 100 CE 80 percent were born in slavery. Historians can derive such statistics about New World slave societies, and they provide crucial information about the working of slavery. But our evidence about the Roman Republic and Empire is primarily anecdotal. It is compatible both with the traditional picture or its opposite. So it may seem that we are left with a likely enough reconstruction, based on the prevalence of war and growth of slavery during the Republic, but without any way to confirm the argument.

Recently, however, some historians have attempted to solve this impasse by drawing on the discipline of historical demography, the quantitative study of human populations. It may seem mysterious or even improbable that any quantitative methodology can solve an issue about which we lack numerical evidence, since no equation or calculation can produce results that are better than the data we plug into it. Historical demography, however, allows the construction of models of the gains and losses of the Roman slave population based in part on the size of the population and the probable life expectancy of slaves. Even granting large errors in the data used to construct these models, their main result is simple and persuasive: as a slave population grows large – as in the Roman Empire – its resupply will necessarily become more and more dependent on reproduction, a finding in agreement with the traditional model. Just as important for our purposes, simply constructing and thinking about a model of the gains and losses of the slave population involves learning a great deal about Roman slavery.

First, a detour to familiarize ourselves with demography before attacking the problem of the Roman slave supply. In the late nineteenth and twentieth centuries, humanity in general (and especially developed countries) underwent a demographic revolution. People started living much longer and consequently did not need to have as many children to maintain the population. Before this revolution, life expectancy at birth was often only 25 years; some of this was due to infant and childhood mortality, but even a person who made it to twenty could only expect to live to fifty – as opposed to eighty in many places today. In societies before the demographic revolution, that is, high mortality/high fertility societies, populations would stagnate if adult women had fewer than five live births on average, or about six births in total.

Demographers do not have direct access to the mortality, birth rate, or life expectancy of the Roman Empire, but they present good evidence from other societies from before the demographic revolution and are thus able to make a number of probable – if rough – inferences about the Roman population. The life expectancy of a Roman at birth was almost certainly between twenty and thirty years. Some historical parallels suggest that slaves – and the poor in general – die younger on average than slaveholders due to differences in nutrition and living conditions. This is not, however, certain. For example, living in cities was extremely unhealthy due to contagious diseases and poor sanitation, and the Roman elite lived in cities. An aristocrat in Rome may even have had a greater risk of dying than did his slaves out on farms in the country. In any case, we can safely assume a life expectancy under thirty for the slave population in the Roman Empire. The payoff of this reasonable assumption is the following: if we can determine the size of the Roman slave population and assume that it is not changing rapidly, then we can calculate how many slaves were needed each year to maintain its size. We can then consider how much of a contribution different sources of slaves might make to this.

A Slave Population Equation

The ancient social historian Walter Scheidel has explored these issues in several important articles (1997, 2005a, 2011). He believes that neither exposure nor import (via war or otherwise) from outside the Empire came close to matching the contribution that natural reproduction made to the maintenance of the slave population during the Empire, our second period. We can best understand this claim by constructing an equation to describe the Roman slave population. This does not mean that we are introducing any difficult math but it will just help us organize our thinking. Nor does the use of an equation imply any degree of precision. In fact, many of the numbers we use will be ballpark estimates. Nevertheless, stating our results in equation form allows us to see more accurately which scenarios are plausible or not.

Scheidel first assumes that the number of slaves was more or less a constant during our second period since we would hear about a dramatic decline in slave numbers. This assumption is liable to minor objections around the edges: a very slow change in the number of slaves might go unnoticed but still make a difference over the course of a century. Nevertheless, such a slow process would only involve a tiny change each year so the assumption of a constant number of slaves is good enough for our rough purposes and allows us to start our equation: the total loss of slaves each year must be balanced by a gain of about the same number, the annual Roman slave supply. This assumption allows us to approach the size of the Roman slave supply by considering the number of people who left the slave population each year and had to be replaced:

Total Loss of Slaves (per year) ≈ *Roman Slave Supply (per year)*

The most common way for people to leave the slave population was for them to die, but some slaves escaped and others gained their freedom when they were manumitted:

Manumissions (per year) + Escapes (per year) + Deaths (per year) ≈ *Total Loss of Slaves (per year)*

The number of manumissions, escapes, and deaths per year all depend on the total number of slaves. Consequently, before we can explore how much the slave population lost in these three ways, we need at least a rough estimate of the total number of slaves in the Empire. The best we can do for this is a very rough figure: about 10 percent of the Empire's 60 million inhabitants were slaves. Slaves may have constituted more than 20 percent of the population in the center of the empire, Roman Italy, and wherever the use of slaves in agriculture became common. In other places agriculture continued to be dominated by different grades of peasants, sharecroppers, or seasonal hired labor rather than slaves. In those areas, slavery may have been mainly an urban phenomenon and concentrated in the households of the affluent: there the proportion of slaves may have been well below 10 percent. For example, some of our best data comes from census returns preserved on papyrus in Egypt. We would not expect to find large numbers of slaves there, since the agricultural economy remained primarily based on peasant labor. Nevertheless, slaves – probably domestic slaves – constituted slightly more than 10 percent of the approximately 1100 people listed. These returns over-represent cities and towns, where the rich with their domestic slaves would concentrate, so the actual proportion of slaves in Egypt as a whole is more likely to be between 5 percent and 10 percent. On the whole, we'll be in the right ballpark and keep the math simple if we assume six million slaves, 10 percent (Scheidel 2011, 288–292).

Manumission: As we shall see in Chapter 8, the Romans manumitted large numbers of their slaves. Impressionistic evidence – for example the epitaphs left by ex-slaves in Rome – suggests that some groups of skilled, urban slaves regularly gained their freedom before they died. We now reap the first payoff from demography: despite the tens of thousands of ex-slave epitaphs, not that high a proportion of slaves can have been freed. Scheidel shows that a high rate of manumission would make the replacement of the slave population almost impossible; particularly costly in this respect is the manumission of women still able to bear children, for their subsequent children would be free and would not contribute to maintaining the slave population. Scheidel's intermediate model of manumission assumes that 10 percent of all slaves gained their freedom at 25 and 10 percent more at five-year intervals. In this simplified model one-third of all slaves would have been freed before they died. Scheidel eventually concludes that even this rate of manumission is too high; the slave population would have declined if so many slaves were freed. We'll want to keep these percentages in mind not only here, but also when we discuss manumission in Chapter 8: it is fascinating and important that the Romans gave freedom and citizenship to some of their slaves, but we should not forget that a large majority of slaves died while still in slavery. Even with low rates of manumission, more than 30,000 new slaves would have been required each year to replace those who gained their freedom.

Slaves who escaped: The number of slaves who escaped and remained free is impossible to estimate. Most scholars of the Roman slave supply have not even made the attempt, but we know that masters were concerned with the possibility of slaves running away. Such slaves hit them in the pocketbook and, as we'll explore in Chapter 9, slaveholders took all sorts of counter-measures to prevent flight or to recapture slaves who had run away. But, although fugitive slaves are well attested, their numbers are difficult even to estimate. A couple of historical parallels may also help us here: during the American Civil War, around 10 percent of slaves in Virginia escaped – and freedom was assured in the North during these years. Closer in time, one of Alexander's finance chiefs, Antimenes of Rhodes, made money from a scheme to insure the masters of slaves in an army camp against the risk of their slaves running away. The annual premium was only eight drachmas, perhaps 4 percent of an average slave's value, suggesting a low annual rate of escape ([Aristotle], *Oeconomica* II 1352b33–1353a4). If, at Rome, only one slave out of two hundred escaped each year, which is quite conceivable, that would still add up to a total of 30,000 slaves that needed to be replaced each year.

Deaths: Demography plays a direct role here. The total number of slave deaths per year is a function of the mortality rate and the population of slaves. If the life expectancy at birth of the six million slaves in the Roman Empire was 25 years, about 300,000 would die each year. Once we have added the number of slaves who were manumitted (at a low rate of manumission) and who escaped, we end up with an annual loss of slaves on the order of 350,000 – I round to the nearest 50,000 to make clear that these are very rough approximations.

Now we need to consider how the Romans might have replaced such a large number of slaves every year. The Roman slave supply can be divided into the enslavement of previously free people and the birth of slaves to a slave mother, natural reproduction. The enslavement of previously free people can be subdivided into the following main categories: enslavements in war, by pirates and other kidnappers, via self-sale, and of children exposed at birth:

> *Roman Slave Supply* ≈ *Natural Reproduction* + *War* + *Piracy* + *Self-Sale* + *Exposure*

Although there is vigorous debate about almost every aspect of the Roman slave supply and we'll never end up with precise numbers to put into our equation, considering each possible source of slaves in turn is revealing about how the system of slavery was maintained.

Natural Reproduction: Some Roman slaves had families and children – a topic we'll explore in Chapter 7 – but the question here is how many on average? W. V. Harris argues that the Roman system of slavery was harsh and that most slaves were males with little chance of a family life. For example, agricultural writers advised slaveholders to give a wife as a reward to the most important slaves on their farms, such as the *vilicus*, who managed the whole farm.[4] This implies that having a wife was a special and rare reward. This makes the most sense if the ratio of male to female slaves was high. On this issue, Harris points to data from the epitaphs in several Roman noble households – including one belonging to a woman, whom we would expect to have more female slaves. These epitaphs suggest that men may have constituted 60–70 percent of the slaves in these households (Treggiari 1975b, 395; cf. Mouritsen 2013, 51). Farms, on which most jobs seem to have been for men, ought to have employed an even greater proportion of male slaves. The fertility rate of a population depends on the proportion of females of childbearing age, so a population containing a majority of males would have little chance of maintaining its numbers, which is not easy anyway when the life expectancy is under 30. Harris argues that Roman slavery was similar to Caribbean slavery, which depended throughout its history on a large proportion of imported slaves from Africa, in part because the population was predominantly male – though the brutal work regime of growing and refining sugar didn't help either. This would not mean that there was no natural reproduction among Roman slaves, but only that a large and continuous influx of new slaves was necessary.

Scheidel proposes, in contrast, that the Roman slave population mainly reproduced itself. He counters the evidence from epitaphs at Rome and jobs by arguing that women were simply less likely to be commemorated. This was merely part of the neglect of women by the men of a patriarchal society. In a similar way, in the free population women and men were probably present in approximately even numbers, but in all our sources of evidence we find more men than women. So, this argument runs, women were there in equal numbers with the men, but are just not as conspicuous in our surviving, biased sources. Another scholar, Ulrike Roth, argues that even large farms provide another case of this phenomenon (2007). Contrary to the impression we get from our authors who concentrate on fieldwork and its supervision, female slaves were present in roughly equal numbers to the male slaves. They produced clothing for the market (especially for the Roman army), prepared food (an important and time-consuming task in ancient conditions), and raised children.

In general, Scheidel does not believe that Roman slavery was so harsh that masters would not accommodate their slaves who wanted to have and raise children, since these activities were in their financial interest – except perhaps when war captives came on the market in such numbers that buying a slave was cheaper than raising a child. When it comes to historical comparisons, Scheidel believes that the Roman slave population in the imperial period was, in this respect, more similar to the slave population in the United States South. This population had a natural, balanced sex ratio. It not only maintained its numbers but grew considerably during the fifty odd years between the end of the slave trade and the abolition of slavery during the American Civil War.

The issue of the gender ratio among Roman slaves and thus the fertility of the slave population is hard to decide, but Scheidel has another, strong argument up his sleeve, this one deriving from simple math. The number of slaves born in slavery is a function of the size of the slave population; the more slaves, the more slave children. A population of

---

4 Harris 1980, 119–120 on Varro, *On Agriculture* 1.17.5–7; Cato, *On Agriculture* 1.143; cf. Chariton, *Callirhoe* 2.3.2.

six million can reproduce itself as easily as a population of one million. External sources of slaves are not a function of the size of the slave population; they *do not* grow in proportion with the number of slaves. Thus the larger the slave population, the more likely it is that natural reproduction will contribute to maintaining it. In the Roman case, Scheidel does not believe that outside sources could produce, year in and year out, anything like the number of slaves required to maintain the slave population of the Empire. Thus natural reproduction must be the main source of slaves. To evaluate this argument let's return then to the ways that free people became slaves, external sources of slaves, and try to quantify them.

War: During the Republic, the ravaging of Epirus by a Roman army reportedly involved the capture of 150,000 slaves, but this and other mass enslavements are reported because they were exceptional events, not something that happened every year – especially after the reign of Augustus. But for the Roman slave population to maintain itself, 350,000 new slaves were needed every single year.

As we saw in the case of Athens, warfare can produce slaves that then are sold far away to parties uninvolved in the war. Wars outside the frontiers of the empire produced slaves that were then sold across the frontiers to the Romans. We sometimes hear as much, and we can also assume that slaves were imported into the Roman Empire whose enslavement occurred in wars that we do not hear about, for example, raids and counter-raids among German tribes a few hundred miles away from the Roman frontier. Scheidel, however, does have a demographic argument against such wars providing enough slaves to maintain a non-reproducing population. After calculating the highest possible population in the areas around the Roman Empire from which slaves might be imported, he concludes that this population was not large enough to maintain itself if, say, a hundred thousand of its people were every year being imported as slaves into the Roman Empire. This argument is not incontestable – perhaps the population of the frontier zones did decline – but it nevertheless adds weight to the strong general impression that war could not resupply the whole Roman Empire with slaves.

Piracy: During the period of the late Republic, pirates were a major threat to the security of the Mediterranean and a notorious source of slaves. Some pirates once even held the young Julius Caesar for ransom. He promised to come back and have them executed once he was ransomed, and he was good to his word. At another point, the famous general Pompey had to be given a special commission with extraordinary powers and large forces to clear the Mediterranean of pirates, who were threatening the grain supply of Rome. Pompey's commission was only one of several such appointments to deal with different groups of pirates. But during the Empire, although smaller-scale brigandage and kidnapping continued to plague some areas, piracy largely dried up as a major source of slaves. Instead of the confused, divided, and violent Mediterranean of the late Republic, by the time of Augustus, Rome had made the sea into a "Roman lake" and had every incentive to keep it safe for commerce.

Self-sale: In legal theory, no free Roman citizen could be enslaved within the Roman Empire, but people might wish to become slaves to escape abject poverty and starvation. Accordingly legal loopholes allowed for the transition from freedom to slavery. Most scholars play this down as a source of slaves, but Harris points out that Romans often refer to their own provinces as the source of slaves; it may be that more enslavement than we think was voluntary – at least in the limited sense that a person facing starvation can be said to make a choice. We also hear about men selling themselves into slavery in order to become business agents for rich Romans (Aubert 1994). There were legal advantages to having a slave as one's business manager, but such self-sales cannot have been significant numerically. Only a few thousand Romans can have been rich enough to need a business agent.

Exposure: As we saw earlier, ancient Romans might "expose" a newborn child if they did not want to raise it. The approximate number of such exposed infants and the proportion raised as slaves is hard to determine. On the one hand, Harris is able to point to several cities such as Paris, Milan, and Moscow with extraordinarily high rates of child abandonment, over 20 percent of births in the eighteenth and nineteenth centuries. On the other hand, Scheidel calculates that for exposure to contribute significantly to a slave population of six million, it would have to have been common – and not just among the poor. He argues that we ought to have much more evidence of such exposure if it were such a standard practice – and likely a traumatic one.

This all may seem frustratingly indecisive and, in some ways, it is. Nevertheless, two results of the recent, demographic arguments are hard to contest and are important. First, the number of slaves required to maintain the Empire's slave population is so large that natural reproduction probably played a dominant role. Scheidel believes that it *must* have provided more than half of the 350,000 slaves needed each year and he favors a higher proportion; Harris is more pessimistic about the birth rate in slavery and favors a higher estimate of the capacity of wars, self-sale, and especially exposure to provide large numbers of new slaves. Even if Harris is correct and the slave population did not come close to reproducing itself, natural reproduction probably constituted more than half of the requisite slave supply and was likely the most important source of slaves by a large margin. Second, once the Empire had grown to its full size, the slave population was so large that not even the most intense warfare on and beyond its borders could provide enough slaves by itself.

Conclusion

Surprisingly, this new thinking about the Roman slave supply reinforces the old view of a shift from war to reproduction as the main source of slaves. Let's focus on the ratio between the size of the Roman slave population, upon which natural reproduction depends, and the population affected by Roman wars and expansion, the main external source of slaves. During most of the Republic, Roman rule comprised a smaller area and its slave population was smaller whereas the conquest of the Mediterranean basin, France, and Spain led, directly and indirectly, to more enslavement than did later wars under the Empire. (And, as we'll see next chapter, the wealth pouring into Italy enabled the Romans to import even more slaves.) To take one example, Caesar's conquest of Gaul in the 50s BCE may have involved the enslavement of one million people over the course of a decade. This would have provided the lion's share of all the slaves needed to maintain the slave population for those ten years. In contrast, the conquest of Dacia by Trajan after 100 CE was one of the most successful and large-scale conquests under the Empire, but it involved a smaller area and population. And, even if the scale of enslavement was the same as Caesar's – a hundred thousand slaves per year during the four years of the Dacian war – that would have still provided less than a third of the slaves required to maintain the slave population of six million under the Empire.

In the Empire, there was a much larger slave population with fewer wars to maintain it, and these wars drew on a reservoir of potential slaves that was no larger than during the Republic and may have been smaller. Natural reproduction has the unique quality of increasing with the size of the slave population and was thus likely to become more and more important as the Empire and its slave population grew. This tendency, however, was a constant and would not lead to distinct periods, as in the traditional model, but a continuous increase in the proportion of born slaves as the size of the Empire gradually increased over the generations.

Suggested Reading

Follett 2011 provides a concise treatment of the demography of New World slavery. Written from a Marxist perspective, Garlan 1999 is an excellent entrée into the problem of the source of Greek slaves. Rosivach 1999 argues for a very high percentage of foreign slaves; Wrenhaven 2013 and Braund and Tsetskhladze 1989, 119–121, emphasize the difficulty of our evidence. The sources of Roman slaves can be traced in the debate between Harris (1980, 1999) and Scheidel (1997, 2005a). Scheidel 2011 provides a summary of the whole issue with bibliography.

4

Economics

> *The work done by slaves, though it appears to cost only their maintenance, is in the end the dearest [most expensive] of any. A person who can acquire no property can have no other interest than to eat as much, and to labour as little as possible.*
> Adam Smith, *The Wealth of Nations* (1937, originally 1776), 365

Introduction

We turn now from the supply of slaves to the demand for them. Societies do not buy slaves in large numbers simply because they accept slavery and a supply of slaves is available. For slaves to be used on a large scale, it usually has to make economic sense to import and exploit them.

Some historians and more classicists, however, have a visceral dislike of economics. Economics works with a simplified conception of human interactions and decisions that can seem improbably distant from how people actually behave and think. According to one witticism, economics describes the behavior of calculating "econs," not people. Economics thus seems to neglect the complexity and nuance that many historians aspire to in their understanding of the past. It is, however, these reductionist features of economics that give it its great explanatory power. Economics allows insight by reducing the actual complexity of a situation: for example, it tries first to understand human actions in terms of the simplifying assumption that people are rational calculators, who try to "maximize their utility." This model, of course, underrates the complexity of human motivations, but it allows economists to explain many actions and tendencies. For example, although we do not live in a world of perfect markets today – and ancient markets were even less perfect – the law of supply and demand does explain a great deal about many transactions. We simply need to remember not to confuse a simplifying model with a full explanation of the real world. Economics has proven invaluable for understanding many trends throughout history, including the growth of slavery in both the ancient and modern worlds.

The economics of slavery may also seem inhumane and callous. First of all, in this chapter we will frequently be interested in the question of why rich Greeks and Romans tended to employ slaves rather than other types of workers. This requires us to take the point of view of the exploiter of labor rather than the worker, who, we can assume,

Ancient Greek and Roman Slavery, First Edition. Peter Hunt.
© 2018 Peter Hunt. Published 2018 by John Wiley & Sons, Ltd.

does not want to be a slave or exploited at all. In other words, when in this chapter we ask what "you" would do, "you" is usually going to be a slaveholder or a potential slaveholder. Second, we will be talking about concepts like labor, resources, incentives, and efficiency, but all this may seem distant from the experiences of individual slaves and masters. These abstractions are, nevertheless, necessary to understand the institution of slavery and to make some sort of sense of the multitude of individual decisions that brought it into existence and maintained it.

We shall begin by exploring the concept of the slave society and some general theories about the efficiency of slave labor. The main part of the chapter will focus on attempts to explain in economic terms the use of slaves in different periods of classical antiquity. We'll finish with a more concrete topic: the slave trade.

Slave Societies

Historians categorize only a few states as slave societies. There have been slaves in all sorts of places and times beyond the simplest hunter-gatherers, but in many cases the role of such slaves was to enhance the status and lifestyle of their masters rather than to do productive work. In slave societies, the institution of slavery not only permeates the culture but also the economy.

Until the industrial revolution, the dominant sector of the economy was agriculture: the vast majority of people worked on the land. For example, Roman Italy displayed a high degree of urbanization for a pre-industrial society, but that means that perhaps only 70 percent of the population lived in the countryside instead of 90 percent or more, as in many other societies (Jongman 2003, 103). Although we'll talk in terms of the whole economy – and slaves were often important in mines and craft production – the organization of agricultural labor will be a key issue throughout the following discussions.

How can we tell if slaves played an important economic role? On the most obvious level, when slaves made up a large proportion of the population, they were almost certain to play a key part in the economy. Slaves can serve as luxuries and status symbols, but you can't have too large a percentage of the population that is not productive. So, since slaves constituted more than 80 percent of the population on some Caribbean islands such as Antigua and about a third of the population in the antebellum South, these were manifestly slave societies. Like the definition of slaves in terms of property, the definition of a slave society in terms of the number of slaves may not be the most sophisticated approach, but it will rarely lead you astray.

But even estimating the number of slaves in an ancient society can be difficult. Fortunately, there are other and perhaps more illuminating ways to define a slave society, for example, in terms of slavery's role in the economy. In *The Class Struggle in the Ancient Greek World*, the Marxist historian G. E. M. de Ste. Croix argues that when we characterize the labor system of a given period, what is most important is how work is organized beyond the family unit (Ste. Croix 1983, 133). Labor beyond the family may be organized in a non-hierarchical way, but it is much more frequent to have bosses and workers in one form or another. In Marxist terms, the organization of labor is thus the way the ruling class "extracts surplus" from an oppressed class. The expression "surplus" indicates that workers, say on an ancient farm, need to produce more than they consume in order to maintain the lifestyle of a ruling class, who do not themselves plant and harvest food. When a state's elite predominantly "extracts surplus" from slaves on their farms – or mines or workshops – that state was a slave society.

This definition can diverge from one based simply on the role of slaves in the economy. In some periods and places in Greek and Roman history, independent farmers did most of the farming with their families. In those periods and places much of the economy did not involve the large-scale organization of labor, but, if the elite used slave labor on their large farms rather than exploiting peasants or serfs, then de Ste. Croix categorizes it as a slave society. In theory, one might thus have a slave society without many slaves. In practice, the elite typically control a large enough portion of the economy so that, if they primarily use slaves, that society contains a significant proportion of slaves, and there is no difficulty in calling it a slave society.

When we come to particular ancient societies, the situation is complicated and hard to discern. Often we hear of more than one way of organizing labor: for example, some rich Romans worked their land with tenant farmers while others used slaves – not to mention that some tenant farmers had slaves of their own. Which system was more common? Our scattered and ambiguous evidence often makes it impossible to tell. As a result, the role of slaves in the ancient economy in different times and places is often a matter of controversy. Nevertheless, a short summary will reveal significant and generally accepted differences between periods.

Of the classical Greek city-states, we know the most about Athens. There the rich employed slaves rather than peasants or serfs: for example, Xenophon's *Oeconomicus*, which provides guidelines and advice to a wealthy farm owner, assumes a workforce of slaves without any discussion of alternatives. Even middle-class farmers had one or two slaves to work for them. In the cities, workshops – making swords or sofas, for example – were staffed largely with slaves. And the lucrative silver mines depended on a large workforce composed predominantly of slaves. So by the Marxist definition, Athens was a slave society. This impression is in line with estimates that slaves made up more than a quarter of the population of Attica. Other city-states such as Corinth and Corcyra seem to have resembled Athens in their dependence on slaves for labor. But in some other areas of Greece, such as Sparta and Thessaly, we find that nobles exploited peasants or serfs rather than owning slaves.

In the Hellenistic period, slavery continued in mainland Greece and may even have increased with the concentration of wealth and emigration of the free that most historians believe characterized the age. The Graeco-Macedonian ruling class in the Hellenistic kingdoms continued using slaves in their households – as we'll see in the section called Running Away in Chapter 9. The land, however, was worked mainly by peasants, just as it was before Alexander made his conquests. So most areas of the Hellenistic world were not slave societies.

The conquests under the Roman Republic involved large-scale enslavement as well as growing concentrations of land and wealth. The Roman elite was fabulously wealthy and their households in Rome could include a few hundred slaves. Slaves were just as important in urban crafts and shops. Some ancient sources claim that large farms worked by slaves began to dominate the countryside in many parts of Italy, a controversial topic we'll revisit later in this chapter. Archaeologists find plentiful evidence for small and mid-sized farms, even after large slave-worked estates had purportedly displaced the peasantry. Yet works of advice for large farm owners once again mainly assume a workforce made of slaves, and a wide array of evidence, including the magnitude of the slave revolt under Spartacus, strongly suggests large numbers of slaves in the countryside. On balance, Roman Italy in the first centuries BCE and CE is usually considered a slave society both in terms of the proportion of slaves and the role they played in the elite's agricultural labor force.

Whether we should classify the whole Roman Empire as a slave society is less obvious. On the one hand, some areas seem to have experienced the same growth of slave-based agriculture as Roman Italy. On the other hand, traditional systems of exploiting the peasantry remained in place in other areas. In Roman Egypt, as we mentioned above, slaves may have constituted less than one tenth of the population and seem to have been concentrated in the households of the wealthy, while peasants worked the land. This may have been a more typical pattern than the slave plantations of Italy. The eventual decline of ancient slavery is a tricky topic that we shall revisit in Chapter 13.

In sum, in at least two separate (and important) periods of classical history, slaves dominated labor when it was organized in groups larger than the family. Such slave societies are rare, so one can hardly avoid the question: why did classical Greece and Rome become slave societies? Given that the role of slaves in the economy is central to the definition of a slave society, it makes sense to look for an economic answer to this question.

Economics of Slavery

On the one hand, slaves are a capital expense rather than a recurring one like wages: you need to invest a lot of money up front to buy a slave. This is risky, especially in a high mortality society. For this reason, in the American South as well as ancient Rome, slaveholders sometimes hired free men to do particularly dangerous work (Varro, *On Agriculture* 1.17). On the other hand, slaves sometimes have children and, as we have seen, slave populations sometimes maintain their numbers. In such cases, an initial investment can produce labor indefinitely. Another strategy was for masters to allow slaves to save up monetary rewards to buy their freedom, a practice that recouped the slaveholder's initial investment and also provided incentives for the slave to work hard – a practice we'll revisit in Chapter 8.

The economics of slavery seem extremely favorable in other ways as well. You don't have to pay slaves at all. You need only to feed and clothe them, and you don't need to do that beyond what will keep them alive and healthy enough to work. You can forget about employee-of-the-month programs or holiday bonuses to motivate your workers; you can whip anybody who doesn't seem to be working hard enough or threaten to sell their family far away or themselves to the mills or mines. Despite these (cruel) economic advantages, Adam Smith, the founder of economic theory, took the opposite view of the economics of slavery in the quotation with which this chapter began. His line of thought is that slaves are unmotivated – indeed hostile – workers who bring little profit to their master. He also implies a contrast between slaves and wage laborers, who are assumed to have incentives to work hard – an idealized picture in many cases. So we have two diametrically opposed positions: slaves are cheap and can be motivated by violence and threats; and slaves may be cheap sometimes, but they cannot be motivated and are thus unprofitable.

As often, the truth lies somewhere between the two extremes, but we don't need to settle for an undifferentiated middle ground on this issue. Stephano Fenoaltea, an Italian economist, had an important insight into the adaptability of slavery to different types of work (1984). His basic argument was that "pain incentives," such as whipping, were sufficient to motivate workers in low-skill activities, such as some types of farming, mining, and construction. In high-skill activities, however, the anxiety caused by the threat of pain inhibits performance and, more important, slaves often have a greater ability to retaliate through sabotage: you don't want to entrust the care of your prize horse to a disgruntled groom or to really infuriate a slave jeweler to whom you need to entrust gold, silver, and gems. According to Fenoaltea, slavery works only in areas of the economy where pain incentives are effective: there slaves will work hard even if their masters provide no more than subsistence. If slaves are employed in high-skill occupations, the system of slavery will have to depend on rewards including eventual manumission. As a result, so he argues, it will not be a stable system.

Although this picture is generally true of New World slavery, where most slaves performed agricultural labor and slaveholders were diabolically clever about how to apply pain incentives to increase efficiency, Fenoaltea's theory does not seem to fit the reality of classical slavery well at all. Slaves were conspicuous in skilled crafts and may well have dominated them in some periods and places. Although manumission was practiced in both Greece and Rome, especially in urban contexts, it is hard to argue that urban, skilled slavery was unstable in the classical world. It is well attested from archaic Greece through the late Roman Empire, a span of about a thousand years.

Although Fenoaltea's theory was originally designed to explain the use of slaves versus free labor, when applied to the ancient world, it ends up telling us more about how masters motivated slaves: with greater reliance on threats where the work was simple and with more reliance on rewards when the work was complex and highly skilled (Scheidel 2008). For example, rewards for skilled slaves often included the promise of manumission, which is not disruptive under two conditions: the society had an inexpensive supply of new slaves; and there were no strong ideological barriers to allowing slaves to gain their freedom. In many periods, Greece and Rome satisfied these conditions, but the antebellum South did not. There, racism and the threat of abolitionism made it hard to allow too many blacks to gain their freedom, and the slave trade had been shut down by the early nineteenth century. Thus, classical slave societies had the flexibility to use slaves in both low- and high-skill jobs, whereas in the antebellum South the vast majority of the slave population was employed in low-skill agricultural work and motivated by pain incentives. Even this is, of course, more of a rule of thumb than an unbreakable law. For example, some slaves in the South did skilled work and were motivated to do it well, mainly by rewards (e.g., Dew 1994, 108–121).

To explain the growth of slavery in certain periods and places in the classical world, Scheidel goes back to a basic model historians use to understand the economics of New World slavery: imported slaves become valuable, and the institution of slavery may become central when a society has an abundance of resources, usually land, and too few available workers. At that point, the import of labor becomes attractive to those who own land that they are not able to work otherwise.

Outside the modern period, this type of situation is not, however, that common. In the absence of technological advances, the population of pre-industrial societies often grew to or above the number that the land could support – as the pessimistic demographer Thomas Malthus posited in *An Essay on the Principles of Population* in the late eighteenth century. A state in such a Malthusian condition would never pay to import large numbers of slaves, who would simply represent more mouths to feed. Throughout history, many elites depended on the exploitation of peasants to maintain their lifestyle. Such peasants reproduced themselves, had few rights, and paid their surplus production to those higher up the social hierarchy, either through taxes, rents, sharecropping, labor obligations, or some related system. Peasants often required less supervision than chattel slaves typically do. Such societies had no economic incentive for the extra, imported labor that slaves provided – though this does not rule out a few slaves in specific niches or as part of the lifestyle of the elite.

In the New World, however, slavery was employed on a grand scale and, economically speaking, it is not hard to see why. Europeans through conquest and disease quickly gained access to huge amounts of land on which they could produce cash crops: sugar, tobacco, and cotton. The supply of free labor to work this land was eventually insufficient. In addition, the very availability of land made free labor less practical:

> The story is frequently told of the great English capitalist, Mr. Peel, who took £50,000 and three hundred laborers with him to the Swan River colony in Australia. His plan was that his labourers would work for him, as in the old country. Arrived in Australia, however, where land was plentiful – too plentiful – the laborers preferred to work for themselves as small proprietors, rather than under the capitalist for wages. (Williams 1964, 5)

Basically, the laborers decided they would rather have their own farms, since land was readily available, than work for Mr. Peel. So the Mr. Peels of the world often turn to coerced labor in situations where land is plentiful or some other factor makes wage labor hard to obtain. Slavery is one alternative, though it was convict labor that played a large role in the early settlement of Australia.

These inquiries into the economic prerequisites for the widespread use of slaves have revealed three main points. First, there must be a supply of slaves available at lower cost than the supply of free labor. To put it more simply, slaves must be readily available and free labor not. Second, there must be new resources, usually land, that require more labor in the first place. This usually occurs in times of rapid change or even turmoil; otherwise labor and resources tend to be more or less balanced. Third, the easy availability of land or some other factor may by itself make coerced labor more profitable than paying wages.

We will consider two case studies in the economics of slavery in light of these factors. We'll first consider the Roman Republic, where the spread of slavery was based not only on conquest, but also on economics. Then, we'll consider the evidence that slaves were cheap relative to free labor in classical Athens but not during the high Roman Empire.

Roman Expansion

At first glance, the massive influx of slaves into Italy during the mid- and late-Roman Republic seems not to have had an economic basis at all. Roman armies were fighting almost constantly and large numbers of people were enslaved in these campaigns. It may seem that the Romans did not buy slaves in order to make a profit with them; rather, slaves were part of the profit they obtained from successful warfare.

Furthermore, rich Romans employed slaves in large numbers to enhance their status or to provide luxury services. You couldn't play the part of the big man in Rome without a large and conspicuous crowd of slaves escorting you wherever you went. Some Roman aristocrats even dressed their slave escorts in fancy matching uniforms. Slaves who were obviously expensive, rare, or exotic – for example, African slaves or matched twins as litter-bearers – also contributed to making a grand and elegant impression. As for luxuries, the lists of slave jobs in great Roman households included masseuse, *nomenclator* (to memorize names and announce guests), and a specialist in setting pearls; whole teams of slaves were assigned to take care of their owner's wardrobes or to help the mistresses of the house do their hair and make-up (Treggiari 1975a, 51–57). Such slaves represented, so the argument runs, a way to spend money rather than to make it. There is something to be said for this view: Roman slavery in the Republic was more directly connected with conquest and war than New World slave systems; Roman slaves often served prestige and luxury functions.

Economics is still in the picture, since slaves were also a profitable investment. Striking confirmation for this picture comes from inscriptions at Delphi in Greece that commemorate the manumission of slaves during the period of the late Republic. These often give the price that a slave paid for his or her freedom. The sociologist and ancient historian Keith Hopkins considers these prices a proxy for a slave's market price; his basic and admittedly rough assumption is that most of the time a slave owner would want to be able to buy a replacement for the slave he or she was freeing. During the late Republic, the prices slaves paid for their manumission increased significantly.[1] But it was during this period that Rome was fighting constant and intense wars and making major conquests all around the Mediterranean basin. Why would the price of slaves be going up when we might have expected the market to be glutted with them?

The most parsimonious explanation of this increase in price is that Roman conquest involved the acquisition of other forms of wealth even more than of slaves. The Roman elite acquired money with which to buy slaves, and it was worth their while to do so even as slave prices rose. Slaves were not just for luxury and display. Rather, Roman aristocrats acquired huge tracts of land as the result of conquest, and slaves provided much of the labor on the farms and ranches they established on this land. We know this from various sources, but especially from the three books on farm management that have survived from ancient Rome. These agricultural dissertations are all addressed to absentee owners whose farms were worked primarily by slaves. Even the overseer, left in charge of running the farm, was a slave, and his main task was the effective management of the other slaves working the farm. In addition, these authors repeatedly make it clear that their goal was to maximize profitability.

None of this is surprising. Roman nobles often reaped great wealth from conquest and empire, either directly or indirectly; it would have been strange indeed if they had spent all of it on show and luxury. They also invested their wealth and expected a return on their investments. The safest and most prestigious way to invest it was to buy land – especially Italian land on which no taxes were levied – and the most lucrative way to work that land was with slaves. This brings us to the key issue in the economics

---

1 Hopkins and Roscoe 1978, 134–171. The large quantities of Roman Republican coins found outside the Empire in Dacia (modern Romania) may represent payment for slaves (Crawford 1977; 1985, 230–235; cf. Lockyear 2004, 66, 70).

of ancient slavery: why was slave labor in this period more profitable for landowners than some other system of labor such as sharecropping or some other way of exploiting native peasant labor?

Hopkins provides an explanation in his classic book *Conquerors and Slaves*. He first outlines the striking difference between the clear economic rationale of New World slavery and the situation in Roman Italy:

> When we compare Roman with American slavery the growth of slavery in Roman Italy seems surprising. In the eighteenth century, slavery was used as a means of recruiting labour to cultivate newly discovered lands for which there was no adequate local labour force. Slaves by and large grew crops for sale in markets, which were bolstered by the incipient industrial revolution. In Roman Italy (and to a much smaller extent in classical Athens), slaves were recruited to cultivate land that was already being cultivated by citizen peasants. We have to explain not only the import of slaves but the extrusion of citizens. (Hopkins 1978a, 9)

Then Hopkins sets out to explain how the two factors crucial to New World slavery – empty land and markets for produce – were also present in the Roman case.

In the New World, plentiful land resulted from the extirpation of native populations through war and disease. Why was land available for Roman nobles to buy up and to farm with foreign slaves? The answer comes in several parts. For starters, the Romans often confiscated territory from the states they defeated in war. This "public farmland" could be farmed by any Roman, but the rich tended to move in and take possession. In fact Roman nobles often exceeded the statutory limit of 500 *jugera* – 300 acres or 125 hectares – which was rarely enforced by the Roman state, dominated by the very men who were most likely to break the rule. This land was like the "empty land" in the New World, which also came from the displacement of prior owners.

More benign processes also played a part: in many rural societies, some peasants fall into debt every generation and are eventually forced to sell their holdings. Bad weather, for example, can easily ruin a farmer whose crops for the year are destroyed. This is true especially if the disaster comes at a bad time in the family life-cycle; for example, a farm is particularly vulnerable when a farming couple has had several children, and thus more mouths to feed and to care for, but the children are not yet old enough to work. All sorts of other possible problems can be imagined and no doubt occurred.

Roman small farmers were even more prone to losing their land than peasants in most states because of the extraordinary military demands of the Roman state. As we have already seen, for a period of a couple of centuries Rome regularly mobilized many of its men for military service. Hopkins makes some reasonable assumptions about the length of military service and the life expectancy of Roman males and concludes that perhaps 80 percent of all Roman men served five years in the army during their life; more recent treatments suggest a less extreme, but still high, military participation rate.[2] Depending on when military service took place, a farm could easily be lost when labor was insufficient. For instance, it could be advantageous for a younger son to go away and make some money in the army. But, if an only son was absent overseas for a few years and his father died, the widow might struggle to hang onto the farm.

---

2 Hopkins 1978a, 34–35; revised downward by, for example, De Ligt 2012, 72–77.

That Roman nobles wanted to invest their money in land could make the decision for a small farmer to sell a struggling farm easier: land was valuable. In addition, other ways to make a living were possible and often attractive due to Rome's imperialism and the wealth it brought to Italy. Nevertheless, the elite's thirst for land to work with slaves occasionally meant that violence and threats were used to force peasants from their land. Although land was not sitting around, plentiful and deserted for their use, one way or another, the Roman elite found plenty of land to work with their slaves. And this seems to have been a profitable proposition.

This profitability brings us to the issue of markets, of how a farm worked by slaves would function efficiently within the larger economy. Most obviously, such farms only make sense if there is a market for agricultural produce. In primitive economies, agricultural production aims mainly at growing grain for subsistence. This obviously would not provide the basis for a profitable investment: Roman nobles didn't want to buy slaves and land in order to eat a lot of bread! Their farms could only make a profit if there was somebody to whom they could sell their surplus. If such farms were to be a large part of the economy, there had to be a large market for agricultural produce. Such a market presupposes an economy that, if not modern, is at least a long way from being primitive. Hopkins argues that this was the case in Roman Italy. As the result of Rome's conquests and wealth, the cities of Italy grew and the proportion of the population living in them rose to a level probably not equaled in Europe until the eighteenth century. Rome in particular may have had a population of one million, a level that London only matched around 1800 (Jongman 2003, 100; Hanson 2016). These urban dwellers provided a large market for agricultural produce; this tendency was increased when the state instituted a grain dole for citizens at Rome, thus subsidizing the urban market out of the profits of empire. The Roman army added to the demand for produce and clothing. These markets made the transformation to large slave-worked farms profitable.

Slave labor was most efficient for certain crops; the production of grain, the staple food of the Roman world, was not usually one of them. Grain cultivation has extremely uneven labor demands. There are a few periods of intense work, most obviously the harvest time. Much less labor is required during the rest of the year, but slaves would still need to be fed. So, if you were the owner of a grain farm, slaves would not be an obvious choice for your workforce. Some slave-worked farms in Italy may have produced grain at a profit nonetheless, but slave labor was most suited for mixed agriculture and cash crops such as olives and wine. Farms with such products are able more efficiently to use slave workers, since the labor demands for orchards and vineyards, for example, are spread out over the year. This effect is amplified if a farmer has several different crops with offset seasonal labor demands. Then the expense of maintaining slaves over the whole year makes financial sense: they can work all year. The historian Ulrike Roth suggests that the production of clothing, on which women could work throughout the year, may also have been a lucrative activity on these estates (2007, 53–118).

So far this is all somewhat hypothetical. It makes sense that rich Romans, trying to invest their imperial wealth profitably, would buy land and work it with slaves to produce cash crops for the market. Hopkins also provides a plausible explanation in the urbanization of Italy, a phenomenon confirmed archaeologically, and the large Roman army for why markets existed for the varied cash crops produced by these farms. But did large farms with slave labor actually displace peasants? Yes, at least according to the martyred reformer, Tiberius Gracchus, in the late second century BCE.

The Greek biographer Plutarch describes how Gracchus got the idea that Rome needed agrarian reform:

> When Tiberius on his way to Numantia passed through Etruria and found the country almost depopulated and its husbandmen and shepherds imported barbarian slaves, he first conceived the policy that was to be the source of countless ills to himself and to his brother. (Plutarch, *Tiberius Gracchus* 8, trans. Jongman 2003, 110)

In a similar vein, the historian Appian describes the situation as follows:

> The rich took possession of most public land . . . and acquired nearby, smaller farms either by purchase and persuasion or by brute force. They ended up with huge tracts of land instead of single farms. To work these lands they bought slaves as farmhands and shepherds, since free men could be drafted into the army and taken away. (Appian, *Civil War* 1.7, trans. White 1913)

These accounts seem to confirm Hopkins' basic model, but they show an obvious moralistic and political slant and derive from Greek authors – albeit well informed ones – of the late first and second century CE. Depicting the displacement of the sturdy Roman peasantry by foreign slaves was part of a general condemnation of the Roman elite for their excessive greed, which according to these authors led to the civil wars and eventually the fall of the Republic. But, though these reports are biased, are they wrong? More specifically, is there any material evidence that could bear on this issue?

In the Italian countryside, archaeologists have excavated large houses from the Republic and early Empire, often referred to as villas. These sites are consistent with the picture painted by ancient authors of extensive estates with a workforce consisting of slaves. Some even contain rooms with shackles in which recalcitrant or suspect slaves might be chained at night or for punishment; others contained cramped little rooms where slaves perhaps slept. The interpretation of these villas is, unfortunately, controversial (Joshel and Petersen 2014, 162–213). They show a great deal of variety in construction, and some are more likely just country or "summer" homes for Rome's elite rather than working farms – not that these categories are mutually exclusive. The existence of large houses in the countryside is consistent with the theory that large farms worked by slaves displaced small farms owned by free peasants; it does not prove that theory.

In contrast to these excavations of specific sites, archaeological surveys – which confine themselves to what is on the top of the soil but cover a much larger area of the countryside than an excavation – reveal ancient field patterns and the location and numbers of ancient farms and villas, all crucial evidence for understanding the organization of the Roman countryside. The results of surveys in Italy are different than we would expect based on the accounts of Plutarch and Appian. First of all, habitation patterns varied from area to area within Italy. Second and most important, a recent synthesis of 27 archaeological surveys indicates that the number of villas was growing over time but that smaller farmsteads were also becoming more common. Some of these farmers may have owned a few slaves, and many may have been tenant farmers of the villa owners (Launaro 2011, 158–162). Still most historians think that the supposed destruction of the Italian peasantry has been exaggerated. The displacement of some peasants by slave-worked estates was balanced – or more than balanced – by all the advantages that come with being at the center of a great imperial power. Rather than just a story of impoverished peasants and the desertion of the countryside, the prosperity of many free Italian farmers and the opportunities available to them may even have raised the cost of free labor and made slave labor more attractive to the rich (De Ligt 2012, 154–157) – similar to the dynamic in Athens we'll explore below. Although some small farmers may have moved to cities, the free population of Italy as a whole probably declined only slightly even while slaves were being imported in great numbers.

Scholars have also questioned the theory that Italian agriculture moved away from grain production towards the market crops, such as wine, which were more amenable to slave labor. Based on calculations of agricultural productivity per hectare, the social historian Willem Jongman argues that a large shift away from grain to vineyards, for example, could not have occurred: "It would have left Italy both fatally hungry, and dangerously drunk" (Jongman 2003, 111). Neither the displacement of smallholders nor the switch to market crops was as extensive as Hopkins originally envisioned. A dramatic switch to slave labor is harder to picture absent these trends. Accordingly, historians' estimates of the Italian slave population have come down from three million or two million (by Hopkins) to under one million. I prefer an intermediate estimate of Roman Italy's slave population: 1.5 million by the reign of Augustus, about 25 percent of a total population of around 5.7 million (De Ligt 2012, 190, 341–342).

Despite these revisions, the overall contours of Hopkins' model won't be replaced anytime soon. The main parts of the puzzle – wars, a growing slave population, the displacement of some peasants, and the agricultural use of slaves – are all well documented. Hopkins' model puts them all together in a way that makes both historical and economic sense. We do need, however, to admit that the displacement of peasants by slave plantations was not as prevalent as Hopkins thought and that there were many other things going on, not all of them detrimental to the free population of Italy.

The Cost of Labor in Athens and the Roman Empire

We do not have good information about the prices of slaves in Italy during the Republic, but Scheidel contrasts the real cost of slaves and of free labor in classical Greece and under the Empire in the first three centuries CE to explain the greater proportion of slaves in the former case.[3] In order to compare costs in such different periods and places, he expresses the price of slaves and of free labor in terms of grain, a proxy for cost of living. Using this basis of comparison, Scheidel shows that free labor cost at least twice as much in classical Athens as in the Roman Empire and that slaves were less than half as expensive in Athens. Given that economic background, the higher reliance on slave labor in Athens is easy to understand.

Scheidel's data varies greatly in quality and type. On the Greek side, there are prices for slaves on the Attic *Stelai* and for wage labor on inscriptions recording the expenditures for various construction projects in and near to Athens. On the Roman side, he finds references to slave prices in legal texts. More important are papyri from Roman Egypt that record both wages and slave prices. Scheidel also collects references to prices or wages wherever they appear in Greek or Roman texts of whatever genre: law-court

---

3 In this section I follow Scheidel 2005b, 1–17 and 2008, 105–126.

speeches, plays, or philosophical works. Although one could argue that one or another of these numbers was unrepresentative – and Scheidel does depend a lot on data from Roman Egypt – his data is coherent and allows the kind of rough estimate that he is looking for. Most decisive, the difference he finds between the prices of free and slave labor in Athens and in the Roman Empire is too great to be a figment of poor data.

These results support a simple economic explanation for the expansion or decline of slavery in the absence of moral compunction: where slave labor is inexpensive relative to free labor, we find that slave labor was used more.[4] Thus, slavery was more common in classical Athens than in the Roman Empire. Some historians estimate that the slave population of Athens could have been as high as 150,000, roughly a third of the population; even low estimates have slaves making up 20 percent of the population. As we saw in the last chapter, most historians think that slaves constituted about 10 percent of the population of the Roman Empire. So, the relative prices of wage labor and of slaves are consistent with the fact that slave labor was more common in classical Athens than during the Roman Empire. But why were slaves cheap and free labor expensive in one society and not in the other?

First, the supply of slaves. As a major port, Athens imported slaves from the whole Greek world and beyond. The presence of peasant/serf labor systems in some other parts of the Greek world like Thessaly, Messenia, and Laconia meant that there was little demand for slaves in those areas, which may have depressed the price of slaves. More important, ancient Greece included colonies throughout the Aegean and Black Sea and the wider Mediterranean. As we have seen, these Greek cities were often on the coasts of lands inhabited by non-Greeks in sporadically hostile relations with the colonies. Thus the ratio of borderland – marked by wars and slave raiding – to the size of Greece and to its population was high. In contrast, Rome was a huge empire with a large population; its borders were distant and had largely stabilized by the imperial period. They were longer than the borders of the Greek world but not to the same degree that Rome's area and population was larger.

The high cost of free labor at Athens was largely a consequence of its democracy. First off, the legal rights of poor citizens were assured to such an extent that rich litigants occasionally complained that they were treated unfairly in court. This was probably an exaggeration, but even the equal legal protection of the poor and rich is rare and remarkable. A large jury of ordinary citizens would have the final say in the case of a disagreement between an Athenian free worker and his employer, and the laws gave every male citizen equal rights – as the Athenians loved to boast. In Roman Egypt, such a dispute would be decided by a magistrate who was of the same class as the employer and who probably despised the poor Egyptian laborers, whose very language he might not understand. We do not have to imagine that such legal cases were very common to understand that the Athenian worker and the laborer in Roman Egypt were in different bargaining positions vis-à-vis their employers and that this contributed to a difference in real wages.

Scheidel emphasizes a second factor contributing to the high cost of free labor at Athens: the existence of other demands on the time and energy of the citizens. In Athens, citizens had many opportunities to take part in politics, something many considered

---

[4] A complication is that the main alternative to slave labor was usually some sort of dependent peasantry rather than wage labor and the cost of such labor is almost impossible to quantify.

important to a full life. In addition, they were required to serve in the military. These institutions made the supply of labor other than slaves smaller and less dependable. The most common competition with slave labor in the ancient world was not free wage labor but rather other sorts of un-free labor such as serfs or bound peasants. But early in the history of Athens' democratic development, the Athenians had eliminated debt bondage and given peasants full title to their land, where previously they were sharecroppers. So these other ways of obtaining labor were not available to wealthy Athenians.

Some scholars also invoke the unwillingness of free Athenians to work for another individual for a salary on the grounds that this was somehow slavish. Several ancient sources equate working for another person with slavery and even specify that the wages paid were the proof of a person's slavery. If this attitude actually influenced people's willingness to take wage labor – and it must have had some effect – it would have diminished the labor pool and made the cost of wage labor greater. The problem is that this attitude could just as easily have been a result of the reliance on slave labor rather than its cause. The hesitation to perform work for others may have stemmed from the fact that many of those who worked for others were indeed slaves. So we can't really tell whether this was an independent factor driving the use of slave labor or a circumstance that, once the slave system was in place, tended to ensure that it stayed.

One can argue about how much weight to put on different explanatory factors for the labor and slave supply in classical Athens and the Roman Empire. Nevertheless, Scheidel's data on real slave prices strongly suggest that the extent of slave use, in the ancient as well as the modern world, was largely a matter of economics.

The Slave Trade and Slave Traders

One modern statistician, waxing poetical in defense of his field, described social statistics as "frozen tears." The preceding discussions may indeed have seemed abstract and cold, but there are plenty of tears there too. Our last topic is the slave trade, an aspect of the economics of slavery that was brutal, but at least brings us back to the concrete experiences of the men, women, and children who suffered under slavery. The slave trade was not only a significant and profitable sector of the ancient economy, but it also shows us in primary colors the terrible effects of slavery on its victims.

The economic impact of slavery included not only all the economic roles slaves filled – in agriculture, crafts, and mining, for example – but also all the people employed, and the money to be made, in acquiring and transporting slaves. Although the overall scale of the slave trade, both the numbers and distances involved, was greater in the Roman than the Greek world, many common features do not require separate treatment. Throughout antiquity, slaves were being moved from one place to another, often in large numbers, to accommodate differences in demand and the vagaries of the supply of slaves. For example, we know that slaves were often sold in war zones for much less than their value in the heartland of Greece or of Rome. Although Trajan's column depicts newly captured slaves locked in holding pens as part of the glorification of his Dacian campaigns (ca. 114 CE), commanders usually did not want to have to guard slaves for extended periods. Occasionally, slaves were distributed among the soldiers. More regularly, merchants followed armies around for the chance to pick up enslaved people at cheap prices and then to transport them, often by foot, to places where they could be sold at a profit.

An important general consideration comes into play here: slaves became increasingly powerless as they were separated from their homelands and people. Tens of thousands of Epiriots in Roman stockades on the outskirts of Epirus after the mass enslavements there in 167 BCE were in a grim position, but they knew that, if they could escape and elude capture, they might have a chance to resume their lives once the Roman army left. They knew the countryside and could both communicate and cooperate with each other. They might even resort to violence if not carefully guarded or chained. Imagine those same tens of thousands, but now scattered on farms throughout Italy, isolated or in small groups among other slaves from other places, in the land of their enemy with no easy way home, and among a population in the millions controlled by the Romans, whose language they could not speak. They would be much more easy to manage and thus more valuable to their owners. In general, new slaves' vulnerability and thus their usefulness went up the further from home they were. This is not just a classical phenomenon: pre-historians and anthropologists observe that slaves were often among the first objects of long-distance trade for this reason (Patterson 1982, 148–149).

In the classical world, the life of slavery often began with a lot of walking. Slaves captured in Britain, in the campaigns under Emperor Claudius for example, might start their enslavement with a boat ride across the English Channel and then by walking more than 1000 miles to Rome, often in coffles – groups chained together. Archaeologists occasionally find the actual chains used for this purpose. Chaining seems not to have been a universal precaution, since several stories in *The Life of Aesop* concern a slave trader traveling with slaves who are not bound (18–19 in Daly 1961). Transport by ship must also have been common around the Mediterranean and the navigable rivers, but no evidence survives of ships specifically designed to transport large numbers of slaves – as were used in the modern Atlantic slave trade.

Figure 4.1 Slave auction scene. Ex-slaves who were rich enough owned slaves themselves; some even engaged in the slave trade. This scene on the gravestone of a Roman freedman shows an assistant (left) displaying a slave's buttocks to customers, while the auctioneer makes a large gesture, whose exact meaning is open to interpretation. *Source*: After a drawing by A. Wiltheim, seventeenth century, in Waltzing 1904, 300.

Many large cities had markets regularly used for the sale of slaves – whether this was their only use is controversial.[5] Some of these markets may have been designed with the control of human merchandise in mind: they seem to be laid out deliberately so that there were only a few narrow exits. Guards could watch these to be sure that no slaves slipped out in the bustling crowds. When they were put up for sale in the market, most slaves were displayed on a platform, where potential buyers could question them or inspect their bodies after having them strip. All of these practices were profoundly dehumanizing to people who had been free and perhaps even noble a short time before. It symbolized the separation of slaves from their past lives that they were often given new names, either by the slave traders themselves or by their new masters. One more-humane Greek practice is attested: newly purchased slaves were marched around their new homes and sprinkled with dried figs and sweetmeats, just as a new bride was, perhaps to symbolize the good things in their new life.[6] I doubt that many slaves were convinced.

In contrast, Xenophon tells a story that illustrates the harshness of the slave trade: the Spartan king, Agesilaus, when he moved camp, made sure that the little children abandoned by slave traders were not just left to die (Xenophon, *Agesilaus* 1.21). Presumably slave traders viewed the children as unprofitable and inconvenient: they could not walk far or fast, would slow and distract their parents, required food, and were not worth much in a world with high child mortality. It was Agesilaus and his army who had enslaved the families in the first place, but he and his admiring biographer Xenophon seem to have seen the inhumanity of leaving children to die of starvation and exposure, something slave traders would sometimes do.

In general, slave traders had a bad reputation. A law-court speech from fourth-century Athens criticizes a certain Timandros for being a terrible guardian to some orphans, whom he separated. To highlight his faults, Hyperides makes two claims about slave traders (*Against Timandros* in Jones 2008, 19–20):

(1) Even slave traders don't separate children from their siblings or mothers (something Timandros purportedly did).
(2) They do commit all sorts of other crimes for the sake of profit.

The first claim was not generally true in the Greek world, as the Agesilaus story shows. Nor does it hold true in the Roman world, where we find evidence such as a sales receipt for a ten-year-old girl sold by herself in Asia Minor and probably bound for Egypt without any family with her (*Papyrus Turner* 22 in Bradley 1994, 2). The threat of separation and that slaves sometimes managed to start and maintain families nevertheless are topics we'll consider in Chapter 7.

The second claim sums up a negative stereotype of slave traders, which seems to be widespread in both the Greek and Roman worlds – as it was in the American South (e.g., Aristophanes, *Wealth* 521–526; Bodel 2005). Several considerations explain why the reputation of slave dealers was so low in antiquity. First off, their relationship with slaves was purely a mercenary one: they had not captured the slaves themselves, which would at least have demonstrated military prowess; nor were they in a long-term relationship that could be palliated by the ideological veneer of paternalism that sometimes

---

5 The identification of designated slave markets with particular architectural features is also controversial. See Roth 2010; George 2011, 394–395.
6 [Demosthenes] 45.74; Aristophanes, *Wealth* 789, 801.

concealed the violence and exploitation in the relationship between master and slaves – see Chapter 11. So, although the elite in Greece and Rome can hardly have disapproved of slave traders on the grounds of their participating in slavery, perhaps the traders displayed slavery in a form more raw than slave owners wished to see.

But the most important factor in the bad repute of slave traders may have been a simple matter of money. The rich landowners, who dominate our sources – as they dominated their societies – had opposing interests to slave dealers: slave dealers wanted to sell slaves for as high a price as possible, whereas the elite wanted to buy slaves for as low a price as possible. Slave dealers often possessed better information than potential buyers about a slave they were trying to sell, and some naturally tried to take advantage of this to sell slaves for more than they were worth. In particular, some sellers concealed problems that made a slave worth less than he or she appeared. Others tried to make slaves look younger, more attractive, or healthier than they really were – using ingredients typical of ancient medicine such as resin from the terebinth tree or the root of hyacinth.[7] Roman legal texts are particularly concerned with these issues and specify a host of "defects" that slave traders must openly declare or else the sale of a slave could be declared invalid. These included latent physical problems, but also whether a slave had ever tried to commit suicide or had a tendency to "wander" (Bradley 1994, 51–55).

We can't tell whether slave traders were actually more dishonest than other merchants, but one result of this negative stereotype was that we know the names of extremely few slave traders from antiquity. Although we have thousands of epitaphs from the Roman Empire declaring the deceased's profession, few proclaim that the deceased was a "slave trader" – and this despite the fact that many people must have made a living in the slave trade. One exception is the gravestone of Aulus Kapreilius Timotheus, a seven-foot-high and well-made marble headstone, which declares Aulus' profession as "slave trader" and includes among other images a depiction of a coffle of eight male slaves walking along chained together at the neck with two women and two children unchained behind them (George 2011, 392; Finley 1977). It is noteworthy that Aulus was himself an ex-slave – that ex-slaves often owned slaves is a phenomenon we'll explore in Chapter 8. Successful ex-slaves did not necessarily share the sensibilities of those born to wealth, and so Aulus may not have realized the social stigma attached to his profession – or he may have just decided to ignore it. In literary sources, it is only the spectacularly gauche Trimalchio, a freedman character in Petronius, who is unembarrassed about trading in slaves (Petronius, *Satyricon* 76) – and that was on the grand scale.

For new slaves the experience of being captured, marched for long distances across the countryside, or shipped across the Mediterranean must have been horrific. To have one's body poked and inspected at a public market – considered a particularly shameful part of slavery in our sources – and to be sold who knows where to who knows whom must have been terrifying. But just as slaves in the New World made lifetime bonds with other slaves from the same ship from Africa – known as *malungo* in Brazil (Hawthorne 2010, 132) – so too we read the following on the epitaph of a Roman ex-slave, commemorated by his friend:

> To his fellow freedman and his dearest companion. I do not remember, my most virtuous fellow freedman, that there was ever any quarrel between you and me.

---

7 Joshel 2010, 97 citing Pliny, *Natural History* 24.35, 21.170; *Life of Aesop* 21 in Daly 1961.

By this epitaph, I call on the gods above and the gods below as witnesses that I met you in the slave market, that we were made free men together in the same household, and that nothing ever separated us except the day of your death. (*CIL* 6.22355A, trans. in Joshel 2010, 109)

Conclusion

It would be misleading to end this chapter on such a positive note. The big and grim picture is clearly that economic forces, unrestrained by moral compunctions about slavery, led both classical Athens and Roman Italy (at least) to exploit slave labor to such an extent that they belong to the small group of slave societies known to human history. The elite in other periods of classical antiquity also possessed slaves with as few qualms, but it was the economic advantages of slave labor that made its use prevalent in those two places and times.

Suggested Reading

Scheidel 2008 provides an overall theory of economic factors that favor slavery and applies it to Greek and Roman slavery. Hopkins 1978a is the classic explanation of how slaves displaced subsistence peasants in Italy during the late Republic. Jongman 2003 criticizes several of Hopkins's main arguments. Analyses of the extent to which large, slave-worked farms did in fact displace free Italian peasants have to take into account the interpretation of ancient census data as well as survey archaeology, estimates of urban populations, and comparative history – all tricky and controversial topics. No fewer than three recent books treat this topic in detail: Launaro 2011, De Ligt 2012, and Hin 2013 – with Scheidel 2013. Finley 1977 uses the gravestone of Aulus Kapreilius Timotheus, described above, as an entrée into a discussion of slave traders in antiquity. Braund 2011 and Bodel 2005 provide more recent overviews of, respectively, the Greek and Roman slave trades.

5

Politics

More bluntly put, the cities in which individual freedom reached its highest expression – most obviously Athens – were cities in which chattel slavery flourished.... One aspect of Greek history, in short is the advance, hand in hand, of freedom and slavery.
    M. I. Finley, "Was Greek Civilisation Based on Slave Labour?" (1982a), 114–115

At the death of Messalina, the imperial household was in an uproar. [The Emperor] Claudius didn't like being single and was submissive to his wives. His ex-slaves fought over who should choose the next one for him.
    Tacitus (Roman historian, ca. 56–117 CE), *Annals* 12.1

Introduction

Slaves were a relatively powerless group, often at the bottom of the social hierarchy. It would seem that they should have nothing to do with politics, which comprises the exercise of an important type of power, typically by those at the top of the totem pole. In fact, slaves played a part, arguably a crucial one, in classical politics in two very different ways. This chapter will focus first on the indirect role of slavery in the growth of Greek democracy and second on the direct participation of slaves and ex-slaves as bureaucrats in the Roman Empire.

A state's economic system often shapes its political structure to a greater or lesser extent. In slave societies like Greece where slaves played a large role in the economy, the political system often reflected the importance of this role – not, of course, in the simple sense that slaves dominated politics since their work dominated the economy! Rather, historians have connected slavery with the egalitarian tendency among Greek free males and even the development of democracy. On the level of ideology, slaves played the role of the "other" against whom all citizens could define themselves as a single class. On the level of economics, the use of imported slaves allowed subordinating economic relations between citizens to be minimized. In simple terms, the rich could allow political equality for the poor because they did not need to exploit them; the maintenance of their lifestyle depended mainly on foreign slaves. Although this dynamic may have been true in many Greek cities, our sources of information are overwhelmingly Athenian, and so, in this chapter, I will mainly be talking about Athens.

Slaves have often served the political ends of others, but rarely their own. Their alienation from the rest of society has sometimes made slaves – like mercenaries – the most dependable tools for various types of despots fearful of giving too much power to their own nobles or citizens. This strategy contributed to the crucial role slaves and ex-slaves played in the administration of the vast Roman Empire during two periods. In the early Empire, the emperor needed to delegate power in order to run the Empire, but could find no other group so loyal, competent, and trustworthy as his own slaves and ex-slaves. In the late Empire, eunuchs – male slaves castrated as children – held crucial top offices. Even though they experienced great resentment and sometimes served as scapegoats, under a succession of emperors it was often a eunuch who held the most power in the empire besides the emperor himself; the court eunuchs as a group were also powerful and dangerous to offend.

The bulk of this chapter focuses on these two different aspects of the entanglement of slavery and politics. A shorter section will deal with state-owned slaves in Athens and the participation of slaves in Greek warfare, a role that their low status and exclusion from political power ought to have made unacceptable, but did not.

Athenian Slavery and Democracy

Karl Marx is most closely associated with the thesis that the economy plays a crucial role in the development of different political systems, but his theories involved oversimplifications about the ancient world and predictions about the modern world that did not come true. When it comes to theory, few historians believe that economics completely determine politics – probably a more dogmatic position than Marx himself held. But just as few would deny important connections between politics and economics. When it comes to ancient Greece, some historians argue that the economic role of slavery had important social and cultural consequences that favored the development of democracy. Paradoxically, slavery was a precondition for a political system in which all male citizens regardless of wealth had equal political rights, an almost unique development in the ancient world and perhaps the greatest of the many contributions of ancient Greece to world culture. More specifically, M. I. Finley, one of the most influential writers on ancient slavery of the past fifty years, proposed a provocative theory: the freedom enjoyed by a citizen in democratic Athens depended in part on slavery. His argument was that the political outcome, democracy, and the rights it assured to free Athenian men was closely related to the socio-economic structure of society including the widespread use of chattel slaves, especially in agriculture.

While today we think of wage labor as the standard arrangement when somebody works for somebody else, in ancient societies wage laborers were rarely central to the agricultural labor supply. Rather, the main alternatives to slaves were peasants of one sort or another. This statement requires a bit of explanation. In general use, *peasant* just means a relatively poor farmer – and this is the way we used the term in the last chapter. Among social historians, however, a *peasant* is a farmer who occupies the land but does not fully own it. Peasants are thus subject to a *rent*: they may need to work for the owner, give him a share of their crop, pay him some money each year, or simply pay high taxes to a government consisting mainly of the upper classes. When peasants are bound (not allowed to leave), they have lost an important part of their freedom and much of their bargaining power. Bound peasants are called serfs.[1]

When peasants, especially serfs, populate the countryside, conditions are unfavorable to democracy: the rich cannot allow equal political rights and freedom to people whom they need as subordinate workers. Peasants have trouble standing up politically to those who are in control of them economically – though they may revolt. Chattel slavery can make these subordinating ties between rich and poor unnecessary. In classical Athens, the rich did not need to impose labor rents or serfdom on other Athenians, since they could simply buy their labor supply: foreign slaves. The rich could allow democratic rights, and the poor could assert them. The livelihood of the rich did not require that the poor be kept closely in check; the livelihood of the poor did not require that they kowtow to the rich.

This helps explain one of the greatest puzzles about Greek democracy: why the wealthy in many Greek cities, but almost nowhere else, were willing to give up their traditional domination of politics and accept legal equality among the male citizens. The rich were a minority of the population in all Greek states, but their power was great – as is usual in the pre-industrial world. They traveled more and had a wider range of contacts. They were more organized. They had long monopolized state power in a world where tradition counted for a great deal. They had the money to hire foreign mercenaries, if push came to shove in a civil war. For all these reasons, the elite retained all sorts of advantages, and the triumph of the mass of the citizens and the establishment of democracy was anything but a sure thing. Democracy prevailed when much of the elite went along with it or, at least, did not fight it nail and fist.

This was partly because the rich continued to provide the most influential politicians and speakers even when a state gave equal political rights to all its citizens. It is also because less was at stake for them economically: the rich held onto their land and wealth, since the Athenian democracy never attempted the radical policies – abolition of debts and redistribution of land – sometimes instituted in other cities. And slaves could provide the labor to work the land, workshops, and mines of the rich. This acquiescence in democracy does not mean that the rich didn't look down on the poor or resent democracy: one elite writer described the poor as ignorant and shameless and another called democracy, "obviously ridiculous."[2] Some rich men plotted to overthrow the democracy and institute an oligarchy. What is striking is how many went along with the democratic compromise, in which the wealthy could maintain their incomes and lifestyles but ceded political rights to the masses. Slavery made this compromise possible.

Finley also argued that two basic types of social structure existed in the ancient world. First, the people in some societies were spread out among many different status levels: from slaves to serfs to peasants of different sorts to more affluent tenant farmers to big landowners to members of the governing elite. Very few people were really free, since each class was bound in various ways to those above. Second and much more rarely, we find societies where people were concentrated at two points in the social spectrum,

---

1 Historians of medieval Europe often use different and more historically specific definitions to delineate serfdom there, a controversial topic.
2 [Xenophon], *Constitution of the Athenians* 1.5; Thucydides 6.89.6.

either they were completely free, possessing equal political rights and subordinate to nobody, or they were utterly un-free, chattel slaves, whose only recognized tie was one of subordination to their masters. According to Finley, Athens in the classical period was among the rare states that fit into this second category. Athens was marked by social dichotomy between free and slave and also by a lack of subordinating economic relationships among the citizens. This does not mean that there were no differences in wealth; rather, poor and middle-class citizens were not economically and thus socially bound to the rich, since they didn't usually work for them.

One phenomenon in Athenian society highlights this lack of subordination among the citizens: the relative infrequency and unimportance of patron/client relations compared to other ancient societies.[3] Patronage exists when wealthy men (the patrons) and poor men (the clients) form bonds based on reciprocal services. Although both patron and client do things for each other, the relationship is not equal. The client sacrifices much of his independence: he is expected to show respect, deference, and even obedience to his patron in return for the benefits he receives. Patronage is an essential ingredient in the way many societies operate. At Rome, for example, it was largely via patronage that some of the poor obtained help when they needed it and the rich exercised informal power over some proportion of the poor. In Athens, however, the poor sought assistance more often from the government and from equals than from patrons. In contrast to Rome, Athenian friendships were supposed to be between equals, not between a patron and his clients (Konstan 1998, 279–280). The avoidance of patronage was an aspect of the lack of subordinating economic ties between rich and poor made possible by the institution of slavery. This phenomenon was part of a self-reinforcing cycle working in both directions: the economic independence and political rights of the poor pushed the rich towards an increasing use of slave labor and slave labor made the independence and political rights of the poor palatable to the rich.

Finley's explanation for democracy makes sense in that it proposes two types of social structure and shows that democracy is more compatible with one of them. But why did Athens go down one path instead of the other? The process was long and complicated, but one crucial step both towards democracy and towards the dependence on foreign slaves rather than peasants within may have come with the reforms of Solon in the early sixth century. Unfortunately, although we possess some of Solon's own assertions about his programs – in poetry! – most of our sources about him are late, unreliable, and hard to interpret. Consequently, historians disagree both about his actual reforms and about their social context. According to one reconstruction, Solon instituted two agrarian reforms that gave more independence to many Athenians in the countryside: he abolished debt bondage and freed some sharecroppers from their obligations. These reforms played an important role in what was no doubt a complicated long-term process in which the countryside became more egalitarian and subordinating ties between rich and other farmers became less common.

Debt bondage remains today a common way that poor farmers fall into a subjection that is close to slavery (Bales 2012, 9). It is one of the reasons that agrarian societies sometimes drift towards greater and greater inequality and subordination until some violent and radical change becomes inevitable. In archaic Athens before Solon, not only was there debt bondage, but people in that condition began actually to be sold

---

3 Millett 1989; cf. Dillon 1995; *contra* Zelnick-Abramovitz 2000.

abroad – a practice sometimes distinguished as *debt slavery*. Perhaps this was a new abuse and led to the social conflict that Solon was called upon to mediate.

At the time of Solon, Athens did not even have its own coinage, so the debt for which people had been losing their freedom could have been a debt in kind: for example, in a bad year peasants sometimes end up eating all their grain and have to borrow the seed to sow for the next year's harvest. The debt might also have come as a result of peasants failing to pay the rent on land that they farmed but did not own outright. This possibility brings us to the *hektemoroi*, a class of peasants in archaic Attica, whose name means "sixth-parters." All we know about the *hektemoroi* is their name, one common interpretation of which is that it implies a sharecropping arrangement. It is a sign of our ignorance that historians can't decide whether the sharecroppers needed to pay over one sixth of their harvest (a surprisingly good deal if the land is somebody else's), only got to keep one sixth of their harvest (a bad deal and probably not enough to survive on), or some third alternative (e.g., one-sixth of a fixed rent is paid in advance).

In any case, Solon's reforms somehow liberated the *hektemoroi* from their obligations. Presumably the *hektemoroi* were given full, unencumbered property rights to the land they lived on and had been farming. Solon also eliminated debt bondage; he even claimed to have brought back to Attica and restored to freedom some people who had been sold abroad. Lending on the security "of the body," that is debt bondage, became illegal, at least for citizens. By the classical period, we find that many independent middle-class farmers – typically even owning a few slaves of their own – and a few rich farmers populated the Attic countryside. It is almost impossible to find any peasants, in the socialhistorical sense, in Attica. Rather, the real poor seem to have lived mainly in the city of Athens. The agrarian social structure of Attica was one in which democracy could thrive.

Finley's picture gains some support from the reverse set-up in some other Greek states, most famously Sparta, which controlled two large areas of the Peloponnese: Laconia and Messenia. Under Sparta, the agrarian economy focused on the production of subsistence crops and grain. Rather than depending on foreign slaves, closely supervised, the Spartans depended on a serf-like class called the Helots to work their farms, mainly on a sharecropping basis.[4] Helots were not slaves but were rather natives who had lost their freedom to the extent that they were bound and subject to labor services as well as owing a share of their crops. How this came about in the poorly known archaic period is obscure and controversial, although the conquest of Messenia by Sparta played a role in the case of the Helots there. The results are clearer: in Laconia and Messenia, the Spartans imposed a harsh subjugation on many of the inhabitants, reducing them to serfs with no political rights; they had no need for – and possessed few, if any – imported chattel slaves. In contrast, would-be peasants in Attica ended up with political rights and economically independent, either as farmers or as working men of various sorts in Athens and other towns in Attica. Chattel slavery played a crucial role in this process, but it would be a mistake to claim that it was the only factor. The institution of slavery and the cheap availability of foreign slaves constituted a *sine qua non* for Athenian democracy, but many other factors – cultural, individual, economic – were also necessary.

Indeed, an apparent problem with Finley's whole theory is that there existed a third class of Greek city-states, for example Chios, that employed chattel slaves on a large scale, but remained oligarchies for most or all of the classical period (cf. Jameson 1992).

---

4 Since they were notoriously rebellious, the main discussion of the Helots is in Chapter 10.

Two approaches can help us deal with what seems at first like a devastating set of counter-examples.

First, many Greek oligarchies are classified as *broad* rather than *narrow*: many people possessed political rights rather than just a few. In a narrow oligarchy, an elected council of ten men from the richest class might wield almost all political power. In contrast, a broad oligarchy might make decisions in an assembly open to the richer half or third of the free male population, numbering in the thousands. In the latter case, the oligarchic citizens were mainly the free, middle-class farmers whose independence was made possible by slavery. In these states, the original narrow aristocracy of birth and wealth had shared its political power, but just not as widely. They had not taken the step of granting active political rights with the poor, who were – at Athens at least – mainly an urban group.

The second and more important response to the objection is to be clear about Finley's argument: slavery was a *necessary* condition for Greek democracy; it was not a *sufficient* one. Slavery made possible the democratic compromise by which the elite's wealth and lifestyle survived the sharing of political power with poor Athenians. This is far from a full explanation of democracy. That would require a detailed consideration of the individual statesmen, their backers and opponents at each critical step. It would also require a consideration of Greek intellectual culture, the political impact of colonization, the fear of tyranny, and the type of wars the Greeks fought. This is not the place to treat these topics, but historians have invoked them all as partial explanations for democracy, a phenomenon not likely to have just one cause.

Our focus on Solon also tends to compress a longer and more complicated process. Slavery could not have been a new phenomenon in 591 BCE: after all, Homer and Hesiod depict or mention slaves at least a century earlier. Instead, we should imagine that, as Solon's ideas for reform were passing around and various rich landowners were deciding how strongly to oppose them, the option of using foreign slaves to work their large holdings made concessions more palatable. We have already discussed in the last chapter the reasons that slaves were so cheaply available in Athens in the classical period; some of these factors were already in place at the time of Solon. The rich probably calculated that as long as they prevented a general redistribution of land, they could do well enough using slave labor on their own lands – as they did.

In addition, more and more farms may have been turning to mixed crops and market farming instead of just harvesting grain for subsistence. As we have seen in the case of Roman Italy, such farms are able more efficiently to use slave workers. Market rather than subsistence agriculture allowed farmers to make money by selling their produce: mainly fruit, olives, and grapes. These shifts in agricultural practices were long-term trends that made the use of slaves become more attractive over generations rather than suddenly and as the result of something Solon did.

Slavery not only affected the political economy of Athens, but also the way Athenian men thought about their social world, their ideology. In particular, slavery was a double-edged sword in its effect on the way Athenians conceived of hierarchy and equality among the citizens.

On the one hand, Orlando Patterson, whose definition of slavery we have met already, argues that slavery commonly leads to a cultural emphasis on honor and a keen sense of rank. Slave owners are used to ordering people around; they do not necessarily lose this habit when they are interacting with people other than their slaves. As a reaction, in a society with slavery, people are in general sensitive to anything that smacks of being treated like a slave and are quick to take offense. Slavery also opens another prospect for inequality in that not all free people are slaveholders. This can become an important distinction between free people. For example, in the American South, it became a mark of respectability to own at least one slave – a mark of respectability that most of the population could not attain.

On the other hand, slaves can also become a group against whom people can define themselves as a unity: "we are all alike – and friends and allies – since we are all superior to *them*." Historians find this interpretation of the effect of slavery persuasive in part because it is easy to find other examples of this social and psychological phenomenon. The scapegoating of Jews by the Nazis allowed them to emphasize the essential unity of the Aryan people; one view of racism against blacks in the United States – not a fully accurate one – insists that racism is attractive to poorer whites because it gives them somebody to look down on and allows them to imagine themselves as part of the ruling (white) class. This way of thinking has been associated with the concept of the *other*, an external group whose existence and difference allows another group to think of itself as united and superior.

Returning to ancient Greece, the Athenian democracy has been described as a free male citizen's club in that democratic rights excluded slaves, women, and foreigners, and the self-conception of the democracy depended on oppositions between the free male citizens and these *others* (Vidal-Naquet 1986, 206). One striking piece of evidence of the position of slaves as the *other* was the tendency, when Athenians categorized the men in the city, to refer to two groups only, "slaves and citizens." In addition to forgetting about the resident foreigners and women, this dichotomy is not a natural one. One would expect slaves versus masters. But all citizens, masters or not, were thought of as a single group in opposition to slaves. Similarly, speakers addressed juries in Athens as if all the jurymen owned slaves. This has puzzled social historians, since they know that many of the jurymen were poor and didn't own slaves. All jurymen were citizens, however, and seem to have felt that they were at least potential slave owners and, as one speaker insists, all had a stake in the good behavior of slaves ([Demosthenes] 45.86). In some ways, this was just an ideology: it served to disguise actual conflicts of interest between rich and poor among the citizens – which sometimes did break out into civil war. In contrast, the rich often viewed the mass of poor Athenian citizens as distinct and inferior to themselves, hardly different from slaves. Nevertheless, the view of the males as divided between citizens and slaves was no more than a simplification of an actual state of affairs: in terms of legal and political rights, classical Athens was a society dominated by one big dichotomy rather than a more complex hierarchy.

A recent book by a French ancient historian, Paulin Ismard's *Democracy's Slaves: A Political History of Ancient Greece*, argues that slavery was crucial to the development of Greek democracy in another way as well (2017 with Hunt 2016a). Public slaves are slaves purchased and owned by the state. Best attested in Athens, they helped build and fix roads, worked in the mint, served as prison guards and executioners, and checked the authenticity of coins in the marketplace. Some even assisted the magistrates and supervised the public archives. These slaves contributed to the smooth running of government: the magistrates themselves were citizen amateurs, usually chosen by lot and serving for a single year, while the slave "assistants" had probably been working at the same post for many years and may have had a much better idea of how things needed to be done.

Ismard goes further and maintains that the longstanding Greek ideal of transparent and direct rule by the community, an important democratic tenet, was only possible because, out of sight, slaves provided the expertise the government required. The citizens did not have to delegate political power to an administrative class from within their ranks. Rather they bought foreign slaves to perform government functions. And, in contrast to a governing elite, public slaves gained little power from their administrative experience and knowledge. Although they enjoyed a higher status than private slaves in several respects, they remained slaves and thus isolated outsiders – not to mention that they could still be whipped.

To modern ways of thinking, the Scythian archers represent the most startling use of public slaves at Athens (see Map 2 for Scythia). These armed slaves served some of the functions of a modern police force, for example, keeping order in the assembly and seizing or removing people at the order of a magistrate. This use of slaves as police was in part a result of the egalitarian ethos among the citizens: for one Athenian to lay hands on another was perhaps too provocative; it symbolized inequality and was likely to lead to violence or at least violent resentment. The Scythian archers, foreign slaves, were somehow out of the game. Of course, individual Athenians resented it when they were manhandled by these foreign slaves (Hall 1989, 47). But such treatment did not threaten democratic equality as similar treatment by a fellow citizen would have.

The oddity of these armed slaves within Athens leads us to the military role of slaves, a problematic one, since military service was a key aspect of being a citizen, slaves were in theory the opposite of citizens, and this dichotomy was central to the way the Athenians categorized people. At first blush, it would seem that slaves could play no role in the many wars that Greek city-states fought against each other. The risks of entrusting such oppressed and often resentful men with weapons are obvious. And many Greeks felt that military service gave a person a claim to political rights, something from which slaves were definitely excluded. The stereotype of slaves as cowardly and childish would hardly recommend using them as warriors. Finally, although wars are the main topic of contemporary historians, references to slave involvement are few and far between. Nevertheless, in my first book, *Slaves, Warfare, and Ideology in the Greek Historians* (1998), I argued the opposite of what one would expect: slaves were important to classical Greek warfare, but their participation was an awkward topic and contemporary historians systematically neglected it as a result.

The patriotic citizen soldier may be an ideal, but reality did not – and does not – always live up to it. From the Persians who (reportedly) drove their soldiers into battle with whips in the Persian Wars (Herodotus 7.223.3) to early modern armies that could not camp in wooded areas for fear their men would desert, armies have often made do with resentful and oppressed soldiers. We cannot rule out the possibility of disgruntled non-citizens serving as soldiers on that count: the frequent military service of the serf-like and sometimes rebellious Spartan Helots provides a striking example. And slaves often served in the navy, where they did not have to be given weapons but rather rowed. Finally, slaves could be motivated by the promise of winning their freedom, in addition to all the other incentives or threats that have motivated previously unenthusiastic soldiers throughout history.

There was nothing impossible about using slaves in warfare. It could also be highly advantageous, since slaves were numerous, could bolster a city's forces considerably, and might escape to the enemy otherwise. For example, the Athenians promised freedom and even citizenship to the slaves they recruited to man a navy in the desperate last years of the Peloponnesian War, a navy that went on to a great victory in the largest sea battle of the war. The grant not merely of freedom but also of citizenship, usually a closely guarded right, may have been a tactic to encourage these freed slaves to remain with the Athenian navy even after the battle rather than deserting to the Peloponnesians, who were paying higher wages at that time (Hunt 2001, 366–370). The practical advantages of enlisting more men – often a lot more – encouraged Greek states to overlook the contradictions between the low status of slaves and the high prestige of military service. When push came to shove, when a navy had to be manned, military advantage trumped ideology.

In the composition of written histories, however, ideology remained dominant. Contemporary historians did not dwell on slave participation, an awkward topic to Greek ways of thinking. Oblique statements occasionally reveal a whole pattern of slave use that contemporary historians otherwise neglect. Thucydides, for example, explains why the crews of the Syracusan and Thurian ships were particularly vocal in demanding their back-pay from their admirals: "since free men made up the majority of their crews" (8.84.2). First of all, this passing reference tells us that *some* of the members of the Thurian and Syracusan crews were slaves. More startling, it also implies that among the other contingents in this Peloponnesian fleet, slaves made up a majority of the crew, something we would not have suspected without this passage. My arguments probably shifted scholarly opinion in the direction of accepting a greater role for slaves in Greek warfare – and for Spartan Helots as well – but particular cases remain controversial.

Slave and Freedmen Administrators in the Early Roman Empire

Some historians believe that slavery played an indirect role in Roman politics, specifically in the fall of the Roman Republic and the establishment of a monarchy in its place, the Roman Empire. If it were true that large estates worked by slaves displaced small farmers, traditionally the backbone of the Roman army, then it would follow that more and more soldiers did not own land or only very little – which seems to have been the case. Such landless soldiers, likely enough, had less of a stake in the Roman Republic and less loyalty to the state. They would be more closely bound to their general, especially when he promised to arrange for retirement bonuses, often land, for his veterans – something the state did not regularly provide. As competition among the elite grew more intense, ambitious generals eventually wanted and were able to lead their men even against Rome and its lawful government, to seize power for themselves, and to obtain the rewards they had promised their troops. This led to a period of civil wars, and eventually one of the competing generals, Augustus, succeeded in establishing a monarchy, in part by regularizing retirement bonuses for the soldiers (Brunt 1988).

According to this reconstruction, slavery's economic impact may have been a partial and indirect contributory cause in these momentous changes, just as it played a role in the Greek development of democracy. The growth of slavery cannot come close to providing a complete explanation for the fall of the Republic, but that is not even the main problem. Rather every step in the theory I outlined above is disputed, either fundamentally (Were landless soldiers any less patriotic?) or with respect to crucial details (When exactly did the soldiery cease to consist mainly of independent middle-class farmers?).[5] To examine all the links in this chain would take us far from Roman slavery and would require a book of its own. This section, therefore, considers slaves who played a direct role in the Roman political system, similar but more conspicuous than Athenian democracy's employment of slave administrators: the slaves and freedmen of the Roman emperor. In the early Empire, these slaves and ex-slaves constituted a powerful and large section of the imperial bureaucracy. In the late Empire, eunuchs, either slaves or ex-slaves, gained immense power from their control of access to the emperor.

The slaves and ex-slaves of the emperor's bureaucracy were known as the *familia Caesaris*: the *familia* of Caesar, that is, of the emperor. *Familia* originally denoted a person's entire household, but it was eventually mainly used of slaves and ex-slaves. Slaves had long acted as accountants or household managers for their masters. The households of rich Romans could include extended families, various clients and guests, and slaves in the hundreds; expenditure and income was on a grand scale, so household managers and accountants held skilled and responsible jobs. By the time a smart, ambitious, and loyal slave had advanced to such a position – in his thirties or forties perhaps – he had often already gained his freedom. As we shall see in Chapter 8, a Roman ex-slave was still attached to his master by bonds of patronage and would often continue to work for him, so in this section we will be talking as much about the emperor's freedmen as about his slaves. At the top levels, we will mainly be dealing with freedmen.

The emperor was not merely any rich Roman. From the beginning of the Empire, the emperor's personal wealth was incomparably larger than that of any other individual and included property in far-flung provinces. It became larger and larger as time went on. In addition, the emperor personally controlled much of the state's revenue and expenditure, including, for example, the salaries of the entire Roman army, more than 300,000 men. Fiscal matters were only part of the story: the emperor was responsible for managing an empire, including more than 25 provinces, with borders thousands of miles away from Rome, and a population of perhaps sixty million. Even a conscientious and hard-working emperor couldn't read and keep track of all of his correspondence on local political matters with the hundred-odd provincial governors, army commanders, and the managers of his estates throughout the empire. Not to mention that some emperors were not, in fact, remotely conscientious and hard working. Ruling this empire was an immense task and early emperors naturally turned to their slaves for help. So the use of slaves and ex-slaves was both a natural extension of their role in managing a private household and essential for the administration of the empire.

Some branches of government were delegated to the Roman elite, the senatorial and the equestrian class. These classes provided military commanders and provincial governors, for example. The emperor wanted to supervise other aspects of the administration more closely. Central government functions, such as managing the imperial budget, needed to be taken care of at Rome. It was natural for the emperor to supervise these tasks himself, but his subordinates could not be senators. For, in the early Empire, Augustus and his successors tried to maintain the façade that important institutions of the Republic continued to exist and to matter. Crucial to these attempts was the emperor's respect for the dignity of the senatorial class. It would have been awkward, to say the least, for an emperor, ostensibly just the first-man, the *princeps*, of the traditional Roman aristocracy, closely to supervise senators and equestrians, to have them read

---

5 E.g., Gruen 1974, 365–384; Rosenstein 2004; Keaveney 2007.

his mail and take dictation, to keep track of his finances, and to draft responses to all the requests that came to him. The sensibilities of the aristocracy would be offended by such direct, daily, and long-term subordination to the emperor.

Finally, relations between the emperor and Senate were sometimes tense – something of an understatement in the case of emperors who had prominent senators executed because they suspected or had discovered plots against themselves. Such emperors might hesitate to give the power that went with these administrative positions to a senator out of fear about how that power might be used for the senator's own gain, for his allies, or even to undermine the emperor.

Thus, for both positive and negative reasons, the emperor turned to his slaves and ex-slaves to constitute his bureaucracy. The slaves who took advantage of this opportunity could expect social advancement. This was the case for a large proportion of the *familia Caesaris* down to minor secretaries and accountants and certainly for the top administrators who enjoyed immense power and wealth, but were also exposed to the bitter resentment of the Roman aristocracy.

We know a fair amount about the social prospects of the *familia Caesaris* – or at least those resident at Rome – from what was engraved on their gravestones, their epitaphs. Roman custom was to engrave not only the name of the person who had died on a gravestone but also the name of the person who had put up the gravestone and his or her relationship to the deceased. In addition, Roman names often reveal legal status: whether the person was a Roman citizen, a foreigner, a slave, freeborn, or an ex-slave. The epitaphs of ex-slaves also reveal the name of the person's former master; for the Roman name of an ex-slave included his or her single slave name as a first name and then the family names of their former masters. When the family names are those of an emperor, we can be fairly certain that we are dealing with a member of the *familia Caesaris*. Several hundred such gravestones have survived for study.

From this evidence, P. R. C. Weaver identified one startling pattern: slave men from the *familia Caesaris* often married freeborn women.[6] Indeed, at least two-thirds of the women married to members of the *familia Caesaris* were freeborn. True love may perhaps strike anywhere, but ancient marriages, largely arranged by male relatives, tended mainly to respect the social hierarchy. Normally, the last thing a free family wanted was for one of their women to have sex with a slave, let alone marry one. In addition to the disgrace, the children from such a pairing – since it would not be considered a marriage – would be illegitimate.

The main exception to marriage taking place between status equals is hypergamy, where a woman marries up the social hierarchy, a common pattern in many societies and in part explicable in terms of evolutionary biology. Paradoxically, it turns out that the pattern Weaver discerned is just another case of hypergamy. Imperial slaves possessed a high enough status that freeborn women were willing to marry slaves, albeit slaves with prospects. Furthermore, many of the wives also carried imperial names, names shared by emperors. This suggests that they were descended from imperial freedmen of earlier generations, a group less likely to consider free birth the decisive indicator of social status.

This surprising marriage pattern was most pronounced among the *familia Caesaris* living in Rome, many of whom must have been accountants and secretaries in the emperor's service. Such marriages had one consequence detrimental to the imperial bureaucracy. By Roman law – and what they claimed was the law of all nations – the status of any

---

6 Weaver 1972, 112–195; Penner 2013, 160–167; *contra* Mouritsen 2011, 297–998.

child not born from a legitimate, official marriage followed the status of the mother. Since marriages of slaves were not legitimate, the children of male slaves of the *familia Caesaris* and free women were free. This deprived the emperor of the next generation of slave bureaucrats, and so a law was passed to discourage such pairings or, at least, to ensure that the offspring would become the emperor's slaves. The details are controversial and obscure, but the important point was that free women who had children with slaves might be liable to enslavement; thus their children would be slaves and potential secretaries and accountants for the emperor. The author of this new law was himself a freedman, Pallas, one of the great administrators and advisors of the emperor Claudius and confidante (and supposedly lover) of Claudius' last wife, Agrippina. We turn now to men like Pallas, the powerful and infamous freedmen at the top of the imperial bureaucracy.

At the head of each of the different departments of the imperial bureaucracy at Rome stood a high-ranking administrator, like Pallas, certain to do much better than merely to marry a freeborn woman. Until the reign of Hadrian (117–138 CE) these officials were typically ex-slaves. The three most important were the *a rationibus*, the *ab epistulis*, and the *a libellis*. The Latin *a/ab* means "from" so the *a rationibus* means something like "[the man put in charge] from accounting." This particular position was something like the Secretary of the Treasury in the United States today, and was like a cabinet-level position in that the *a rationibus* answered only to the emperor, as was the case with all of the major bureau chiefs. The *ab epistulis* handled the emperor's official correspondence (*epistulae*) – with governors throughout the Roman Empire, for example – and seemed to have played an advisory role in making appointments and promotions. In fact, the future emperor Vespasian owed his first major appointment to Narcissus, the *ab epistulis* under the emperor Claudius. The *ab epistulis* has been likened to the Secretary of State. Finally, the *a libellis* administered a large and important part of the emperor's responsibilities, his responses to letters that petitioned for a favor or requested the emperor to redress some grievance. These requests were answered with a reply on the bottom of the original petition. The *a libellis* or one of his subordinates wrote the responses and had them signed by the emperor. Given the responsibility and discretion of all three of these posts and that they answered only to the emperor, they arguably held more practical power, if lower prestige, than all but the most important governorships or magistracies.

We gain an idea about the scope of their powers from the poet Statius in an elegy addressed to the wife of the deceased freedman Abascantus, *ab epistulis* to the emperor Domitian:

> Your husband's job was to send out, far and wide into the great earth, the orders of the emperor, the successor of Romulus, and to control with his hand our imperial armies and the methods of our empire . . . he must disclose to the emperor who deserves to be a centurion and to ride on horse among the companies of infantry, who is to command a cohort, who merits the higher status of noble tribune. (Statius, *Silvae* 5.1.86–97)

Similar praise of Polybius, *a libellis*, comes from the hand of Seneca, an exceptionally rich and powerful senator, an intellectual and philosopher, and top advisor to Nero – by whom he was eventually executed:

> You must hear so many thousands of men and decide so many petitions. You have to examine such a mass of problems streaming in from the four corners of the

> world, for the purpose of submitting them in the due order to the judgment of our supreme ruler. (Seneca, *Consolation to Polybius* 6.5, trans. in Duff 1928, 155)

Seneca thus provides us with a description of the work of the *a libellis*, but this passage's interest to historians does not end there. Seneca had been exiled for (purportedly) committing adultery with a member of the imperial family – any sex with an unmarried woman was considered adultery. The *Consolation to Polybius*, written in response to the death of Polybius' brother, was part of Seneca's campaign, eventually successful, to have himself reinstated at Rome. That he composed a lengthy work for an ex-slave in hopes that he could intercede with the emperor shows clearly the power that the top freedmen were thought to possess.

Seneca's flattery of Polybius is thus easily understood; his admiration was probably feigned. When he had risen to become one of Nero's top advisors, Seneca represents the deceased Emperor Claudius as a dupe of his own ex-slaves, as Tacitus does in the quotation with which we started this chapter. In a satire on Claudius' supposed divinization after his death, Seneca describes Claudius trying to give an order in heaven: "They paid him no more attention than his freedmen had" (Seneca, *Apocolocyntosis* 6).

Pliny, writing under the emperor Trajan (98–117 CE), gives us another and more blatant example of senatorial resentment of powerful, imperial freedman, in this case of Pallas, the *a rationibus* under Claudius and Nero, more than a generation earlier. Pliny had noticed a monument to Pallas with an inscription describing some honors that the senate decreed for him: the insignia of a praetor and fifteen million sesterces. Pliny, himself a wealthy and prominent senator, was moved to go through the Senate's official records and located the actual decree, which was filled with flattery of Pallas. He was indignant and ashamed of the Roman Senate:

> But who is so crazy as to desire advancement won through his own and his country's dishonor, in a State where the chief privilege of its highest office is that of being the first to pay compliments to Pallas in the Senate? I say nothing of this offer of the praetorian insignia to a slave, for they were slaves themselves who made the offer. (*Letters* 8.6, trans. Radice 1969)

The historian Tacitus was also aghast at these proceedings: "And the senatorial decree was made public, inscribed in bronze: an ex-slave, now worth three hundred million sesterces, was loaded with praise for his old-fashioned thriftiness" (*Annals* 12.53). Members of the senatorial class were bitterly competitive and quick to resent any of their peers who surpassed them in rank and prestige; it's easy to imagine the smoke coming from their ears when ex-slaves eclipsed them in the emperor's eyes and in public honors. It probably never occurred to them to consider how competent, useful, and loyal to the emperor such ex-slaves were.

Powerful freedmen were particularly prominent under Claudius, whose relations with the Senate were tense and whose claim to the throne was at first tenuous. Even reputedly good and strong emperors used them high in their administration until the time of Hadrian, whose reign started in 117 CE. At that point, the Empire had been established for many generations and service to the emperor had become an honorable profession. Although many of the minor bureaucrats and secretaries were still slaves and freedmen, the top positions were reserved for members of the equestrian class, the wealthy class next to the senators in rank. Many of these equestrian officials in the second century CE carried the same family names as earlier emperors. Since they were definitely not actual relatives, they were almost certainly the descendants of the *familia Caesaris* of earlier emperors. Indeed, the consul of 167 CE could claim the great freedman *a rationibus* Pallas among his ancestors. Even though the honor of the consulship was one of the pinnacles of the most successful senatorial careers under the emperors, this consul's actual power was likely only a shadow of that of his infamous ex-slave forebear.

Eunuchs in the Late Empire

Beginning in the fourth century and lasting through the Byzantine Empire, eunuchs played a large role in the imperial government, arguably even greater and certainly longer lasting than the role played by early imperial freedmen. For example, the Grand Chamberlain of the Emperor, typically a eunuch, possessed the fourth highest rank in the whole imperial administration. The bribes that even lesser eunuchs regularly demanded and received reflected the fact that they could get things done or prevent them from happening. The resentment that they provoked among the traditional aristocracy was bitter and probably proportional to the influence they had on the emperor. Although some emperors were criticized for allowing the eunuchs too much power, all sorts of emperors – the good, the bad, and the mediocre – used eunuchs in their administration.

Eunuchs are men or boys who have been castrated. This surgery was generally only performed on slaves, although naturally most high-ranking eunuchs had received their freedom earlier in their careers and were thus freedmen when they became, for example, Grand Chamberlain. The exact physical and biological results of castration depend on the age at which the operation is performed and whether just the testicles or the penis too is excised. One certainty is the danger of the operation, performed without sterile instruments, antibiotics, or modern painkillers. According to one story, the emperor Justinian (ca. 482–565) was outraged at hearing that only three children lived out of ninety undergoing the operation. This would seem like sensationalism, except that better statistics from nineteenth-century Africa also reveal a 90 percent mortality rate for slaves undergoing castration (Lovejoy 2012, 35). The mortality rate associated with castration had an economic consequence too: eunuchs must have been extremely expensive slaves – since it might require the waste (painful deaths) of about ten slave children to produce one eunuch. Paradoxically, this may have contributed to their impressiveness as expensive and exclusive status symbols.

Ancient eunuchs are described as effeminate, smooth skinned, and fat. Their voices might have been high or unusual, depending on the age of castration. Their inability to procreate may have been their original attraction: the Greek word *eunuch* means "those who guard the bed" and one early function was as trustworthy supervisors of the harems of eastern monarchs. In such monarchies, eunuchs also possessed great power; Roman emperors may in part simply have been imitating a model they encountered in states such as Sassanid Persia.

In a patriarchal society, the sterility of eunuchs marked them as unnatural and outside of society, except for their bond with the king or emperor. Paradoxically, some eunuchs purportedly retained a sexual appetite; indeed, some were described as insatiable. Without the possibility of paternity, this only made them seem unnatural and monstrous. Most eunuchs probably had their origins outside the Empire, so they were barbarians too. As sterile men, as biologically altered, as slaves, and as barbarians, eunuchs would seem far from ideal holders of power in the Roman world. But it was eunuchs' difference and alienation that provided the rationale behind their power. Before we can understand this claim, we need to explore the nature of that power.

Keith Hopkins has argued persuasively that the eunuchs of the late Empire derived their importance primarily from their own intimacy with the emperor and from their control of access to him (1978b). The titles of the great eunuchs reflected this role. The position translated as "Grand Chamberlain" in Latin is *praepositus sacri cubiculi*, which literally means, "the man put in charge of the sacred bedchamber." Such intermediaries became more important as the emperor represented himself more and more as divine and an increasingly elaborate court ceremonial tended to separate him from mere humans. Eunuchs thus provided, and sometimes controlled, communication between the emperor and his subjects. They often provided the emperor's most trustworthy intelligence about the empire he ruled. They would communicate requests from his subjects or set up audiences – often only upon receipt of a hefty bribe. But, given that the emperor needed – as all rulers do – to communicate with his subjects and needed courtiers to moderate, channel, and ensure this communication, why did the late Roman and Byzantine emperors choose eunuchs for this function?

Recent interpretations of eunuchs in the Byzantine Empire view them from the perspective of gender studies: Were they a third sex or gender? How did their sterility affect how they were perceived as men? Was their supposed androgyny part of their power? (Stevenson 1995, 495–511; Ringrose 2003). But our focus is instead on eunuchs as slaves and thus Hopkins's political interpretation of their power is most apt and, in my opinion, most convincing overall. Hopkins makes the argument that the eunuchs were particularly trustworthy and thus useful to the emperor because their allegiance was undivided (1978b). They were slaves, natally alienated: their prior families, alliances, and other social bonds had been severed. They had no loyalties other than to the emperor, upon whom their entire position depended. Their biological difference from other men, that they seem to have been regarded with disgust and suspicion, severely limited their ability to ally with (or potentially to plot with) the imperial aristocracy. Most crucially, their sterility meant that they could not contract marriage alliances. One main, if not *the* main, purpose of elite marriage was alliance between families, and children or the expectation of children cemented the alliances. Unable to contract marriage alliances, eunuchs remained, individually and as a class, in isolation from the rest of society and in dependence on the emperor. They were his perennial tools.

This position could bring great power, but it also had its risks. In particular, eunuchs often provided scapegoats for unpopular imperial policies. If an emperor's policies evoked too much resistance – widespread riots, for example – the emperor could blame his eunuch chamberlain and execute him. Again the isolation of eunuchs was key to their usefulness as scapegoats: there were no families and allies who would have to be placated, destroyed, or distrusted if an emperor dismissed or executed a eunuch. It might worry other eunuchs, but the matter was essentially between the emperor and his victim.

This scapegoating of eunuchs means that it was sometimes in the emperor's interest to attribute power to a eunuch when he was actually just carrying out an order that the emperor later decided to wash his hands of. In the fourth century, a eunuch of Constantius II reportedly prevented the future emperor Julian from obtaining an audience with the emperor, but perhaps it was Constantius himself who didn't want to meet with Julian and later found it convenient to blame his eunuch (Hopkins 1978b, 173). Such shifting of blame may leave us with an exaggerated view of eunuchs' actual initiative and importance. Nevertheless, because of their incapacity to be assimilated into the aristocracy, eunuchs provided a crucial tool for semi-divine and otherwise isolated emperors and accrued much practical power as a result.

Conclusion

That classical Athens, like many of the cities of ancient Greece, was a slave society meant that its politics were profoundly affected by slavery. Just as some historians trace the segregation and growing use of African slaves in the United States South with the growth of the notion of equal citizenship for whites, the equality of citizens in the Athenian democracy may have roots in slavery. Economically, slavery reduced subordination among citizens; on the level of ideology, slaves provided the other against which all citizens, be they rich or poor, could define themselves as a unity, however diverse their real interests.

Although slaves by definition lack power with respect to their owners, they can obtain political power through their bond with a powerful master, especially when that master is the emperor of Rome. In the early Empire, slaves and ex-slaves provided a bureaucracy for emperors who needed one. In the late Empire, eunuch slaves watched over the divine emperor's person and facilitated his relations with his subjects. In theory both groups of imperial slaves were merely tools, extensions of their master, whose power they merely transmitted. In practice, quite a bit of power tended to stick to these men, so regularly used as the tools of such a powerful monarch.

Suggested Reading

Finley 1982a and 1982b present the main arguments about democracy and chattel slavery that I summarize in the section on Athenian democracy and slavery. I strongly believe that Finley had the big picture right and his basic conception of the relationship between Athenian democracy and slavery remains influential (e.g., Scheidel 2008). But, for example, Vlassopoulos 2016a provides a critical overall assessment and Harris tries to attack important aspects of this model (2002 and 2012). Divergent interpretations of Solon's reforms and their socio-economic context and impact are as numerous as what we know for sure is little. The topic is, nevertheless, a fascinating one and essays collected in Blok and Lardinois 2006 and the commentary of Noussia-Fantuzzi 2010 provide an entrée. Hunt 2006 provides a short and accessible summary of some main arguments from Hunt 1998, my book on slaves in Greek warfare. On the slaves of the emperor, Weaver 1972 is detailed and scholarly. His breakthroughs resulted from his statistical analysis of the epitaphs of members of the *familia Caesaris* rather than on trying to reinterpret the well-known literary evidence. Duff expresses a contempt for powerful freedmen that resembles the attitude of the Roman aristocracy: "imperial freedmen gained an ascendancy in the Empire the like of which has never in another nation fallen to a series of low-born upstarts" (1928, 174). Yet his descriptions of the growth and decline of the power of ex-slaves, the various offices they held, elite resentment, and the lives of famous or notorious freedmen are clear and detailed. My treatment above closely follows Hopkins 1978b on the political context for the rise of powerful eunuchs. Tougher 2008 provides a more general treatment of eunuchs in the Byzantine Empire.

6

Culture

> *The Macrones, with shields and spears... were in battle formation on the other side of the river [from us]... But just then one of our javelin-men approached Xenophon, explaining that he had been a slave at Athens and that he understood the language of the Macrones. "In fact," he continued, "I believe this is my homeland. I would like to talk to them unless you have an objection."*
>
> Xenophon (Greek historian and mercenary commander, ca. 430–354 BCE) *Anabasis* 4.8.3–4 (see Map 2 for Macronia)

> *... I cannot, citizens, stand*
> *A Rome so full of Greeks. Yet what fraction of these sweepings*
> *Derives, in fact, from Greece? For years now Syrian*
> *Orontes has poured its sewage into our native Tiber –*
> *Its lingo and manners, its flutes, its outlandish harps*
> *With their transverse strings, its native tambourines,*
> *And the whores who hang out round the race-course...*
>
> Juvenal (Roman satirist, active in the early second century CE), *Satires* I.60–65, trans. Green 1999 (modified)

> *But now that we have foreign tribes among our slaves, who have different customs from our own and practice foreign religions or none at all, it is only possible to restrain that motley bunch by fear.*
>
> Speech of a senator, Gaius Cassius, in Tacitus (Roman historian, ca. 56–117 CE) *Annals* 14.44

Introduction

In this chapter we look at slaves as immigrants, as foreigners in a new country. Thus we are concerned with imported or captured slaves more than with those born in slavery. We'll focus on the periods and places when such slaves dominated the slave population, especially classical Athens and the Roman Republic. Such first-generation slaves were outsiders and different from their masters and from the native population in general. Not only were they subject to slavery, but they were also distinct in their birth cultures,

Ancient Greek and Roman Slavery, First Edition. Peter Hunt.
© 2018 Peter Hunt. Published 2018 by John Wiley & Sons, Ltd.

their ethnic identities, terms that encompass language, religion, music, art, legends, family structure, a particular system of values – and the list could go on. Our first theme will be slaves' ability (sometimes) to retain their ethnic identity despite the dislocation of slavery. The second theme will be the relationship between the culture of slaves and that of their masters and of free society. We'll be examining these themes first in classical Athens and then among Greek slaves in Rome.

At least three factors affected slave culture as a whole: the birth culture of the slaves, the culture of the enslaving society, and slavery itself. First off, we often do not know much about the birth culture of slaves in the classical world. Many of them came from societies that were not literate or whose writing has not survived; these cultures are known only from the material remains uncovered and interpreted by archaeologists. When the original culture is poorly known and, as usual, the perspective of the slave is poorly attested, it is hard to discover in what ways a birth culture has been maintained or lost in slavery. Consequently, while we will be able to show that some slaves at Athens retained a sense of their ethnic identity, we cannot provide a detailed picture of which aspects of Thracian culture, for example, were maintained, which changed, and which were lost in slavery at Athens. One case where we do know a fair amount about the original culture of a group of slaves was when the Romans enslaved large numbers of Greeks in the second and first centuries BCE. In this case, our interest will be the complexities of Roman attitudes towards Greek culture, a culture they generally admired, and towards Greek slaves, and, on the other side, the roles and attitudes of Greek slave and ex-slave intellectuals.

Greek slaves, of course, shared a similar cultural background. Generally, however, slaves were not only foreign to their new societies, but also different from each other. They came from various areas and experienced dissimilar lives in slavery. For instance, at Athens, a Thracian mine slave and a Phoenician slave banker probably felt little kinship based on both being foreign slaves. When first-generation slaves predominate and when they come from different places, as in classical Athens, slave culture is not likely to be homogenous.

Second, slave culture inevitably reflected the culture of their masters and of the rest of their new society; for slaves were a minority group possessing little power and prestige. Those of one particular ethnicity were an even smaller group, even more isolated in the larger Greek or Roman society. As a result, slaves needed quickly to learn at least some basic Greek or Latin both to understand their orders and even to communicate with each other. Those slaves who had frequent personal contact with their masters were most likely to assimilate to their master's culture, as opposed to slaves in mines or on large farms with absentee owners. And those who assimilated were most likely to please their masters, to gain their freedom, and to possess the resources to leave us some evidence of their lives – such as the epitaphs of freedmen and freedwomen at Rome. Thus slaves who assimilated to a greater extent are overrepresented in our evidence. Yet traces remain of some slaves retaining their birth cultures and sometimes even passing aspects of these cultures on to their children. This was one way in which slaves could assert control over the world in which they lived. Their work was coerced and their lives might be harshly circumscribed, but some would hold onto their birth culture. They would at least remember who they were.

Third, the experience of slavery affected the culture of slaves. For example, stories celebrating weak but clever "tricksters" might rise in prominence among slaves, whose lack of power made them value ingenuity. In contrast, those myths that glorify the powerful might have less appeal to slaves, even if such stories had been important to their home cultures – as such myths often were. Many urban Roman slaves took pride in their skilled labor, a development contrary to Roman elite ideology and arising from the condition of their slavery – that they were skilled craftsmen – and not from any particular ethnic origin (Joshel 1992, 49–61). We'll see that even the function of language could change in slavery. A slave's language was originally simply part of the culture of a certain place and people. It could become a tool of resistance in ways dramatic or subtle and quotidian – as the quotation from Tacitus that opened this chapter suggests.

In many cases, however, the culture of slaves is not well described by a dichotomy between the assimilation of a new culture and the retention of an old one. Like immigrants and the subjects of colonialism, slaves might adopt some new practices and ways of thinking and retain some old ones; which features were retained, which adopted, and how was in part determined by their own needs and desires in the context of their slavery. The meeting of the culture of masters and the birth cultures of slaves in the context of slavery gave birth to cultural phenomena that were new and different from each of the original cultures. Such a process of partial assimilation and dynamic cultural interaction is sometimes described as *hybridity*. Several of the phenomena we'll consider fall best under this heading rather than along a simple spectrum between retention of birth cultures and assimilation to their master's culture.

It would, finally, be a mistake to consider only the adaptations slaves made to the culture of their masters and not also the reverse. Cultural interchange is usually a two-way street. Even in less complex societies, captured slaves might bring aspects of their birth culture to their new societies (Cameron 2011, 169–209). As we'll see, Greek slaves represented an important conduit through which Romans, from elite landowners to the urban poor, were exposed to Greek culture in the middle and late Republic.

Slave Culture in Classical Athens

Slaves constituted a large proportion of the population of classical Athens and far outnumbered the male citizens. As we saw in Chapter 3, the majority of these slaves seem to have been imported from non-Greek societies, from a wide variety of different places. Many came from Thrace and the coast of Asia Minor. Consequently, if you count people, consider their places of birth, and their native languages, Athens was a radically multicultural society. With the Piraeus, its bustling port, it was a magnet for all sorts of foreign visitors. By far the most populous group were the unwilling foreigners, the slaves. Did these slaves retain a sense of their ethnicity? Did they continue to see themselves as Thracians or Phrygian or Macronian – as in the quotation at the beginning of the chapter – even after they had lived in Athens for years?

It is hard to answer this question, since we possess little evidence of slave ethnicity in Athens; much of that comes from slaveholders and is probably distorted as a result. Consequently, Ian Morris concluded that Athenian slaves retained almost no sense of their birth cultures while in slavery (Morris 1998, 193–220; 2011, 176–193). He reached this conclusion after surveying archaeological evidence from burials, house design, and pottery in the area of Laurion, the silver mining region, which had a population consisting predominantly of slaves. Morris finds no sign of the retention of ethnic identity and suggests that slaves at Athens quickly lost any strong sense of their birth cultures. I believe that Morris is just looking in the wrong places: mine slaves did not design houses or make pottery; nor are we likely to find signs of slave culture in the gravestones of the free population (Hunt 2015). Though the families of a few deceased ex-slaves managed a gravestone – as we'll see – most slaves were buried without any commemoration on materials that survive for archaeologists to find. So where and how can we find evidence of the birth culture of slaves? It requires the combination of several types of evidence and lines of reasoning, but their cumulative weight is decisive. The content of this ethnic identity is hard or, in some cases, impossible to reconstruct, but its existence can be demonstrated.

First of all, when an Athenian man wanted to describe a slave, the first thing he would provide was his or her place of origin. The Athenians even gave slaves ethnic expressions as names: many Thracian female slaves had the name *Thraitta*, which just means *Thracian* (feminine). Some literary sources contain more detailed descriptions of the ethnicity of a slave than just a name. For example, in the "New Comedy" of the late fourth and early third centuries BCE, the ethnicity of slave characters is a conspicuous part of their overall characterization. They not only act in ways stereotypical of their birthplace, but occasionally they define themselves in terms of their nationality. For example, Menander depicts a Thracian, presumably a slave in Athens, boasting of his origins:

> All Thracians, and especially we Getae – for I myself proudly claim to be of that tribe – are not terribly self-controlled . . . for we never marry fewer than ten or eleven women – and some marry twelve or more. And if somebody dies with only four or five wives, he is regarded among the people there as an unmarried, unhappy bachelor. (Menander, fr. 877 (*Incertae Fabulae*) in Kassel and Austin 1983–, Vol. VI)

In Menander's *Aspis* another slave makes the ironic comment that "I'm Phrygian. Many things that seem good to you seem utterly evil to me – and vice versa. Why should you pay attention to me? Your opinions are superior, of course" (Menander, *Aspis* 205–208). Later, a different slave, a Thracian, describes this Phrygian's loyalty to his master and honesty as really just the cowardice he considers characteristic of that people (Menander, *Aspis* 238–248).

Some of these statements, though ascribed to slave characters, are suspect: they represent slaveholders' caricatures of ethnic types. The Thracian slave talking about how many wives men have back home is probably meant to be outlandish or a teller of tall tales – or both. But the question is not whether these portraits are distortions – they are – but whether they involve attributing difference and some retention of native culture to slaves who possessed neither or – what seems more likely – putting a negative or humorous spin on actual differences between Thracians, Phrygians, and Athenians.

We can even go further. In one fragment, Menander seems to be responding to a positive self-identification adopted by Thracians: "The Thracians, O Libyan, are called Trojans; so nowadays everything is equal."[1] The speaker of these lines probably did not approve of the equality of Athens "nowadays." Yet, from this criticism we can infer that

---

1 Menander, fr. 359 (*Hydriai*) in Kassel and Austin 1983–, Vol. VI.

some Thracians wanted to be called Trojans. It is possible that the Thracians mentioned here are merely foreigners in Athens. But given how many of the foreigners we meet in New Comedy are slaves and how many actual slaves were Thracians, I suspect that what we have here is a mocking reference to a claim of Trojan descent by slaves. The assertion of Trojan ancestry was a common way for nations on the edge of the Greek world to claim membership in that world, while still emphasizing their independence. The most famous case is that of the Romans, who claimed to be descended from a Trojan noble, Aeneas. To return to Athens, from this passage we have learned something about Thracian slaves' assertion of ethnic identity, albeit indirectly and from a hostile source.

The practice of their native religions was another way that slaves affirmed and reinforced their sense of ethnic identity and sometimes left evidence of it. Scholars who have studied the epigraphic evidence for foreign religions in Attica generally agree that many of the people involved were slaves (Parker 1996, 171, 174, 194). We even possess an early Hellenistic dedication to the Thracian goddess Bendis by a man who does not list his father – as free-born citizens did – and had the archetypal slave name Daos: "Daos, having won the torch race, dedicates [this] to Bendis" (*SEG* 39:210). Another piece of evidence for foreign religions among slaves at Athens comes from the remains of an edifice, Building Z, located near the city walls. Loom weights, the types and amounts of broken pottery, and the many small rooms all suggest that the building was at one time a brothel. Most prostitutes in Athens were foreign slaves. In this building, the excavator, Ursula Knigge, also found a large number of foreign religious artifacts and concluded: "It was therefore foreign slave women who lived in the large Building Z and worshipped their gods" (Knigge and Kovacsovics 1981, 388). Even slave prostitutes, whose lives must otherwise have been horrible, wanted and were able to maintain some connections with religious practices of their homelands. Indeed, perhaps the grim coercions of a slave prostitute's current life would make her cling even more tightly to such religious symbols of her past self and life.

Since the cults practiced in Athens and its port, the Piraeus, ended up representing all the main areas from which slaves were imported, slaves may have had a choice about which cult to participate in. On the one hand, one can easily imagine a lone Egyptian slave in a smallish household joining her three Thracian fellow slaves at the Thracian festival of Bendis. On the other hand, most slaves probably tried to practice a cult imported from their native lands. I would guess, for example, that slaves from Asia Minor often chose the cult of the lunar god, Mēn, and Thracians chose the cult of their goddess, Bendis.

Greek religion was polytheistic so participation in a foreign cult at Athens did not imply a rejection of Athenian gods or Athenian culture, but merely a preference for one's own gods – and likely the companionship of one's compatriots. Indeed, the inscriptions left by foreign cults clearly show Athenian influence. First of all, the language of these inscriptions is Greek. Second, the officers of cult organizations acted to a large extent like any Athenian governing body. To begin with, they put up inscriptions to commemorate and make public their actions. This was not an obvious or universal procedure nor practiced much in the areas from which most slaves came. They recorded the proposer of the motion, just as on an Athenian decree. They honored their former officers for good conduct with wreaths. We do not know the ratio of slaves, ex-slaves, or resident foreigners among these cults, but to all three groups the forms of Athenian government seem to have had an appeal. Or, at the very least, they wanted to represent themselves as official, lawful, and perhaps even democratic, according to Athenian forms. Thus, these religious inscriptions attest to hybridity, rather than simply to the retention of an original ethnic identity.

While the average slave has left little trace of his or her life, some exceptional slaves have left us more interesting and detailed evidence. The epitaph of a certain Atotas, a miner who does not list his father's name and who came from Paphlagonia, dates to the second half of the fourth century BCE. As far as we know, even the most skilled, managerial foreigners in the mines at Laurion were originally slaves. For example, the Athenian general Nicias *bought* Sosias the Thracian, to act as manager of his thousand mine slaves.[2] Atotas, too, was probably a slave who had risen to a position of responsibility – perhaps he eventually managed a mine for an absent owner – became affluent and gained his freedom. We can infer most of this from his gravestone, now lost, which was made from elegant, white marble with fancy decorations and must have been expensive. The epitaph is worth quoting in full:

> Atotas, miner.
> Great-hearted Atotas, a Paphlagonian from the Hospitable [Black] Sea, far from his land has rested his body from toil. Nobody rivaled [me] in skill. I am from the race of Pylaimenes, who died, conquered by the hand of Achilles. (*IG* I²/III² 10051)

The language and style of the epitaph is like something out of the epic poetry of Homer rather than ordinary speech. Its language, Greek, makes it clear that Atotas has adopted aspects of Athenian culture. It is just as certain that he does not consider himself an Athenian, nor is he ashamed of his foreign origins. Atotas places particular emphasis on his homeland with four references: he's Paphlagonian, he's from the Black Sea, he died far from his land, and he is from the race of Pylaimenes – a mythical king allied to Priam of Troy. With this last reference, Atotas seems to be doing something similar to the Thracians who claimed Trojan descent. He was from outside the Greek world, but the reference to Pylaimenes implies that he came from a proud and ancient people. He claims to be a descendant of a hero just as many Greeks claimed to be.

Apollodorus was the son of an ex-slave, Pasion. We'll revisit their family history in Chapter 8 and here we'll focus just on his name. Apollodorus was born after his father gained his freedom and thus was named by him rather than by Pasion's master. The name Apollodorus sounds Greek enough: it meant gift of Apollo and was not a rare name for an Athenian citizen. Scholars have also noticed, however, that Pasion counted Phoenicians with similar names, Theodorus and Pythodorus, among his associates (Trevett 1992, 17 n. 1). Inscriptions from the Hellenistic period reveal that Phoenicians in Athens often used names representing Greek translations of Phoenician names. These names were often derived from the name of a god, just as Theodorus, Pythodorus, and Apollodorus are. If Pasion was a Phoenician like his friends, Apollodorus could well represent a Greek translation of a Phoenician name. It was perhaps the same original name as Pythodorus; for Apollo was commonly called Pythian Apollo. Pasion may have cleverly combined an allegiance to his homeland and an accommodation with Athenian

---

2 Xenophon, *Memorabilia* 2.5.2, *Poroi.* 4.14; Plutarch, *Nicias* 4; see also Demosthenes 37.25.

culture in his choice of a name for his son. And who knows whether, when he was a boy, Apollodorus' parents called him to dinner with Abd-Reshef (the most likely Phoenician original) or Apollodorus. In Athens under the Roman Empire, we find a similar case of hybridity: a chief smelter in the mining district, likely a Semitic slave or ex-slave, had his epitaph written in Greek, but from right to left, the direction of his native writing system and not the direction Greeks wrote (*IG* II² 11697).

Factors in the Retention of Birth Culture

Atotas and Pasion were obviously exceptionally successful slaves and, in general, it is hard to tell whether this scattered evidence for slave ethnic identity is representative. Which aspects of the lives of which slaves are illuminated depends largely on what evidence has survived. Nevertheless, parallels with New World slavery and our knowledge of Athenian slavery can help us sketch out the factors that influenced the chances of different slaves to retain their non-Athenian birth culture to a greater or lesser extent. Exploring these factors sheds light not only on the ethnic identity of slaves but also on important features of slave life at Athens. A picture emerges of a huge range of possibilities depending on a slave's circumstances.

First, the age at which a person was enslaved was crucial. Even born slaves might pick up from their parents a sense of foreign identity, but in general, the older a person was when enslaved, the more likely that his or her ethnic identity was something firmly established and less likely to fade away entirely over time.

Second, the more independence slaves had from masters, the more easily they could maintain their own culture. Studies of the autonomy of slave culture in the antebellum American South make a distinction between the slaves living in the household of the master and those living in separate slave quarters (e.g., Genovese 1976, 327–365). Slaves in the master's house experienced greater pressure to conform to their master's expectations, since masters took a much greater interest in the subtleties of their behavior and were able to exercise a more penetrating surveillance. Such slaves had a greater opportunity and more reasons to assimilate. The slaves living in separate quarters – mainly agricultural workers in the South – were allowed far more autonomy in their demeanor, way of life, and customs. They were more likely to retain aspects of African culture. The proportion of Athenian slaves in situations similar to the house and field slaves of the South is hard even to estimate. And in reality, there were not two distinct classes – slaves with or without autonomy – but rather a complex spectrum of degrees and types of independence.

Slave ownership at Athens extended further down the social spectrum than in New World slave systems. Consequently, a greater proportion of slaves lived with their masters in small groups with little personal space, either physical or metaphorical. Nevertheless, the concentrations of slaves in large urban workshops, on large farms with owners living in the city, and in silver mining, may have equaled in number the slaves in the many mid-sized farms and households of Attica.

Third, if slaves were to maintain more of their culture than a mute awareness of foreign origin and difference, not only independence from their masters but also some reinforcement from a larger ethnic community was necessary: they needed continued contact with their birth culture, either in the form of other slaves or of foreign communities in Attica. What slaves had such opportunities? Well, the notion that slaves were always working, or at least on call, is too simple. Some direct evidence exists for Athenian slaves at leisure or free to move about the city. Isocrates, a moralistic intellectual of the fourth century BCE, states that, in the good old days, not even an honest slave would be seen in a tavern (7.49). This claim implies that in his time, one might find slaves at leisure and allowed some freedom of movement – and they might well want a drink. Brief and informal meetings with other slaves were possible for those whose work required them to do errands such as shopping, delivering messages, and going to the fountain – all of which are attested. Slaves accompanying their masters to a symposium, a drinking party, would get to meet the slaves in the host home and perhaps get to spend much of the evening with them – as, in Aristophanes' *Frogs*, the slave Xanthias chats with Aeacus, doorkeeper of Hades, while his master meets with the god of the underworld himself (738–813).

Even in situations that were at least as systematically exploitative as Athens was, such as cotton plantations in the United States South and the sugar farms of Brazil, slaves were given between sixty and one hundred and ten days off from work each year, mainly for various religious occasions including Sundays (Schwartz 1985, 99–106). Athens did not have the Sabbath, but it was famous for the number of its religious festivals. On some of these days domestic slaves probably assisted their owners as usual. Nevertheless, festivals were considered a perk even for slaves at Athens. Like everybody else, they might simply have enjoyed a hearty meal – blood sacrifice was the main occasion on which Athenians ate meat – when they were allowed to join in. But, perhaps, it was even more of a boon when the masters were celebrating those festivals at which slaves were not welcome; domestic slaves would necessarily get time off from work – or at least off from supervision. When it comes to slaves attending foreign cults that did not take place on the same days as Athenian festivals, it may seem odd to picture a slave asking his master for permission to take the day or even the evening off to go celebrate Bendis or Mēn. I suspect that such negotiations were more frequent than we at first imagine. Piety was an important Greek virtue, and, in any case, the slaves whom we know played a part in foreign religious cults at Athens must somehow have managed the time to do it.

Two final factors in the retention of ethnic identity among slaves are simple, but extremely important: a slave living among a large group of slaves would have a greater chance of having compatriots among his fellow-slaves; a slave from an area that supplied Athens with many slaves would also be more likely to find compatriots. To take an example, Phrygians are the most common ethnic group among mine slaves in the fourth century BCE, making up about one third of the probable slaves of known origins – attested mainly on epitaphs and plaques recording religious dedications (Lauffer 1979, 124–128). If this represents the actual proportion, in a typical mine site worked by thirty to fifty slaves, a Phrygian slave could expect from nine to sixteen fellow Phrygians. Such a slave could probably speak his own language daily and share his culture with his compatriots. And, to a certain extent, this is confirmed by the foreign religious dedications and inscriptions found in the mining district. There were plenty of reasons that the life of even a Phrygian mine slave was horrible – I doubt they got many days off – but cultural alienation was probably not one of them.

On the other hand, almost half of the slaves of known origin came from groups that provided Athens with only a small proportion of its slaves. Such slaves would be unlikely to have many compatriots except in the largest groups of slaves – or in town or city centers. And perhaps half of the slaves in Athens lived in small households with one to five slaves. Such slaves probably had to adopt the Greek language to communicate with anybody at all. Their ability actively to maintain the culture from which they had been severed was likely to be diminished. This does not mean that they would have had to become Athenian in their outlook. Rather, I suspect they are likely to have shared in a slave culture – similar to that in New World slavery – in which aspects of different original cultures and of Greek culture were adapted to the experience of slavery.

Compatibility and Resistance

I want to finish this section by considering two sides of the relationship between slave and Athenian culture: first, the ways in which the two were compatible and, second, the implications of the fact that Athenian slaveholders saw slave ethnicity as a danger.

Athenian slaves, and especially those with access to the cosmopolitan worlds of Athens and its port the Piraeus, were never completely separated from their homelands in the way modern slaves transported across the Atlantic were. Athens was a few days' sail from and was in active and continuous contact with most of the areas from which slaves were imported. Athens and the Piraeus were famous for their diverse peoples and culture. The presence in Athens of communities – including ex-slaves – from the very areas from which slaves came meant that slaves in the urban areas were never fully isolated from their homelands. An Egyptian slave might buy food in the market from an Egyptian fish-seller. Thracian slaves might see Thracian mercenaries in town. One historian has even suggested that there was a district dominated by Thracian immigrants, a "Thracetown," in the Piraeus (Middleton 1982, 299).

And slaves brought to Athens from Thrace or western Asia Minor were not transported to such an alien world. Differences in environment, social structure, work regime, and religion were less than those between western Africa and the regimented slave systems of the New World. The climate of coastal Asia Minor and Thrace was similar to that of Athens. The same three crops – olives, grapes, and grain – were the mainstay of agriculture in both places. Whereas African slaves moved from peasant economies into semi-industrialized plantations, the work regime of agricultural slaves in Athens was probably not that different from what they were used to. Enslaved Lydians, for example, must have suffered a horrible shock upon being yanked from community and family. Upon arrival in Athens, however, they found themselves in a recognizable world and society, one with significant and continuing links to their homeland. Neither was their old culture utterly inappropriate to their new circumstances, nor did the adoption of aspects of Athenian culture represent a complete break from their origins.

Slaves were not, of course, just another subset of immigrants to Athens. Their lives were probably determined less by Athenian culture or their own ethnic identity than by slavery and their reactions to it. Such reactions were varied and complex. As we'll see, some slaves expressed loyalty or even affection for their masters; others felt hostility and resentment. Was there any connection between these attitudes and slave ethnicity? Perhaps there was. As the Tacitus quotation at the start of the chapter suggests and as we'll see in Chapter 10, having a large proportion of foreign slaves makes rebellion more likely. On a more everyday level, slaves with a common language not understood by their masters could plot resistance or just gossip and badmouth their masters behind their backs. It was in response to this threat – or annoyance – that masters in both Greece and Rome were advised not to purchase too many slaves from one place.[3] Whether slaveholders could take this precaution or not probably depended on the vagaries of the supply of slaves: did most slaves come on the market as the result of one particular war, or were people being enslaved in many places and in many ways each year? In any case, the advice rests on two assumptions. First, it continued to matter where slaves came from: slaves must have retained a sense of ethnic identity. Second, any single ethnic identity, if shared too widely among a slave population, could be a threat to their masters.

In conclusion, Athenian slaves retained a sense of their birth cultures; many of them were able to confirm this ethnic identity by contacts with compatriots. The attitudes slaves adopted varied widely from assimilation to various degrees of assertion of ethnic identity – such as manifestations of hybridity – all the way to hostility towards their Athenian masters. Unfortunately, all our evidence allows are glimpses into what must have been a much richer picture.

Greek Intellectuals as Roman Slaves

We could look at this same aspect of slavery in the Roman as in the Athenian case: did slaves in Rome bring with them and maintain in slavery aspects of their birth cultures? In some cases – for example, slaves from Spain captured during the Republic – we might have to look as hard for clues as we did in the case of foreign slaves at Athens. But, in one case, the answer is obvious: Greek slaves at Rome maintained their own culture while in slavery and even afterwards, in the case of those who won their freedom. These slaves and ex-slaves profoundly influenced the culture of the lower classes in Rome and other Italian cities. In addition, a smaller number of highly educated Greek slaves and ex-slaves became famous intellectual and literary figures at Rome. They played a role in the Roman adaptation of Greek high culture, a phenomenon of immense significance to Western civilization.

Rome's enslavement of Greek slaves was not the usual situation, where a belief in the inferiority of the people enslaved justified slavery. Rather many Romans, elite and common alike, admired and imitated the culture of the Greeks. As the Latin poet Horace famously put it: "Although Greece was captured, it captured in turn its uncouth conquerors and brought the arts to rural Latium" (*Epistles* 2.1.156–157). This section will survey the historical context of the widespread enslavement of Greeks starting in the third century BCE and briefly outline the history of Greek cultural influence on Rome – which, of course, had many aspects and causes besides the enslavement of Greeks. Then we'll discuss in more detail a couple of prominent ex-slave intellectuals who contributed to Roman high culture and the masses of Greek slaves and ex-slaves and their impact on the culture of the common people in Rome. Finally, we'll discuss the other side of the coin: Roman resentment of the Greeks and how slavery might have contributed to that feeling.

---

3 *Laws* 6. 777c–d; see also [Aristotle], *Oeconomica* 1.5.6 (1344b); Varro, *On Agriculture* 1.17.5. Similar advice is attested in the New World: Mattoso 1991, 90.

Greek Slaves and Culture at Rome

After Rome's decisive victory over Carthage in the Second Punic War in 201 BCE, it was by far the strongest military power in the Mediterranean. Nevertheless, the Hellenistic states of the Eastern Mediterranean did not go down easy. Starting immediately after the Second Punic War, Rome had to fight numerous wars against Greek leagues, the Macedonians, the Seleucids, and the smaller kingdoms of Asia Minor. It was not until 30 BCE that Ptolemaic Egypt, the last of the Hellenistic monarchies, after becoming embroiled in a Roman civil war, was annexed by Rome. During this long period, Roman armies captured many Greek slaves, some of them highly educated. The Juvenal quotation at the beginning of this chapter reminds us that Greek culture permeated the whole Hellenistic Eastern Mediterranean and not just mainland Greece; it included the Orontes River, which flows by Antioch, an important Hellenistic city in Syria. Culturally Greek slaves might come from a much larger area than mainland Greece, but for convenience, in this chapter, I just refer to them as Greek.

In addition to the direct effects of conquest, Rome's rise brought about a period of widespread violence and chaos in the Eastern Mediterranean, conditions favorable to the enslavement of individuals in a variety of ways. Pirates plagued the seas; armies marched back and forth; states and cities fell into debt to pay the tribute imposed by Rome. All these problems were exacerbated by the civil wars of the first century BCE. Already by the late second century, King Nicomedes of Bithynia, a minor Hellenistic kingdom and an ally of Rome, claimed that he was unable to supply troops to assist Rome against Gallic invaders because "most of the Bithynians had been seized by tax collectors and were slaves in the Roman provinces" (Diodorus 36.3.1–2). This was, no doubt, an exaggeration, but huge numbers of people ended up in slavery due, in one way or another, to Rome's disruptive and violent entry into the Eastern Mediterranean.

Greeks were not the only ethnic group that suffered from the violence and anarchy brought about by Rome's expansion: in the same period, Rome fought repeated brutal and long wars in Spain and against the Gauls; it finally extirpated Carthage. The enslavement of Greeks, however, presented an unusual situation given the high prestige of Greek culture. Greek cultural influence at Rome had a long and complicated history, beginning early in Rome's expansion. The Etruscans, who dominated early Rome well into the fifth century BCE, had traded extensively with Greek cities. In fact, a large proportion of the Greek painted vases extant today come from Etruscan cemeteries. The Romans came into direct contact with the Greek colonies of southern Italy and conquered them in the first half of the third century BCE. Already during this period, the Romans developed legends of their founding by Greeks as well as by Trojans; both stories indicate a consciousness of and reaction to Greek legends about Troy (Gruen 1992, 8).

The Romans developed their own literature but were almost always conscious of and reacting to Greek models. Examples are numerous. Roman comedies by Plautus and Terence (active from ca. 205–160 BCE) were adaptations of Greek originals. The first Roman historian, Fabius Pictor, a senator of the third century BCE, wrote in Greek, presumably since it was the language of history and of intellectual discourse in general. Roman aristocrats with philosophical aspirations tended either to follow the Epicureans, Stoics, or Skeptics, all Greek schools of philosophy. The plunder from Rome's wars with Hellenistic states included thousands of Greek sculptures, many of them masterpieces, brought back to decorate Rome. Some scholars even believe that most "Roman" portrait sculpture was actually made by Greek artists.[4] One last piece of evidence is perhaps the most decisive: by the mid-second century BCE, many, if not most, members of the Roman ruling class could understand Greek. In the early first century BCE we even hear of Greeks addressing the Roman Senate in Greek without a translator.[5]

Livius Andronicus

One surprising result of this situation was that Roman nobles with cultural aspirations or pretensions bought highly educated Greek slaves to be tutors for themselves, for their children, or just for the prestige of having a philosopher in the household. Even outside the home, most schoolteachers were Greek slaves or ex-slaves. This makes sense, because a large part of Roman formal education focused on Greek culture. The average schoolteacher did not leave much evidence of his life, nor did the average household philosopher. We do have considerable textual evidence about two famous Greek ex-slaves: Epictetus and Livius Andronicus. Epictetus will figure in our treatment of Stoic philosophy in Chapter 12. Livius Andronicus deserves treatment here. How did being Greek figure in his life? How did his experience as a slave affect him as an author?

Livius Andronicus was active in the second half of the third century BCE. His name, like that of other Roman ex-slaves, includes the name of his former master, Livius, and ends with his name as a slave, the Greek name Andronicus. We can't be sure whether the latter was just a Latinization of his original Greek name, which would have ended in -kos, or whether he was renamed by his master. His life story was not unusual, although his success was. He was born in the Greek city of Tarentum in Italy, which the Romans sacked in 272 BCE, presumably the occasion on which he was enslaved. After serving as the tutor to the children of a Roman noble, he gained his freedom and started a school. His writing consisted mainly of the translation or adaptation of Greek literary works into Latin. He wrote a version of Homer's *Odyssey* and produced Latin versions of Greek tragedies and comedies. This may not sound that creative, but these are the first known works in Latin literature and some of the first translations of long literary texts in history. As Susan Treggiari sums up, "The distinction of founding Roman drama and of being the father of Roman literature thus belongs to an ex-slave" (Treggiari 1969, 111). The linguistic prerequisite to his contribution was that he possessed an excellent Greek education and – presumably after his enslavement – learned Latin extremely well. Given the popularity of Greek culture, Andronicus lived at an especially favorable time not only to maintain his Greek culture in Rome but also to achieve success by sharing and propagating it among his captors. His job as a tutor and teacher probably involved teaching the language and literature of Greece; his success was based on transferring Greek models into Latin.

We possess only fragments of Andronicus' work, and these are typically adaptations or translations of Greek originals. This makes it hard to detect his own attitude about anything, much less slavery. Even if more of his work had survived and it had been more

---

4 E.g., Pollitt 1978; Richter 1951; *contra* Conlin 1997, 11–44 with discussion in P. Stewart 2008, 11–18.
5 Valerius Maximus, *Memorable Doings and Sayings* 2.2.3; cf. Cicero, *De Finibus* 5.89.

directly expressive of his views, it is unlikely that we would have found much criticism of slavery. This may at first seem surprising: ex-slaves from the United States South, for example, were usually vehement critics of the institution of slavery. This seems to make perfect sense; these men and women had suffered through slavery themselves and knew its violence and injustice. Although we shall explore some honorable exceptions in Chapter 12, there were few attacks on the institution of slavery in the ancient world. It was not a controversial institution – as slavery in the United States South became – but one that seemed to exist everywhere. In particular, Andronicus' life story was not conducive to any degree of abolitionism. Tarentum was a Greek city and thus practiced the institution of slavery. If we make the likely assumption that Andronicus had a good Greek education before he was enslaved, then it follows that his family was rich enough to own slaves. His first experiences with slavery were probably from the perspective of a master – or the master's son. Later, he probably owned slaves himself, like other successful ex-slaves.

Greek Ex-Slaves and the Lower Classes

Interactions between Greek and Roman culture at the level of literature and philosophy are relatively easy to trace, since we sometimes possess the texts at issue. For example, we can directly compare the epics of Homer and Virgil, in Greek and Latin respectively. We have fragments of Livius Andronicus and the *Discourses* of Epictetus. Although harder to investigate, the influence of Greece on the culture of the lower classes in Rome and Italy was also pervasive. Most striking, the ability to speak and understand Greek was not confined to the elite, but was also a mass phenomenon. For example, according to one scholar the freedmen depicted in Petronius' Satyricon speak "a half-Greek patois" (Horsfall 2003, 52) – an example of hybridity to which one might compare the "Spanglish" spoken in various parts of North America and Puerto Rico today. More common, perhaps, was "code-switching," an example of which is full bilingualism: a person would switch from one language to another depending on the people present and what was appropriate in the circumstances (Wallace-Hadrill 2008, 57–70). Yet Greek culture among the Roman common people was not just a matter of language. We hear also of Greek actors and theater, Greek athletics, Greek dance, and Greek music, for all of which there seemed to be a large audience among the general public at Rome (Horsfall 2003, 53).

Many factors contributed to the larger picture of the embrace of Greek culture and language: Greek colonies in southern Italy, the service of Roman soldiers in the Hellenistic world, government service in these areas, trade, and immigration resulting from the wealth and power concentrated in the city of Rome. If we confine ourselves to the means of transmission of Greek culture, to how and why a Roman commoner would learn Greek, then slaves too must have played a large part. The numerous slaves of the noble households interacted with free people, sometimes while at work but especially in their leisure time. More important was the Roman practice of freeing a proportion of their slaves as a way of rewarding good service – something we'll discuss in Chapter 8. Household or skilled urban slaves were most likely to gain their freedom with the result that, generation after generation, a constant and significant influx of ex-slave Greeks joined the lower classes, particularly in cities and towns.

Statistical analyses of the names and status indication on the epitaphs of the lower classes of Rome during the early Empire suggested to early twentieth-century historians that only a sixth or a tenth of the population of Italy descended from Italians; the rest were immigrants, mainly slaves, ex-slaves, and their descendants. Historians like Tenney Frank and A. M. Duff put a negative interpretation on this phenomenon: the simple, manly Roman and Italian culture lost its vigor among a population deriving mainly from the over-sophisticated, decadent Greek Eastern Mediterranean (Frank 1916, Duff 1928, 199–209). This cultural shift, so the argument ran, led to the decline and fall of the Roman Empire after some centuries – a delay somewhat inconvenient to explain. More recent historians believe that the proportion of ex-slaves on gravestones is much greater than their proportion of the population – a topic we examine in Chapter 8. And Romans tended to give their slaves Greek names regardless of their actual ethnicity. Still, historians cannot escape the impression that many Greek ex-slaves and their descendants, a large minority of the population perhaps, lived in Italian cities. Nor is there any plausible way to minimize their role in the mixed Greek and Roman (and sometimes local) cultures of Italian cities and towns.

Ambivalence

Second-century Rome produced leading politicians who were unabashed *philhellenes*, lovers of Greek culture, such as Titus Flamininus. After defeating Philip V of Macedon in 197 BCE, he took great pleasure in declaring the freedom of Greece at the Isthmian games, to ecstatic acclaim by the assembled Greeks. Scipio Aemilianus (185–129 BCE), the leading statesman and general of his day, cultivated several famous Greek intellectuals among his entourage. The Roman embrace of Greek culture, however, was neither unanimous nor un-ambivalent – as is obvious in the Juvenal passage at the beginning of this chapter. Conservative Romans anticipated (or inspired) early twentieth-century historians like Tenney Frank, since they thought that Greeks undermined traditional values and were corrupting Rome. Cicero's grandfather, for example, claimed, "the better a Roman knew Greek, the more worthless he was" (Cicero, *De Oratore* 2.265). The great general and populist politician Gaius Marius (157–86 BCE) didn't bother learning Greek – or so he said – because he didn't see any point in learning a language that had to be taught by a subject race (Plutarch, *Marius* 2). In the late first century BCE, even the poet Virgil drew a famous contrast between the martial and imperial Romans and the Greeks:

> For other peoples will, I do not doubt,
> still cast their bronze to breathe with softer features,
> or draw out of the marble living lines,
> plead causes better, trace the ways of heaven
> with wands and tell the rising constellations;
> but yours will be the rulership of nations,
> remember Roman, these will be your arts:
> to teach the ways of peace to those you conquer,
> to spare defeated peoples, tame the proud.
> (*Virgil, Aeneid* 6.847–53, trans. Mandelbaum 1971)

Despite this distinction between Greek and Roman abilities and its appeal to Roman pride, Virgil does give some credit to Greek culture. And indeed all his works responded to Greek models. I imagine that Virgil himself was more familiar with Greek poetic traditions than with the business of ruling and fighting, in which the Romans were supposed to excel. Nor would most Greeks agree that their greatness lay only in their culture; military prowess and bravery played a prominent role among Greek virtues just as it did in Rome.

The Roman statesman, intellectual, and orator Cicero (106–43 BCE) also shows ambivalence towards Greek culture and Greeks (Guite 1962). Cicero went to Greece to study oratory in that language because he thought that the best teachers of oratory were Greek. He even named his speeches against Marc Anthony the *Philippics* in homage to, and emulation of, the fourth-century Athenian orator Demosthenes, whose most famous speeches consisted of attacks on Philip II of Macedon. And Cicero's other works included detailed explanations of the main Greek philosophical schools. One might expect such an intellectual, steeped in Greek culture, to be an un-ambivalent and enthusiastic *philhellene*. But no: Cicero was perfectly capable of playing upon anti-Greek and anti-intellectual prejudice in his speeches; even in his letters, where he cannot be trying to sway a jury by appealing to prejudice, he sometimes slips into the stereotype of Greeks as clever but lightweight, slick talkers without substance, and basically dishonest.

Among intellectuals like Cicero, rivalry or envy could provoke hostility towards Greek culture. That many Greeks were slaves probably also made contempt for Greeks easier in general. In particular, a ubiquitous stereotype of slave personality cohered with the way Romans caricatured the Greeks: slaves were regarded as trivial, tricky, and cowardly. Some part of this stereotype was based on the actual behavior of slaves. Slaves have little power, so they are forced to be devious. They fear their masters, reasonably enough, since their masters could beat them, order them tortured, send them to the gladiatorial games or to the mines, or sell their families away forever. Masters who wanted to feel superior to their slaves could interpret this fear as cowardice – though we never hear of a master wanting to settle things with a slave in a fair fight! As Orlando Patterson noted, masters in many slave societies have a need "to despise those they oppress" and thus are prone to negative stereotyping (Patterson 1971, 217). In Rome, this common caricature of the cowardly and trivial slave resonated with the way the Romans thought of the Greeks as possessed of a superior culture, but dishonest, tricky, and inferior when it came to manly, soldierly qualities. Exactly how much the slave stereotype contributed to the ethnic one and vice versa is hard to gauge.

Conclusion

The foreignness of slaves is a feature of any system of slavery with many first-generation slaves; indeed, masters sometimes represent even born slaves as different and foreign. Our evidence about ancient slavery, coming primarily from slave-masters, often provides only caricatures of slave culture: "they are despicable barbarians." But we do not have to believe in the content of masters' stereotypes to accept that foreign slaves did, in fact, come from a different culture and knew it. The culture of Athenian slaves provides a typical case where we can try to recover from scanty hints some evidence of slave ethnic identity. The case of the Greek slaves in Rome is exceptional. It provides an opportunity to explore in more detail the relationship of slavery and cultural interaction. The high prestige of Greek culture among Romans did not depend on Greek slaves; Romans wanted Greek slaves as teachers and intellectuals because of the esteem in which they held their culture. Nevertheless, Greek slaves were common as Rome expanded into the Hellenistic Eastern Mediterranean and contributed immensely to the Greek influence on Rome, both on its highbrow and its popular culture. This may not be that surprising, if you recall the profound influence of African culture on American popular music, most directly jazz and the blues.

Suggested Reading

Contrary views on whether slaves at Athens retained a strong sense of their birth culture are found in Morris 1998, Morris 2011, and Hunt 2015. Hodkinson and Geary 2012 contains essays on the intersection of slavery and religion in the ancient world – and in Brazil. McKeown 2007, 11–29, discusses Tenney Frank's now notorious theory that the decline of Rome was due to the admixture of foreign blood and culture due to the manumission of so many slaves from the Eastern Mediterranean. McKeown puts Frank in the political context of early twentieth-century racism and reactions to immigration, but also puts more recent perspectives in the context of the current embrace of multiculturalism. Treggiari 1969, 110–142, provides a survey of the many ex-slave intellectuals, writers, and artists who contributed to Roman high culture in the late Republic. Horsfall 2003 treats the culture of the Roman common people whereas Wallace-Hadrill 2008 provides a sophisticated treatment of Greek and Roman cultural interactions with an emphasis on bilingualism and "code-switching" but does not focus on slaves and ex-slaves.

7

Sex and Family Life

Tecmessa: Ajax, my master, life knows no harder thing
Than to be at the mercy of compelling fortune.
I, for example, was born of a free father;
If any man in Phrygia was lordly and prosperous, he was.
Now I'm a slave. Such, it seems, was the gods' will,
And the will of your strong hand. But since I've come
To share your bed with you, my thoughts are loyal
To you and yours.
    Sophocles (Athenian playwright, ca. 495–405 BCE), *Ajax* 485–491, trans. Moore 1969, modified

Introduction

The topics of this chapter, sex and family life, are related biologically. They are also both areas of slaves' personal life into which the violence of slavery could penetrate. Coerced sex with masters, unwilling prostitution, and the separation of families, especially the sale of young children away from their parents, inflicted harsh emotional traumas. Nevertheless, some slaves could be active or resilient, *if* they had the opportunity – a big *if*, unfortunately.

First consider sex. To spend one's life – from the age of twelve, for example – as a slave prostitute was a horrible fate. Not for prostitutes only, but in general, the sex life of slaves was not under their control. Masters could coerce male or female slaves to have sex with them. Or, without warning or consultation, a female slave could find herself "given" as wife to reward a favored male slave. In all these ways, slavery could permeate even what we consider a particularly intimate part of a person's life and identity, their sexuality.

In contrast, emotional relationships were possible even between slaves and masters. Such relationships were extremely unequal and, we can assume, often shaped by the institution of slavery. Yet, slaveholders freed slaves for love; some Roman masters even married their own freedwomen. In return, slaves might feel loyalty and even affection towards masters who were their sexual partners, as in Sophocles' portrayal of Tecmessa,

Ancient Greek and Roman Slavery, First Edition. Peter Hunt.
© 2018 Peter Hunt. Published 2018 by John Wiley & Sons, Ltd.

Ajax's slave mistress, in the quotation above. Of course, Sophocles, who wrote those lines, was a male slave owner and not a female slave, a fact that hints at some of the methodological difficulties we'll encounter in this chapter.

Let's turn to slave families. In law and in theory, slaves could have no legitimate family ties. In practice, too, slavery interfered with or even precluded slave family life. Many slaves – for example, male mine slaves – lived in conditions which prevented them from marrying or having children. And all this was in a world to which family life was of central importance. Other, more fortunate slaves did form emotional bonds with each other and even affectionate families: their epitaphs commemorate their mutual affections and their feelings of loss at the death of a husband, wife, parent, or child. But, even in this life, slave families were precarious and insecure. The forced separation of husbands from wives, or of children from their parents, was one of the most wrenching experiences of slavery, as horrible and feared as whippings, deprivation, or other humiliations. In the antebellum South, the words, "I'll put you in my pocket" – meaning, "I'll sell you and put the money in my pocket" – was one of the scariest threats a master could utter. The threat of sale inspired fear not only because of the degradation of the slave market, but also because being sold meant leaving spouses, parents, children, siblings, and friends. Historians of classical slavery, too, have found evidence of slave children being sold away from their parents and of couples separated forever.

This chapter contains three sections. The first focuses on slave prostitutes and mainly uses evidence from classical Athens. The second explores sexual and amorous relations between masters and slaves. These relationships varied greatly, but they tend to raise the same issues; examples from throughout classical antiquity can contribute to the depth and vividness of our understanding. The final part of the chapter addresses the family life of slaves in the Roman Empire; the epitaphs of slaves and ex-slaves provide much of our best evidence.

Ancient stories about the *hetairai* or "escorts" of classical Athens and about slave women who attracted their masters' affections provide us with unusually detailed stories about the lives of individual slaves, both real and fictional. Although we typically have these life stories from the point of view of the master rather than the slave, I will not shy away from this rare, if tricky, chance to explore the lives of individual ancient slaves. Roman epitaphs provide another unusual opportunity, this time to draw upon the actual words of slaves and ex-slaves. This chapter is more anecdotal than earlier ones, both because it can be and because the topics involve stark contrasts in the experiences of individual slaves. These are better reflected in different stories than in generalizations.

Prostitution in Athens

Prostitution was surprisingly common throughout the classical world. Judging from the number and size of probable brothels excavated in Pompeii, one historian suggests that the town supported one hundred prostitutes, roughly 1 percent of its population (McGinn 2004, 173–174). Social historians of classical Athens lack the complete archaeological record preserved at Pompeii by the eruption of Mount Vesuvius and the burial of the town in volcanic ash, but references to prostitutes appear frequently in Athenian sources too. One historian has even argued that the ex-slave women identified as "woolworkers" in one series of manumission inscriptions – about 80 percent of the women listed there! – were probably prostitutes, described as woolworkers to avoid the stigma associated with their profession.[1] Whether we accept this interpretation or not, prostitution was the fate of many slaves at Athens, especially of women slaves. The reasons are obvious: slaves were cheap in Athens and men would pay to have sex with them, a lucrative business for their owners. Slave prostitutes often needed to continue this work even after they gained their freedom, so ex-slave prostitutes are also well attested. Poverty must have also forced free women and men to become prostitutes, but our evidence depicts slave and ex-slave prostitutes with few and uncertain exceptions.

Although this chapter focuses on female prostitutes, romantic and sexual attachments between grown men and male youths are conspicuous and common in our sources for classical Athens. Numerous passages refer also to male prostitutes. For example, Phaedo of Elis, the philosopher after whom a famous Platonic dialogue was named, reportedly worked as a slave prostitute after being enslaved in war; later a friend of Socrates ransomed him (Diogenes Laertius, *Lives of the Philosophers* 2.105). Most of our evidence, however, concerns women, who probably constituted the majority of prostitutes.

While prostitutes could be male or female, virtually all of their customers were men. Greek sexual mores involved a stark double standard: men were allowed sexual outlets (such as prostitutes) before or in addition to marriage whereas the chastity of free women was strictly enforced. Not only were women not free to patronize prostitutes – hardly a surprise – but free-born women were generally inaccessible or, at least, dangerous for men to pursue outside of marriage. As a result, several authors even argue that men *should* frequent prostitutes rather than engaging in the perilous pursuit of free women, whose husbands or relatives were permitted to kill on the spot any man caught in the act.[2] Athenian authors viewed prostitution as immoral mainly when men squandered their fortunes on expensive *hetairai* (Xenophon, *Oeconomicus* 1.13; cf. Isocrates 12.140).

Prostitution at Athens spanned a wide range of conditions and arrangements. At one end, prostitutes worked either within brothels or as streetwalkers, who would service their clients in semi-public places. At the other extreme were the *hetairai*, the feminine of the Greek word for "friend" or "companion." Rich men could rent *hetairai* for periods ranging from a single evening – say for a party, a *symposion* – to many months. Rather than renting, some wealthy men bought slaves as mistresses for long-term relationships that might last years. So, slave prostitution could be short or long term. The longer-term and hence more expensive arrangements were likely the prerogative of richer customers and, on average, meant a less horrible life for the slave.

Slave *hetairai* seem to have been expensive, but the best stories, those most likely to be preserved, involve the most extravagant prices. So our information is skewed. The more typical, cheaper end of the price range was within the budget of relatively poor Athenian men (Loomis 1998, 166–185). And, surprisingly, even male Athenian slaves frequented prostitutes – as did slaves throughout classical antiquity. This may seem surprising. First, why were Athenian slaves willing to pay for sex? Second, where did they get the money?

Part of the answer to the first question is that men outnumbered women among the slave population at Athens. And many lived in households with only a handful of slaves

---

1 Cohen 2003, 218-227; Wrenhaven 2009; *contra* Rosivach 1989 and Futo-Kennedy 2014, 130–133. Meyer 2010 argues that these inscriptions are not actually manumission records, but see the objections of Vlassopoulos 2011b.

2 Xenarchus, fr. 4 in Kock 1880–1888; cf. Horace, *Satires* 1.2.31–36.

and thus few potential partners; prostitutes might constitute their only option. Xenophon recommends bolting the door between the sleeping quarters of the male and female slaves, so they could not breed without the master's permission (Xenophon, *Oeconomicus* 9.5). If this was a common practice, it would be a significant interference in slaves' sexual lives and another possible reason that male slaves turned to prostitutes.

The answer to the second question is that some slaves were allowed to possess property and money, although without full, legal ownership. Slaves could even save up in order eventually to buy their freedom, a practice that we explore in the next chapter. It is a faulty assumption, however, that all slaves had perfect self-control and only saved their money for their freedom: they seem also to have patronized prostitutes.

A puzzling set of vase paintings reveal another unexpected aspect of Athenian prostitution. These vases show women being accosted at their looms by men with gifts or money bags in hand (Davidson 1997, 86–90). The most persuasive interpretation of these images is that efficiency-minded brothel managers put prostitutes to the

Figure 7.1 Greek symposium scene depicted on a vase found in Campania. The hosts of a *symposion*, a drinking party, could rent a *hetaira* to liven up the gathering. They could also hire a flute player, either a free or slave woman. Flute players were obviously musicians – which is why they made more than regular prostitutes – but several passages indicate that their job often included sex acts with guests, perhaps for additional payment. In this vase painting, the masks and instruments on the wall suggest a theatrical context as in Plato's *Symposium*, set at the celebration of Agathon's victory in a dramatic competition. In Plato's *Symposium*, however, the host sends the flute player home, an indication of the group's intellectual seriousness – and because they were tired from the previous night's party (176e). *Source*: INTERFOTO/Alamy Stock Photo.

archetypical "woman's work" of spinning when they were not busy servicing customers – thus "wool-worker" for "prostitute" might not be entirely inaccurate. These vases show the moment when such slaves were switching from one type of work to another, apparently a moment that appealed to the buyers of painted vases. As we saw in the last chapter, Building Z in the Ceramicus was at one time a brothel, staffed with foreign slave women. And, indeed, loom weights were found in it. Building Z had an unusual floor plan with many small rooms, the main evidence that it was a brothel. The building also included larger rooms, in which shards of fine drinking bowls have been found, so its owners may have tried to provide a party (*symposion*) atmosphere for its customers and not just sex.

If we turn to the slave's point of view, Building Z was anything but a good time. Historians may need to imagine the details, but even slaves considered prostitution a particularly terrible fate. Some of this was a matter of material conditions: sexually-transmitted diseases were less common in ancient Greece and Rome than in the modern world, but contraception was primitive and ineffective by modern standards and both abortion and childbirth were dangerous. The most horrible thing about being a slave prostitute was probably the loss of control over your own body, having to have sex with whoever paid your pimp – though one wouldn't want to play down the misery of being tied up and whipped either. Last but not least, the ancient world was one in which the chastity of women and their fertility within a marriage were their cardinal virtues and to be forced into prostitution was to be made worthless in the eyes of much of society. This is confirmed by the predictably derogatory way that our literary sources refer to prostitutes, associating them with sewage, for example (Davidson 1997, 78–83) – though the prostitutes' own opinions were likely very different.

Neaira's Story

Even though the majority of prostitutes were *pornai*, slave women hired to perform sex acts, our best evidence concerns the higher levels of the profession, the *hetairai*, whom rich men, our main sources, patronized. For instance, one law court speech by Apollodorus, *Against Neaira*, narrates the life story of Neaira in some detail.[3] Apollodorus repeatedly vilifies Neaira for her profession even though it is absolutely clear that she had no choice in the matter. To modern sensibilities it is hard to imagine a more blatant case of blaming the victim. Still, Apollodorus' account is worth dwelling on, since it is rare that we have so much information about the life of any ancient slave.

Nikarete, a former slave prostitute herself, bought Neaira when she was a small child in Corinth. Nikarete reportedly had a keen eye for which little girls would blossom into beauties and knew how to train them to command high prices as *hetairai*. Nikarete's own experiences do not seem to have made her a sympathetic owner: according to Apollodorus, Neaira had to start working as a prostitute – "with her body" in the Greek – before she even reached puberty. One story about Lysias, a skilled writer of law-court speeches and a rich man, sheds a slightly more positive light on the lives of Nikarete's

---

3 The stories about Neaira in the paragraphs below can be found in the following sections of [Demosthenes], *Against Neaira* 59: 18, 20, 21, 22, 24, 30, 33–35, 51 – but the whole speech is worth reading.

slave girls. He paid to have Metaneira, another *hetaira* owned by Nikarete, travel with him from Corinth to Athens to celebrate the Eleusinian Mysteries nearby, probably an assignment lasting a couple of weeks. Lysias reportedly wanted to do something nice for Metaneira herself and to gain her gratitude rather than merely paying money that Nikarete, her owner, would pocket. In ancient Athenian terms, he was a gentleman in another respect too: to avoid offending his wife and his mother, he put Metaneira up at a friend's house during her stay at Athens rather than bringing her into his own home. Neaira herself went on a trip to the Panathenaic Festival, also at Athens, with a prominent member of the Thessalian aristocracy. Both of these assignments probably involved sex and, for a slave, there was no question of consent. But serving as an "escort" to a prominent and wealthy man at a festival was better than working in a brothel – depending in part on his behavior.

Back in Corinth, two young men bought Neaira for three thousand drachmas, more than ten times the cost of an average slave. They realized that even at this price it would be more economical to buy her outright from Nikarete and to share her company rather than constantly to pay Nikarete's high prices. For men to share a courtesan does not seem to be unusual, though our other evidence comes from law-court speeches on occasions when the arrangement went sour. When the two men of Corinth were about to get married, they allowed Neaira to buy her freedom for two thousand drachmas, one thousand less than they had paid for her. They may have done this partly out of affection, but they insisted on the condition that she leave Corinth. For Neaira to continue working there would apparently have caused them embarrassment or regret or raised the hackles of their prospective wives and their relatives. Apollodorus adds in passing that all seven of Nikarete's *hetairai* were rented out during their prime, then sold, and finally freed. This claim implies an enviable 100 percent manumission rate.

In another case, an Athenian man, Olympiodorus, never married or had children. Instead, he lived with a *hetaira*, whom he freed and spoiled with jewels and fancy clothing, rather than paying what he should have to his brother-in-law in an inheritance dispute – so the latter claims ([Demosthenes] 48.53–56). Not all relationships ended so well for the purchased mistresses. One man, described as a "gentleman," grew tired of his slave mistress and decided to sell her to a brothel (Antiphon 1.14–15). The mistress, so the accusation went, was then duped into giving him a "love potion," since she hoped to regain his affection and avoid the brothel. The concoction turned out to be poison – part of a complicated plot – and after his death, she was tortured and executed even though she did not confess to any malice. This story is valuable for showing the callous treatment that *hetairai* might often expect as they aged. It also highlights the relatively humane behavior of the Corinthian pair of young men, who at least allowed Neaira to purchase her freedom at a discount.

Neaira later endured an abusive boyfriend, Phrynion, who had leverage over her, because he had lent her some of the money with which she bought her freedom. When things became intolerable, she fled from Athens to get away from him. After more travel and difficulties, Neaira eventually returned to Athens and settled down in a long-term relationship with a prominent Athenian citizen, Stephanos. Since she was not a citizen, they could not officially marry, but their relationship was a long-lasting and affectionate one, as far as we can tell.

Stephanos claimed to have had children with a former wife before Neaira moved in. If so, he fit into a pattern attested among other wealthy men, including the philosopher

Aristotle and the Roman emperor Vespasian.[4] When a rich man with children divorced or his wife died, he might not remarry but would rather find an ex-slave mistress; the two would not contract an official marriage nor have legitimate children. Among the motivations for this practice was the man's sense of loyalty and responsibility to his children by the first wife. He would not father any more legitimate children to compete with his original set when it came to inheriting his estate; nor would his original children have a step-mother, a relation with a sinister reputation in the ancient world. The gain of the early children was, of course, to the detriment of any children that the ex-slave mistress might bear, whose legal status and monetary position would be worse – although emperors, of course, could afford to see their illegitimate children well off too!

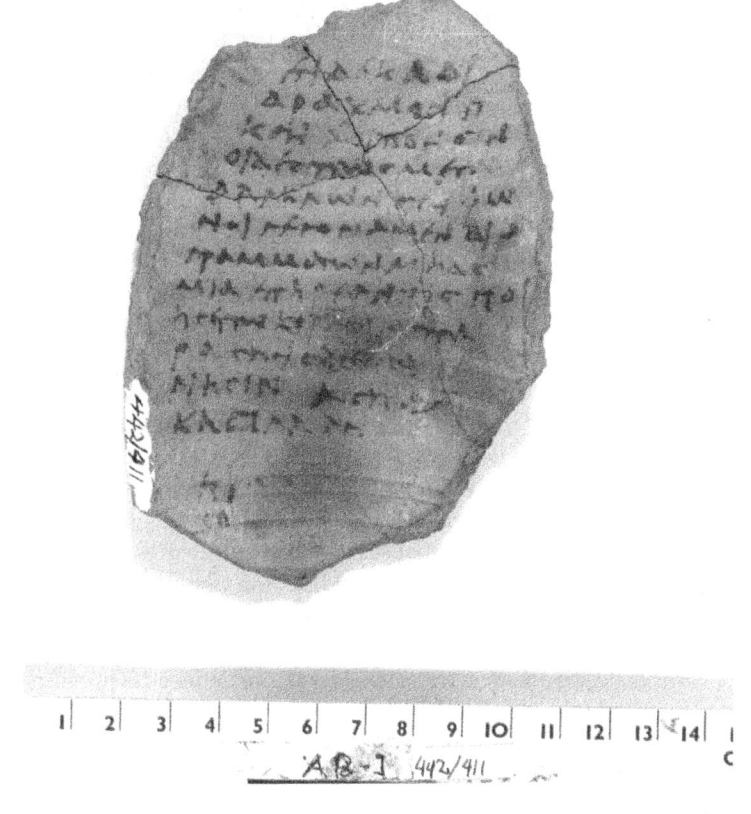

Figure 7.2 Letter about rent for live-in *hetaira*. Early second-century CE. Roman Egypt also provides evidence of the long-term rental of a slave woman for sex – and perhaps other domestic work. In this letter, written in Greek on a piece of broken pottery (9 × 12 cm), the slaveholder, Philokles, is angling to increase the amount he is charging a customer to rent a live-in slave *hetaira*. Scholars describe Philokles as "pimp and green grocer" after the two lines of work that his surviving letters frequently mention. In the second line, you may be able to make out the word *draxmas* from the Greek unit of coinage, the drachma. *Source*: Bülow-Jacobsen 2012, 315, #390, reverse. Reproduced with permission of Adam Bülow-Jacobsen.

---

4 Athenaeus, *Learned Banqueters* 13.589c; cf. Diogenes Laertius, *Lives of Eminent Philosophers* 5.1.13–14; Suetonius, *Vespasian* 21.

Coerced Sex and Emotional Relationships

In one law-court speech, Demosthenes is trying vividly and humorously to depict the greedy brutality of his opponents' methods of collecting back-taxes: he complains that if they broke into the house of a man who happened to be having sex with a slave woman, they would confiscate her (Demosthenes 24.197). This piece of wit raises several questions for the historian of slavery. Were sexual relations between masters and slaves this common in real life or were they merely good for laughs? How often did masters force slaves to have sex? Were sexual relations ever really consensual, given the difference in power between a slave and a master? What about affection or even love? The first two questions cannot be answered in quantitative terms. References to sex between masters and slaves, often coerced, are frequent and do not give the impression that this was anything exceptional. Still, we are nowhere near able to tell, for instance, what percentage of female domestic slaves were raped. The second set of questions cannot be answered with the depth we would like: what emotions did a slave woman feel upon being freed to marry her former master? But before going further, I need to clarify two issues.

First, in the paragraph above, I assumed a male master and a female slave. Ancient sources mention such cases more often, but we also hear about sex with male slaves. One crucial difference between the two situations is that women slaves can get pregnant, which greatly complicates matters, as we'll see. When it comes to the sex of the slaveholder, the situation was one-sided. From the beginning to the end of classical antiquity, it was considered a scandalous abomination for a woman to have a sexual relationship with her own male slave. The protagonist of the *Life of Aesop* mocks the desire of his owner's wife for a good-looking male slave, whom she'd end up seducing. Eventually Aesop himself has sex with her ten times in exchange for a new shirt, leading to a ridiculous dispute over the terms of the deal – arbitrated unknowingly by his master (32, 75–76 in Daly 1961). Outside of humorous, fictional cases – which are admittedly common – relations between free women and their slaves attracted strong disapproval and punishment: in a fourth-century BCE law court speech, Apollodorus says that such a marriage involves great shame and outrage; in the fourth-century CE, a law required that both the woman and her slave be killed, the slave by being burned alive.[5] Women and slaves who acted contrary to this taboo – I imagine there were some – tried very hard to do so secretly, so the vast majority of our evidence concerns male slaveholders, consequently our main focus of attention.

Second, in the patriarchal societies of the classical world, coercion or pressure on women respecting their personal and sexual lives was not specific to slavery. Most conspicuously, this was a world where fathers and brothers arranged, and enforced if necessary, the marriages of free women, usually in their teens. It would be anachronistic to imply that it was only *slave* women who were not in control of their bodies and relationships.

With these points in mind, let's turn to a particular case, reconstructed from two related manumission inscriptions from Hellenistic Delphi. The first document records that a slave woman named Eisias bought her freedom for two *mina* (200 drachmas) subject to *paramonē*. Often translated as "conditional" or, better yet, "deferred" freedom, *paramonē* was a common arrangement at Delphi. Often a woman in *paramonē* would

---

5 [Demosthenes] 45.39; *Codex Theodosianus* 9.9.1; cf. Petronius, *Satyricon* 45.

only gain her full freedom upon handing over a child to be a slave in her place. In this case, despite her legal manumission Eisias was still required to serve her master, Kleomantis, for the rest of his life. She would be freed only after his death. This particular *paramonē* contract is explicit in its requirements: "If Eisias does not remain or does not do what is ordered, let Kleomantis have the power to punish her in whatever way he wishes, by beating her and selling her" (Daux 1909–1954, 3.3.329, trans. Tucker 1982, 230). Only one of these terms was unusual in its harshness: other contracts did not give masters the option of selling a slave in *paramonē*, since that could effectively negate the whole manumission, for which the slave had paid good money.

The plot thickens with the record of Eisias' release from *paramonē*, a strikingly generous one. Instead of serving him until he died – as per the first inscription – Eisias was released from *paramonē* while Kleomantis was still alive. She even received back the two *mina* that she had paid for her freedom. Most revealing, Kleomantis freed the son Eisias had while in *paramonē*. Even though his mother was "free," he had been a slave according to a stipulation common in *paramonē* contracts. His name was changed to Kleomantis. Kleomantis also put Eisias and Kleomantis (Jr.) in his will, but after his wife.[6] The release from *paramonē* and renaming of the son after Kleomantis makes it almost certain that Eisias had borne Kleomantis' child.

Kleomantis' will, also recorded, reveals that either he did not have a legitimate son by his wife, Sosula, or that that son had died – perhaps in the time period between the two documents? The great importance of having a son to continue his line, conduct his funeral rites, and perform the ongoing rituals at his grave may explain why Kleomantis was willing to offend his wife and embarrass himself by acknowledging a son by his former slave even while he remained married.

Despite these probabilities, the two documents are consistent with a wide range of possible backstories. On the one hand, Eisias may have been raped – repeatedly for all we know – and eventually received some slight compensation, only because she became pregnant and bore Kleomantis' only son. On the other hand, perhaps Eisias seduced Kleomantis – whose wife may have been barren – with an eye to the advantages she would gain from having his child. Or they may have fallen in love and gradually became more mutually committed and courageous about acknowledging their relationship. The default assumption has to be that Eisias and Kleomantis' wife were rivals for his attention and his property – every *mina* that went to Eisias did not go to Kleomantis' wife – but it is not inconceivable that they were, on the contrary, best friends.[7] Our two inscriptions illuminate possibilities and allow us to imagine several possible life stories; they do not reveal what actually happened nor how common such relationships were. We cannot even differentiate rape from true love. And, it is the issue of rape that particularly interests historians of slavery. Especially for domestic slaves in close contact with their masters and their master's families, coerced sex or just the threat of it could exacerbate the misery of slavery.

---

6 At Athens and probably elsewhere in Greece, a will could be challenged on the ground of being written "under the influence of a woman" ([Demosthenes] 46.14; 48.56); for Eisias and Kleomantis (Jr.) to inherit instead of Kleomantis' wife (and eventually his wife's family) was exactly the sort of situation this law was designed to prevent.

7 The development of a relationship between an Afghan man's two wives is a main focus of the novel, *A Thousand Splendid Suns*, by Khaled Hosseini.

In the United States today – where there are sanctions against the use of power to coerce sex as well as general and strong disapproval and where power disparities are much smaller than between slave and master – many people in positions of authority still use their power, more or less explicitly, to pressure subordinates into having sex with them. In the classical world, the power a master had over a slave was enormous: not only the power to physically punish the slave, bind her, or deprive her of food, but also to sell her away from family and friends to a mill or a brothel.

There were also fewer and weaker restraining factors. A master's legal rights over his slaves included the right to have sex with them, just as it included the right to force them to work as prostitutes. Only in some circumstances were there even social restraints, and these were often toothless. For example, wives might not like their husbands to fool around with the slaves, but they might not care if their sons accosted the slave women. Philosophers, whose impact on ancient culture should not be underestimated, disapproved of the lack self-restraint such conduct demonstrated and illegitimate children were always potentially awkward. For instance, an early Hellenistic-period intellectual advised: "don't put your seed in just anybody" or you'll disgrace your wife and children, who may be confused with their slave half-siblings ([Aristotle], *Oeconomica* 3.2 (p. 144, 10–15); cf. Plato, *Laws* 11.930d–e). These issues, rather than the possibility of coercion, were behind what little criticism we find.

Ancient intellectuals often deplored the use of violence for selfish ends, but the institution of slavery was in general a blind spot – as we'll see in Chapter 12. This is not to say that all ancient men were too callous to prefer an affectionate relationship to rape or could not restrain themselves. For instance, Menander's *The Man She Hated*, a romantic comedy written in early Hellenistic Athens, survives only in fragments on papyrus. The main character, Thrasonides, owns a captive slave woman, Krateia, with whom he falls in love and treats with generosity and consideration. He does not want to rape her, although he believes it is his right and implies that other men would have done just that:

> It's almost midnight, and I could be in bed and in possession of the girl I love. For she's in my house, and I have the right, and I want this as passionately as any raving lover – and I don't do it. I prefer to stand outside, in the winter air, shivering with cold and talking to the night! (Menander, *The Man She Hated* A8–A12, trans. in Miller 1987; cf. 39–40)

This whole situation and its characters are, of course, fictional: the play would end before it even started if Thrasonides just forced himself on Krateia. Nevertheless, the tender feelings that he expresses highlight the emotional complexity even of highly unequal relationships. Unfortunately, his statement also highlights how feeble were the protections slaves possessed.

Indeed, the plots of a whole genre of literature, the Greek romance novel, often revolve around the threat of coerced sex. These novels typically narrate the adventures of a pair of star-crossed lovers, originally of high birth. After they are separated and one or both is captured by pirates or brigands, the lovers sometimes remain in slavery for much of the novel. As slaves, their noble good looks typically attract unwanted sexual attention. Amazingly enough, they escape coerced sex or forced marriage, at the last minute, again and again. This is far from historical evidence for how often slaves avoided coerced sex; more realistic is the constant threat. A passing remark by a freedman in Petronius' *Satyricon* provides some confirmation: he paid a high price to free his wife from slavery so nobody else could put his hands on her (Petronius, *Satyricon* 57). He assumes that unwanted, hard-to-refuse advances would always be a threat as long as she was a slave.

If many slaves suffered coerced sex, others took advantage of their masters' attraction to them. Slaves willing to accommodate or even to attract their masters' sexual interest could often obtain a better life; in some cases, this even extended to gaining freedom. In Petronius' *Satyricon*, the outrageous freedman Trimalchio claims that his own rags-to-riches story began with his accommodating both his owner and his wife: "Nothing that a master orders is shameful; nevertheless, I did enough for my mistress too. You know what I'm saying."[8] Even short of freedom, it is easy to imagine all the ways that a well-disposed, post-coital master could make a slave's life easier and a rejected master make it wretched. To take a humorous and everyday ancient example, Theophrastus, an early Hellenistic philosopher, describes the kind of things that the "country bumpkin" does: he secretly seduces the slave woman who works as his cook and then helps her grind the grain (Theophrastus, *Characters* 4.10). Presumably, he was a bumpkin for pursuing a regular house slave rather than a lovely *hetaira* and then in forgetting his dignity and helping with the slave's work.

Help grinding grain is far from getting one's freedom, but it could be worse. A master who "needed" to use force with a slave could end up angry with his victim. And whether a slave was a willing partner or not, he or she could end up vulnerable to vengeance from the master's wife, a scenario replete with drama and frequently depicted in literature: in one Greek novel, the pirate's cover story for why the beautiful Callirhoe is on the slave market is that the wife of her master had her sold out of jealousy (Chariton, *Callirhoe* 1.12.8; cf. Menander, *The Necklace*, fr. 333 in Sandbach 1972). Callirhoe is a fictional character, whose subsequent adventures are anything but realistic, but the pirate's cover story was intended to be a plausible one.

Outside Pompeii, archaeologists found a golden bracelet on the arm of a thirty-year-old woman, who died in the eruption of Mt. Vesuvius. It carried the inscription, "The master [gives this] to his very own slave girl." Although several interpretations of the bracelet are possible, the most likely explanation is that it was a gift from a master – married? – to his slave mistress (Edmondson 2011, 353). Such generosity may have been an expression of deep and sincere affection for all we know, but even when a relationship between a master and his slave seems to have been mutual and affectionate, skepticism is in order. On the one side, even if a slave did not reciprocate the master's affection, he or she had very good reasons not to say so, but to pretend. On the other side, no doubt many masters proclaimed love and made promises just to get their way with a slave they found attractive. This scenario is hardly specific to slavery, but slaves lacked legal or family protection. And many female slaves must have attracted not only their master's brief interest, but also his wife's enmity, and ended up pregnant and sold away.

It is not surprising that a slave might do and pretend whatever in hopes of obtaining freedom. Nor is it surprising that masters distrusted the professions of slaves who had such a huge interest in feigning affection. This distrust could have teeth, since slaveholders constituted the ruling class. The best illustration comes from the Roman legal category "manumission for the purpose of marriage." Men of the senatorial class were

---

8 Petronius, *Satyricon* 75; see also 69. Compare the story in Seneca the Elder, *Controversiae* 4 pr.10.

not allowed to marry freedwomen, but otherwise marriages between a master and his manumitted slave-woman were fully legitimate. These marriages show up in two legal contexts.

First, laws limiting manumission were enacted during the reign of Augustus. Among other regulations, these established a minimum age of thirty for the slave and twenty for the master for a full manumission to be legal. There were, however, certain exceptions (Gaius, *Institutes* 1.6.18–19). Some of these evince nothing more than sex between masters and slaves: there were exemptions for slaves who were the natural sons and daughters of a slave owner (the offspring of masters and female slaves) and for natural brothers and sisters (the offspring of relations between the master's father, probably deceased, and female slaves). Of course, a master did not have to free his own children or siblings from slavery; he was merely permitted to.

Intended marriage was also one of these legitimate grounds for early manumission. So far, so good: true love did not need to wait upon the law; masters could manumit slave women to marry them. Indeed, we possess many gravestones put up by ex-slave women to their "well-deserving husband and patron" – in this context, patron denotes the former owner of a slave, a meaning we'll meet repeatedly.[9] These inscriptions sometimes go well beyond conventional expressions of respect for the dead and seem to express affection and grief.

A more cynical note comes up in the second legal context. A patron could not force his freedwoman to marry him, *unless* he had freed her for this purpose. In that case they had to marry or else the manumission would be void. Nor did freedwomen have the right to divorce their patrons and marry somebody else, a right Roman women normally possessed (Justinian, *Digest* 23.2.28–9, 24.2.11 with Treggiari 1991, 450–451). These laws were manifestly designed to prevent a slave woman from feigning affection only until she was freed and then leaving her former master heartbroken. In a comedy of Plautus, a slave mistress with a heart of gold insists that she will be no less affectionate to her lover, "now that I've got what I wanted [my freedom]" (*The Ghost* 220–221). Roman slaveholders did not depend on such good faith alone.

In the story that began this section, Kleomantis' motivations may have included a desire to continue the male line and not simply generosity to his slave mistress. And in general, it remains notoriously hard, if even possible, to distinguish sexual desire from love. One of the few situations when we can risk such judgments is when the public avowal of a relationship incurs a high and predictable cost. For example, in antebellum Mississippi, Thomas Foster Jr., a slaveholder, openly preferred his slave mistress, Susy, to his wife, Susan, and eventually moved away with Susy: "Susan called the affair base and degenerate, but Susy meant more to Thomas than she, their children, his family, or the opinion of society. At that price the relationship earns its true characterization. Thomas was in love" (Alford 2007, 95). In one case from Athens, too, a man seems to have fallen in love with his retired ex-slave-prostitute, Alke, who managed an apartment building for him. Despite having a legitimate son himself, he began to live with her rather than at home and eventually acknowledged her sons as his own and had them enrolled as

---

9 See Perry 2014, 96–128. In some cases such epitaphs commemorate a relationship that began when the man and woman were both slaves. The man may have received his freedom first and then purchased and freed his partner, thus becoming technically his wife's patron (Treggiari 1975b, 396–397).

citizens (illegally). According to his original family, who wanted to retain his estate, he had lost his mind because of "drugs or disease or something else."[10] The willingness of a master or former master to alienate his family and offend polite society is probably a sign of sincerity; even in this case, we cannot tell if his affections were reciprocated.

Roman Slave Families

Slaves had sexual relationships with other slaves. Some of these were casual affairs. In other cases, the partners thought of each other as husbands or wives and, if they had children, they considered themselves a family, regardless of the lack of legal acknowledgment of their ties. Although slaves formed families throughout the classical world, this section focuses on Rome and Roman Egypt, where our evidence is richer and more revealing. First we'll consider the difficulties slaves faced starting families and then the challenges such families faced in staying together.

At first blush, it seems that calculating masters would want their slaves to have and rear children. From the slaveholder's point of view, slaves were valuable property; if they had children, it was like getting more property for free. But this consideration was not as dominant as one might expect. Before the twentieth century child mortality was so high that raising slave children was not uniformly a good investment. That unwanted children, mainly of poor parents, were often exposed to die rather than sold, suggests that a baby slave was not worth much money; on the Greek side, we have already seen that Xenophon refers to slave traders who did not bother to transport and sell newly captured children, but just let them starve (Xenophon, *Agesilaus* 1.21). On the other hand, some people did find it worth their while to take and raise exposed infants as slaves. And Columella, a Roman author of a book about farm management, writes that he rewarded women slaves for rearing three children by letting them retire from other work; he freed them after they'd raised four (*On Agriculture* 1.8.19). Thus, the calculations of masters probably varied over time and place depending on various factors including the price and availability of slaves and the cost and risks of raising children. For example, Roman legal sources reveal that slave children were sometimes sent from the city to the country to be raised – this assumes rich masters who owned both city houses and country farms (Justinian, *Digest* 32.99.3 with Treggiari 1979, 189). For big cities, especially Rome, were expensive and disease-ridden. Stable family units were not crucial for slaves to reproduce – masters themselves fathered children on their slave women – but allowing slaves to form families both encouraged them to have children and gave these children a better chance of surviving the perils of infancy and childhood in an ancient society.

These considerations informed the calculations of slaveholders; let us turn to the point of view of slaves. When slaves wanted to start families, it was not for the sake of their masters' profit; it was because rearing children was immensely important in Greek and Roman society, as in practically every ancient society about which we have evidence. Unfortunately, aspects of slavery made even starting a family difficult,

---

10 Isaeus 6.19–22. The whole story comes from his original family and may contain other distortions and exaggerations.

particularly for male slaves, who may have outnumbered female slaves during some periods both at Athens and at Rome (see Chapter 3).

First, the pool of potential spouses in small households could be limited for either men or women: in the *Life of Aesop*, all the female house slaves in a philosopher's medium-sized household quarrel over who would get first shot at the new, reportedly good-looking slave their master had purchased (30, trans. Daly 1961): "The master has bought me a husband . . . Oh, no, he's for me. I saw him in my dreams . . . I'll go out and get myself engaged to him first." Of course, this is meant to be silly – and Aesop turns out to be spectacularly ugly – but romantic options for slaves were often limited or non-existent in real life (cf. Hopkins and Roscoe 1978, 169). Their chances were, of course, better in large households, such as those of Roman senators. And, in cities, the pool of available mates was larger, since slaves could have amorous relationships with or even "marry" slaves from other households. But just because some slaves could start families does not mean that their family life was secure.

The fundamental reason that slave families were precarious is that it was in slave-holders' financial interests that their slaves, considered a form of property, be as liquid and disposable as possible. As a result, Roman law did not acknowledge the marriages or families of slaves. A male and female slaves could only contract *contubernium*, informal marriage, and never an official marriage. One legal consequence of this was that a child born from *contubernium* followed the status of his or her mother – the child was a slave if the mother was – rather than the status of her father, as was the case in a legal marriage. Indeed, slaves had no official parents at all – part of their natal alienation – and even ex-slaves could be mocked for this. For instance, the poet Martial attacks an ex-slave, "Zoilus, even if the right of seven children is granted you, a mother and father you'll never have."[11]

Since the familial ties of slaves had no legal and little customary force, they could be severed at the discretion of a master or as the result of various sequences of events. As we mentioned, to separate a family was a severe punishment; other actions or events lacking any malice could have the same terrible side effects on slaves. The divorce of a master and mistress could lead to the break-up of families throughout a large slave-holding unit – and divorce was not rare among the Roman upper classes. Masters sold slaves just to raise money and, if they were in debt, they could be forced by their creditors to sell them. And once slaves were on the market, their family ties would count for little. One papyrus from Roman Egypt (second century CE) reveals that, to pay a debt, a certain Casianus sold a female slave, Demetrous, away from her five-month-old son (Straus 2004, 272–273 on *BGU* III 859). After some months Casianus found that he had nobody to nurse the child and paid Ammonios, his former creditor and the new owner of Demetrous, a fee to have the mother raise the child "with great care." We would seem to have arrived at a happy ending when Casianus was unable to pay the nursing fee and sold the child to Ammonios: mother and child were reunited. But, according to one of two plausible interpretations of the Greek, Casianus was the child's father. He had impregnated his slave, Demetrous, then sold her to pay a debt but held onto his son, and finally had to sell his son also. Not a complete victory for family ties.

---

11 *Epigrams* 11.12; see also Plautus, *Captives* 574. The "right of seven children" is a reference to various legal privileges conferred on Roman citizens and ex-slaves based on how many children they had; the "seven" is an exaggeration for the sake of humor.

The death of a master often meant that several heirs split the estate, including the slaves. We know a fair amount about this situation, since the division of estates could lead to litigation and is thus discussed in Roman legal texts. These show that the fate of slave families could depend on the peculiarities and exact wording of the will. On the one hand, if the deceased left a farm "with its equipment" as a legacy, then the slave families on that farm would stay together under a new master (Justinian, *Digest* 33.7.12.33 in Watson 1987, 78). Despite referring to slaves as equipment, the reasoning behind this decision is humane, since it recognizes the brutality of separating slave families: the jurists preferred this interpretation, "so that the deceased not be thought to have commanded a cruel separation" (33.7.12.7). On the other hand, the bequest of a slave business manager did not include his wife and children at another house unless they were specified (33.7.20.4). Nothing prevented masters from breaking up slave families either while they lived or in their wills: the law merely required that they express themselves clearly and favored the more humane alternative when they did not.

The practice of giving a particularly useful or otherwise favored male slave a "wife" as a reward for good work seems more the carrot than the stick and did create a family of a sort. Male slaves must have welcomed such a "gift" or it would not have been a useful incentive. No consideration, however, was given to the preferences of the female slave. Historians possess fairly detailed information about a Brazilian case. There a slave woman with great difficulty managed to avoid a marriage her master had arranged as a reward for a male slave (Graham 2002, 1–82). But both in Brazil and in the classical world, the more common result was acquiescence, whether willing or not: a fictional ancient case even includes the order to the "husband" to use force if the "wife" refuses (Xenophon of Ephesus, *Anthia and Habrocomes* 2.9.3). Nor would a master be under the slightest obligation to take into account any informal marriage that his slave women felt she had already contracted.

As one might expect, some slaves insisted on the validity of their familial ties, despite their legal non-existence. Again epitaphs provide our best evidence. Most obviously slaves and ex-slaves commemorated their family members when they died; historians have found many thousands of such epitaphs. Wealthier ex-slaves celebrated their family ties with expensive reliefs on large tombstones showing the whole family together. Some historians even speculate that this desire to commemorate the family may be a reaction to the lack of family, the natal alienation, of slavery (Mouritsen 2011, 285–287).

On epitaphs, slaves also ignored the legal distinction between official and unofficial marriages: they used the official terms for husband and wife for their slave spouses. Conversely, they sometimes retained *contubernalis* (unofficial spouse) even when both partners were freed and they could have used the official term (Treggiari 1975b, 396). In a couple of cases, slaves used naming practices to indicate family ties and paternity, something that Roman law denied them. In one memorial for a slave baby we find the following:

> ... Spendo ... and Primigenia made this for their most sweet daughter, Spendusa, who lived for five months and twenty-seven days. The space for this commemoration was granted by our masters ... (*CIL* 7303, trans. Treggiari 1975b, 400)

We know that Spendo and Primigenia were slaves since each has only a single name and since they refer to their "masters." Nevertheless, Spendo and Primigenia – presumably with the cooperation of their master – managed to include the father's name in their daughter's name, Spendusa, so it was obvious even from the slave child's single name that she did have a father and who he was. From a feminist point of view, for a girl to be given the feminine version of her father's name might not seem very liberating. In an ancient context, however, it was an assertion of a key family tie, paternity, usually denied to slaves.

Historians would like to get beyond such anecdotal evidence and to be able to generate at least some basic statistics about slave family life – as historians of slavery in the United States South can (e.g. Gutman 1976, 9–21, tables 1–5). Three important transitions – sale, manumission, and death – produced lasting evidence of large numbers of ancient slaves and potentially of their family ties.

Unfortunately, in records of sale or manumission, there was no regular requirement to report familial relationships, much less whether the slaves named were being sold apart from parents, siblings, children, or (unofficial) spouses. For instance, the French papyrologist Jean Straus lists 154 documents referring to slave sales in Roman Egypt (Straus 2004, 272–276, 344–349; cf. Bradley 1978, 246–247). On these we find references to 21 children below 14 years of age. Alas, in only three cases are we sure that the child was sold without a mother; in another three cases, we know that a child was sold with a mother. This result is liable to opposite interpretations. On the one hand, the optimistic view is that the sale of families together indicates that slavery in Roman Egypt was particularly humane. Straus objects that the only children sold with their mothers were very young, probably not weaned, and likely to die without their mothers – or a wet nurse. They were only of any value together with their mothers and this was what buyers and sellers cared about. On the other hand, although the sale of children by themselves certainly looks sinister, Straus rejects the inference that all slave children sold alone were separated from their mothers – hence he puts only three in that category. Many children sold alone may have been orphans, a common fate due to the high mortality rate in the ancient world – not that selling an orphan child is particularly kind treatment either.

One striking feature of the slave sale contracts on papyrus is the absence of references to fathers in what was, for the free at least, a strongly patriarchal world. This impression is confirmed in the manumission records from Hellenistic and Roman Delphi. This set of inscriptions refers to almost a thousand individual slaves and includes 133 group manumissions, where we might expect to find related slaves being freed together. Hopkins and Roscoe find references to 29 mother–child relationships, but only a single acknowledgment of paternity and one of a marriage between slaves – unofficial of course (1978, 165). The explanation for this focus on mothers and children is twofold. One factor is relatively innocuous: maternity is a concrete and obvious relationship, whereas unofficial marriage and paternity are not. Slaveholders had strong and selfish motives to ignore all family ties: recognizing them could have inhibited them from selling their slaves in whatever units were most convenient and profitable. They sometimes made an exception for mothers and children, since the mother needed to nurse and raise the child and her status as a slave was the basis for the child's slave status. Thus, records produced by slaveholders – of manumissions and sales, for example – acknowledge only the maternal bond. Another scenario must have played a role in some cases: some children may be the result of casual encounters rather than long-term relationships. The biological fathers may not have been in the picture at all for their children. All the Roman epitaphs memorializing slave wives, husbands, fathers, and children prove that this was not the whole story.

Taken en masse, these Roman epitaphs might seem to open the door to statistical analysis. More than two hundred thousand epitaphs survive from various regions of the Roman Empire – mostly from the first two centuries CE and with the largest set from Rome itself. Although the norm throughout the Roman world was for members of the nuclear family of the deceased to commemorate him or her – around 80 percent of the time (Saller and Shaw 1984, 134) – this number is far less in the case of ex-slaves. In particular, they seem rarely to have had legitimate children to commemorate them when they passed away even though having children conferred legal advantages for ex-slaves and for their children (Hasegawa 2005, 64, Table 5.1; Mouritsen 2011, 87). Various factors help explain this contrast: for example, if they had children while still slaves, those children would often still be slaves when their parents died and thus be less able or likely to commemorate them. The difficulties that slaves encountered in starting families and keeping them together probably also played a role. The ex-slaves who appear on epitaphs generally came from a favored subset of the slave population: they managed to gain their freedom and had the means to commemorate themselves. If even this relatively fortunate group of slaves suffered lasting negative effects from their time in slavery, we can fairly assume that the majority of slaves were much worse off when it came to family life.

We noted earlier the likelihood that male slaves experienced greater difficulty in starting families than female slaves did. Historians find some confirmation of this too in the statistics from Roman epitaphs: female ex-slaves are much more likely than males to be commemorated by family members (Hasegawa 2005, 68). Again several factors may be at play; one was that slave women, and thus ex-slave women, enjoyed a gender ratio conducive to finding an (unofficial) husband. They were more likely to have a family to commemorate them when they died.

Conclusion

Slavery drastically impinged on even the sexual and family lives of slaves. Slave prostitutes suffered repeated invasions of their bodies and often, we imagine, their sense of self. Working in a brothel was the female equivalent of being sent to a mine. Not that all prostitution was the same: Neaira was an elite *hetaira* and eventually gained her freedom. Almost certainly, she had a better life than a prostitute in a brothel or a streetwalker. Nevertheless, although we know many details about the course of her life, we are almost completely in the dark about her own views and feelings. Some of these would probably surprise historians in one way or another.

Like slave prostitutes, many slaves, especially female domestic slaves, endured sex that was coerced whether by violence or by threats. Such cases did not exhaust the sexual and emotional possibilities between slaves and masters. Modern Western societies put a high premium on equality in relationships, but hierarchy and affection are compatible. Still, when the power differential is as great as between master and slave, historians need to be sensitive to the ways power shaped relationships and to be especially skeptical about whether public statements and actions reflected private feelings at all.

Depending on their circumstances and masters, some slaves were able to start families. To some extent, these slaves were active agents rather than victims in this part of their life, but again the situation is complex: when a slave had children, these were slaves too and increased the wealth of the slaveholder. We have seen that during some periods natural reproduction was the main source of slaves, but family life in slavery was insecure and being sold apart was always a terrifying possibility.

Suggested Reading

Davidson 1997, esp. 73–138, provides a sophisticated treatment of how Athenians conceived of the exchange of money for sex with detailed evidence about the practice and types of prostitution. Hamel's clear and readable account of the trial of Neaira (2003) investigates the lives of slave prostitutes and provides a general introduction to Athenian society and its legal system. McGinn 2004 focuses on Roman prostitution, mainly using evidence from the excavation of Pompeii. For recent collections of engaging scholarly articles, see Glazebrook and Henry 2011 and Glazebrook 2015. See Tucker 1982 for evidence of slave families in the Delphic manumission inscriptions and especially the requirement that women, freed but subject to paramonē, had to surrender their babies into slavery. Two classic articles, Rawson 1966 and Treggiari 1975b, analyze the epitaphs of lower-class Romans, predominantly slaves and ex-slaves, to discern the variety of and patterns in their familial relations. Hasegawa 2005 provides a statistical analysis of what can be gleaned about slave and ex-slave life from the epitaphs of several large aristocratic households. Golden 2011 discusses major issues in the study of slaves within the Greek household and their family ties. Jones 2008 discusses a recently recovered text that provides our only evidence that Greeks, like the Romans, sometimes professed a reluctance to separate the families of slaves.

8

Manumission and Ex-Slaves

Many who are not even free now tomorrow will be citizens from Sounion [a town in the mining district of Attica].
Anaxandrides (fourth-century Athenian comic playwright), fr. 4 in Kock 1880–1888

And there were people in the house who put out a foot to trip me up here and there. But still – God bless my master! – I struggled through. These are real victories: for being born free is as easy as saying, "Come here"... you will see that my iron ring [of a freedman] commands credit.
                                                Petronius, *Satyricon* 57–58, trans. Heseltine 1987

Why Manumission and Ex-Slaves?

Some ancient slaves legally obtained their freedom before they died. Regardless of how much of their lives they spent in slavery, historians typically refer to such men and women according to their status at death as "ex-slaves" or "freedpersons." Evidence about or produced by these men and women has already played a role in this book: the frequency of manumission plays a role in our equation quantifying the slave supply (Chapter 3); the top administrators of early Roman emperors such as Narcissus and Pallas won their freedom well before they reached that pinnacle of their careers (Chapter 5); other ex-slaves include the Paphlagonian miner, Atotas, at Athens, and Livius Andronicus and Epictetus, Greek intellectuals at Rome (Chapter 6 and 12); the *hetaira* Neaira obtained her freedom as did Eisias, the probable mistress recorded in the manumission inscriptions at Delphi (Chapter 7). These ex-slaves are legitimately part of our story since they experienced slavery, often for most of their lives.

How and how often slaves obtained freedom and their position in society, if they did, tell us a great deal about how slavery functioned within Greek and Roman society. And, fortunately, historians possess more evidence about ex-slaves – often much more – than about slaves. First, as a major change of status, the freeing of a slave usually required legal regulation, rituals of transition, publicity, and sometimes a written record, all of which may leave evidence for historians. Second, freedpersons were more successful than other slaves in one obvious respect: they won their freedom, something most slaves wanted their whole life long but never got. Ex-slaves were thus more likely than other slaves to

Ancient Greek and Roman Slavery, First Edition. Peter Hunt.
© 2018 Peter Hunt. Published 2018 by John Wiley & Sons, Ltd.

possess the resources to commemorate themselves in stone when they died; the surviving epitaphs and grave monuments of ex-slaves show us how they wanted to represent themselves – and provide evidence of their family life as we've seen. Finally, ability, drive, and good relations with their masters contributed to slaves' chances of manumission. These qualities sometimes allowed freedmen – more obviously than freedwomen – to enjoy considerable economic success in their free lives also. When freedmen did become rich, they attracted intense, and usually negative, attention in our literary sources, typically written by highborn, free men. These regarded all self-made men, and especially ex-slaves, as base interlopers. Historians do not, of course, adopt this attitude, given the modern admiration for those who owe their station in society to hard work and ability rather than to birth and inherited wealth. Still, we may be grateful for how much we learn, at least about the most successful ancient freedmen, as an unintended result of resentment.

The process of manumission is our first topic. How often and why did Greek and Roman masters free their slaves? How did ancient societies conceive of and formalize such a momentous change in status? We'll then consider the position of ex-slaves after manumission: the continuing, usually subordinating, ties of ex-slaves with their former masters; their political and legal rights and liabilities; and their social status. These issues become vivid and concrete in the stories of two exceptional freedmen: Pasion, an Athenian ex-slave banker, and Trimalchio, a fictional Roman freedman, outrageously wealthy and gauche. I'll use these characters to some extent as colorful illustrations, but more often as foils for experiences of more typical ex-slaves. For just as ex-slaves represent a relatively fortunate subset of the slave population, Pasion and Trimalchio were utterly atypical of ex-slaves, most of whom achieved freedom but still endured the hard and poor life of the common people. The chapter will conclude by summarizing the important contrasts in manumission and the status of ex-slaves in classical Athens versus Rome. Not only in the conclusion, but throughout our treatment, it will be obvious that manumission and the treatment of ex-slaves was an aspect of ancient slavery more marked by differences than by similarities between Greece and Rome.

How Common Was Manumission?

Both at Athens and at Rome, manumission was a well-known and unremarkable process. Consequently, historians have often observed that there must have been "many" ex-slaves in each city. This is only true because "many" is so vague. The slave populations of the two cities may have numbered in the hundreds of thousands; the presence of "many" ex-slaves does not tell us whether slaves had a large or a miniscule chance of obtaining their freedom. To gauge the effect of manumission on the experience of slavery and the role of ex-slaves in the societies of Rome and Athens, we would like to quantify both the proportion of slaves that gained their freedom and the proportion of the whole population that ex-slaves constituted. A ballpark estimate is the best we can hope for and even that is impossible for Greece, even Athens and those areas of Greece – Thessaly and Delphi – with numerous manumission inscriptions in the Hellenistic period (Hopkins and Roscoe 1978; Zelnick-Abramovitz 2013). So we will focus on the city of Rome, where historians have enough evidence to attempt rough estimates of the manumission rate and the proportion of ex-slaves among the population. Although each individual argument or set of evidence has potential problems, they all point in the same direction and leave the strong impression that manumission was common in Roman cities and that the urban population of Roman Italy (from about 100 BCE to 200 CE) contained a large proportion of ex-slaves.

In a political speech in 43 BCE, Cicero implied that "frugal and hard-working" captives typically recovered their freedom within six years (Cicero, *Philippic* 8.32). This argument would be ridiculous if manumission was rare, but, for several reasons, historians suspect that Cicero is exaggerating its ease and regularity (Wiedemann 1985). For starters, he uses "six years" instead of five or ten or even twenty, simply because that is how long, in Cicero's opinion, Rome has been suffering under tyrannical government, beginning with Julius Caesar's march on Rome. The qualification "thrifty and hard-working" means that Cicero extends his claim only to a subset of Roman slaves. Finally, Cicero's letters describe how his beloved personal secretary and confidante, Tiro, obtained his freedom. But this was a major event, which took place, almost certainly, after far more than six years of service. Other slaves mentioned in the letters, even those with long tenures in positions of trust and responsibility, did not obtain their freedom as a matter of course. By itself, Cicero's statement cannot bear much weight, but a different class of evidence may.

It is again the numerous epitaphs of the Roman Empire that may provide the key. A Hungarian ancient historian, Géza Alföldy, tabulated the fraction of slave and ex-slave epitaphs that include the deceased person's age. He noticed that the proportion of slaves dying above forty was extremely small (0.6 percent), much less than the proportion of ex-slaves dying at that age (18.3 percent). From this Alföldy inferred that, by the time they reached forty, most slaves had gained their freedom. In other words, slaves did not die old, since they were ex-slaves by that time. This argument is, again, not quite decisive for several reasons. First, the ex-slave population would be somewhat older than the slave population in any case, since people are slaves before they become ex-slaves. Additional skewing of the age distribution may result if old ex-slaves were more likely to be commemorated with their age than were old slaves for whatever reasons (Mouritsen 2011, 133–134). It's unlikely, however, that these factors can account for the entirety of the effect Alföldy observed, 0.6 percent versus 18.3 percent; his research provides additional evidence that manumission was not unusual, at least among the urban slave population with epitaphs. This last limitation is an important one. If the slaves and ex-slaves with an epitaph were a favored subset of these populations – as seems likely – then we cannot extend our conclusion to the whole slave and ex-slave populations.

In several cases, historians possess sets of epitaphs numbering in the hundreds of the slaves and freedpersons, the *familia*, from a particular Roman noble household. The epitaphs of one such *familia*, the Statilii, a house headed by wealthy and powerful senators, seem particularly comprehensive: even slaves with low-status jobs within the household have epitaphs. The social historian Henrik Mouritsen has estimated that between one-quarter and one-third of this household obtained their freedom before dying, whereas the remainder died while still slaves (Mouritsen 2011, 139 n. 96; 2013, 49). This is a relatively high manumission rate, since a significant minority of slaves won their freedom. It only applies, however, to the household, urban slaves of a particularly rich and important family, who had unusually favorable prospects. The slaves in the richest and most important *familia*, the *familia Caesaris*, regularly received their freedom in their thirties, but that situation is even less likely to be typical.

As a result of the large numbers of slaves and the regularity of manumission, we would expect a substantial population of ex-slaves. Indeed, ex-slaves or probable ex-slaves erected a majority, sometimes a large majority, of the inscribed gravestones in Rome and in the towns and cities of Roman Italy. In some places and contexts it is hard to find any inscriptional evidence of freeborn citizens. This last phenomenon is surprising, if not impossible. For example, didn't the previous generation of ex-slaves have any freeborn children? So commemoration habits rather than mere numbers must be involved: ex-slaves tended to put up epitaphs more than the free-born. One possibility is that ex-slaves and their families took pride in displaying their new status and the accomplishment it represented (Taylor 1961, 129–130). An epitaph could also provide the children of ex-slaves evidence of their relationship and thus of their right to inherit, something that the ex-slave's *patronus* might otherwise contest – as we'll see below. Whatever the reason, historians have given up on the idea that ex-slaves so greatly outnumbered the free-born. Nevertheless, it remains difficult to avoid the inference that ex-slaves made up some large proportion – greater than 30 percent, perhaps much greater – of the urban population. And not only epitaphs, but other types of lists also show a majority of ex-slaves – for example, one list of uncertain purpose, which seems to have included most of the free male population of Pompeii (Mouritsen 2011, 130).

All this evidence points in one direction: in Rome and the cities of Roman Italy, manumission was attainable for many slaves; ex-slaves constituted a large, perhaps a dominant part of the urban population. Mouritsen, for example, concludes that slaves in Rome enjoyed "a strikingly high manumission rate, which was probably unparalleled by any other slave society" (Mouritsen 2013, 53). This is certainly an important fact to remember about Roman slavery and a stark contrast with the American South, where manumission was exceedingly rare. At least two serious complications remain.

First, to have a good chance of obtaining freedom before forty does not have the same significance in a high-mortality society as it would today. Recall that life expectancy at birth was probably around 25 and that even twenty-year-olds, who had made it past their dangerous infancy and childhood, could only expect to live to 45 on average. Many slaves did not survive to gain their freedom; even those who died free had often spent the vast majority of their lives in slavery.

Second, the observant reader may have observed the words "urban," "cities," and "Rome" popping up frequently in the arguments above. Historians have far less evidence about agricultural slaves, most conspicuously almost no epitaphs. In our discussion of slave families, we noted that the agricultural writer Columella recommends his own practice of freeing women for raising four or more children (*On Agriculture* 1.8.19). But other references to manumission in the countryside are scanty, even in other agricultural writers who devote great attention to the rewards needed to motivate slaves to work hard. The chance of manumission for slaves working in the mines or as shepherds or cowherds were perhaps each different, but we have almost no evidence to determine this. Most historians suspect it was only urban slaves who enjoyed the high manumission rate that produced such a large and conspicuous class of ex-slaves.

Reasons for Manumission

Manumission was something that individual slaves wanted, but it was granted at the discretion of slaveholders and only to those slaves who worked hard and behaved themselves – in the view of their masters. Manumission encouraged obedience and made resistance and revolt less likely; it was a potent tool of social control (Bradley 1987, 81–112). In contrast to this paradoxical and sinister function, the conscious motivations for freeing slaves were much more varied, even if we confine ourselves to individual masters and exclude emancipation by the state.

First of all, freedom was a great reward, but you can only free a slave once. The common practice of allowing slaves to save their money and to purchase their freedom enhanced manumission's effectiveness as an incentive: it allowed owners to divide up the big reward, freedom, into many small rewards and to use these to motivate slaves day after day, year after year. By no means was purchase the only way that slaves obtained their freedom, but in both Athens and Rome, it was an important one that repays exploration.

We possess, for example, the pay records for the slaves, *metics*, and free citizens who worked together on the Erechtheion temple on the Acropolis and other public works. Although the slaves sometimes did lower-skill jobs than their masters, they were paid at the same rate for a given job as the free workers, either citizens or *metics*. This did not indicate equal treatment of slaves and free, since a master could pocket however much of the slave's wages he pleased. For instance, a shrewd master of a slave carpenter making a drachma (= 6 obols) per day might allow the slave to keep an obol every other day as long as he worked hard and didn't cause any trouble. Assuming a work year of 250 days – since full employment year-round is unlikely – such a slave might save 125 obols each year and in less than a decade would have the 200 drachmas (= 1200 obols) he needed to purchase his freedom. The master would enjoy and profit from a motivated slave for many years and, at the end, could buy a replacement with the money the slave paid him for his freedom. Of course, reality was usually more complicated. Not to mention the round and simple numbers and continuous employment, I assumed that the slave did not spend his money on anything else at all, an unlikely scenario. Finally, masters might let their slaves buy their freedom for less than their market value, but they could also demand more.

One contradiction between the practice of slaves saving to buy their freedom and the theory of slavery is blatant but easy to understand. Legally, slaves were themselves property rather than owners of property: no law prevented a slave owner from simply confiscating his slave's savings at any point. In practice, however, the system of allowing slaves *de facto* possessions and money – called *peculium* at Rome – was greatly to the advantage of the slaveholder for various commercial reasons as well as for its potential as an incentive for loyal service. A master could confiscate a slave's *peculium*, but only at the cost of not being able to use this system of incentives effectively in the future. In one case, we even hear of a further pseudo-contract between master and slave: in 61 CE a slave murdered Pedanius Secundus, the prefect (mayor) of Rome; one explanation was that he and Pedanius had agreed on a price for the slave's freedom and Pedanius had then reneged (Tacitus, *Annals* 14.42).

Many slave jobs are not ones that we would normally think involved any access to money, for example, a woman's hairdresser or litter bearers. The system of monetary rewards could still work for such slaves, if they received occasional or regular bonuses for good service, or for any slaves in a position to receive tips from third parties, for example, *hetairai*, messengers, and doorkeepers. We have mentioned last chapter how many of the ex-slaves on the manumission inscriptions at Athens were women described as woolworkers. Such household slaves could sell leftovers or their own meals, but this was plainly a hard way to save money for one's freedom (Seneca, *Epistle* 80.4; cf. Apuleius, *Golden Ass* 10.14). The workers on a large Roman farm or in the mines are not likely even to have access to extra food; they were probably motivated more by punishment than by rewards and the hope for freedom.

We may, however, be focusing too much on just one way that slaves won their freedom, saving up money and buying it. Slaveholders also freed slaves as a reward for long and faithful service without any purchase being involved at all. The common practice of freeing slaves in one's will provides an obvious example of this motivation. In another case, an Athenian litigant says his father freed his nurse for her faithfulness ([Demosthenes] 47.55). Masters could free slaves out of love or because they were related to them, as we have seen in Chapter 7. Slaves might also win their freedom for some exceptional service or for loyalty in the face of danger. All these possibilities favored slaves in close contact with their masters; many mine, pastoral, and agricultural slaves were again out of luck.

Just like the use of manumission as a reward, these are all rational reasons for freeing slaves. It is not hard, however, to imagine that rich slaveholders might free slaves on whims, just because they could. So we should imagine a spectrum of reasons for manumission from the most calculating to the most spontaneous and emotional. According to one account, Cicero freed a slave, simply because he was the messenger who brought Cicero the good news that a court case, which Cicero wasn't yet prepared to argue, had been delayed (Plutarch, *Sayings of Kings and Commanders* 90.21 = *Moralia* 205e). Presumably, manumission on a whim or out of momentary enthusiasm was most common among the rich for whom the loss of a slave's value was not a big blow. Nevertheless, we ought not to rationalize manumission too much.

Rituals and Processes

The emancipation of a slave constituted a momentous transformation, from non-person to person, and was marked by rituals just as other transitions such as birth, death, coming-of-age, and marriage. For example, the most dramatic Roman procedure was a collusive lawsuit before a *praetor*, the judge in this case. It was called *manumissio per vindictam*, "manumission by the staff." An "assertor of liberty" – often the *praetor's lictor*, his orderly – uttered a formal phrase: "I declare that, by the law of the Quirites [an old-fashioned name for the Romans], this man is a free man." He then touched the freedman with his staff, his *vindicta*, to symbolize his assertion; the master said nothing to contradict the *lictor*, and the slave was declared a free man. In celebration, the slave put on a special cap, called a *pilleus*, which he would wear on special occasions thereafter – see the *pilleus* in Figure 12.1 below.

Like this one, most manumission procedures involved publicity. In this way, masters both advertised their generosity and reassured slaves that they would not renege on the manumission – an otherwise worrisome possibility, for who would take a slave's word against his or her master? At Athens, for example, we hear of one way of publicizing manumission only because it was eventually banned as a public nuisance: Athenians had taken to having the emancipation of their slaves proclaimed before the crowds in the theater before the tragedies were performed (Aeschines 3.41, 3.44).

Closed and Open Slave Systems

Athens is classed among *closed* systems of slavery in that slaves, even when freed, did not regularly become full Athenians.[1] Legally, they did not gain citizenship but merely the status of *metics*, resident foreigners. *Metics* were not allowed to possess real estate; they needed to rent the houses they lived in or the land they (occasionally) farmed (Lysias 7.10). Most crucially, neither male nor female metics could contract legitimate marriages with Athenian citizens. While *metics* and citizens worked next to each other on public works like the Erechtheion and presumably socialized with each other, they could not legally intermarry. Consequently, ex-slaves and their descendants remained a class apart and separate even from the poor citizens at Athens.

This practice was an outgrowth of the general exclusivity of Athenian citizenship. Even during the high point of the fifth-century Athenian Empire, the Athenians did not share citizenship with their subject allies – as Argos and Corinth did a generation later – but, on the contrary, tightened the requirements for Athenian citizenship and its imperial perquisites by requiring that both parents be Athenian instead of just the father. And the ideal of egalitarianism among the male citizens – though not the only strain in Athenian thinking – made the incorporation of slaves more difficult. Their promotion to citizenship would have been an all-or-nothing matter: a former slave would suddenly have the same legal and political rights as the most blue-blooded Athenian aristocrat. The quotation from Anaxandrides, with which we opened this chapter, exaggerates the likelihood of slaves advancing to citizenship. In some cases, slaves and their descendants managed to assimilate and their families to intermarry with citizens despite the letter of the law and the Athenians' exclusive, egalitarian ideology; for the vast majority of ex-slaves the reality was not citizenship at Sounion or anywhere else, but rather something like "freedom but never membership."

Rome in contrast was an *open* slave society. When Roman slaves were freed, they maintained strong relations with their former masters and became citizens. In terms of Orlando Patterson's definition of slavery as social death, Roman ex-slaves were reborn to society with civic rights and a pseudo-familial connection to their former master that decisively ended their natal alienation. They could own land and intermarry with the freeborn, which they often did. They suffered some political and legal disabilities, but their children did not. This was in line with Rome's willingness to expand its citizenship, a contrast to Athens' reluctance. Although the process of inclusion was slow and often violent – and occasioned a bitter war in first-century BCE Italy – eventually almost all the free inhabitants of the vast empire became Roman citizens.

Turning to ex-slaves in particular, some historians argue that the origins of Rome's unusual, but longstanding, policy of giving them citizenship originated in early Italy, before the fifth century BCE. Competition for manpower among warring states – a circumstance that often favors open slave societies – gave an impetus to incorporating former slaves among the citizens. And the hierarchical structure of Roman citizenship meant that ex-slaves were not immediately the equals of their masters: they were barred from the top classes of the citizens, from becoming state officials, and were all assigned to the four urban voting blocks (*tribus*), which diminished the force of their votes. Romans loved to relate that in 169 BCE Sempronius Gracchus did not make any

---

1 See Watson 1980 on the concepts of closed and open systems of slavery.

long speeches for this last measure, but with "a nod and a word" deprived all the uppity freedmen of equal voting rights (Cicero, *De Oratore* 1.38). In contrast to Athens, Roman society approved of hierarchical bonds between citizens, which historians describe as patron–client relations. So, ex-slaves fit without much awkwardness into the lower ranks of the citizen body and into personal subordination, if no longer slavery, to their former masters.

In summary, ex-slaves of modest means were integrated more fully and easily into the lower classes at Rome than at Athens. Rich and successful ex-slaves, on the other hand, experienced similar problems as they tried to gain acceptance among the snobbish upper echelons whether at Athens or at Rome. In both cases, the modern expectation that ex-slaves would oppose slavery or at least not own slaves is disappointed: as soon as they advanced socially, ex-slaves aspired to all the symbols and instruments of wealth in the ancient world, including the possession of slaves. We'll explore three issues – the relationships of ex-slaves with their former masters, their legal and political rights, and their social position – in the cases of the family of Pasion in Athens and then the fictional Trimalchio, whose dinner party in Petronius' *Satyricon* is set in Roman Italy.

Pasion and His Family

Pasion, an ex-slave banker, became immensely wealthy. He possessed over 70 talents at a time when 3 talents put one in the highest, the liturgical class, of citizens, who were obligated to perform expensive tasks for the state (liturgies). His son, Apollodorus, even tried to play an active role in Athenian politics. Their banking activities, Apollodorus' political ambitions, and a disputed inheritance involved them in many lawsuits. Nine law-court speeches by Apollodorus or concerning his family survive.[2] Neither this amount of evidence nor their lives are remotely typical of ex-slaves at Athens.

Relationship with Former Masters

We've seen (Chapter 7) that in Hellenistic Delphi slaves might pay for "freedom" and still be required to serve their former masters and be subject to punishment just like a slave for a period that could extend for years. No evidence of such *paramonē* contracts survives from Athens. There did exist, however, a legal suit that could be brought against ex-slaves for "abandonment" (Harpocration, *Lexicon*: Apostasiou). If found guilty, ex-slaves could be re-enslaved; if found innocent, they were entirely free of ties to their former masters. For example, all *metics* needed to have an official guardian, a *prostatēs*; ex-slaves were required to have their former master as *prostatēs* and were liable to this law if they did not. Ex-slaves were also subject to punishment if they "did not do the things the law commands," but it's not certain that these laws are specific regulations for ex-slaves and, if so, of what they consisted. Finally, a single passage can be interpreted to imply that, if an ex-slave did not have an heir, his former master could claim his estate (Isaeus 4.9). All of this is not much to go on and, as we'll see, vastly less than what historians know about the relations of Roman slaveholders with their former

---

2 Isocrates, *Trapeziticus*; Demosthenes, *For Phormio*; and [Demosthenes], *Against Stephanus I, Against Stephanus II, Against Timotheus, Against Polycles, Against Callippus, Against Nicostratus, Against Neaira*.

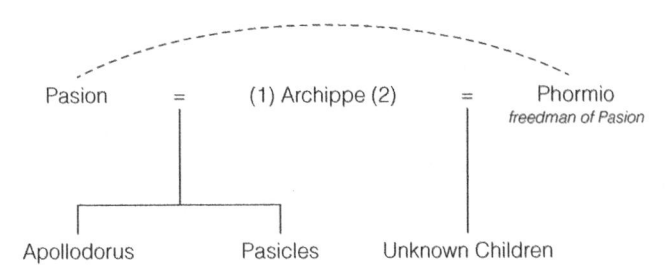

```
                    ┌─────────────────────────────────────┐
Pasion      =      (1) Archippe (2)      =      Phormio
                                                 freedman of Pasion
    │                     │                        │
    │                     │                        │
Apollodorus          Pasicles              Unknown Children
```

Figure 8.1 Family tree of Pasion. *Source:* Courtesy of Wesley Wood.

slaves. This apparent disparity may simply be the result of poor evidence for Athens, in contrast to the survival of extensive Roman legal texts. But most historians suspect that formal and legal bonds between ex-slaves and their former masters were, in fact, far weaker and less regular in Athens than at Rome.

The relationship between Pasion and Phormio, his freedman, is a single, extraordinary case. In some ways, their relationship could hardly have been closer. When he got old, Pasion leased his banking business to Phormio, whom he had already freed. When he died, Pasion's will instructed Phormio to marry Pasion's widow, Archippe, and to become the guardian of Pasion's children, Pasicles and Apollodorus. This is surprising to us and was shocking to some Athenian jurors. We need, however, to understand this measure in its historical context: it was not rare for an Athenian man to arrange the marriage of his widow in his will and to appoint the husband-to-be as guardian of his children. For example, the orator Demosthenes' father made a similar arrangement for his widow (Demosthenes 27.5). That the conservation of family property took priority over the widow's free choice was simply one aspect of Greek patriarchy. What was shocking to Athenians was that an ex-slave married the widow of his former owner ([Demosthenes] 45.39). Phormio's explanation was that a measure that would be shameful for free-born Athenian citizens was necessary in the case of ex-slaves whose position depended on their wealth: the continued prosperity of Pasion's family depended on binding the bank's current manager, Phormio, as tightly to the family as possible, something the marriage accomplished (Demosthenes 36.28–30, 32).

Apollodorus, Pasion's son, bitterly resented Phormio's marriage to his mother. He quarreled repeatedly with Phormio over money and the terms of his father's will; in one place, he even impugns his own mother's chastity and his younger brother's legitimacy ([Demosthenes] 45.73–75, 83–84). It is hard to be sure which side was in the right, though modern sympathies are generally with Phormio. What is important here is that none of the claims and counter-claims are based on general laws governing the relations of former masters and slaves; they all concern specific terms in Pasion's will and the contract according to which Phormio first leased Pasion's bank. These speeches confirm the impression that, in contrast to Roman practices, Athenian law did not regularly impose much in the way of duties or financial obligations on former slaves.

Wealth and Status

Little evidence about the average freedperson at Athens survives. We can assume that he or she did not have a huge inheritance to fight over in court nor the money to hire

Demosthenes nor the education to prepare his own speeches, as Apollodorus did. Most ex-slaves must have remained in their former owner's service or eked out a modest livelihood in the city, as did some of the craftsmen recorded on the work records for public building projects. Another example is telling: a man took back into his house his former slave nanny – whose manumission we mentioned above. When her husband died, he says he felt obligated to take care of her in her old age and to keep her from poverty, the likely fate of many less fortunate ex-slaves ([Demosthenes] 47.55–56).

In contrast, Phormio's advocates needed to preempt potential indignation at his wealth among the jurymen, who were Athenian citizens, but unlikely to count their wealth in talents. They used the argument that Phormio's success in business was due to his being both hard-working and honest, "an amazing combination" among businessmen (Demosthenes 36.44)! The speech *For Phormio* not only attributes Phormio's success to these qualities but even questions heredity as a determinant of a man's worth (Demosthenes 36.41–48). Either these arguments proved effective or the legal position was indisputable: the jury was unwilling even to listen to Apollodorus' accusations – though this didn't stop him from renewing the dispute later ([Demosthenes] 45.6).

Even these fabulously wealthy ex-slaves, Pasion and Phormio, had a difficult and expensive road to become citizens rather than remaining *metics*. The full assembly had to vote on every grant of citizenship. Often such an honor expressed gratitude for generosity to the state and the hope that the new citizen would continue to be generous. For example, Pasion reportedly gave five triremes and one thousand shields to Athens; he paid special taxes and performed liturgies costing him well over ten talents in total.[3]

Citizenship may have been worth the price, since it served a crucial function for a banker. Then, as now, many loans were made on the collateral of real estate. But a typical ex-slave possessed only *metic* status and could not take possession of real estate if the debtor defaulted, a big problem for a banker. Pasion and Phormio were ambitious and successful men and would have probably aspired to citizenship even without this concrete advantage. Their rise from slaves to wealthy citizens made Pasion, Phormio, and even Pasion's son, Apollodorus, *nouveau riches* in the extreme. As ex-slaves, Pasion and Phormio had little chance to assimilate and did not seem to try hard; Apollodorus, the son of an ex-slave, tried very hard indeed.

Pasion and Phormio were men of the Piraeus, the cosmopolitan commercial port of Athens, the sort of place Plato, for example, regarded as a source of foreign moral contamination (Plato, *Laws* 4.705 a–b). Even when they became citizens, they kept their residences where they had made their money and, presumably, felt at home. Apollodorus on the other hand, moved into the Athenian countryside after his father's death (Demosthenes 53.4). There his neighbors would be overwhelmingly citizens and he would no longer be associated with the mixed population of the Piraeus.

Pasion's wife was a *metic*, Archippe, whether an ex-slave or not we do not know. She and Pasion were married for at least 24 years before his death in 370 BCE. Pasion never felt the need to trade up and then Phormio married Archippe as per Pasion's will. In contrast, Apollodorus married a woman from a prosperous native Athenian family, "who supported the [Athenian] people's grant of citizenship to Pasion" ([Demosthenes] 59.2; Demosthenes 36.17). The contacts and friends of Apollodorus mentioned in the

---

3 [Demosthenes] 45.85 with Trevett 1992 n. 10, 24–25; cf. [Demosthenes] 45.76, 59.2.

law-court speeches came also from the free-born elite of Athens. He seems to have lived an aristocratic life in other respects, at least according to his opponents in court:

> You wear a fine wool mantle, and have bought the freedom of one mistress, and have given another in marriage – all this, even though you have a wife – and you go around with three attendant slaves, and live so extravagantly that that everybody can see it. (Demosthenes 36.45)

If these accusations are true, then Apollodorus was an owner, apparently a generous one, of the same class of slave-mistresses as Neaira, against whom he brought charges of pretending to be an Athenian wife, as we've seen (Chapter 7).

Apollodorus had political aspirations and collaborated – with the prominent statesmen Hyperides and Demosthenes no less – to promote an anti-Macedonian foreign policy for Athens. His career did not go smoothly. He ended up taking the risky step of advocating a controversial measure: to use the budget surplus for war. Accused of proposing an illegal motion, he ended up paying a large fine and was at one point in danger of financial ruin. Perhaps this risky assignment fell to him because he was an ex-slave's son.

Apollodorus had to try harder in other ways: his liturgies cost him, like his father, at least 10 talents, a huge fortune to devote to the state (Trevett 1992, 39–41). On one occasion, when he was assigned to be a *trierarch*, the commander financially responsible for a warship, he seems to have tried to do a particularly good job – which involved additional expenses – and still he was taken advantage of. His replacement did not take over for him at the end of the year when he was supposed to. Rather he mocked Apollodorus and reportedly said, "The mouse is now tasting the pitch; for he wanted to be an Athenian." This must be a reference to some fable, now lost, about a mouse; the main point is that Apollodorus shouldn't expect to have things easy, since he was reaching above his station ([Demosthenes] 50.26 with Trevett 1992, 12).

Apollodorus himself was hardly a poster-boy for inclusivity. In his legal dispute with Phormio, he tried to play on the jurors' hostility and contempt for slaves with every derogatory comment possible about Phormio:

> You must each of you consider what slave he left at home, and then imagine that you have suffered from him the same treatment that I have suffered from Phormio. Do not take into consideration that they are severally Syrus or Manes or whoever, while this fellow is Phormio. The thing is the same – they are slaves, and he was a slave; you are masters and I was master.[4]

Apollodorus argued that Phormio was an ungrateful, despicable barbarian, lucky rather than capable or hard-working.

Despite his wealth, his attempts to act the elite Athenian, and his distasteful attacks on ex-slaves, Apollodorus' bearing may have revealed his upbringing. He admitted that people found him annoying because he talked loudly and walked fast; another banker in a law-court speech admitted these same two habits and worried that his lack of social grace would alienate the jury ([Demosthenes] 45.77; Demosthenes 37.52). These were perhaps the manners of merchants and bankers in the Piraeus. In contrast, Aristotle portrays the noble man as behaving in a dignified and unhurried manner (*Nicomachean Ethics* 1125a12–16). It may be too much of a stretch to imagine Apollodorus as a loud

---

4 ([Demosthenes] 45.86, trans. Murray 1939; cf. 30, 81–85.

and successful New York immigrant, who moved to the suburbs and has trouble fitting in with the snooty WASPs at the country club, but we can easily imagine him at the famous, extravagant dinner of Petronius' Trimalchio. He could not compete with the fictional ex-slave billionaire himself, but with his mistresses, ambition, loud voice, and litigiousness, he certainly would have earned a place at the table.

Trimalchio's Wild Party

Before Nero executed him in 66 CE, Petronius, a senator and former confidant of that emperor, wrote a long episodic novel called the *Satyricon* (Tacitus, *Annals* 16.17–20). Much of the work has been lost, but the longest and most famous surviving section relates a dinner party hosted by Trimalchio, a fabulously wealthy and extravagant ex-slave. Many of the guests are also ex-slaves. The dinner party of Trimalchio, the *Cena (Trimalchionis)*, seems at first to give us direct access to a stratum of society rarely depicted in Roman literature: ex-slaves in Campania, an area in Italy south of Rome. And in some ways the *Cena* is indeed realistic: the speech of the freedmen, for example, reflects everyday spoken Latin better than any other literary source. But Trimalchio himself is obviously a larger-than-life caricature, and the *Cena* can lead historians astray in subtler ways too. As we'll see, "Trimalchio vision" predisposes art historians to scan works of Roman art for signs of ostentation or excess and then to declare them examples of "freedman's art," unconsciously duplicating the contempt the Roman elite felt for parvenus like Trimalchio (Petersen 2006, 10). For us, the *Cena* provides a colorful starting point for explorations of key issues in freedman life; our conclusions based on wider evidence will usually constitute a correction or modification of the picture we get from Petronius.

Relationships with Former Masters

First of all, Mouritsen points out that the ex-slaves in Petronius are unusual in that they were not closely bound to their former masters, their patrons, *patroni* (singular: *patronus*) (Mouritsen 2011, 291). Rather than the independent freedmen at Trimalchio's table, most Roman freedmen maintained close relationships with their former masters, if they were still alive. Some even continued to live with their former masters and performed the same, specialized jobs even after they won their freedom. After all, where else was a "dresser," a "keeper of the pearls," a "mirror woman," or a "guest announcer," to work if not in the house of a Roman aristocrat? And why not the one where they were already working and where their friends and (perhaps) family lived and worked?

The bonds between Roman ex-slaves and their *patroni* could be legal and explicit or moral and general. Some ex-slaves had contractual obligations, imposed at the time of manumission, to work for their former masters a set number of days each year. These *operae* attracted a great deal of attention in legal texts – for instance, a prostitute could not legally be required to continue that profession (Justinian, *Digest* 38.1.38) – but they are not mentioned as often elsewhere. In other sources, more general, moral obligations dominate: former slaves were supposed to respect their *patroni*. For example, ex-slaves could not bring their former masters to court and were required to support their patrons if they fell into poverty – a reciprocal obligation, since *patroni* had to take care of their *liberti,* their ex-slaves. Ex-slaves who failed to behave properly could be indicted as *liberti ingrati*, "ungrateful ex-slaves," and were subject to severe penalties. This process, of course, required taking a former slave to court, something elite Romans felt was beneath them. Tacitus reports a proposed change in the law that would have enabled former owners at their own discretion to reduce their ex-slaves to slavery again:

> It was no imposition to require them [former slaves] to keep their freedom by showing the same respect that had won it for them in the first place. No, those who were obviously guilty ought to be re-enslaved, so that those who were not moved by kindness could be coerced by fear. (Tacitus, *Annals* 13.26)

This proposal was apparently too severe and arbitrary, even in a society dominated by slaveholders. Normally, Roman citizens, including freedmen, could only be reduced to slavery for severe crimes and through due legal process, not simply because an interested party took offense. The measure was rejected. Nevertheless, it reveals the strong expectation, sometimes disappointed, that freedmen show respect to their masters.

The word *patronus* is related to *pater*, the Roman word for father. Ex-slaves were supposed to remain close to their former masters, but in a subordinate position, like a son to his father in the hierarchical Roman household. Roman nomenclature exemplifies this way of thinking, paternalism – which we'll revisit in Chapter 11. The full names of free-born Romans included their father's name, for example, *Marci filius* or *M.f.*, son of Marcus. In that place in their names, ex-slaves indicated whose freedman (*libertus*) they were, for example, *Quinti libertus* or *Q.l.*, freedman of Quintus.[5] Historians say that Roman citizens indicate "filiation" in their names whereas ex-slaves indicate "libertination" or "pseudo-filiation" – recall that slaves did not have official fathers and their biological fathers did not figure in their nomenclature.

The pseudo-familial connection of ex-slaves and ex-masters had legal consequences for the estates of deceased ex-slaves. The laws changed over time, but, for much of the classical period, a former master could claim a portion of the estate of his or her ex-slaves. The *patronus* lost this right only when the ex-slave had three legitimate children, natural not adopted. Only then, finally, did the ex-slave's real family fully replace his pseudo-father, his *patronus*, in the allocation of his estate.

We might extrapolate from the modern fantasy of telling your boss to "take this job and shove it" and imagine that ancient slaves would be overjoyed to sever their ties with an owner who had bossed them around, yelled at them, humiliated them, and, quite possibly, hit them, sexually assaulted them, or had them whipped. But, in the first place, slaves who won their freedom were, on the whole, the ones with the best relationships with their masters. The freedmen in the *Cena*, for example, all talk about their former masters with admiration and respect: "I tried to please my master, a fine dignified gentleman whose finger-nail was worth more than your whole body" (57.10).[6] Even for the (secretly) disgruntled slaves – and I'm sure there were plenty of these – another consideration played a role: in the same way that most people today refrain from burning bridges and telling off their bosses when they quit, calculating ex-slaves realized that their economic survival might well depend on having a powerful and wealthy backer to protect them

---

5 When the former owner was a woman – for Roman women possessed property including slaves – a backwards C, standing for Gaia (the Roman Jane Doe) indicated that the patron was a woman.

6 References and quotations in this section are from Petronius, *Satyricon*, trans. Heseltine 1987.

in court, to invest money in their business – as Trimalchio himself does with his own ex-slaves (76.9) – or merely to send customers their way. Mouritsen sums up this side of the story: "Since the one advantage which the freedmen enjoyed was their familial background and the patronal connection, an 'independent' freedman would generally have been a disadvantaged freedman" (Mouritsen 2011, 234). Conversely, one factor that contributed to the success of many ex-slaves was that they automatically had a patron.

Wealth

Trimalchio and several of his freedmen friends are wealthy, even by the standards of the Roman senatorial class. The number and specialization of his slaves is one mark of this. Trimalchio has so many slaves that not one in ten of them knows him by sight and seventy slaves were born on one day on his estates (37.9; 53.2); his household slaves are assigned to numbered groups of ten of which there are at least forty (47.12). Huge household establishments in Rome with slaves numbering in the hundreds are attested for actual Roman senators (e.g., Tacitus 14.43). Trimalchio's household is also realistic in the specialization of the slaves with 23 different slave jobs mentioned, including, for example, a slave whose job is to carve meat at the table – in time to music (36.6). On epitaphs in Rome, historians have counted almost a hundred separate job titles for slaves in actual aristocratic households; one grand household by itself had slaves with at least 47 different job titles (Joshel 1992, 74–75; Treggiari 1975a, 57–58).

Trimalchio owed his rise to large-scale trade – including the importation of slaves (76.6) – a pattern that may often have distinguished rich freedmen from senators, prohibited by law from taking part directly in overseas trade. For this reason, economic historians used to consider ex-slaves a mercantile class. We shouldn't exaggerate this tendency: wealthy but non-senatorial free-born Romans also took part in trade; even senatorial families profited indirectly, often by lending at interest to their freedmen, something Trimalchio does (76.9; cf. Rauh 1993, 235–237). And, by the time of the *Cena*, Trimalchio possessed immense landholdings, the traditional source of wealth for the Roman elite: he claims that he wants to buy Sicily so he can travel to Africa without leaving his own property (48.3)!

There were certainly some fabulously wealthy non-fictional freedmen. Elite resentment ensured that we hear about them: for example, one freedman reportedly owned 4116 slaves (Pliny, *Natural History* 33.134–135; Brunt 1975, 624–635) – and in Chapter 5 we saw the hatred the rich ex-slave bureaucrats of the emperor attracted. Throughout Italy, many impressive and expensive grave monuments commemorated rich freedmen and their families. These conspicuous works attract attention, but do not represent the average ex-slave. For one of the purposes of the many associations or clubs, *collegia*, which Roman ex-slaves and slaves joined in great numbers and to which they paid dues, was to provide burial for those whose bodies would otherwise be unceremoniously discarded. Nevertheless, the corpses of tens of thousands of poor Romans – including ex-slaves no doubt – ended up in huge lime pits without any commemoration at all (Bodel 1994, 38–54). The many simple grave monuments, a name and perhaps a few words inscribed on a small, stone plaque, make it obvious that even those ex-slaves whose surviving families or *patroni* put up a gravestone were usually poor. Ex-slave epitaphs often mention the deceased's job, which may well indicate a sense of pride, in striking contrast to elite contempt for labor (Joshel 1992, esp. 85–91). They also reveal

Figure 8.2 Columbaria 1 in the Codini Vineyard near Rome. No billionaire ex-slaves displaying their wealth here! Columbaria were communal tombs, either partially or entirely underground, perhaps already a rejection of competitive, public display (Borbonus 2014, 3). They housed many niches, each of which could house two small urns for bone ash. These niches were sometimes decorated with plaques containing short epitaphs. Some columbaria were built to house all the slaves and ex-slaves of a great household, a sign of continued connection within this community and a display of the paternalistic care of the noble master; this particular one contained burials from many different households. It had a capacity of about 900, and was in use during the first and second centuries CE (Borbonus 2014, 169). *Source*: Alimari/Art Resource, NY.

that many ex-slaves made their living from humble jobs such as barber, doorkeeper, messenger, meat carver, masseur, and mule driver. In the *Cena*, it is not Trimalchio and his rich friends who are typical, but rather the ex-slave Ganymede with his complaints about how the high price of grain is breaking his budget (44.15).

Status Conscious?

Trimalchio and two of his friends are proud of their position as *seviri Augustales*, members of the town's six-man board of the Augustan priests (30.1, 57.4, 65.5, 71.9). There is plenty of evidence outside of Petronius for these respected local panels, which supervised some religious practices – including the cult of the emperor – and sponsored public events. Since ex-slaves were prohibited from holding many other public offices, affluent freedmen tended to congregate in the *Augustales*, which they eventually dominated. Membership in the *Augustales* was an important way that freedmen, both in the *Satyricon* and in real society, displayed their success and new status in society.

Such displays attracted resentment from free-born Romans, perhaps especially those who were not as wealthy. In one of his *Epodes*, the poet Horace, himself the son of a freedman, attacks a rich ex-slave:

> Your flanks are scorched by Spanish lashes,
> your legs by iron chains,
> And though you strut about in pride of wealth
> good fortune does not mend low birth.
> (*Epode* 4.3–6, trans. West 2008, modified)

Horace blames the former slave for what he suffered in slavery – whipping and fettering – perhaps on the assumption that it was deserved. These lines provide a virulent example of the scorn mixed with envy that rich freedmen attracted. So, too, Trimalchio's ridiculous attempts to impress his guests not only with his wealth, but with his class and sophistication, provide one main theme in the *Cena*: he wants to be seen as a sophisticated Roman nobleman, but fails utterly and laughably. For example, only members of the senatorial and equestrian classes were allowed to wear gold rings and penalties were established if others, especially slaves or ex-slaves, usurped the *ius anuli aurei*, "the right of the gold ring." So Trimalchio sports one huge ring, only plated with gold, and another smaller one of pure gold, which he keeps within the letter of the law by decorating with iron stars (32.3). The statue of himself he has planned for his huge and extravagant gravesite will wear five gold rings (71.9); a statue, presumably, is out of reach of the law. But it was considered gauche to wear more than one ring, much less five gold ones. And, in general, Trimalchio's attempts to look classy and educated fail hilariously – not to mention his other eccentricities such as having all his slaves constantly singing as they serve dinner. Petronius' portrait is at least amusing and less obviously bitter than what we find in Horace. Consequently, it is easy to fall into the trap of joining (in spirit) the educated elite and laughing at rich freedmen like Trimalchio as crass, materialistic, and status-conscious. But several lines of thinking and classes of evidence should give us pause.

First, an important aspect of many cultural practices is elite self-definition. On the one hand, every elite tries to mark the distinction between themselves and everybody else with their dress, house decorations, way of speaking, dining habits, education, and what they read – the list could go on. On the other hand, those people who have acquired the resources required try to imitate the elite and to cross the boundaries they have set up. Although this would be reductive as an overall theory of culture, it does identify one of its important functions (Wallace-Hadrill 1994, 143–174). In the Roman case, rich ex-slaves wanted to assimilate into the free-born upper classes, the members of which tried to maintain and publically signal their difference and superiority.

The free-born elite maintained some distinctions by law. In addition to the restrictions on gold rings, it was also illegal falsely to claim to be free-born: ex-slaves, no matter how rich, could not write their names with "son of" but only "freedman of." Ex-slaves could not become Roman magistrates or *decurions*, town councilors, elsewhere. One result was that freedpersons couldn't display their status with statues or inscriptions in the town center, the most prestigious venue. This disability may explain why they lavished such attention and wealth on commemoration after death (Mouritsen 2005, 53–54). Petronius may be aware of this feature of freedman culture: one of the characters at the *Cena* is described as "Habinnas of the *seviri Augustales*, a monumental mason with a reputation for making first-class tombstones" (65.5).

In addition to these legal disabilities, many cultural attributes are hard to acquire as an adult. Trimalchio studied accounting as a child (29.4) – something noble Romans might never bother learning. He claims to have both a Greek and a Latin library (48.4), but his knowledge of literature and basic mythology is laughable: he mangles famous stories from the Odyssey (48.7). Considering culture in terms of elite self-definition suggests that ex-slaves were not particularly crass and materialistic, but rather that they were barred from some status symbols, did not enjoy the classical education of the Roman elite, and that the elite deliberately made of itself a moving target. As Orlando Patterson himself pointed out:

> The native Roman elite was arguably one of the most rapaciously materialistic and ostentatious in the entire history of ruling classes. It is the plutocratic elite which is the main source of Roman materialism. (Patterson 1991, 244)

Indeed! Freedmen were status conscious – as almost everybody is in one way or another – but we shouldn't follow our elite sources in focusing on only this feature of their culture. For example, although some grave monuments aim to display wealth and taste, many more are simple monuments that did not aim at a wide audience but mainly expressed the grief and affection of the bereaved – you may recall the one cited at the end of Chapter 4. We have mentioned that ex-slaves were particularly inclined to celebrate their families with grave reliefs. This may represent a reaction to the denial of family life in slavery and an assertion of Roman citizenship, but it's overly cynical to reduce such depictions of family on gravestones to merely another display of status.

Modern art historians sometimes unconsciously adopt ancient elitist attitudes when they characterize as "freedman's art" works that display great wealth but are somehow eccentric, overdone, or inelegant. In addition to the inevitable subjectivity involved and the possibility that "good taste" changed from decade to decade, we often do not know the actual status of a work's commissioner. For example, the tomb of Eurysaces or "the Baker's Tomb" is admittedly huge, extravagant, and eccentric: the top contains scenes from inside a huge bakery; the tube-like structures that make up the body of the tomb may be representations of kneading barrels. But is this any stranger or more original than the huge, pyramidal tomb of Cestius, a blue-blooded Roman senator, albeit apparently a fan of things Egyptian? And, as so often, historians suspect, but do not even know for sure, that Eurysaces was a freedman (Petersen 2006, 87–88).

Patterns in nomenclature raise further complications for the stereotype of the status-obsessed freedperson (Bruun 2013). First, Greek names are extremely common on Roman epitaphs. The arguments are complex, statistical, and only reveal overall probabilities, but most historians believe that Greek names on an epitaph do not indicate that the person in question was ethnically Greek, but rather that he or she was a slave, a former slave, or descended from slaves. For example, almost 90 percent of the slaves mentioned in Cicero's letters have Greek names, a higher proportion than can actually have been Greek in terms of language or ethnicity. As a result of this naming practice, Greek names were associated with slavery and low status; few free-born Romans would give their child a Greek name and risk having him or her mistaken for an ex-slave. But, surprisingly enough, some people made this very choice: on epitaphs, 10 percent of the children born to free-born parents received Greek names. Such a choice could signal family continuity: for example, parents might name a child after an ex-slave grandfather with a Greek name. Giving children Roman names, on the other hand, would make their origins less conspicuous and perhaps help their chances of social advancement. Among extant inscriptions the proportion of Greek names declines with each generation out of slavery, so most families either decided to go with the higher-status Roman names or unconsciously assimilated into Roman society. Some did not and persisted in using Greek names despite their association with slavery.

A second intriguing phenomenon is decline of both libertination and filiation in imperial epitaphs. Historians often explain the failure of ex-slaves to include libertination in terms of embarrassment about being ex-slaves, an explanation in line with the stereotype of freedmen as status conscious. Thus, historians believe that most of the *incerti* – those whose legal status is uncertain from their epitaphs – were actually former slaves. But, in some cases, historians can tell that ex-slave parents did not include their children's filiation even when they could and when it would have signaled their freeborn status. Perhaps some ex-slaves rejected putting a high value on free birth and were proud of their success in advancing in society (Mouritsen 2011, 282–283).

Even Petronius, who generally seems to mock the pretensions of ex-slaves, may be more complicated than he appears. None of the freedmen at the *Cena* show the slightest inclination to cover up their past in slavery, but rather they discuss it openly as if to say, "and look at me now." One of them, Hermeros (in the quotation from Petronius at the beginning of the chapter), even claims that the struggles he went through to gain his freedom make him superior to the free-born. Unfortunately, we cannot quite rule out the possibility that Hermeros was supposed to be ridiculous, and it is only modern readers who find him, in some ways, a sympathetic and admirable character.

Conclusion: Contrasts Between Greek and Roman Practice

Despite a few similarities, manumission and the experiences of ex-slaves were different at Athens and at Rome. Manumission was permitted in both places and for similar reasons. But manumission and urban ex-slaves are much more conspicuous in the Roman evidence, both literary and epigraphic. It is hard to escape the impression that manumission was indeed more usual for Roman slaves (even though that may be due to skewed evidence), less common in Athens than in Roman cities, and very rare among rural slaves in Roman Italy.

At Athens, ex-slaves were not closely tied to their former masters. The weakness of these bonds helps explain why ex-slaves were not incorporated into Athenian society. In particular, neither ex-slaves at Athens nor their descendants obtained political rights – with rare exceptions such as Pasion. They remained *metics* and could not intermarry with Athenian citizens. In contrast, Roman ex-slaves often maintained strong, pseudo-familial ties with their former masters, their *patroni*. They were incorporated within Roman society and became citizens, albeit disbarred from magistracies and the army.

Descendants of rich ex-slaves could advance socially to join the equestrian and eventually the senatorial class. More relevant for the average ex-slave was the possibility of contracting marriages with free-born Romans, an important form of integration, well attested on epitaphs. This contrast had its roots in basic differences in the outlooks of the two societies: Athenian citizenship was (ideally) egalitarian, but exclusive; Rome was more openly hierarchical, but was thus more able to incorporate outsiders, like ex-slaves, at appropriate levels in its social hierarchy – a practice essential to Rome's success as an empire.

Suggested Reading

Hopkins and Roscoe 1978 is a classic article on the Delphic manumission records, whereas Sosin 2015 argues that people in *paramonē* were still slaves, albeit of Apollo, and provides up-to-date bibliography. Trevett 1992 is a clear and detailed book, which provides an account of the life of Apollodorus, the son of the ex-slave banker Pasion, and of his family quarrels as well as an examination of his speeches. Three recent works challenge aspects of the traditional views about citizenship in Athens and the position of ex-slaves there: Cohen 2000 argues that Athens was actually a large and diverse society and that ex-slaves and foreigners were more readily assimilated than traditional scholarship holds; one section (130–154) focuses on the slaves and ex-slaves involved in banking. Kamen 2013 provides a judicious and concise introduction to the legal and civic status of conditionally and fully free ex-slaves at Athens. Her main argument is that the slave/citizen dichotomy was just one of several important status distinctions at Athens. Zelnick-Abramovitz 2005 is dense and technical, but also wide-ranging and ambitious. It emphasizes the legal and social liabilities that Greek ex-slaves endured. Mouritsen 2011 is an insightful, general treatment of Roman ex-slaves, which focuses on the discordant pictures in different sources, especially legal, literary, and epigraphic texts. Several of Mouritsen's views are iconoclastic – for example, that self-purchase was rare – but he represents fairly and clearly the views he criticizes as well as the evidence on both sides. Perry 2014 focuses on freedwomen and the importance of marriage to their assimilation to Roman society. In a series of case studies, Petersen 2006 critically examines the role attributed to ex-slaves' artistic patronage in Roman art history.

9

Everyday Conflict

> *Great heavens, what poor specimens of humanity the men [slaves grinding grain in a mill] were! Their entire bodies formed a pattern of livid bruises. Their backs, which bore the marks of the whip, were not so much covered as shaded by torn shirts of patchwork cloth. Some wore nothing except a thin covering over their private parts; all were clad in such a fashion that their bodies were visible through the rags they wore. They had letters branded on their foreheads, half-shaved heads, and chains round their ankles. Their faces were a ghastly yellow, and their eyes had contracted in the smoke-filled gloom of that steaming, dank atmosphere, making them half-blind.*
>
> Apuleius (Roman novelist, second century CE),
> *The Golden Ass* 9.12, trans. Walsh 1994

Resistance and Agency

We have seen in the last three chapters how some slaves made tolerable lives for themselves within the system of slavery and the obstacles they faced. Some slaves tried to maintain their birth cultures or to assimilate to the culture of their masters or both. They might enjoy amorous relationships or raise families. They aspired to and sometimes succeeded in gaining their freedom. In all these ways, slaves demonstrated that they possessed *agency*: they were not merely passive victims but played an active role in creating a life for themselves. This sounds like a good thing and social historians sometimes aspire to "give agency back" to the oppressed people they study. Although this approach has played a large role in recent work on slavery and provides a corrective to the view of slaves as passive victims, two issues remain problematic. On the one hand, an emphasis on agency tends to overrate the options available to many slaves – for example, the mill slaves described by Apuleius above.[1] On the other hand, agency is very common, encompassing much that all humans do all the time: choose among available options. Let's examine these two issues in more detail.

First, we should not exaggerate the options available to slaves or underrate the difficulties of their position. Take for example, Lesis, a slave in Athens, who wrote a letter

---
1 See Joshel and Petersen 2014, 125–142 on slaves in mills and bakeries.

Ancient Greek and Roman Slavery, First Edition. Peter Hunt.
© 2018 Peter Hunt. Published 2018 by John Wiley & Sons, Ltd.

on a sheet of lead in the fourth century BCE, which was excavated and then published in 2000.[2] Lesis addressed the letter to his mother and a certain Xenokles, whose status and role are unknown. Lesis was trying to get somebody to help him, since his masters seem to have rented or apprenticed him to the owner of a foundry, a metalworking shop.[3] He describes his plight and concludes: "I've been handed over to a very evil man; I'm being whipped to death; I am tied up; I am abused. Worse and worse." Unfortunately, we don't know how Lesis managed to send a letter, what he hoped his mother and Xenokles could do, and what, if anything, they actually managed to do. And that assumes they received the letter: it was found in a dump, but was it discarded after delivery or instead of being delivered? This situation may seem grim enough, but Lesis at least had his mother and Xenokles and the resources and opportunity to send a letter. Whether successful or not, he was exercising agency.

But imagine yourself a boy of fifteen born somewhere in the second-century BCE Mediterranean. Your city joined an unsuccessful revolt against recently imposed Roman rule and was taken by storm. Your father was killed. Your mother and sister were both raped by soldiers before being sold separately from you. You were branded or tattooed with a symbol of your city, an extremely painful and humiliating process, and sold to a slave merchant. You endured a three-month journey by foot and ship in a large group of fettered slaves and were then sold to a wealthy farm owner in Italy. None of the other slaves on this farm, thousands of miles from your home, even spoke your language; you were reduced to speaking in whatever rudimentary Latin you were able to learn. The field hands were overwhelmingly male so you had no chance to raise a family; you almost never laid eyes on money, much less had any chance to save to purchase your freedom. Like the other slaves there, you worked hard to avoid whipping. You didn't cause trouble, so you wouldn't be chained day and night. Positive incentives were few and meager. Isolated and lonely, poorly clothed and fed, worked hard and whipped for any disobedience, mistakes, or just when the overseer got drunk and angry, you died of a disease after ten years of slavery.

Such a life may seem unspeakably grim, and this case is admittedly fictional. But it cannot have been an unusual one: ample evidence survives for all of its elements and, as we've seen, the Romans enslaved defeated people by the tens or hundreds of thousands for centuries as the Greeks had done before on a smaller scale. Indeed, historians agree that during the late Republic far more slaves ended up living hard lives and dying on large Italian farms and leaving no trace of their existence than were able to preserve their birth culture, marry and raise families, and buy their freedom. Some degree of agency is almost always possible – our imaginary slave *chose* to work hard and keep quiet to avoid whipping and chaining. We should not mistake options and agency with the pleasant, vague notion that you can't keep a good man or woman down, a myth mainly persuasive to people who have been watching too many feel-good, Hollywood movies recently. But throughout history untold millions of good men and women have been kept down and exercised agency only among limited and harsh options.

The results of slaves' agency that we have explored so far – their cultural and family life and their striving for freedom – can all be described as ways that slaves accommodated

---

2 Jordan 2000; Harris 2004. Lead was a major byproduct of silver production, so it was cheap at Athens. It can be beaten into a thin sheet on which one can scratch a letter.

3 Roman legal texts consider slave discontent and flight in similar situations (*Justinian's Digest* 21.1.3 and 5).

themselves to the system of slavery. Slaves could simply make the best life for themselves within the system, but they could also resist the system of oppression to which they were subject. This chapter explores the day-to-day resistance that individual slaves or small groups of slaves practiced and the counter-measures of masters; the next chapter explores the massive and dramatic revolts of the Spartan Helots and of slaves during the late Roman Republic, which pitted slaves in a life-or-death struggle against their oppressors.

As we turn to resistance and revolution, the second potential pitfall with the concept of agency is worth noting and avoiding: it is easy to slip without noticing from the unobjectionable claim that somebody exercised agency – something very common – to saying or implying that there is something admirable about them, especially if he or she belonged to an oppressed group. If one slave won his freedom with outstanding loyalty and years of hard work and started a family as a Roman citizen, he exercised agency. If another slave, undeterred by punishment and threats, stymied and resisted her exploitation at every turn, she also exercised agency. Are we to admire both of these opposite patterns of behavior?

Some historians would reject the question all together: they aim simply to understand the people they study and not to judge them. But sympathy or antipathy, admiration or condemnation, are hard to avoid; it's not clear that avoiding them is even desirable. For more than a generation, most historians have generally sympathized with slaves, since they were manifestly victims of severe oppression. This is not to say that no slaves were ignorant and hateful, backstabbing and violent, alcoholic and cruel; all populations include people with these unpleasant qualities. Nevertheless, historical writing about slavery – mainly in the New World – went through a phase, "neo-abolitionist historiography," which began in the 1950s and emphasized the harshness of slavery and celebrated resistance (e.g., Stampp 1956). More recently, the ways slaves fashioned lives within the system has garnered more attention and, again, usually admiration. Regardless of the flow of historical sympathy in one decade or another, good historians are always attentive to the details and complexities of individual cases. As we turn from those slaves who did their best within the system to those who opposed it, a couple of complexities involved in evaluating either group deserve mention.

A focus on slaves getting ahead by cooperating with their owners risks portraying slavery as a meritocracy, in which loyalty (or obedience), hard work, and competence were rewarded. Many slaves, however, worked hard their whole lives motivated by threats and punishments with little hope to improve their lot. When we consider those slaves who did advance themselves, we need to consider the possibility of collaboration in the negative sense. For example, any system for rewarding slaves was necessarily competitive: slaveholders wanted to motivate their slaves to work hard for them, not to free them or give them money or even feed them too well. So any incentive bestowed on one slave was one not bestowed on others.

Hard-working slaves made slavery profitable and contributed to the strength of the institution. Even worse, those agricultural slaves, for example, who worked exceptionally hard for their masters made life more difficult for other slaves, perhaps less healthy, smaller, or weaker ones, who could not keep up a faster pace or longer hours. This may seem relatively benign, but evidence from other slave societies reveals how important the pace of work is to people who do little else. If they can, not only slaves but many oppressed groups ostracize and retaliate against people who seek individual rewards at a cost to their class.

This dynamic provides the context for the fragment from Euripides, with which we began this book: "slaves who love the class of masters provoke a great war with the other slaves" (Euripides, *Alexander*, fr. 50 in Nauck 1889). Competition for a master's favor and rewards might extend to slandering fellow slaves or informing against them, if they were resisting slavery or planning revolt or flight. For example, we hear that Roman authorities were able to suppress several abortive slave revolts when one slave informed on his or her fellow slaves and we can assume that other cases went unreported (Thompson 2003, 249–251). The stakes were high: informers often gained their freedom as a reward while conspirators were burnt alive and rebels sometimes crucified. Conspiracies were, admittedly, not a frequent occurrence, but to return to daily life, it was often a slave rather than the master him- or herself who carried out a whipping. In sum, plenty of evidence survives of the sinister meaning of "collaboration," not the sort of agency some historians celebrate.

Resistance, too, comes in a large variety of forms. Some involved great dangers or sacrifices: for example, trying to prevent or stop a brutal whipping or causing trouble when children were sold apart from their families. Other activities included in the category of resistance were surreptitious and overlapped with self-interest: can we distinguish between admirable resistance and arson motivated by malice or slow work motivated by laziness? And what about theft, perhaps the slave activity most troublesome to slaveholders? Historians cannot distinguish resistance from self-interest with any general rule. Our information almost never allows us to distinguish, for example, between theft as a reaction to slavery – if we knew that Daos, for example, would never steal from a fellow slave but only from his masters, whose wealth his own work produced – and theft in order to get something. We are best off conceding that this issue is intractable and defining resistance for our purposes as all deliberate slave activities that made slavery more difficult and less profitable for slaveholders and for which a slave might be punished.

Historians sometimes describe the moves, countermoves, and compromises between weak and strong groups and individuals as *negotiations*. In some ways this terminology is apt: in longstanding slave systems, especially where most slaves are born in slavery, masters and slaves learn what they can and cannot do without provoking damaging retaliation from the other side; both sides, more or less, come to a tacit agreement about the terms on which they can live with each other. Nevertheless, even in this chapter, which does not deal with slave rebellions, I prefer the older term *conflict* instead of *negotiation*. There are three reasons for this. First, in many places and times in the classical world, most slaves were first-generation slaves, often foreigners barely able to understand basic commands, much less to negotiate about the treatment they expected in exchange for the work they would do. Second, violence and the threat of violence were too frequent and serious for a metaphor from a verbal process, negotiation, not to involve a major distortion. Finally, our three most serious cases, slaves who ran away, killed themselves, or killed their masters, had nothing to do with mutual accommodation, but rather aimed at ending the relationship between slave and master one way or another.

In contrast to most previous chapters, this one does not include sections devoted to distinct places and time. Slave resistance was not constant throughout the classical world, but the greatest differences were between different types of slaves rather than between different periods. The types of resistance practiced by household slaves in fifth-century BCE Athens and in first-century CE Rome had more in common than either had with the resistance practiced by agricultural slaves. Almost every tactic of resistance and almost every method of controlling slaves are attested throughout the classical world. They may not have been equally common or worked the same way everywhere. For instance, running away was easier from a Greek city-state at war with its nearby neighbors or when a fugitive slave could blend in and find work in a big city. Resistance on a large farm supervised by a slave manager for an absentee owner must have been different from that on a smaller farm with the owner in residence. Yet the ancient evidence is too thin for us to investigate such differences in detail: for instance, statistics about the frequency of whipping or slave flight in different places are non-existent. So my approach will be to survey the repertoire of options that slaves and masters employed and to choose examples for their vividness and the insight they yield, rather than restricting myself to this or that particular place or time. I'll begin with less serious infractions and punishments, move to more and more serious conflict, and finish with slaves who murdered their masters and the brutal reprisals they provoked.

Throughout the classical world, our evidence is best for the lives of domestic slaves, those slaves in daily close contact with the elite authors who provide so much of our evidence. But thanks to handbooks of advice about farming, this is one case where we know a fair amount also about the difficulties of managing slaves on farms. I will emphasize this evidence whenever possible in partial compensation for our sources' usual focus on household slaves.

Weapons of the Weak

The difficulties faced by slave rebellions will concern us in the next chapter, but even on the individual level, masters possessed far more power than their slaves. Slaveholders could easily inflict great harm on any slave who opposed them. Hence most resistance was based on cunning rather than strength; it rarely took the form of open conflict. As Harriet Jacobs put it in her account of her life as a slave, "Who can blame slaves for being cunning? They are constantly compelled to resort to it. It is the only weapon of the weak and oppressed against the strength of their tyrants" (Jacobs 1987 [orig. 1861], 100–101; see also Scott 1985). When they acted against their masters' will, slaves either tried not to get caught at all or did things that were exasperating, but that did not quite rise to a level that would justify punishment.

Phaedrus, the Roman freedman who put together the earliest collection of fables, claimed that this genre had its origins in slavery: slaves wanted a way to talk to each other without being understood by their masters (Phaedrus, *Fables* III pr. 33–37). Appropriately enough, the *Life of Aesop,* a loosely organized collection of amusing stories about the legendary slave and first writer of fables, provides us with many examples of the small ways that slaves could stymie their masters. When ordered to cook a lentil dish for dinner, Aesop cooks a single lentil (39–41). When asked to give some fine food to his master's "love" (meaning his wife), Aesop feeds it to his master's dog with the claim that only his dog really loves him (44–46). These stories are meant to be amusing rather than realistic. But a passing remark by Aristotle suggests that his audience was familiar with deliberately difficult slaves in real life: like speakers with a bad case, "[S]laves never answer questions directly but talk in circles and don't get to the point" (Aristotle, *Rhetoric* 3.14.10). This type of resistance may seem at first to resemble no modern situation more than that of a parent trying to get a clever and contrary 12-year-old to collect and take out the garbage. But modern parents don't normally depend on their children as a work force; nor are they likely to have their children tied up so they can whip them. Despite the humor of Aesop, resistance was usually a serious business.

Ancient slaves tried to avoid work by feigning illness, malingering, a tactic still familiar today. In a case reported by Galen, a doctor and medical writer, a slave malingerer had the goal of staying with his girlfriend rather than accompanying his master on a long trip. This story comes from a work entitled, *How to Catch Malingerers*, which Galen introduces with the statement that many people have an interest in being able to detect malingers; slave owners certainly did (Kühn 1821–1833, 19.3–7).

On the one hand, several works on agriculture mention the need to take care of slaves who are ill. Slave owners did not want sick slaves to die unnecessarily or to recover slowly because they had been forced, by whipping for instance, to continue to work while ill. On the other hand, to allow one slave to avoid hard work by falsely claiming illness might put slaveholders or farm managers on the slippery slope to supporting many "sick" and unproductive slaves. Cato's notorious advice that such slaves not be fed full rations or simply be sold would have ensured that malingering was an unattractive option, but who would buy sick slaves and for how much (Cato, *On Agriculture* 2.4, 2.7)? So a duty assigned to the wife of the estate manager, the *vilica* – a slave like her husband – was to take care of sick slaves, but also to be sure that they really were sick (Columella, *On Agriculture* 12.3.7; cf. Xenophon, *Oeconomicus* 7.37). Illnesses with demonstrable symptoms were probably more readily accepted as excuses; so the malingering slave in Galen rubbed mustard seed on his knee to make it swell up. Presumably claiming a hurt knee without swelling would not have done the trick – and Galen found him out anyway.

Another way to avoid work was to "wander," an option mainly available to household slaves whose jobs already involved some independence. We know about "wandering" mainly because Roman law codes discussed the distinction between a fugitive slave and a "wandering" slave, an *erro*. While fugitive slaves intended never to return to slavery, the *erro* was "a slave who does not actually run away, but who often wanders aimlessly about and comes home late after wasting his time" (*Justinian's Digest* 21.1.17.14). Picture a "good" slave who efficiently does the master's shopping and rushes home with the change to take further orders; compare him with a "wandering" slave who watches a procession on the way to the market, buys a drink in a tavern, and talks with his friends there. On his way back from shopping, he checks to see if his girlfriend, a slave in another household, is available. He returns home ready with a series of lies about why he was delayed and exaggerates the prices he paid for groceries to cover his drink – such a ploy explains why Theophrastus' *Suspicious Man*, "sends out one slave to buy groceries and then another slave to check what everything cost" (*Characters* 18.2). The "good" slave in my example might be aiming for manumission; the "wanderer" caused his master annoyance and expense, took advantage of his opportunities, and hoped not to be punished too harshly – or perhaps knew exactly what he could or could not get away with and at what cost.

On a farm, deliberately slow work or general carelessness was a major problem. Xenophon points out that motivated slave work-gangs can do twice as much work in a day as disgruntled or apathetic ones do (Xenophon, *Oeconomicus* 20.16). On the Roman side, Columella discusses all the ways a farm deteriorates if worked by bad slaves: for instance, they don't feed the animals enough and some grain disappears every day during threshing either because it's been stolen or out of carelessness (Columella, *On Agriculture* 1.7.6).

Our wandering slave whimsy included some minor embezzlement, the money for the drink. Real slaves seem often to have stolen or embezzled from their masters. One Athenian slave, Moschion, embezzled a sizeable fortune from his old and trusting master and hid it in different places ([Demosthenes] 48.15–18). When the old man died, the heirs were suspicious and threatened to torture Moschion: he revealed that he'd stolen and hidden away a thousand drachma, about three years salary for a skilled worker. Later one of the heirs came back alone and actually tortured Moschion: he revealed the location of even more stolen money, seven thousand drachmas!

This case also illustrates how much variation there might be depending on the individual slave and master: the slave fools and robs the old man, but he is found out by a ruthless heir taking advantage of his right to torture a slave. Old masters may often have been at a disadvantage: after a long series of recommended precautions and inspections, Columella promises that the slaveholder who follows his advice will never be despised by his slaves when he gets old; presumably this was a common worry (Columella, *On Agriculture* 1.8.20). We may also find one such case in an Egyptian census document on papyrus. An elderly woman listed a household of nine slaves comprising two mothers and their four young children as well as three other adults; only the two mothers and their children were left since the other adults had run away (Papyrus Berlin Liehg. 15 in Shaw 2001, 55).

Roman agricultural handbooks give the impression that anything not nailed down was likely to be stolen. They recommend that everything that can be locked-up should be. And good masters will keep complete, duplicate inventories of tools, equipment, and containers – one copy at the farm and one at their home in town – and should check these regularly. The watchman needs to minimize comings and goings from the storeroom, cellar, and pressing-room and to be careful that nobody steals oil (Cato, *On Agriculture* 66.1, 67.2). Buyers of a slave could require assurances, legally enforceable, that he or she had not been guilty of theft or sabotage – the latter of which cannot have been that rare either (Varro, *On Agriculture* 2.10.5).

In the case of stolen tools and equipment, we must imagine that slaves could sell them somehow; the theft of foodstuff had a more obvious and direct appeal among slaves, whose rations were otherwise strictly limited. In the American South, slaves did not feel that the foodstuffs produced by their own hard work were the property of their masters in any moral sense.[4] Unfortunately, our evidence from the ancient world is entirely one-sided – advice to masters about how to prevent slaves from stealing – and the slave viewpoint is irrecoverable. And there were plenty of free-born thieves in the ancient world. All we can say for sure is that slaves were thought to be particularly prone to stealing.

In Chapter 2, we discussed Vegetius' warning that slave grooms not be allowed to ride horses or they might lame them (*On Veterinary Medicine [Mulomedicina]* 1.56.12–13). It is hard to tell how deliberate such damage was, but there is plenty of evidence of sabotage by slaves. Crops may at first seem harder to damage than horses, but that is only until fire and hay come to mind. And, sure enough, legal sources discuss arson committed by slaves.

Like their property, the reputations of masters were subject to damage from their household slaves, notorious as gossips. James Scott points out that "We are more familiar with gossip as a technique of social control among relative equals – the stereotypical village tyranny of the majority," but "[g]ossip is perhaps the most familiar and elementary form of disguised popular aggression" (Scott 1990, 143, 142). Household slaves

---

4 Genovese 1976, 599–612, a chapter entitled, "Roast pig is a wonderful delicacy, especially when stolen."

were everywhere in Greek and Roman elite houses, and they knew all the dirt about their masters. For example, in Aristophanes' *Frogs*, two slave characters list what they most enjoy in life: meddling, eavesdropping on the master's conversations, and spreading slanderous stories (Aristophanes, *Frogs* 748–753). When slaves gossiped, colorful and embarrassing stories would get out, a major blow to masters, given how important reputation was to social standing. Even worse, under a paranoid Roman emperor, stories originating among a senator's household slaves could end up as evidence of treasonous activities (Tacitus, *Annals* 15.54–55; *Histories* 1.2). Such cases were extreme and rare, but irritation at or fear of gossiping slaves is real enough and finds parallels in other times and places in the ancient world.

Figure 9.1 Slave holding chamber pot. Oinokles Painter c. 470 BCE, (Getty Museum). Like Trimalchio when he plays ball (Petronius, Satyricon 27), this Greek master doesn't want to interrupt whatever he's doing just to urinate. Household slaves were intimates of their masters to an extent quite foreign to modern ideas of privacy (Hunter 1994). They might remain in a room while a master or mistress was having sex (as on the cover illustration), hold a drunken master as he throws up, or let their master wipe off his hands on their hair. Although archaeologists have identified slave quarters in some large Roman houses – halls or courtyards surrounded with small, low, sleeping cubicles with dirt floors (George 2011, 388) – many slaves just slept on the floor. Personal attendants would sleep right outside the slaveholder's bedroom door or even at the foot of the bed, so they would be close at hand if their master or mistress wanted something in the night. *Source*: Digital image courtesy of the Getty's Open Content Program, http://www.getty.edu/art/collection.

The Tools of Oppression

This catalogue of slave resistance and misbehavior may leave the impression that owning slaves was more trouble than it was worth. That can't have been the case: although the price of slaves varied from period to period, they were almost always expensive, and not because all they could do was steal, burn, work poorly, gossip, and malinger. Slaves were valuable because there were ways to make slavery work. Slaveholders' tactics did not eliminate resistance – we've seen too much evidence to the contrary – but they did have at their disposal rewards and punishments robust enough so that most slaves most of the time did more or less as their masters wanted. And some, perhaps many, were hard workers.

The importance of rewards and clever management is clear in Xenophon's contrast between well and poorly managed farms in classical Athens: "In some places pretty much all the slaves are chained and still they keep trying to run away; in other places they are not bound but willingly work and stay" (Xenophon, *Oeconomicus* 3.4). Varro confirms that control without violence was also the ideal on Roman farms: the farm manager ought not whip the slaves when less violent tactics could be equally effective (Varro, *On Agriculture* 1.17.5). Among other considerations, slaves were valuable and harming them could reduce their value: even if a master or overseer did not injure a slave permanently, a slave with a scarred back had a lower market value and even a previously hard-working slave could become sullen and uncooperative after a beating.

We have already discussed one obvious reward, freedom, which could motivate slaves to work hard. The possibility of manumission also served as a check on resistance. One display of anger, one case of pilfering food, or one evening spent "wandering" could undo years of service in terms of a master's willingness to manumit. Indeed, some masters became so irritated with certain slaves that in their wills they bequeathed them only on the condition that they would never be set free (Bradley 1994, 165). In smaller ways too, calculating masters could encourage good behavior every day: some even provided clothing of different quality, so that the more or less obedient slaves would be reminded of their master's power to make their lives better or worse, whenever they put on their clothes in the morning – especially, one imagines, when it got cold in winter (Xenophon, *Oeconomicus* 13.10).

Another important power of masters was their ability to minimize solidarity among their slaves by giving some of them not only concrete rewards (like better clothing) but also more responsibility and higher status in the house. We often hear of slaves supervising other slaves: in the great Roman households, some slaves had other slaves – sometimes many of them – in their *peculium*. Presumably, these were the slaves they managed every day (Mouritsen 2011, 151). Both in Greece and Rome, the men who ran farms for absentee owners were often slaves. Another striking case is the *silentiarius* in great Roman households. In the late Roman and early Byzantine Empire this was the title of an important official of the emperor, but originally the *silentiarius* may have been the slave responsible for maintaining silence among the other slaves (Hasegawa 2005, 35). This would have been especially important among the slaves serving guests at dinner parties and the *silentarius'* responsibility might extend to all aspects of "good service" among the waiters, water-boys, foot washers, and other luxury slaves at such occasions. It was probably a *silentarius* or a similar slave, rather than the master himself, who enforced with blows strict silence among the slaves serving dinner, a harsh practice that Seneca deplored (Seneca, *Letters* 47.3–4).

This brings us to the concrete physical punishments masters had at their disposal to counter resistance and encourage prompt obedience and hard work. In a dialogue by Xenophon, a philosopher, Aristippus, argues for a life in which he would neither dominate others nor himself be dominated. But Socrates points out that he might be enslaved and then resisting would be hopeless:

> "Let's examine how masters treat such slaves. Don't they starve them to rein in their horniness, lock things up to prevent them from stealing, chain them up to stop them from running away, and whip them to keep them from being lazy. Or what do you do if you get slaves like that?" [Aristippus replies,] "I punish them harshly in all ways until I reduce them to submission." (Xenophon, *Memorabilia* 2.1–16–17)

The most obvious punishment is whipping, which usually first involved having a slave tied down. But masters also punished their slaves on the spur of the moment with whatever was handy: characters in Greek comedy threaten their slaves with all sorts of violence and sometimes just hit them. These passages are meant to be funny, but Galen provides more serious confirmation of this practice.[5] He relates that his mother would sometimes get angry with her maids and bite them; the emperor Hadrian put a slave's eye out with a stylus; other masters injured their own hands when, in a rage, they punched their slaves in the mouth. They did all this when they could just have the slaves tied down and whipped, the procedure Galen recommends. We have been considering violence against slaves as part of a rational system of rewards and punishments; these stories remind us not to forget that people are often emotional and irrational. Slaves were always at the mercy of ill-tempered or drunken masters or overseers, who need not have gained anything concrete by abusing them.

Slaveholders' control of the food supply of their slaves was another potent weapon in their arsenal. The Xenophon passage above states that masters curb their slaves' horniness – and presumably the trouble this could get them into – by starving them.[6] More generally, control of slaves' food could display each day the extent to which masters determined the lives slaves led.

Xenophon also mentions fetters, and archaeologists have found various ancient chains for binding slaves' feet or hands, individually or in groups. Physical constraint could take other forms. For example, some areas of the Greek countryside are dotted with classical-era stone towers, to which farmers could retreat in the event of enemy raids or bandits. Or so historians used to think. But some of the towers had *external* bolts, suggesting that they were designed as places to lock up the slaves at night (Papadopoulos and Morris 2005). In the Roman world, there are frequent references to slaves who were not only chained up at night, but who did their work in chains; it is unclear how widespread this practice was. Chaining at work and confinement at night were obviously potent means of controlling slaves and also severe punishments. Columella advises that the owner himself investigate the case of every individual slave whom the farm manager either puts in chains or removes from them (*On Agriculture* 1.8.16). Historians rightly

---

5 *The Diseases of the Mind* 1.4, 517, 1.8, 540–541 (Kühn 1821–1833) in Bradley 1994, 28–29; Seneca, *De Ira* 3.32.2.

6 In Menander, *Heros*, 14–17, a character assumes the converse: that a slave who falls in love has been getting too much food.

point out that the advantages household slaves enjoyed in terms of their living conditions and chance of manumission came with greater exposure to violence at the hands of their owners. But we shouldn't forget, as Columella's advice indicates, that slaves on large farms with absentee owners were also subject to corporal punishment and abuse, but at the hands of the farm manager rather than their owner. Thus, Columella also warns that chained slaves were particularly vulnerable to abuse because they were subject to so many people. He adds that, if abused, their hopeless situation could make them desperate and dangerous (*On Agriculture* 1.8.17).

All these types of punishment were concrete and sometimes temporary ones, but masters had the power in one fell swoop to blight a recalcitrant slave's whole life. In large households, a slave could be demoted to a more difficult type of work with less chance of manumission: for instance, a master could punish a skilled domestic slave by sending him away to work in the fields. Even more drastic, a slave could be sold as a punishment. As we have noted, this presented a special threat to slaves with families. For all slaves, the threat of sale to a particularly hard workplace was a terrifying possibility. In one speech by Lysias, a master forces a slave woman to confirm his wife's adultery by threatening to sell her to a mill (Lysias 1.18). In the Republic, Roman slaves could be sold to gladiatorial schools, to producers of animal shows (to be eaten alive by wild beasts for the entertainment of the crowd), or to the mines. Later, masters could only sell slaves to these places after they had justified their decision to a magistrate, presumably on the grounds of some serious misbehavior on the slave's part, as we'll see in Chapter 12. But there were no ploys or tactics a slave could use to escape being sold somewhere bad, if their masters were angry enough, a fact that would give most slaves pause before they decided to resist and exasperate their owners.

The ability to sell slaves was one advantage that masters gained by virtue of their position within a larger society dominated by slaveholders; yet it was not the only one. In a famous example, Plato describes how helpless a rich master of fifty slaves would be if he were isolated from society. The master would have to give some of the slaves perquisites and eventually "be slave to his slaves" to control such a large number of slaves (Plato, *Republic* 9.578d–579b). As Plato was well aware, the real situation was different, because slaveholders were not isolated. As Xenophon bluntly puts it, citizens protect each other from being murdered by their slaves (Xenophon, *Hiero* 4.3, 10.4). If push came to shove, masters in both Greece and Rome could call in the armed forces to put down conspiracies or rebellions. The state supported slaveholders even on an individual level. Most striking, a first-century BCE inscription from Puteoli describes the tasks for which the public undertaker and his assistants were responsible: these included the torture, whipping, or even the crucifixion of misbehaving slaves upon payment of a fee by the slave's master (Bodel 1994, 73).

Running Away

One type of resistance, running away, had the advantage, if successful, of terminating the relationship between slave and master and thus the possibility of retaliation by the master. The extent of "wandering" is hard to gauge, but slave flight was a recurrent and costly problem for masters throughout the classical world. After sampling some of the evidence, we'll consider the difficulties of running away, the potent counter-measures that masters could take, and, finally, why other people sometimes helped fugitive slaves.

References to runaway slaves are ubiquitous. Peaceful relations between classical Greek cities involved collaboration in returning fugitive slaves, whereas states at war often tried to encourage slave desertion. Hence slaves contemplating flight are listed by Aristophanes as among those who want the Peloponnesian War to continue; another character complains that he can't beat his slaves anymore on account of the war, that is, because they could run away (Aristophanes, *Peace* 451; *Clouds* 5–7). In Theophrastus, the "paranoid" character makes his slave walk in front of him in case he tries to run away, hardly a convenient precaution (*Characters* 18.8). A fascinating set of tablets record questions asked of the oracle of Zeus at Dodona in the fifth and fourth century BCE. Several of these ask about the recapture of fugitive slaves; other questions are asked by slaves, perhaps including, "Should I run away?" (Eidinow 2012, 247, 259–264). On the Roman side, Cato includes the claim that slaves had run away among the standard excuses incompetent managers give for poor productivity on a farm (Cato, *On Agriculture* 2.2–3). Perhaps the best evidence for the frequency with which slaves ran away consists of the laws against harboring fugitives; these tended to be promulgated again and again during the Empire, a sign that they were not successful.

Papyrus documents from Hellenistic and Roman Egypt provide a unique and direct source of information about fugitive slaves. Papyrus, the original paper, can survive for thousands of years in the desert climate and some documents survived from as early as the fourth century BCE. To begin with, census records provide statistics about slave ownership, at least among the households whose records happen to have survived. During the Ptolemaic (Hellenistic) period, slavery in Egypt was mainly confined to the Greek population, since slavery was a Greek institution, uncommon in Egypt in this period. Even among the ruling class of Greek immigrants, slave ownership was not common and it was almost unknown among the Egyptians. By the Roman period, slavery had become more common: about 15 percent of all households possessed at least one slave (Bagnall 2011, 57–58). In both periods, we find evidence of runaway slaves on papyri: public notices described them and offered rewards; letters requested assistance in tracking and capturing them. For example, three papyri in different hands contain identical and detailed descriptions of the runaway slave Thorax, a Cilician, round-faced with a scar under his left eyebrow, eighteen years old. Another, later papyrus refers to Thorax and may indicate that he'd been caught and been sent to work on a farm as punishment for running away (Scholl 1990, #61–63, 170). The WANTED posters for Thorax date to the third century BCE, but other such documents are as late as the fourth century CE – seven centuries of primary evidence for fugitive slaves!

From another third-century BCE papyrus, historians learn that a slave stole a horse and sold it to fund his escape attempt (Scholl 1990, #66). Whenever they could, fugitive slaves stole something when they took off – some coins for their journey or something valuable to sell. This particular fugitive had done well, since a horse might have a market value twice as high as the slave himself. Another pair of runaways, in the second century BCE, managed to make off with a tidy stash: three minae of gold coins, five thousand bronze coins, ten pearls, and an expensive jewelry box (*Papyrus Paris* 10 in Shaw 2001, 56).

Another payoff from the papyri references to slave flight under the Ptolemies is statistical: a large majority of the fugitives are male even though most slaves in Egypt seem

Figure 9.2 Egyptian WANTED poster for runaway slave. "If any person finds a slave named Philippos ... about fourteen years old, light in complexion, who speaks haltingly, has a flat nose ... wearing a ... woolen garment and a used shoulder belt, he should bring him to the army post and receive ... " You may be able to make out *Philipon*, in the first line: the lambda and second iota run together, but if you can identify phi and pi, the rest is clear. *Source*: P.Oxy. LI 3616, trans in Shaw 2001. Courtesy of The Egypt Exploration Society and the Imaging Papyri Project, Oxford.

to have been women (Scholl 1990, #61–85; Bagnall and Frier 1994, 158). Male slaves seemed more likely to run away than women – as is the case in almost all New World slave societies and even among slaves today.[7] Women may have been unused to traveling on their own or unable to do so without attracting unwanted attention; their ability to find work other than prostitution may have been limited – and even male fugitives faced an uncertain future. Another factor may be the stronger family ties of women slaves, especially those with children: a fourth-century Greek text advises allowing slaves to have children, "as hostages for their good behavior" ([Aristotle], *Oeconomica* 1344b18; contrast Xenophon, *Oeconomicus* 9.5). In the Egyptian household we mentioned above, it is only the women with children who have not run away. And remember the unchained women and children, depicted following the coffle of male slaves on the gravestone of Aulus Kapreilius Timotheus (see the section in Chapter 4 on The Slave Trade and Slave Traders).

Naturally, masters used any means possible to recover what they thought of as their valuable property. In addition to the WANTED posters we find in Egypt, masters tried to get their slaves back on their own: one unlucky master from Athens went abroad in pursuit of three runaway slaves and ended up captured by a privateer and enslaved himself ([Demosthenes] 53.6). In the late Roman Republic, Cicero, a powerful and well-connected

---

7 E.g., Gaspar 1985, 207–208; Walwin 1994, 286, Bales 2012, 111–112.

former consul, was able to write to a provincial governor, whom he knew, to ask him to arrest a slave Cicero believed was hiding out in his province (*Letters to Friends* 13.77). The degree of state assistance varied. In Roman (and probably Hellenistic) Egypt, officials not only posted public notices but were also supposed to arrest fugitive slaves themselves (Llewelyn 1997; Watson 1992, 1347). Roman officials were finally assigned this responsibility in the second century CE. Earlier the government only took active measures when a master suspected that somebody else was harboring his fugitive slave on their property.

If they recovered them, masters punished runaways severely. A slave in Aristophanes, contemplating flight, notes that it can be bad for the skin (Aristophanes, *Knights* 21–28). He may be referring to whipping, but masters also tattooed or branded runaway slaves, often on the face (Kamen 2010; e.g., Petronius, *Satyricon* 103). Such marks were both a punishment and a way to make flight much harder, by marking a person permanently as a slave. Later, slave collars served the same function (see Figure 12.2 below). The Apuleius quotation with which we started this chapter mentions tattooing, as well as revealing another tactic of masters: to keep half of their slaves' heads shaved. It would be hard for a fugitive slave to blend into a crowd with a half-shaven head and everybody in the Roman world must have known what that particular hairstyle meant.

Roman laws governing the activities of the slave catcher, the *fugitivarius*, shed light on some unexpected tactics used by owners and by fugitive slaves (Daube 1952). The expertise of *bona fide* slave catchers made freedom more precarious for a runaway slave: one can imagine them as ancient "bounty hunters" and perhaps pretty effective. What worried our legal sources was that some slave catchers colluded with slaves to con their masters – not that we need to have much sympathy for them! Instead of a mix of pay and reward, a slave catcher could offer to buy a fugitive slave for a low price from a master content to recoup some of his loss. In theory the slave catcher would then profit by finding and capturing the slave and selling him at market price. But suppose the slave and slave catcher were in cahoots? Then the slave catcher would pretend to catch the slave and then manumit him for a price. If the manumission price was more than what *fugitivarius* paid for the "runaway" slave but less than what the slave would otherwise have had to pay for his freedom, then both slave and slave catcher gained. The slave gained legal freedom at a discount – and maybe he used money he'd stolen from his master rather than just his *peculium*. The "slave catcher" profited from the difference between the price he paid to buy the slave and the amount he'd taken for manumission – and he didn't actually have to track down the slave. Roman jurists repeatedly tried to prevent this scam with laws against the purchase of an absent slave. Their lack of success probably explains why these laws needed to be reenacted and improved.

Even without worrying about real slave catchers, it was hard enough to be a runaway slave, trying to make a fresh start in a dangerous world with few resources or connections. The destitution of runaway slaves was proverbial: for example, one letter preserved on papyrus begs for help, "so I don't perish penniless like the runaway slaves" (Scholl 1990, 1.267–268, #76). But fugitive slaves sometimes found somebody to help them. One puzzling case emerges from a curse tablet. Curse tablets were usually inscribed sheets of lead buried to enlist the assistance of supernatural entities against an enemy. Many survive, including one written in the Hellenistic period and found on Amorgos, a Greek island. It invokes the aid of Demeter and contains the following complaint:

> [Epaphroditus] has taken off my slaves, has led them into evil ways, indoctrinated them, advised them, misled them, he/rejoiced (in my misery) . . . he has them wandering round the market place, he persuaded them to run away. . . . The same man has bewitched my handmaid so he could take her as his wife against my wishes. And for this reason he had her flee together with the others . . . may he come to an evil end together with all that belongs to him." (*Survey of Greek Defixiones* [Jordan 1985] #60, trans. in Versnel 1999, 125–126)

As curse tablets often do, this seems to express the anger and hatred of a person otherwise lacking power. It is a mystery why the writer is unable to take Epaphroditus to court or to punish and retain his own slaves, a humiliating situation. Different scenarios can be imagined, but all of them involve some unusual lack of the power one would expect of a slaveholder.

The behavior of Epaphroditus seems like an exceptional case, but the Romans repeatedly enacted laws against the sheltering of runaway slaves, apparently a recurring problem. People might harbor a runaway for various reasons. We shouldn't rule out sympathy for slaves, especially those with particularly pitiful tales of abuse. But, some later laws specify, "whoever hides a fugitive slave is himself a thief" (*Justinian's Digest* 11.4.1–3). This implies that the person sheltering the runaway might be aiming to acquire a worker, not to help out a victim of oppression. Other laws allow those searching for fugitive slaves to enter other people's properties and even specify that they can enter the lands of Roman senators, all of whom were extremely wealthy slaveholders. Some of the enactments also promised amnesty for the guilty in a way atypical of Roman treatment either of slaves or of thieves, but explicable if the culprits included prominent men. All this suggests the possibility that large landowners, competing for labor, sometimes tried to attract other people's slaves as workers. That laws against this needed to be reasserted suggest the wealth and power of those breaking them and the competition for agricultural labor that presumably motivated them.

Escape to a free life was often impossible or too difficult either for immediate reasons – chains, locked doors, and guard dogs – or more distant fears such as recapture and punishment, separation from friends and family, destitution and hunger. As a result, many Greek and Roman slaves committed suicide, a phenomenon observed also in New World slave societies. In some cases, this was prompted by the threat of punishment or the humiliation of it. In Apuleius' *The Golden Ass*, a dog took and ate some expensive meat from the slave cook: "his master was demanding his dinner right away, so the wretched and terrified cook said farewell to his little boy and picked up a cord to hang himself" – but his "wife" intervenes with a better plan (8.31; cf. Seneca, *Epistles* 4.4). Theophrastus depicts a man watching another's house slave being whipped and remarking that "one of his slaves hanged himself after a beating like that" (*Characters* 12.12). By this point, you will not be surprised that Theophrastus does not disapprove of whipping, even if it sometimes led to suicide. Rather his target is the tactlessness of bringing up this unfortunate and costly possibility.

In another case, Symmachus, a leading noble in the late Roman Empire, was preparing to display his beneficence and wealth by producing a gladiatorial show, but 29 of the captives managed to kill themselves while still in training. Symmachus felt neither sympathy at the wretched prospects that made these slaves kill themselves nor admiration at their resolve. He was furious at "this band of slaves, worse than Spartacus" (*Letters* 2.46). To modern sensibilities, this seems an odd comparison of miserable suicides with the famous leader of a terrifying slave rebellion. But these unhappy slaves had wasted Symmachus' money by inconsiderately killing themselves rather than fighting and dying in the arena to amuse the populace and bring him glory. In contrast, Seneca, a Roman senator and Stoic philosopher, views a similar case as an example of the control over fate one can exert even in the most desperate circumstances:

> While one of the Germans was engaged in a training session for the morning [gladiatorial] spectacles, he went off to relieve himself. No other opportunity was ever allowed to him to have an unguarded moment of privacy. In the latrine, he picked up the stick tipped with a sponge, which was provided for the purposes of cleaning one's private parts. Then, jamming the whole thing down his throat, he blocked his windpipe and suffocated himself to death. What a joke to play on death! (*Letters* 70.20–21, trans. Shaw 2001, 49)

Among gladiators, the danger of suicide was apparently high and strict precautions were taken to prevent it; these cases were reported because they were so exceptional. In the slave population in general, suicide was more often an option, but it represented a rather grim assertion of agency.

Murder and Reprisal

Slaves killed their masters for many reasons. We cannot assume that every case falls into the category of slave resistance – just as with theft and embezzlement. Because of the status of the perpetrator and of the victim, such homicides were shocking, scary, and likely to be reported in our sources. The customary reprisals also made it clear that slaveholders viewed a master's murder in terms of control over the slave population rather than as the act of an individual. We know the most about two Roman cases.

Pliny, a wealthy and powerful senator, relates in a letter the murder of Larcius Macedo. Macedo was also a senator of high status, son of a freedman but a cruel master to his slaves: "he forgot that his own father had been a slave or, rather, he remembered it too well" (Pliny, *Letters* 3.14.1). Some of his slaves surrounded him while he was washing in his baths. They choked and beat him until they thought he was dead and then threw him on the hot tiles to check. When he didn't move, they brought him out pretending that he had passed out from the heat. More loyal slaves and his mistresses – mentioned without further explanation – received him and began to shout and wail. He came to and the slaves fled; most of them were caught and the others were still being hunted down when Pliny wrote his letter. Macedo died from his injuries a few days later, but he "enjoyed, while alive, the consolation of vengeance that is customary for those who are murdered." Even though Pliny noted that Larcius was cruel, he concludes with a complaint about the hard lot of masters: "nobody is safe just because they are gentle and kind." But what was the customary "consolation of vengeance"? And why did *all* the slaves run away?

Throughout classical antiquity, the state exacted savage and collective reprisals whenever a slave murdered his master. Already in the fifth century, the Athenian orator Antiphon mentions the collective punishment of slaves in such cases. He relates that a twelve-year-old slave attempted to kill his master but lost his cool and fled, leaving the knife in the wound. Antiphon adds that if the master had died and the culprit was not found out – for nobody would have suspected the boy – all of the slaves in the house would have been executed (5.69).

The Romans took this collective punishment a step further with a practice codified in a law called the *Senatus Consultum Silanianum* and known both from legal discussions and one particular case narrated by Tacitus. The basic idea is that all slaves who might conceivably have prevented a murder – all those who were under the same roof or close enough to hear shouts – were to be interrogated under torture and then executed. Two lines of thinking, not entirely consistent with each other, justified this brutal procedure and the details of its application.

First, slaves were supposed to protect their masters with their lives. Those who failed to do this deserved death – and the law applied even for slaves who failed to prevent a murder by an outsider. The law was interpreted strictly: even if an armed assailant threatened a slave with death, he or she had no excuse for not shouting for help. The slave should be executed to prevent other slaves from "worrying about their own safety when their master was in danger" (*Justinian's Digest* 29.5.1.28). This was a harsh standard, but it at least attempted to find culpability in those to be executed. The old and infirm, children, the blind, deaf, and insane were all off the hook.

The security of masters among numerous and hostile foreign slaves provided the second line of justification of this law. In the case that we'll consider below, Tacitus recreates a speech in the Senate by the jurist Cassius that refers to the threat that the slave population presents and the necessity of terror to keep them in line. Cassius counters the complaint that the innocent will die if the law is enforced with a reference to the process of decimation: the execution of every tenth man in a Roman army unit that fled in battle. Cassius argues that in both cases the public benefit of exemplary punishment more than makes up for the injustice to some individuals (Tacitus, *Annals* 14.44). In the case of Larcius Macedo, it is quite possible that even the slaves Pliny describes as loyal were rounded up, tortured for information, and executed along with the murderers.

An even more notorious case involved the murder of Pedanius Secundus and the execution of his household slaves (Tacitus, *Annals* 14.42–45). One of Pedanius' slaves killed him, either because Pedanius refused him manumission after agreeing on terms for it or because of a love triangle. Pedanius was a former consul and the city-prefect (something like a mayor) of Rome itself; many slaves lived in his house in Rome. The *Senatus Consultum Silanianum* required them all to be questioned under torture and then executed. The Roman Senate met to reconsider the decision, obviously an unpopular one, but, in the end, decided to enforce this brutal law. Rioters with stones and torches at first prevented the verdict from being carried out – recall the number of ex-slaves and their descendants in the urban population – but the emperor Nero ordered the Praetorian Guard to line the streets through which the slaves were marched. The death sentence was carried out on about four hundred innocent slaves, quite possibly by burning them alive.

Conclusion

The murder of Pedanius Secundus and the spectacular and brutal punishment of his slaves was a real occurrence. Yet historians need to be careful not to fall into the "man bites dog" trap by emphasizing too much this extraordinary event, reported for that very reason. You might even be tempted to argue that such a murder and the spectacular and violent reprisal had little to do with the lives of most Roman slaves, who did their best within the system and worked towards manumission; it was not even relevant to the remaining slaves, who resisted their oppression as best they could in less dramatic and often surreptitious ways, the tactics we have focused on in this chapter.

This may be going too far. Even if only a fraction of slaves successfully ran away, the chance that they could played a large role in how masters thought about and treated their slaves, whether more kindly or with suspicion. It was the same with murder. Masters like Pliny were fascinated and upset by cases where slaves had killed their masters. For their part, most slaves would have heard about the *Senatus Consultum Silanianum* and would know how brutal the slaveholding class could be, even if their own master seemed fair to them most of the time. I suspect that the awareness of such unusual events shaped the way slaves and masters lived together and thought and felt about each other. And, speaking of exceptional events that cast long shadows, it is unlikely that either slaves or masters ever forgot the bloody rebellions of Spartacus and his predecessors in Sicily, our next topic.

Suggested Reading

The debate over slave agency can be followed in Brown 2010 (in favor of even greater attention) and in the critique in Johnson 2003. Bradley 1990 is a classic article, which finds evidence of resistance to slavery in the ubiquitous ancient references to slave misbehavior. McKeown 2011 provides a balanced treatment of resistance to Greek slavery with a prudent emphasis on the difficulty of our evidence. Eidinow 2012 investigates the light that tablets with questions for the oracle of Dodona in northwestern Greece shed on slave life there in the classical period. Joshel and Petersen 2014 investigate how archaeology can inform our reconstruction of Roman slave life, for example, how different house designs provided opportunities for resistance or at least places where slaves could escape their master's surveillance. Kajanto 1970 and Williams 2006 analyze Tacitus and Pliny's accounts of the murders of Pedanius Secundus and Larcius Macedo respectively and the application of the *SC Silanianum* in both cases. I have written two essays that treat many of the topics in this chapter in more detail: Hunt 2016c and 2017.

10

Revolts

Nothing could be more naïve – or arrogant – than to ask why a Nat Turner [leader of a violent slave revolt in Virginia in 1831] did not appear on every plantation in the South, as if, from the comfort of our living rooms, we have a right to tell others, and retrospectively at that, when, how, and why to risk their lives and those of their loved ones. As the odds and circumstances become clearer, there is less difficulty in understanding the apparent infrequency of slave revolts throughout history and less difficulty in appreciating the extent of the rebels' courage and resourcefulness and the magnitude of their impact on world history.

Eugene Genovese, *From Rebellion to Revolution* (1979), 1

Introduction

Large slave revolts are rare. They do not occur in societies with a small proportion of slaves, but only in true slave societies. Even in slave societies, rebellions only spread under extremely favorable circumstances. The rebellion that eventually resulted in the state of Haiti may have been the only successful slave revolt in history. The classical world, too, saw long stretches of relative calm and only a few major slave revolts during the late Roman Republic. The everyday patterns of resistance and accommodation we discussed last chapter mattered more directly to a far greater number of slaves than did slave revolts. But we should not underestimate the psychological impact of the revolts on contemporary masters and slaves. After all, some masters and some slaves were, or had recently been, locked in a life-and-death struggle. Slaves had tortured, raped, and killed masters and those rebels who didn't die in battle usually ended up publically crucified or executed in some other horrible way. In his account of 64 CE, Tacitus notes an attempted uprising of gladiators. It was quickly put down, but the Roman commons were already talking about Spartacus and ancient disasters.[1] This was more than a hundred and thirty years after Spartacus' death; closer to the time of the great revolts the possibility of slave rebellion must have played a larger role in people's hopes, fears, and attitudes. Slave revolts, like murders committed by slaves, had effects extending far beyond the participants.

---

1 Tacitus, *Annals* 15.46; cf. Horace, *Odes* 3.14.19 and *Epodes* 16.5.

Ancient Greek and Roman Slavery, First Edition. Peter Hunt.
© 2018 Peter Hunt. Published 2018 by John Wiley & Sons, Ltd.

We should be careful to avoid, however, one false inference: neither slave revolts nor their absence tells us what slaves really felt about their masters. Slaves in revolt often killed their masters, but this does not mean that slaves usually wanted to kill their masters and could only act on these feelings during a revolt. The stakes were high and so uprisings were typically conducted on both sides with the utmost ferocity. But occasionally even slaves in revolt distinguished between kind and brutal masters and spared the former. And consider an obvious point: high estimates of the number of slaves under Spartacus reach beyond a hundred thousand, but low estimates of the total number of slaves in Italy at that time are over a million. So even when Spartacus was at his height, marching up and down the peninsula, only a fraction of the slaves in Italy had gone to join him.

Likewise, we cannot infer that slaves loved their masters or accepted their slavery, just because they didn't revolt. Rebellion was almost hopeless. Indeed, most uprisings were quickly put down. By the time of Spartacus, more than a half-dozen earlier revolts had failed with almost invariably fatal results for the slaves involved – and those are only the ones important enough for us to hear about. Given these bad odds, it is not surprising that slaves, however much they hated slavery, did not rise up more often; what needs to be explained is why they ever did. To be more precise, historians aim to understand why slaves revolt in some places and times and not in others. Why didn't Greek chattel slaves rebel? Why did the Helots? And, most of all, why was the late Republic the scene of some of the largest and most sustained slave revolts in history?

Classical and Hellenistic Greece

In the 130s BCE, the slaves around Laurion, the mining area of Athens, rose up and killed their overseers. They took the town of Sounion and ravaged the countryside for a long time before the revolt was suppressed (Athenaeus, *The Learned Banqueters* 6.272f). This rebellion had a great deal to do with the violent chaos of the second century BCE and the contemporaneous slave revolt in Roman Sicily, but it had no antecedents in Athens or Greece in the classical period. Classical Greece seems to have been one of those slave societies in which slaves were unable to mount significant armed revolts on their own. Of course, slaves fled their masters. Wars between city-states could make flight easier. For instance, Thucydides reports that more than 20,000 slaves – a large proportion of them skilled slaves – fled Athens after the Spartans established a fort nearby at Decelea (7.27.5).

On the rare occasion when slaves openly defied their masters, it was in the context of an enemy invasion. For example, when the Athenians were besieging Syracuse in 414–413 BCE, some slaves within Syracuse refused orders, came together, and demanded to be allowed to fight as hoplites and to receive equal rations of food. We only hear of this because of the stratagem that allowed the Syracusans to defuse the mutiny, the unscrupulous and unimaginative trick of seizing and killing the slave leaders during a conference to discuss their demands (Polyaenus, *Strategemata* 1.43.1).

We also hear of a Greek slave *maroon*, a term growing out of Latin American slavery. A maroon is a community of escaped slaves, usually living in rugged or otherwise inaccessible country. As you might imagine, slaveholding classes hated maroons and usually tried to destroy them. So, maroons were often at war with their masters and can be hard to distinguish from revolts. To some extent, a slave revolt is a maroon on the offensive, and a maroon is an unambitious slave revolt. The mountainous Greek island of Chios, for example, had longstanding problems with slave discontent. Thucydides reports that the Chians had more slaves than any other Greek city – except for the Lacedaemonians (Sparta) – and that consequently these slaves were punished harshly when they misbehaved. When the Athenians set up a fort to besiege Chios in the last phase of the Peloponnesian War (412/411 BCE), many of these slaves deserted to them and, knowing the countryside, did a great deal of damage to the estates of their former masters (Thucydides 8.40.2 with Hunt 1998, 102–115). Later, in the Hellenistic period, we hear of a maroon on Chios and its legendary leader, Drimakos (Athenaeus, *The Learned Banqueters* 6.265d–266d). Relations between the Chians and this maroon were naturally hostile. The slaves raided the estates of the Chians and welcomed fugitive slaves; the Chians tried to find and kill the members of the maroon. Under Drimakos, the slaves held their own. They were even able to arrange a truce: in return for being allowed to live unmolested, the slaves limited their plundering, and they would only accept new fugitive slaves if Drimakos determined that they had really been mistreated. But the truce did not last: the Chians put a price on Drimakos' head and, when he grew old, he convinced his young boyfriend to kill him, to cut off his head, and to claim the reward and his freedom. This sounds more like a good story than the truth; we know that Drimakos became a cult figure in Chios with his own shrine and sacrifices – and legends (Forsdyke 2012, 37–89).

That we find so few similar cases from Classical and Hellenistic Greece suggests that the slave population was not volatile. Most Greek slaves were newly captured males (see Chapter 3) and thus the type most likely to revolt – as we'll explore below. But other factors were not favorable for rebellion. The proportion of slaves, between one quarter and a half of the population, was too small. And the slaveholding units were not large either. Plato mentions a man with fifty slaves as exceptionally rich (Plato, *Republic* 578d–e). In contrast, three quarters of Jamaican slaves lived on plantations with a larger number of slaves than this; on Caribbean islands in the eighteenth century, slaves often constituted 80–90 percent of the population (Kolchin 1993, 101). It is not surprising that Caribbean slave systems were notoriously prone to violence and rebellion whereas classical Greek slavery was not. Finally, Greek slaves were heterogeneous relative to other slave societies and would have found it hard to unite and collaborate. At Athens – to take the best-known case – slaves came from many different ethnic groups. And their different and separate experiences of slavery precluded solidarity: skilled slaves in various crafts were numerous and probably had little fellow-feeling for or even contact with the slaves working on farms in the countryside, much less the mine slaves. Greek slaves could not match the superior numbers, resources, weapons, and organization of the free population, dominated by slaveholders. But the Helots of Sparta were a different story.

The Helots

Neither the Spartans nor their Helots much resembled the Athenians and their chattel slaves. The Spartans were the ruling class of a large, overwhelmingly agricultural area in the Peloponnese including Laconia and Messenia. Their numbers were relatively small – perhaps around 10,000 men in 500 BCE – and declined throughout the classical period. Yet they controlled the most powerful Greek state throughout most of the archaic and classical period. Part of the explanation is that the Spartans were professional, highly trained warriors. Unlike the amateur soldiers who constituted other Greek armies, the Spartans did not practice any other trades or farm the land themselves. As a result, their military prowess, bravery, and willingness to sacrifice their lives for the state were legendary. Presumably, the Spartans needed to spend some of their time managing their estates, but they could devote themselves primarily to military training because Helots performed the actual farm work and then handed over a portion of their harvest each year.

Rather than "bought barbarians," the Helots were Greeks. They were not a homogeneous population but fell roughly into two groups: the Helots of Laconia, the Spartan homeland, and those of Messenia, a large area of the western Peloponnese, which is separated from Laconia by a mountain range. There is evidence of discontent among both groups, but it was primarily the Messenians who mounted large, long-lasting revolts against the Spartans. Early in the archaic period Sparta conquered Messenia. A generation later, in the seventh century BCE, an uprising by Messenia provoked the legendary and hard-fought Second Messenian War, the context for the martial poems of Tyrtaeus, still recited in the classical period:

> Do not fear throngs of men or run in flight, but let a man hold his shield straight toward the front ranks, despising life and loving the black death-spirits no less than the rays of the sun. (Tyrtaeus, fr. 11 (Stobaeus, *Anthology* 4.9.16), trans. Gerber 1999)

Despite Tyrtaeus and his exhortation about "loving the black death-spirits," we know few or no reliable details about either war: even the dates are highly uncertain. More surprising is our poor information about insurrections in the classical period when we would expect better information. Helot revolt was apparently not a congenial topic of conversation for the Spartans, a taciturn and secretive bunch to begin with.

The most famous uprising took place after an earthquake, probably around 464 BCE, and may have lasted ten years.[2] The Messenians reportedly wiped out a Spartan unit of 300 men, and they threatened Sparta itself. The rebels eventually fell back to a base near Mt. Ithome in Messenia. To put down the revolt Sparta called on its allies for armed assistance, as various city-states reminded the Spartans for generations to come. At one point the Spartans began to suspect that an Athenian army, also called in to assist them, might do something revolutionary, that is, change sides. They sent the Athenians home, alone of their allies. This offended the Athenians and led to our first definite case of a continuing pattern where Sparta's enemies took advantage of Helot discontent (Hunt 1998, 62–82). We can't tell whether the Spartans' original suspicions of the Athenians were justified or not. Yet, when the last rebels at Ithome were allowed a safe conduct out of the Peloponnese on condition that they would never return, the Athenians settled them in Naupactus, a small city on the Gulf of Corinth that the Athenians had captured. During the Peloponnesian War (431–404 BCE) the Athenians also established a fortified base at Pylos, on the coast of Messenia, and with Messenian help captured a Spartan detachment of several hundred men. The Athenians then posted some of the Messenians from Naupactus at Pylos to raid and make trouble for the Spartans. This dismayed the Spartans, who feared further revolts (Thucydides 4.41.2–3). Adding insult

---

2 Thucydides 1.101–103, Diodorus 11.63–64; Herodotus 5.49.8, 9.35.2, 9.9.64.2.

to injury, the Messenians and Naupactians even commissioned a Nikē (victory goddess) by the famous sculptor Paionius. This statue, prominently displayed at Olympia, must have galled the Spartans, even though the inscription doesn't actually mention them – reportedly out of fear (Pausanias, *Description of Greece* 5.26.1). But the Athenians were not fully committed to the Messenian cause. During a break in the war, they even agreed to a short-lived treaty with Sparta that included the clause, usual in Spartan alliances, that the Athenians were to help the Spartans "if their slave population [the Helots] revolted" (Thucydides 5.23.3). In the end, the Athenians lost the Peloponnesian War and even Naupactus with its Messenian exile community fell into Spartan hands.

A generation later, however, the Thebans succeeded where the Athenians had failed. A year after they defeated the Spartan army at the battle of Leuctra (371 BCE), they marched into the Peloponnese. Among other activities aimed at destroying Spartan prestige and power, Thebes liberated Messenia and helped build strong walls for its new capital, Messene, an act that greatly reduced Messenia's vulnerability to Spartan reconquest. The epitaph of Epaminondas, the great Theban general boasts:

> By our plans was Sparta deprived of her glory, and holy Messene received back her children at last . . . And all Greece was independent and free. (Pausanias, *Description of Greece* 9.15.6)

The loss of Messenia cemented the decline of Sparta from the dominant political and military power in mainland Greece to a second-tier city, always hoping to retake Messenia but never succeeding.

Even when there was no open revolt, the need to keep the Helots down loomed large in Spartan thinking. Every year the Spartans' *ephors*, their most important elected officials, declared war against the Helots so that Spartans would not incur the ritual guilt attached to murder committed outside of war (Plutarch, *Lycurgus* 28 citing Aristotle). It is unlikely that most Spartans had occasion to murder a Helot, but terror did play a large role in the Spartans' treatment of the Helots. For example, Thucydides relates one shocking incident (4.80). During the Peloponnesian War, the Spartans offered freedom to any Helot who claimed to have done outstanding military service for Sparta. These Helots went around the temples, garlanded as if they were celebrating their freedom, but they were later all killed – "And nobody knew how each one died." In this account the threat presented by good Helot soldiers outweighed their demonstrated loyalty. Modern historians don't even agree that this massacre really took place, but Thucydides was a contemporary and usually reliable historian (Paradiso 2004; *contra* Harvey 2004). That Thucydides would believe such a story, whether true or not, is evidence of the Spartans' well-founded distrust and fear of the Helots and the brutality they relied on to keep them down. Why were the Helots such a threat? Why were they more capable of revolt than the slaves in the rest of Greece? At least four main factors played a role: potential allies both inside and outside of Spartan territory, the number of Helots, their military service, and their organization.

The Spartans were called the *homoioi*, "the equals," because they espoused an egalitarian lifestyle with the aim of minimizing internal conflict. Some historians consider this ideal a response to the threat the Helots posed and trace it all the way back to the bitter Second Messenian War. Spartan practice did not always live up to this ideal of unity. One case was particularly startling: Thucydides reports that Pausanias, a victorious Spartan general, promised the Helots freedom and citizenship if they supported his planned coup against the government. The authorities, however, discovered and foiled the plot (1.132–34; cf. Herodotus 6.74–75). And between the full Spartan citizens and the Helots lay several subordinate classes, about whom we usually know little beyond their names. Cinadon, an "inferior," conspired against the Spartans in the early fourth century, but he was betrayed, captured, and executed. The historian Xenophon, who lived with the Spartans and ought to have known, depicts Cinadon as claiming that all the subordinate classes hated the Spartans (Xenophon, *Hellenica* 3.3.6) – it was not just the Helots. This claim could well be an exaggeration, but the discontent of the Helots was obviously not the only tension within Spartan society.

Even more significant were the foreign interventions we have already noted: Sparta's external enemies, most conspicuously Athens and Thebes, made common cause with the Messenians in order to harm Sparta. Even after the liberation of Messenia, Aristotle likened the remaining Laconian Helots to enemies waiting in ambush to take advantage of Spartan misfortunes and emphasizes that this situation is made worse by the fact that Sparta is surrounded by hostile states willing to ally with rebels (Aristotle, *Politics* 1269a 39–b5).

The sheer number of Helots compared to the Spartans was another important factor. At the battle of Plataea against the Persians (479 BCE), seven armed Helots reportedly accompanied each Spartan soldier (Herodotus 9.10.1 with Hunt 1997). This may overestimate the actual disproportion of population between the two groups, but this was still significant: a calculation based on the total agricultural capacity of Spartan territory and number of Spartans suggests that Helots outnumbered Spartans by more than two to one (Scheidel 2003, 242–243).

As the story about Plataea suggests, the Helots served in the army more regularly than did slaves in other cities. On the one hand, the Spartans were professional soldiers, the most formidable infantry in Greece, and typically campaigned with numerous allies. None of this was likely to encourage would-be rebels. On the other hand, when Helots accompanied the Spartans on campaign, they would have become aware of their superior numbers vis-à-vis the Spartans. They would also have gained military experience and confidence.

Finally, several features of Helot society made communication and concerted action easier than is usual in slave populations. The Helots all spoke the same language; many shared a sense of themselves as Messenian. In the areas more distant from Sparta, including all of Messenia, the Helots may have run their farms themselves and just handed over a portion of their produce to their Spartan lords. We hear hints of Helots in positions of authority, probably appointed to supervise this process, but natural leaders in times of revolt. Most Helots probably lived in their own villages and families. All these aspects of social organization made the Helots more dangerous.

To historians, these factors in the Helots' tendency to revolt are all familiar and common sources of power: what group or state is not stronger when it has a large and unified population, available allies, and its enemies are divided? But some of the factors that made the Helots a threat do not correspond closely with those that typically make slave populations prone to rebellion. Most conspicuously, in the New World – and in Roman Sicily and Italy as we shall see – it was newly enslaved men who are most likely to rebel; the Helots remained dangerous generation after generation. Their uprisings seem more like the insurrections of serfs, peasants, or subordinate ethnic groups than like slave rebellions.

Although this is a complicated and controversial issue among historians, I believe that the Helots resembled serfs more than chattel slaves. Like many classes of peasants, they owed the Spartans "rents," both a share of their harvest, like sharecroppers, and some personal service. That they could be described as gaining freedom or running away shows that they were normally not free to leave: they were not just peasants, but bound peasants, like serfs. That they primarily lived in stable villages and families made them unlike slaves in Orlando Patterson's definition in terms of natal alienation (see Chapter 2). But, although ancient Greeks usually referred to the Helots as Helots, some Greek texts refer to them as *douloi* (for example, Thucydides 4.118.7, 5.23.3) – which is the common and usually unambiguous Greek word for slaves. In addition, one tricky passage may imply that Helots could be sold, only not across the border, that is, outside of Spartan territory; if such sale were common, the Helots would be slaves (Ephorus [*FGrH* 70 F117] in Strabo, *Geography* 8.5.4).

Whether we think of the Helots as slaves of a particular kind, subject to "Helotic slavery," or as a serf-like class, they were different from the largely imported, non-Greek slaves in most other city-states.[3] They were much more capable of revolt, but this ability does not have the same roots as it does in other slave populations. So we have considered one population of slaves, the chattel slaves in typical Greek cities, who didn't often revolt, and another population, the Helots, who were not really slaves – in my opinion. In contrast, the late Roman Republic was marked by huge rebellions by people who were incontrovertibly slaves; it thus provides historians with richer material for understanding and explaining slave revolts.

The Roman Slave Wars

Although we hear of insurrections as early as the start of the second century BCE and as late as 27 CE, major Roman slave revolts were primarily a feature of the late Republic (133–30 BCE): the first Sicilian revolt lasted from 137 (perhaps) to 132 BCE, the second Sicilian slave war from 104 to 100 BCE, and Spartacus' rebellion from 73 to 71 BCE. Each of these uprisings involved armies of rebel slaves numbering in the tens of thousands. Each inflicted defeats on regular Roman army units over the course of several years. The Romans only prevailed after they had committed the same impressive military resources to fighting their own slaves that they typically devoted to important foreign wars. For example, to defeat Spartacus, Crassus commanded a special force of at least eight legions, around 40,000 legionaries as well as auxiliary forces probably equally numerous (Appian, *Civil Wars* 1.118). About twenty years later Julius Caesar would conquer Gaul (approximately modern France) with an army of similar size.

The geography of the revolts was equally impressive. Sicily was the first overseas Roman province, a large and rich island dotted with famous and populous Greek and Phoenician cities and a major source of grain for Rome. For two four-year periods barely a generation apart, slave rebels overran large swathes of the island's countryside. Spartacus and his army marched all the way up and down the Italian Peninsula itself, from Cisalpine Gaul to the Straits of Messina. This was a horrifying spectacle for the Romans and reminiscent of the devastation wrecked by Hannibal in the Second Punic War (218–201 BCE). And, as in that famously bitter conflict, after one defeat, the Roman Senate even feared an attack on the city of Rome.

---

3 Some Greek states did have subordinate groups, poorly known to us but perhaps similar to the Helots, e.g., the *penestae* of Thessaly.

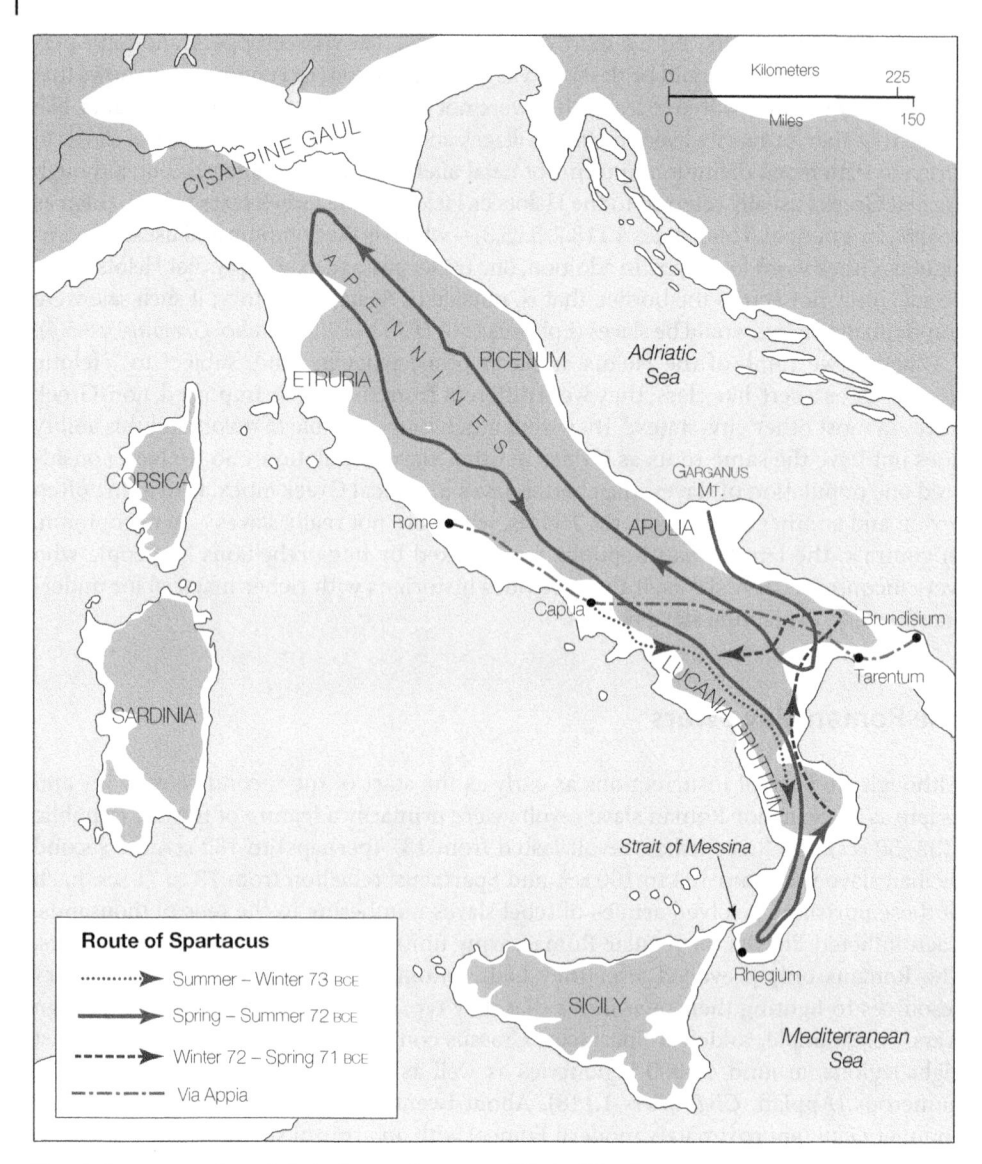

Map 5 Spartacus at large in Italy. *Source*: Courtesy of Wesley Wood.

Thus these rebels intruded into the world of military and political events, the traditional subject matter of history, in a way that most slaves never did. It is not surprising that several historians related the stories of the big three slave revolts and of various smaller uprisings as well. What is surprising is that some of these ancient accounts show sympathy for the slaves; thus, we find not one, but at least two, attitudes towards the rebels (Urbainczyk 2008, 81–90).

Some sources portray them as purely evil, violent, and even bestial, the typical reaction of slaveholders to rebellious slaves. Sallust, for example, was a Roman senator and historian. He was a teenager at the time of Spartacus' revolt and provides a lurid account of the slaves' entry into Lucania in Italy: they immediately began to rape the women, young and old, and mutilated the men, whom they left lying half-alive; they plundered and burned houses; the local slaves revealed where their masters had hidden valuables or where they themselves were hiding (Sallust, *Histories*, fr. 44 b–c [Book 3] in Ramsay 2015). Such violence finds parallels in modern slave revolts, such as the Haitian revolution of 1791; in nineteenth-century Virginia, Nat Turner and his rebels spared neither women nor children. Rather than considering the reasons for the slaves' anger, Sallust ascribes their brutality to the band's "barbarian and servile natures." Yet he adds that Spartacus himself could not hold them back. Why is Spartacus depicted as trying to hold back the slaves? Rather than the arch-villain, Sallust represents Spartacus as superior to the mass of rampaging slaves.

Two later Greek authors, the biographer Plutarch (ca. 45–120 CE) and the historian Diodorus, (mid-first century BCE) go further and almost excuse the slaves for their violence. First of all, Diodorus puts the blame for the outbreak of the first Sicilian revolt on two particularly abusive slaveholders, Damophilos and his wife (34/35 2.10). The slaves killed them, but they protected their kind daughter and escorted her to safety. Diodorus claims that this showed that they were not naturally savage but were only getting revenge for what they had suffered (34/35 2.13–14). In another place, Diodorus draws the moral that sensible men should treat their slaves kindly to prevent plots and rebellions: "The more power is perverted to cruelty and lawlessness, the more the character of those subject to that power is brutalized to the point of desperation" (Diodorus 34/35 2.33, trans. Walton 1967). Even though Romans typically thought of gladiators as violent criminals who deserved their fate, Plutarch claimed the opposite of Spartacus and his original band: "They were locked up to be gladiators because their owners were unjust, not because they were guilty of anything" (Plutarch, *Crassus* 8.1). It may be significant that Plutarch and Diodorus were Greeks subject to Rome; their loyalties were mixed, and they subscribed to a view of the late Roman Republic as brutal and arrogant, deserving the disasters it suffered, both the great slave revolts and the civil wars that brought down the Republic. As a result, historians today possess more balanced narratives of the rebellions than we might otherwise expect, accounts that treat the slaves as violent, but not irrationally so.

The three great revolts shared a similar trajectory. First of all, the numbers of slaves in revolt grew quickly: Spartacus' original band of seventy gladiators soon numbered in the tens of thousands, an indication that at that place and time slaves were numerous and that many were discontented enough to risk death rather than stay in slavery. Even in distant places – such as the mining district near Athens – slaves began insurrections when they heard about what was happening in Sicily or Italy and thought the revolt's initial success presented an opportunity for them too, a false hope it turns out.

The rebels' military victories were astonishing and repeated. Although the Romans assigned commanders of higher and higher rank with increasingly powerful forces to fight the slaves, they met with little success. Roman armies were defeated and noble Romans disgraced again and again. Eunus in the first Sicilian revolt captured the camps of three praetors, Roman officials and sometimes commanders of one rank below the two consuls. Two other praetors were exiled for their failures during the second Sicilian revolt. In one campaign Spartacus defeated both of the year's consuls and the governor of Cisalpine Gaul. When he was finally defeated, the Romans recaptured the eagles (sacred standards) of five Roman legions and the *fasces* (the rods and axes, symbols of state authority) of five Roman generals, who had to abandon them when they ran away from the slaves (Frontinus, *Stratagems* 2.5.34 citing Livy).

We can only imagine the joy, pride, and relief that the slaves felt when they defeated a Roman army; after all, slaves were regarded with contempt, and the Roman army was the most fearsome one in the world. For the haughty Romans, to be defeated by slaves was particularly humiliating; a later historian considered it his duty to name the disgraced generals, all members of the Roman elite: "I will not hesitate to name the generals responsible: Manlius Lentulus, Piso, and Hypsaeus. These commanders with the rank of praetor fled the battlefield, pursued by men who ought to have been arrested by slave-catchers" (Florus, *Epitome of Roman History*, 2.7). In another case, to restore discipline, Crassus took the rare step of decimation, the execution of every tenth soldier, as a punishment for some units who fled from Spartacus' army (Plutarch, *Crassus* 10.2–3; Appian, *Civil Wars* 1.14 [118]).

Still, for centuries Rome had lost battles but always won its wars. Its resources and determination were immense. For example, in case Crassus with his ten legions did not defeat Spartacus and his followers – which he did – the Senate had called back Pompey, their most famous general, with another large army from Spain. He arrived in time to hem Spartacus in and to kill some of the slaves who had escaped Crassus. The slaves could not defeat Rome and had no other viable exit strategy. For example, Plutarch reports that when Spartacus was victorious in northern Italy, he proposed that the slaves should disperse and return to their homes in Gaul and Thrace. Plutarch regards the slaves as foolish and bloodthirsty, since they reportedly preferred to pillage Italy and did in fact turn back south to eventual destruction (Plutarch, *Crassus* 9.5–6). But Plutarch's story overrates the slaves' options. If the slave army had dispersed, most of the slaves, traveling through foreign tribes in small groups would have been helpless prey. They were more likely to have ended up dead or re-enslaved than able to assert their rights in the scattered and distant homelands that they may have left decades earlier – and usually in poor circumstances. But, if the army stayed together or in large contingents, it was unlikely to be welcome anywhere. Had the rebel slaves continued out of Roman territory, they might just have ended up fighting battles against the enemies of Rome instead of against Rome itself.

Some slaves may just have wanted to pillage Italy and take violent revenge on anybody associated with their hated masters. Others may have hated the brutality of slavery as the Romans practiced it. In Sicily, Eunus had his men put on pantomime shows for a city's inhabitants just out of range of their weapons. In these dramas, slaves rose up against their masters, whom they portrayed as deserving their fate on account of their brutality and arrogance (Diodorus 34/5 2.46). Mixed up with this hatred and outrage at slaveholders was a stream of ethnic hostility towards the Romans; for many slaves came from formerly proud states that had suffered defeat and harsh treatment at the hands of Rome. They often identified themselves as Syrians, Thracians, or Gauls, Rome's victims and enemies. In Chapter 12, we'll see how hard it is to find categorical opposition to slavery in the ancient world; if any group in the ancient world contained abolitionists, rebellious slaves would seem a likely bunch. Unfortunately, other than the story about Eunus' plays, we have almost no information about the rebels' ideals. And these ideals were unlikely to have been put into practice as they struggled just to supply themselves and fight back against Roman armies.

For the Romans, the slave revolts meant the destruction of immense numbers of slaves – whom they considered valuable property – not to mention harvests lost, houses burnt, and fellow slaveholders slaughtered. The results were even worse for the rebels. At

Figure 10.1 Coin commemorating the suppression of the second Sicilian slave revolt. The descendants of the proconsul Manius Aquillius were proud even of a victory over slaves. By chance, two of them on separate occasions (70 and 18 BCE) were in charge of a Roman mint and oversaw the production of coinage commemorating their brave ancestor's deeds and his service to Sicily – or at least to the slaveholders of Sicily. The front of this coin has the word *virtus*, "manliness"; *III Vir* indicates the "three-man" mint board. The reverse depicts a Roman soldier helping up an injured or ailing woman, identified as the incarnation of Sicily, "Sicil." It also has the name, M(anius) AQUIL(lius); M(anii) F(ilius) M(anii) N(epos) is his filiation: "son of Manius and grandson of Manius." *Source*: Courtesy of Gorny & Mosch GmbH.

the end of the first Sicilian War, the Roman general tortured and then threw over a cliff all of the slaves he captured (Diodorus 34/35 2.21). At the end of Spartacus' insurrection, Crassus had the 6000 captives crucified along the entire Appian Way, a famous and busy road from Rome to Capua, about 125 miles. Until they rotted away, a traveler on the Appian War would have passed the corpse of a crucified slave every 35 to 40 yards.[4] These displays were not the only deterrent measures the Romans took. After the second Sicilian War, slaves were forbidden ever to have weapons; in theory this applied even to slave herdsmen who often needed them to protect their herds from rustlers or wild animals. The Romans loved to tell the story of a stern Sicilian governor who, upon being given a huge boar as a gift, asked who had killed it. When he discovered that a slave shepherd had speared it, he had the unlucky slave crucified (Cicero, *Verrine Orations* 2.5.7).

Nor was there much glory or profit in a war against slaves. Successful Roman generals and their armies were often honored with a triumph, a ceremonial victory march through Rome, celebrated with great fanfare. The defeat of any of the large slave uprisings would have merited a triumph, except that slaves were considered inferior and unworthy opponents. For example, Manius Aquillius put down the second Sicilian revolt as proconsul in 100 BCE. He performed the heroic feat of killing the slaves' leader Athenion in single combat (Diodorus 36.10.1). He even sustained a head wound during the fight but obtained only an *ovatio*, a less prestigious honor than a triumph. Crassus received only an *ovatio* for defeating Spartacus and was even criticized for accepting this (Plutarch, *Crassus* 11.8).

---

4 Appian, *Civil Wars* 1.14.120 with Shaw 2001, 144. Slave rebels in the New World were punished with equal ferocity well into the nineteenth century: penalties including burning alive and "live gibbetting"– and corpses were often publically displayed (Walvin 1994, 253–278).

Challenges of Revolt

Even starting a revolt was a deadly and difficult gamble. Imagine you were a slave contemplating revolt. On the one hand, you'd want to prepare as much as possible for the revolt and, in particular, to sound out your fellow slaves. You'd have a better chance with a large number of slaves when you had to fight against whatever local muscle the slaveholders threw against you first. On the other hand, the more slaves who knew about the plan, the greater the chance that one would turn you in. An informer could win his or her freedom while you and your co-conspirators were put to death in a slow and painful way.

If you actually succeeded in starting a rebellion, you and every single slave in your band would immediately be considered a murderer of the worst kind, and the armed force of the Roman state would be mobilized to see to your defeat and punishment. The dangers and difficulties of your situation would be numerous and severe. Any functional state held a great advantage over a bunch of rebellious slaves, who started out with almost no organization, resources, money, weapons, or training. And Rome was not just any state. Even if we knew them all – which we don't – we don't have space here to cover all the challenges the slaves had to overcome. We'll focus instead on just three areas: military capability, leadership, and unity.

The Roman army had evolved over many generations of warfare. Its soldiers were well trained in battle tactics, highly disciplined, and possessed effective and versatile weapons. But, in that violent age, some of the slaves had also experienced army service, and they knew what was at stake for them. They could find or make rudimentary weapons such as sickles, knives attached to sticks, hunting spears, and axes. Slave rebels could overcome local Roman forces – often incompetently led – by sheer weight of numbers or though surprise attacks and other tactics of guerrilla warfare. Our detailed accounts of the great revolts usually describe such early victories. They may, however, give us the wrong impression here for a simple reason: those rebels who didn't acquire arms and defeat local forces were quickly beaten and the survivors executed; their uprising became one of the small revolts that one ancient source or another sums up in a sentence – or one that never gets into the historical record at all.

Once they acquired more effective weapons from defeated soldiers, rebellious slaves had plenty of motivation to train hard and obey orders. For example, the historian Sallust reports that Spartacus' band followed regular army procedures, including the stationing of night watches (Sallust, *Histories* fr. 42.4 [Book 3] in Ramsay 2015). Eventually they were able to match the Romans even in set battles. In siege warfare, however, the rebels could not compete. Siege towers, battering rams, catapults, and undermining required some of the most advanced engineering in the ancient world, something the slave armies lacked. Thus slaves could sometimes win set battles and dominate the countryside, but they were only occasionally able to capture fortified and well-defended cities. This made it hard for them to consolidate their power even after victories in the field and left them more vulnerable to counter-attacks once the Romans had fielded another army.

Effective leadership was another crucial factor in maintaining a revolt: if a leader could make his decisions stick, then the rebels could overcome many other difficulties. Fortunately, our sources focus on the leaders of the slave revolts and describe how they acquired leadership and how well they wielded it once they had it. One striking pattern is how often these leaders sought supernatural support for their leadership. Most conspicuously, Eunus, the leader of the first Sicilian revolt, cultivated a reputation as a miracle worker and fortune-teller when he was still a slave. As his gifts became known, his master had him amuse the guests at dinner parties. Eunus would prophesize that he would become king of Sicily and agreed to be merciful to the guests then, if they gave him presents or some of their food. A hearty laugh all around, no doubt, but when he actually gained control of large parts of Sicily, he spared those who had been kind to him at these dinners – or so this story goes (Diodorus 34/35 2.8–9, 34/35 2.41). Legends of the supernatural surrounded Spartacus too:

> They say that when he was first brought to Rome to be sold, a snake was seen coiled around his face while he slept, and that his wife . . . a prophetess subject to the mystical ecstasies of Dionysus, declared that this showed that a great and formidable power would accompany him to a fortunate destiny. (Plutarch, *Crassus* 8.3, trans. Warner 1958)

In fact, of all the main slave leaders, it is only Cleon to whom no supernatural stories attach – but perhaps we just don't know them. The Roman aristocracy had divine connections too: for instance, Julius Caesar held the prestigious priesthood of the *pontifex maximus* and his family claimed descent from the goddess Venus. Nevertheless, the elite's right to leadership rested also on secular criteria: family prestige, great wealth, connections, government positions, and military exploits. At the start of a revolt, slave leaders could claim none of these. It is not surprising that they turned more to divine support.

This is not to say that slave leaders did not also rely on customary rituals and symbols of leadership rather than trying, like some modern revolutionaries, to make a clean break with the past. Eunus gave himself the title Antiochus, a traditional name for the king of the Seleucid Empire, one of the main Hellenistic kingdoms. He also called his followers "Syrians," since many inhabitants of the Seleucid Empire and even the wider Eastern Mediterranean identified themselves as Syrians regardless of their actual ethnicity and language (Diodorus 34/35 2.24). Athenion, a leader of the second revolt, preferred, somewhat paradoxically, Roman rituals of leadership: he wore a toga with a purple border like a senator and had *lictors* (official attendants) with axes, as a Roman general would on campaign (Diodorus 36.7.4).

Unity was crucial for the slaves. The major insurrections spanned large areas and often groups of slaves operated at great distances from each other in circumstances when communications were uncertain and slow. The slaves didn't just need a king but also obedient subordinate leaders who would coordinate their plans and follow orders – or at least not fight each other! This last requirement may seem pretty minimal, but in times of revolution, local leaders may emerge in different places; they often disagree about who should be subordinate to whom and on what terms they should unite. There are many modern examples – the bitterly divided opposition to the Syrian dictator Bashar al-Assad is topical as I write this – but the ancient Romans were already aware of this possibility. During both Sicilian revolts, a second group and leader emerged in a different area after the first main revolt with its "king." The Romans expected or hoped that these groups would fight each other, but in both cases one leader submitted to the other and willingly served as general for the main leader of the slaves (Diodorus 34/35 2.17, 36.7.2).

Figure 10.2 Coin of the slave king Antiochus (originally Eunus). Striking coins was a traditional activity of autonomous states, something to which the Sicilian slave rebels aspired. This coin combines Sicilian themes – the ear of wheat and a veiled face of Demeter, the goddess of agriculture – with a title more at home in the Seleucid Empire: Antioch(ou) Basil(eō), "of King Antiochus." Numismatists believe that the explanation is that Eunus had coins made with his new name and title together with the traditional Sicilian motifs of the town of Enna, the slaves' main base. *Source*: Figure from Robinson 1920, 175.

No doubt dread of the Romans played a role in keeping the slaves united and, much of the time, disciplined: as Samuel Johnson famously observed, "when a man knows he is to be hanged in a fortnight, it concentrates his mind wonderfully" (James Boswell, *The Life of Samuel Johnson*, September 9, 1777). Only in the case of Spartacus' rebellion do we hear about disagreements and different subsets of slaves, for example, a German group. Plutarch reports several occasions when contingents camped or operated separately and the Romans managed to defeat them (Plutarch, *Crassus* 9.7, 11.1, 11.2–3). But even here, another explanation of this apparent foolishness is possible. In the ancient word, it was extraordinarily hard to supply a large stationary army, even with the organization and resources of a state; this would have been even harder for a numerous band of slaves with no state to support them. Perfect harmony among the slaves is not probable, but logistical considerations would in any case have forced them to divide up and operate in smaller groups at times.

The Ability to Revolt

In the long run, rebellious slaves could never overcome the advantages of the slaveholding class and the Roman state and army. Slaves must have been well aware of this. Many of them came from places that had first-hand experience of Roman brutality and power. Those without direct experience of the Roman army had heard about it – who hadn't? Intolerable oppression probably played a large role in explaining why many slaves were willing to risk their lives. It can't be the whole story: we can probably assume that many slaves in every period bitterly resented their oppression and would have liked to revolt, had they any chance of success. The question is why slaves in the late Republic thought they had a chance and why they met with success for a while.

Ancient authors had their own explanations. For example, Diodorus stresses the role of slave herdsmen in the first Sicilian revolt (34/5 2.29–30; cf. Tacitus, *Annals* 4.27). These were particularly dangerous slaves for several reasons. The work was physically demanding so the strongest young men were assigned to it and allowed considerable independence (Varro, *On Agriculture* 2.10.1). And to protect the herds from predators, like wolves, slave herdsmen often carried spears, clubs, or rods. In Sicily, their owners made the situation worse by not providing enough food or clothing and forced their slaves into banditry to support themselves. Finally, since the large slaveholders were rich and powerful, even the governor of Sicily was afraid of curbing these dangerous practices and overlooked the consequent breakdown of law and order in the countryside (Diodorus 34/5 2.31). There must be some truth to Diodorus' picture: slave herdsmen, already accustomed to brigandage, were a source of strength for the rebellions. Yet Sicily's economy had long been based more on grain production than on livestock, so the majority of the rebels were likely agricultural slaves; the herdsman may have been more conspicuous than numerous. Our sources also focus on shepherds because they found an obvious and somewhat comforting moral there: don't mistreat *and* arm slaves.

Modern scholars need to consider comparative history to explain why slaves succeeded in rebelling in Roman Sicily and Italy during the 75 years from 135–60 BCE and not at other times and places. For example, Eugene Genovese's influential book, *From Rebellion to Revolution* (1979) identified the factors that enabled large-scale revolts to get off the ground in Brazil and the Caribbean, but not in the American South (Genovese 1979; cf. Cartledge 2003).[5] There is no *a priori* reason to think that these same factors all apply to the Roman Republic, but several of them are worth considering. Here, I'll consider the circumstances that favor slave rebellions under four larger categories: the proportion of slaves in the population, their organization, their alienation from their masters, and disunity among the free.

As we mentioned above, slaves needed to be present in overwhelming numbers to revolt successfully. Already the ancient Romans made a connection between the proportion of slaves and the danger of revolt (Tacitus, *Annals* 4.27). Taken as a whole the population of Roman Italy and Sicily comprised at most 35 percent slaves, but these slaves were not evenly distributed. Some areas were still dominated by free Italian peasants. Other places more resembled a Caribbean island, with a large majority of slaves, even if we allow for exaggeration in the claim of Tiberius Gracchus that in some areas large slave-worked farms had entirely displaced the native Italian peasantry (Plutarch, *Tiberius Gracchus* 8). Such areas provide the explanation for how Spartacus' tiny band grew so quickly into the tens of thousands. Even when slaveholders had plenty of warning and were presumably taking every precaution, there was little they or their overseers could do to keep their slaves from deserting to the rebels where there were large concentrations of slaves and few free people.

Other factors make it possible for slaves to overcome some of the disadvantages they suffered in terms of organization. We've already seen that the promotion of some slaves above others can be a way to divide and weaken a slave population: it can backfire when slaves favored by the masters also have the stature of leaders among the slaves. For instance, Eunus' claimed supernatural powers made him an amusing status symbol for his master, but he had enough of a reputation among the slaves to take a leadership role in the revolt. His power also seemed to rest on the ethnic identity of his "Syrian" slaves. For centuries, masters repeated the standard advice not to buy too many slaves

---

5 This contrast does not imply that Southern slaves were more docile, but only that their resistance usually had to take other forms.

from one area, but the slave supply depended on the vagaries of war and violence. In any given decade during the late Republic, large landowners could not buy cheap slaves evenly spread over many nationalities; they had to acquire them from the places where people were then being enslaved in great numbers. So the "Syrians" in Sicily and the Gauls and Thracians under Spartacus were able to organize themselves more easily because of their common culture, language, and feelings of kinship.

In addition to slaves of various ethnic origins, Roman slavery encompassed slaves whose experience of slavery and relations with their masters were radically different from each other: the bilingual and educated tutor of an aristocrat's son in Rome, who had never been whipped and who expected manumission, had little in common with a Gallic slave working in a chain gang on one of his master's large farms. Perhaps this imaginary tutor bitterly resented slavery, and it is not inconceivable that he would run away to join Spartacus after a Roman defeat; it was just not very likely. Rather the strength of the Roman slave rebellions came from the large number of farm slaves living away from their masters on large estates and, in the main, sharing a similar experience of slavery and a similar, hostile relationship with the slaveholding class. It seems to be a general principle of resistance and revolution that the more alike the lives and situations of the oppressed the less difficult it is for them to organize against their oppressors (Scott 1990, 135).

By alienation, our third factor, I mean all the ways in which slaves and masters were physically, socially, or culturally distant from each other. The last two chapters showed that classical slaveholders deployed a variety of methods to co-opt and control slaves, including selective manumission and other rewards for obedience and hard work. The more closely slaves and masters interacted, the easier it was for masters to deploy these tools of social control; the more alienated slaves were, the more difficult it was. In the late Republic, Roman slaveholders were often absent from their agricultural estates. They lived most of the time in cities, such as Rome itself, and only visited their farms occasionally. Of course, an absentee owner would appoint a *vilicus*, an overseer – often a slave himself – to manage his or her farm. Some of these *vilici* were probably better managers than the owners would have been, but in general they lacked the permanent and vested interests of a slave owner resident on his farmland.

Genovese found that alienation and thus revolts were more likely when most slaves were male, foreign, and newly captured. Male slaves were individually more dangerous on account of their size, upbringing, and possible military experience. New slaves were likely to experience hard work and violent coercion more than any more subtle forms of social control. There was little room for "negotiation" between such slaves and their masters. Foreign slaves might not even understand the language in which they were ordered about. That newly enslaved men were considered dangerous contributed to a vicious circle of punishment, chaining, and desperation.[6] In contrast, when most slaves are born into slavery, both masters and slaves had the time and motivation to find a way of coexisting – not that this rules out violence or coercion. This situation, where most slaves are born in slavery, generally occurs only when some accommodation is made for slave families. And slave family ties also tend to limit the willingness of a slave population to resist or rebel, a theme we encountered in Chapter 9 (cf. Scott 1990, 24). Indeed, one ancient Greek source claims that masters should allow slaves to have children to provide hostages for their good behavior ([Aristotle], *Oeconomica* 1.5.6).

---

6 Columella, *On Agriculture* 1.8.16–17 urges special precautions for chained slaves.

The traditional model of the sources of Roman slaves (see Chapter 3) posits a shift from importation to natural reproduction. Such a shift would help to explain when the great slave revolts occurred. Until slave numbers reached a certain level, they were not capable of mounting a large rebellion. In the second century BCE, however, Roman wars and consequent anarchy were producing new slaves in the hundreds of thousands – arguably mostly male. This produced the type of slave population most willing and able to revolt. By the early Empire, the size of the slave population had stabilized. Slaves were still numerous, but more of them were born into slavery and more were women or children rather than the most dangerous slaves, first-generation foreign males. It would be rash to put too much emphasis on just these two factors or to imagine that we are certain about the gender ratio in the slave population at different times. Still, the great slave revolts did, in fact, occur just when the traditional model of the slave supply predicts a population both large and composed of the types of slaves most likely to rebel.

The Roman state was strong in ways we have already mentioned: revenues, organization, and an unmatched army. But, elements of disunity made it weaker in the late Republic than it was before and after. In Sicily, for example, the interest of individual, powerful slaveholders trumped the communal interest in law and order when it came to feeding and clothing shepherds well enough so that they did not turn to robbery. This was also a time of vast disparities of wealth; the free poor were often resentful of the rapacious Roman elite. For example, in Sicily we hear that the free poor took advantage of slave revolts to plunder country estates themselves (Diodorus 36.11.1; cf. 34/5 2.48). In passing, the historian Appian implies that the Italians had sided with Spartacus against the Romans (Appian, *The Mithradatic War* 109). It's unclear what exactly this could refer to, since we don't hear of any Italians on the side of the slaves. But large regions of Italy rebelled and fought a savage war against Rome from 90–88 BCE. It is quite plausible that pockets of resentment remained twenty years later, another case of disunity in the late Republic.

We need to give due credit to the rebels for the determination, courage, and resourcefulness in taking on Rome. But the deck was not as stacked against them as it was against rebellious slaves in most other times and places. The slaves were able to mount a revolt and maintain it for several years. But I'm not sure that that quite counts as a victory for the vast majority of the rebels, who either died in battle or were executed.

Conclusion

Classical Greek slaves could desert or help the enemy during times of war; the mountains of Hellenistic Chios formed the backdrop for an ancient maroon, but slave revolts were unheard of. Among the Greeks, the Messenian Helots may have fought hardest and longest for their freedom, but they were more like serfs than like chattel slaves. Only the slaves of the late Roman Republic were able to sustain revolt on their own for long periods. These uprisings were on the grandest of scales and accomplished great victories over the Romans, even if their end was as unhappy as it was inevitable.

Most slaves in every period want freedom. Why else would they buy it – often at the cost of years or decades of extra work and self-deprivation – or take it by running away? Resentment of masters is a common and unremarkable phenomenon too. In the more alienating and brutal forms of slavery, the feelings of many slaves may often rise to the level of murderous hatred. So, even if we condemn some of the brutalities that the slaves committed, we do not condemn their decision to rebel against such a horrible system of oppression. Indeed, in 1769 Voltaire described Spartacus' rebellion as "a just war, indeed the only just war in history."[7] This formulation takes the point of view of actual or prospective slave rebels as we have in this chapter. In the next two chapters, we turn to the opinions of slaveholders and try to understand their perspective. But we should not forget that when they thought they had any hope at all, many slaves were willing to fight to the death against these masters, perhaps even the "good masters."

Suggested Reading

The first part of Genovese 1979 contains the comparative treatment of the ability of slaves to revolt mentioned above. Cartledge 2003 (originally 1985) applies Genovese's categories to Greek chattel slaves and to the Helots. Cartledge 2002 discusses the Helots within a general history of Sparta; he also includes a helpful appendix with translations of all the main sources about the Helots. Kennell 2010 provides a recent and accessible survey of Spartan history. Hodkinson 2008 uses comparative material on New World slavery and Russian serfdom to understand the lives of the Helots. Luraghi 2002 provides an influential argument that the Helots were slaves, which I try to counter in my chapter on Orlando Patterson's influence on the study of ancient Greek slavery (2016b). Ogden 2004 discusses the legends surrounding the legendary Messenian hero, Aristomenes. Finally, Gillen, Kelly, and Bellair 2014 is a (violent) graphic novel about three helots on the run from the Spartans. On the Roman side, Shaw 2001 collects and discusses the sources that describe or provide context for the great slave revolts. Bradley 1989 is lively and provides a detailed account of the three main rebellions. He argues that their original aims were limited and they may have started as maroons. Urbainczyk 2008 provides a thematic treatment of the Roman slave revolts, the maroon on Chios, and even the Helots. On several points, she argues against Bradley's emphases and arguments. The movie Spartacus (1960) is a classic epic based on the novel by Howard Fast; I discuss it in Chapter 13.

---

7 Voltaire, Letter 283, 5.4.1769 in Urbainczyk 2004, 11.

11

Representations

Many slaves have in the past proved superior to brothers and sons in every respect and have saved their masters and their property and their whole houses; for people say these things about slaves.
Plato, Laws 6.776d–e

You have as many enemies as you have slaves.
Roman proverb in Seneca, Epistles 47.5

I am truly delighted with what you have done: Tiro [Cicero's personal secretary] did not deserve that lot in life and you [Cicero] preferred to have him as a friend rather than as a slave.
Cicero, Letters to Family 16.16

Introduction

In these next two chapters, we turn from the institution of slavery to the ways that masters represented slaves and to their justifications or criticisms of slavery. It is impossible to make a sharp distinction between these topics, but overall this chapter focuses more on attitudes, often unexamined, and it uses the representations of slaves in drama and material culture as evidence. Next chapter, we look at philosophical and legal texts for explicit arguments about slavery. Compared to previous chapters, we have relatively copious evidence for the representation of slaves. For we are no longer trying to recover the feelings or typical actions of slaves based on scanty and difficult evidence. Rather our goal here is to understand the attitudes of masters, who were the producers, commissioners, or audience of most of what has survived of classical culture.

The main methodological difficulty of this chapter lies in deriving attitudes towards slaves from how slaves were represented in drama. A slave character may display certain traits because that is how slaves are supposed to be, how they are not supposed to be, or because such traits contribute to the plot, important themes, or the humor of the play.

Ancient Greek and Roman Slavery, First Edition. Peter Hunt.
© 2018 Peter Hunt. Published 2018 by John Wiley & Sons, Ltd.

Similar issues arise when fictional characters make statements about slavery: we cannot take these sentiments at face value as what the author thought or what he expected his audience to think. In the case of a successful playwright, like Plautus, it is pretty safe to assume that everything in his plays served some purpose, helped his play to appeal to its audience. The nature of this appeal will need to be evaluated carefully in each individual case; we cannot at all assume that the audience was expected to approve of everything done or said in the play.

Ancient views about slavery varied greatly. Some people viewed it as simply an appalling catastrophe, terrible luck. Period. You shouldn't blame somebody for being a slave any more than we today would blame somebody for having pancreatic cancer. This view encouraged sympathy for slaves, but it almost never implied that slavery could and should be abolished: that was just the way the world was. More common was a partial version of this view: some slaves were merely unlucky, but many were inferior, "slavish." If a person considered the good but unlucky slaves as exceptional – or just didn't think about them much – he or she might still hold a negative stereotype of slaves, perhaps the most common attitude. Belief in the inferiority of slaves had a variety of rationales. Male captives who had been enslaved could be viewed as cowards, who had surrendered rather than fighting to the death. In a world with little social mobility and a high premium on "good birth," being born into slavery implied inferiority without much thought about how the parents became slaves. Ethnic prejudice went a long way to justify the enslavement of foreigners, even though it was not nearly the dominant justification that racism provided in New World slave systems. The results and causes of slavery could be mixed up: slaves often had good reason to be afraid of their masters; they could rarely resist slavery openly and needed to be indirect. These circumstances led to a stereotype of slaves as sneaky, dishonest, childish, and cowardly. Finally, slaves had to do work that the elite regarded as demeaning; they were (illogically) faulted for what they were forced to do. All of these different negative images of slaves tended in a vague way to justify the system of slavery and the harsh and exploitative treatment of slaves. They provide the background for the explicit justifications of slavery that we consider next chapter.

It was not only slaveholders who had a stake in negative representations of slaves. The depiction of slaves as different and inferior also marked them as "the other," as a group in contrast to whom all the free could feel united and superior. Poor citizens did not possess slaves and had no direct need to justify the institution of slavery, but they did have a stake in feeling different from and superior to slaves. In fact, the border between slaves and free was possibly most important to the poor, who in some cases lived precariously close to it and might be regarded as "slavish" by the elite. Elite slaveholders could picture themselves as occupying the top rung of many in a hierarchical society; the poor could at least derive satisfaction from their position on the right side of the crucial divide between slave and free. This line of argument is intrinsically plausible, finds historical parallels in phenomena such as the "wages of whiteness" (Roediger 1999), and is supported by indirect evidence in some periods of classical history (see Chapter 5 above and, e.g., Hunt 1998, 126–143). Nevertheless, our direct evidence of the attitudes of poor free men is notoriously scanty, a problem we encounter repeatedly – and the evidence for poor free women is even worse. And we find the odd report of the poor and slaves making common cause, not impossible apparently (Thucydides 3.73.1; Aristotle, *The Athenian Constitution* 40.2).

You may have noticed that the previous paragraphs contained no places or dates. I believe that these various attitudes were ubiquitous in the classical world; they show up wherever and whenever we have good evidence. I will sometimes note that a certain way of viewing slavery seems more or less prominent in one period than another, but our main goal is to understand particular attitudes more deeply rather than to try to trace changes in emphasis over time. We'll focus first on the portrayal of slaves in Greek tragedy: at first enslavement appears to be merely a catastrophe, but on closer inspection we can find evidence of several different negative views of slaves – or at least of most slaves. Evidence from vase painting and slave names will support this picture. Household slaves often play a large role in Roman comedy especially in Plautus' plays, where a type of character called the "clever slave" sometimes takes the leading role. Finally, we'll explore paternalism in the Roman worldview. In paternalism, slavery was not an evil to be endured or justified but rather a benevolent, albeit hierarchical, system of mutual obligation and even affection, like the relation of a father and his children. Naturally, we will not just describe the paternalistic ideal but also note the limits and distortions of this ideology.

Tragedy and Slave Stereotypes

Euripides, an Athenian playwright of the classical period and almost certainly a slaveholder, wrote three tragedies based on legends about the Trojan War: *Hecuba*, *Andromache*, and the *Trojan Women*. These focus on the suffering and struggles of captives enslaved during the sack of Troy. As is usual in tragedy these characters are royal or at least high-born; the degradation of slavery is in sharp relief. Hecuba, for example, exclaims: "I must work the bolt that bars their doorway, I whose son was Hector once; or bake their bread; lay down these withered limbs to sleep on the bare ground, whose bed was royal once" (*Trojan Women* 492–495, trans. Lattimore 2013). Such passages emphasize the reversal of fortune involved when elite women suffer capture and enslavement. We find less concern with the justice or injustice of slavery for most slaves. So when Hecuba bemoans her lowered state, she does not conclude with an anti-slavery statement, but rather with a more general lesson: "Count nobody lucky until they have died" *(Trojan Women* 509–510).

Ancient drama represents slaves as well as masters and can thus provide a "worm's eye" view of slavery far different from what we find when slave owners speak in their own voice (Hall 1997, 123). Typical tasks – grinding, kneading and baking bread, cleaning the floors, nursing and raising their master's children, bolting and guarding their master's bedroom doors, or sharing his bed – are depicted from the point of view of the slaves doing them. We hear about the humiliation of being put up for sale, the hopelessness of arguing with a mistress or master, the discomfort of sleeping on the ground, and the long, weary days of work.[1]

In addition to representing the slave's experience, tragic characters sometimes express a critical attitude towards slavery: "Alas, what an evil slavery has always been / It endures

---

1 Aeschylus, *Libation Bearers* 749–762; Sophocles, *Ajax* 489–491; Euripides, *Trojan Women* 190–196, 506–508; *Hecuba* 357–368; *Andromache* 186–191.

what is not right, overcome by force" (Euripides, *Hecuba* 332–333). In addition, the basic worth of some slaves is repeatedly asserted in Euripides, apparently in opposition to the claim that slaves are intrinsically inferior to the free or noble.[2] This assertion of basic equality is in line with the conception of slavery as simple bad luck. Some scholars have tried to portray Euripides as almost a proto-abolitionist. Admittedly these criticisms and this empathy are of great interest, since they tell us what opinions and sentiments were possible in Athens. They do not, however, turn out to be the dominant strain of thought even within the dramas of Euripides, much less those of the other two great tragedians, Aeschylus and Sophocles. Rather, the notion of intrinsic worth dominates tragedy: nobles are born different from and superior to the rest of us; born slaves are, and will always be, inferior.

For starters, the particular type of nobility that slaves most often claim consists of determined loyalty to their masters: "It is most glorious for noble slaves to die for their masters" (Euripides, *Helen* 1640–1641; cf. 726–733). This brand of nobility was obviously more comforting to masters than subversive. The complaints of the enslaved noblewomen of Troy have even less of a bite. Slavery is horrible and unfair for those who were originally and naturally noble, but that isn't relevant to the average slave, who was not, after all, the daughter of a mythical king. And in *Hecuba* (365–366), the newly enslaved Polyxena fears that she might suffer the horrible and degrading fate of having to share the bed of a "money-bought slave," a real slave, not a fallen princess. Tragedy generally maintains a distinction between born or longstanding slaves and the sad fate of nobles newly reduced to slavery. The former – who most resemble actual slaves in Athens – may voice their petty complaints, but their lives reveal no tragic fall nor are they the equals of the nobility in any way.

Slaves in tragedy may assert their worth, but other characters display contempt for them. It is completely unremarkable when, for example, a character asks, "Are we slaves?" to exhort his fellows to avoid cowardly passivity: as in Greek culture in general, to act like a slave has entirely negative connotations throughout the whole genre.[3] The notion that slavery was bad luck is far from the whole attitude of tragedy: they were also inferior. Some historians believe that this prejudice against slaves was a new, classical-period attitude, not found in Homer. This theory neglects the central role that military prowess and bravery played in determining the worth of a Greek man. Let me explain. Homer can indeed treat the enslavement of women as a blameless catastrophe, deserving only sympathy: in the passage with which we started Chapter 3, Odysseus himself is likened to a woman facing slavery after her husband has been killed in war (8.523–530). Slavery is also regarded as a disaster for a man. But, since men, were supposed to die fighting – like the husband in the simile – their capture was never quite blameless. It requires explanation. For instance, Eumaeus, Odysseus' swineherd, a brave and sympathetic character, has to explain how he was kidnapped as a child and sold to Laertes (15.381–388, 15.415–484). Military prowess remained a cardinal virtue in the classical period, so defeat – and especially surrender and enslavement – could hardly fail to suggest inferiority. In Plato's *Republic* those guardians who fail in courage and surrender to the enemy will not be ransomed, presumably because they deserve to be

•

---

2 Euripides, *Ion* 854–856, *Helen* 728–731, 1640–1641, fr. 495, 40–43, fr. 511, fr. 831 (Nauck).

3 E.g., Sophocles, *Philoctetes* 995–996, 1006; *The Women of Trachis* 453–454; Euripides, *Alcestis* 675–678.

enslaved (5.468a–b). So far, then, we have seen the tragic view of slavery as bad luck, but also a sense that most slaves are inferior. For men, that inferiority may be connected with the fact that captives were enslaved and real men ought not ever to be captured – or so the reasoning ran.

In classical Athens, that most slaves were non-Greek bolstered the sense that they were different and inferior. This attitude probably grew in prominence during the course of the fifth century BCE (Isaac 2004, 257–303). A concise presentation of this view comes from Euripides' *Iphigenia in Aulis*: "It is proper for Greeks to rule barbarians and not for barbarians to rule Greeks, mother, for the one [the barbarian] is a slavish thing while the other [the Greeks] are free people" (1400–1401). That this statement was not an outrageous or idiosyncratic declaration is clear, since the chorus immediately praises Iphigenia. One character in Aristophanes' *Thesmophoriazusae* is a Scythian archer – one of the public slaves we mentioned last chapter: "Besides his barbarised Greek, his most obvious attribute are cruelty, sloth, aggression, abusiveness, libidinousness and eventually credulity" (Hall 1989, 52). Such attitudes towards foreigners – and especially foreign slaves – became more and more common and vehement as Greeks increasingly thought of themselves a group in opposition to non-Greeks during the fifth century BCE and especially during and after the Persian wars. Greek authors sometimes portrayed the subjects of the Persian Empire in particular as slavish both for climatic reasons – the weather was too nice! – and because they were subject to a monarchy (Isaac 2004, 60–69 on [Hippocrates], *Airs, Waters, Places* 16). Although neither popular nor intellectual opinion about non-Greeks was homogeneous nor consistent, this prejudice provided a convenient rationale for slavery. Indeed, the belief in Greek superiority was the closest classical Greece came to a racist justification of slavery.[4] All of this emphasis on the slavishness of barbarians tended to justify slavery, because a majority – perhaps a vast majority – of slaves at Athens were in fact non-Greeks. But, as this justification of slavery grew more prominent, the enslavement of Greeks become an increasingly awkward anomaly. Plato provides a famous statement of this view: his model city will consider wars among Greeks as deplorable, intestine struggles and will not enslave the defeated (*Republic* 5.470e–471c). Such sentiments did not represent the first step towards the elimination of slavery altogether, but rather the sharpening of ethnic distinctions.

Two very different bodies of evidence confirm the impression that Greeks often viewed their slaves as somehow inferior: slaves on vase paintings and slave names. Pseudo-Xenophon complains that you can barely tell the difference between the poor and slaves at Athens (*Constitution of the Athenians* 1.10). There was no standard dress that distinguished slave and free nor any obvious physical marker such as skin color. So, on vase paintings it can be hard, sometimes impossible, even to tell who is a slave. In some cases, however, scholars can identify a slave based on what the person is doing: for example, slaves are often depicted carrying things on their heads, and slave women might be weaving under their mistress's supervision. Some tombstone reliefs depict a deceased woman attended by her slave, who is helping her get dressed up to go out as in Figure 11.1 below. We have already seen a slave holding a chamber pot for his master in Figure 9.1. Another clue is that vase painters often distinguished slaves by painting them smaller than free persons. Art historians demonstrated this convention from

---

4 Isaac 2004 uses "proto-racism"; Lape 2010 explores racial identity in the Athenian democracy.

Figure 11.1 Grave relief of Hegeso. In this famous and beautiful grave relief of the late fifth century, the deceased, Hegeso, is seated and her slave woman is holding a box, from which Hegeso has taken something, probably a piece of jewelry and is examining it. In such scenes, the slave is much smaller than her mistress – you have to imagine Hegeso standing up for this to be obvious. The slave women have practical, short haircuts, whereas their mistresses have more elaborate hairdos and more complicated clothing. Only Hegeso is named on the inscription even though two women are depicted on the relief, but it is clear who is the important person (the deceased) and who is the slave.
Source: Chris Hellier/Alamy Stock Photo.

cases when we can be sure that a slave is depicted – rather than a child – by what he or she is doing: grave reliefs sometimes show a deceased small child with his or her slave attendant, in one case an adult, "fully formed but unnaturally small" (Wrenhaven 2011, 106). Such artistic depictions parallel a striking linguistic practice: a common word for a slave of any age in both Greece and Rome was "child" or "boy."[5] This usage implies that

---

5 The Greek *pais* could be applied to male or female slaves, but the Latin *puer* referred only to males.

slaves are never full adults. This sort of terminology for slaves finds many parallels in various times and places, such as in the antebellum South. As a result, "boy" remains, even today, an extremely derogatory way to address an African-American.

In other cases, obviously foreign persons are depicted performing the type of work slaves did. These cannot be poor Athenians or family members, so they are unambiguously slaves. Occasionally we see slaves who may look African.[6] Others have tattoos, a barbarian custom according to Herodotus and particularly associated with the Thracians, a common slave ethnicity at Athens (5.6.2). Among women, slave women typically have short hair in a relatively simple style, "the slave bob." These criteria often, but not always, allow scholars to identify slaves on vase paintings.

This detective work is important, because the way artists depict slaves reveals the traits associated with slavery. Many vase painters were themselves slaves or ex-slaves, but still they needed to appeal to the free citizens who bought the vases (Lewis 1998–1999). Most obviously, slaves are small because they were considered less important, just as mortals are smaller than divinities. The notions that slaves and foreigners were inferior tended to reinforce each other; on vase paintings, we find foreign slaves serving their larger, Greek masters. In contrast to the depictions of free Greeks as graceful and beautiful, slaves in vase paintings are often ugly in one way or another. They are placed in inelegant positions, twisting awkwardly or squatting at their work. This was both an intrinsic quality – we saw that in novels enslaved nobles can be distinguished from "real" slaves at a glance – and an acquired trait. Elite authors, at least, believed that the crafts that many slaves performed warped their bodies and made slaves – as well as free craftsmen – incapable of achieving real excellence (Aristotle, *Politics* 3.1278.a22–23; Xenophon *Oeconomicus* 4.2). Finally, the faces of slaves do not fit the Greek ideal and their expressions are likely to be emotional rather than classically restrained. A poem ascribed to Theognis sums up this vein of contempt:

> Never is a slave's head by nature straight, but it is always crooked, and he holds his neck aslant. For from a sea onion grow neither roses nor hyacinth and the child of a slave mother is never free in spirit. (Gerber 1999, 535–538)

Thus, the way that vase painters depicted slaves is in line with the attitude that slaves are intrinsically inferior and especially with the growing emphasis on the ethnocentric justification of slavery (Thalmann 2011, 87–88).

One of the humiliations of slavery was that masters would usually name or rename their slaves. The rationale behind their choice of names could vary greatly.[7] Strabo, a later writer, points out that the Athenians often named their slaves after the country from which they were bought or with names popular in that country (*Geography* 7.3.12). We have plenty of evidence of the first case, slaves named after their country: there are many simple epitaphs as well as other references to slaves whose names seem simply to have been "Thracian": *Thrax* for a man or *Thraitta* for a woman. Slaves who had names popular in their own countries might have retained their original names; that is probably too optimistic. Foreign slave names were few and stereotypical. For

---

6 Greek vase painters adopted the convention that men, who were supposed to spend their time outside and be sun tanned, have dark skin and women, who were supposed to stay inside, have white skin – as in the Roman painting on the cover of this book. Thus sub-Saharan Africans are not always easy to identify.

7 In this section I follow Robertson 2008 and Vlassopoulos 2010.

example, Athenian owners seemed to give slaves from Phrygia the name Manes, rather than respecting their original and more various names. If somebody today referred to every Mexican male he saw as José, this would be considered extremely insulting. Ancient Greek slaves may also have taken offense, but they were not in a position to complain. Another common class of slave names were those indicating qualities that masters wanted to see in their slaves: for example, *Pistos* means obedient, trusty, or loyal. These names were not derogatory in a simple sense – loyalty isn't a bad trait – but are best understood in terms of the ideology of paternalism, which we'll examine below.

As a result of these practices, the most common slave names were not shared with Athenian citizens: no citizen father would name his son Daos or Manes, for example. And in fictional contexts, such as comic plays, most slaves carry one of these stereotypical slave names. The names of actual slaves appear in literary sources, on lists of trireme crews, in the Attic *Stelai* (see Chapter 3), on manumission lists, and on gravestones. Kostas Vlassopoulos found that about half of the real slaves do not have one of the stereotypical slave names, but rather have Greek names that are also attested among citizen males. Masters sometimes did and sometimes did not try to distinguish and mark their slaves as different, foreign, and inferior to the free. The reasons why they sometimes went one way and sometimes another are likely various and complicated – and are unknown to us. In any case slave names provide evidence for contempt for slaves, but also of more complicated and, just possibly, more respectful individual attitudes.

The Clever Slave in Roman Comedy

Complete comic plays survive from both Athens and Rome and span more than two and a half centuries. Already in the late fifth century BCE, Aristophanes reveals that having a slave beaten was a cliché way to get a laugh (*Peace* 743–750) – again we are obviously not talking about entertainment for or by slaves. But Aristophanes also presents impertinent and witty slave characters. It is about a century later that we first find evidence of plots revolving around what we'll call the "clever slave" character. Such a slave seems to be the speaker of a fragment from Menander's *Perinthian*, "A slave who has a good-natured and dim-witted master and tricks him hasn't done anything so great by making a bigger fool of somebody who was a fool already" (Menander, *Perinthian*, fr. 3 in Sandbach 1972). The mother lode of such material lies within the 21 surviving plays by Plautus, most of them performed in Rome in the early second century BCE. In eight of these comedies, a clever slave plays a central role.[8] Plautus' comedies are often set in Greek cities and based on earlier Greek models and plots, sometimes plays of Menander. That such plots could work in the growing Roman imperial state, just as they did originally in the city-state of Athens, suggests considerable cultural sympathy. Some degree of continuity in relations between masters and those slaves who served as personal attendants in the household is also likely. What we know for certain is that Plautus aimed to please a Roman audience in the early second century and that he succeeded. That is what we aim to understand.

---

8 Although Terence was himself an ex-slave, his plays tend to be more naturalistic and don't revel in the outrageous reversals of Plautine comedy.

In some ways, comedy reflects social reality: the household servants are slaves rather than free men and women; they can be beaten or sold; prostitutes or courtesans were often slaves. But this realism on big, basic issues rarely tells historians things they do not already know. And, in other ways, the plays are far from realistic: the clever slave character spends his time helping a son to fool and swindle his wealthy father and to marry his true love. This can hardly have been the main occupation of any real slaves. Indeed, some ancient comedies are humorous precisely because they are not realistic: rather they present a world turned upside down where, for example, slaves disobey and baffle their masters with impunity. What is entertaining and funny is not what is true or typical. It can also be hard to understand or explain, especially when the joke comes from a foreign culture more than two thousand years ago. Fortunately, some ancient humor fits categories still familiar from movies today: parody, the world turned upside-down, the flouting of authority, and the breaking of social conventions.

The eight plays with clever slave characters show many similar patterns, but we'll focus on Plautus' *Pseudolus,* which was performed in 191 BCE and may be based on a Greek original of the late fourth century. The play gets its name from its main character Pseudolus, literally "Liar," an improbable and humorous slave name. His trickery not only goes unpunished, but is richly rewarded in the end. His place in the household dynamics is typical of the clever slave: he is recruited by his master's son (the young master) to help him in a love affair without his father, Pseudolus' master, finding out. The son is in love with a slave courtesan but does not have the money to buy her. His father, who controls the family finances, refuses to help him out. Even worse, a soldier has paid the pimp, Ballio, a deposit on the courtesan and has arranged to send his own slave with a letter and the final payment to take her away. Finally, both the father and pimp Ballio have been forewarned about Pseudolus' plans. They are on their guard.

Despite these considerable challenges, Pseudolus pulls it all off successfully. He dupes the nasty Ballio, the father (his own master), and the slave of the soldier. The son can now manumit and marry his love interest, but the play ends with the triumph of the scheming slave, the main focus throughout. Pseudolus had made several large side bets on his success, and his master is prompt in paying up and even expresses admiration of him.[9] For his part, Pseudolus is not a gracious winner. He comes on stage totally drunk. He burps at his master and crows "Vae Victis," "Woe to the losers" (1318; all translations de Melo 2012). These were the legendary words of a Gallic chief who sacked Rome in the early fourth century BCE, an arrogant and offensive way for a slave to address his Roman master! The master endures all this, does not assert himself, and, in fact, the play ends when the two decide to go out drinking together.

The Conservative and the Subversive Reading

This synopsis does not do justice to the play's humor, but it should show why historians of slavery find the clever slave character so intriguing: why did the free and the powerful members of a slave society enjoy seeing a slave mock and triumph over his master?

---

9 Since he doesn't have much money, Pseudolus has to wager his body: if he loses, he will be whipped (two bets, 513, 545) and sent to a mill for a miserable life of hard labor (534).

Our main discussion of this question will focus on why plays such as Pseudolus might not offend but rather appeal to an audience dominated by slaveholders ("the conservative reading"). We'll conclude, however, with the contrary perspective ("the subversive reading"): Plautus was critical of slavery and was potentially offensive to slaveholders; he appealed to a mixed audience that included many slaves and ex-slaves.

Let's begin with several ways in which clever-slave plays are not as subversive as they seem at first. At one point Pseudolus brags of his lineage (!) and glory: "Such is the stock from which I was born; I ought to do great deeds that bring me great and long renown afterward" (590–591). In fact, his trickery is not at all the traditional stuff of glory; the clever slave shows boldness and low cunning, but not nobility or wisdom. Pseudolus' boast is mock epic, and the audience is meant to smile at his chutzpah but not to admire him. At the end of the play, he is drunk and has just come from partying with his young master and a prostitute; he wanted her to have sex with him, but he was too drunk and fell down (1246–1284). Even in his hour of triumph, Pseudolus reinforces common

Figure 11.2 Terracotta of a comic slave mask (National Archaeological Museum, Athens). Comic actors wore standard masks for common character types: the old man, the young lover, or the slave. Wiles points out that the masks for slave characters had arched and distorted eyebrows suggesting emotions like fear, surprise, or malice (1988, 63). Their right brows were raised; this asymmetry probably indicated a lack of moral balance. Their mouths were huge, in line with the propensity of comic slaves to eat, drink, and gossip. Comic slaves also wore red hair, marking them as foreign and different. A character describes the slave Pseudolus as "Someone red-haired, paunchy, with fat calves, darkish, with a big head, sharp eyes, a ruddy face, and very big feet" (Plautus, *Pseudolus* 1218–1120). Almost all of these physical characteristics were considered foreign or ignoble. *Source*: Yanni Archive/Art Resource, NY.

stereotypes of slaves as interested only in food, wine, and sex (Joshel 2011, 220). In addition, the triumph of the clever slave is not a simple victory of slaves over masters. Almost invariably, the clever slave is the ally of the son, the young master, in a conflict with his father, the *paterfamilias* and thus his legal master. Pseudolus, for example, excuses himself for not telling the father about his son's love affair on the ground that he did not want to accuse one master to another (491–494). So Pseudolus is still very much a slave in that he exerts all his efforts to serving the interest of somebody else.

The classicist Holt Parker points out that Plautine comedy is often socially conservative: "The plays end ... with marriage and legitimate children, the son and the father in harmony again, and the slave still a slave" (1989, 241). Pseudolus, for example, wants his freedom (358), but he ends the play in slavery. Such endings are common but not invariable: for example, another clever slave, Epidicus, humiliates his master and obtains his freedom as a reward for finding said master's long-lost daughter – the result of an improbable coincidence (*Epidicus* 724–733). But manumission was a common way to reward obedient and hard-working slaves; it played a key role in the successful functioning of Roman slavery. Epidicus also demands that the old master continue to feed him, suggesting that he plans to stay within the household, but as a freedman. So, even those plays that end with the slave gaining his freedom are hardly revolutionary.

This set of arguments shows that plays celebrating clever slaves may not have seemed as offensive and radical to slaveholders as we might first assume. Clever slaves had a positive appeal too because seeing authority flouted is often a source of humor. You will probably have little difficulty in thinking of movies or television shows much of whose humor comes from seeing various types of authority figures humiliated. In Republican Rome, slaves were not the only ones likely to laugh and cheer for a Pseudolus or Epidicus; there were all sorts of people who could in one way or another see themselves as underdogs. Most directly, Roman sons remained subject to paternal power until their father's death. The father's control of the family's purse strings probably chafed many grown sons.[10] One may hope that few of them consciously wanted their fathers to die (cf. Ovid, *Fasti* 2.625), but the alliance of a clever slave and a son to outwit the father and take his money would have held an obvious appeal to sons. And the common people resented the elite and government officials. Soldiers resented their officers – and there were a lot of soldiers and ex-soldiers in Roman audiences in the early second century. Ex-slaves may already have constituted a significant part of the urban population, and thus Plautus' audience; they might resent their former slavery or their continuing subordination to their former owner. As David Wiles sums up, "The Plautine slave is a kind of algebraic symbol for the underdog in Roman society. Anyone in a relationship of servitude ... could relish the triumph of the downtrodden slave and his fantastical inversion of all structures of power" (1988, 66). Many Romans could both enjoy the triumph of the underdog slave and be reassured by the reassertion of the master's control at the end (McCarthy 2000, x).

Although much of the humor comes from the clever slave's insolence, Plautine comedy contains another, incongruous theme: the dialogue is peppered with references to all sorts of violence against slaves, "an obsession" of Plautus.[11] Some plays contain more

---

10 Admittedly, high mortality rates meant that fewer adults than today had living fathers (Saller 1994, 189).

11 Parker 1989, 233 endorsing the view of Segal 1968. The comic slave himself seems immune to actual punishment on stage; that would stop his wisecracks, which Plautus does not want to do.

than a dozen references, often graphic and witty, to the corporal punishment of slaves. For example, Plautus delights in jokes based on the resemblance between the bright colors of a beaten slave's body and various artistic creations, such as Campanian coverlets and Alexandrian carpets (*Pseudolus* 145–147). There are two ways to view these references. In the subversive reading, all this violence against slaves in Plautus "forms part of the plays' general work of pointing out and denigrating, through mockery, injustices against the enslaved" (Richlin 2014, 183). This function is sometimes clear. Ballio, the pimp in *Pseudolus*, is thoroughly nasty. He delivers a lengthy series of threats against his slaves, whom he represents as lazy parasites (136–137). And he repeatedly threatens his slave courtesans with regular prostitution (228–229):

> Unless I'm brought your whole keep here today from the estates of your boyfriends, Phoenicium, you'll go to the common brothel tomorrow, with a hide that's Phoenician purple [another reference to beating or whipping].

Pseudolus and his master listen in on this extended display of brutality and comment harshly on Ballio; the audience is expected to share their disapproval. The subversive reading doesn't work as well for all of the violence and threats in Plautus. As a pimp and slave trader, Ballio is a scapegoat – who wouldn't hate him? But the fathers in Plautus are also whipping enthusiasts, and they are represented as regular Romans and are often sympathetic characters by the end of the play. Indeed, in five of the eight plays with prominent clever slaves, the slave himself refers to his vulnerability to brutal punishment near the start of the action (R. Stewart 2008, 75).

Accordingly, a conservative reading is more persuasive here. Most references to whipping are not critical of violence but rather serve as comforting reminders to the slaveholders in the audience of the coercive power they held over their slaves (Parker 1989, 238). So too, depicting slaves as abject and terrified of punishment also reassured masters of their control and their slaves' inferiority (cf. Hunt 1998, 160–164). These reminders may have been particularly apt in the context of the play's ancient performance. In Rome, there was a mid-December festival, the Saturnalia, in which we see some of the same role reversal as we see in comedy: everybody wore the *pilleus*, a freedman's cap and symbol of freedom (see Figure 12.1); slaves either ate with their masters or before them; and the whole festival was considered a slave festival, perhaps harkening back to a mythical golden age before slavery. The plays of Plautus that revolve around a clever slave recreate something like this Saturnalian atmosphere of reversal, disorder, and revelry. The frequent references to the punishment of slaves make sense in this context of a ritual of reversal that needed to be strictly limited. Thus, Parker argues that the constant references to past and future punishments underline that, "It is only today, while the Saturnalian spirit reigns, that they hope to get off" (Parker 1989, 238).

Plautus' insistence on the vulnerability of slaves to violence was well suited to an age when Roman slaveholders themselves felt vulnerable. Plautus wrote and produced his plays a couple of generations before the three great slave revolts. But already, the absence of so many Roman men on military service and an increasing influx of slaves made for a dangerous situation: Livy reports four separate slave revolts in Italy during Plautus' lifetime.[12] Army units were required to put down the rebels and, in some

---

12 Livy 22.33.2, 32.26.4, 33.36.1–3, 39.29.8–10.

cases, the Romans executed thousands of slaves. As a precaution, the state ordered extra vigilance and street patrols, and required that captives wear chains that weighed no less than ten pounds (Livy 32.26.18). A comparison allows us to judge the possible psychological effect of all this: before the American Civil War, the Nat Turner rebellion involved only around fifty slaves, who killed about sixty persons of the slaveholder class, but it caused a wave of paranoia, violence against blacks, and panics throughout the South. In second-century BCE Rome too, we can well imagine that slaveholders were on edge (cf. Plautus, *Pseudolus* 471–476). Slaves were clearly capable of more trouble than merely conning their masters out of money in order to repair their sons' love affairs. Such trickery was relatively benign, perhaps almost soothing, in the context of violent rebellion. The frequent references to the torture and beating of slaves may also have assuaged these more serious anxieties.

So far we have mainly been considering the attractions or the non-offensiveness of Plautus as if the audience consisted entirely of free citizens and slaveholders. This must be part of the story. The *Pseudolus*, for example, was first performed at an important public and official occasion for the Roman Republic, the dedication of the completed temple of the Great Mother. But Amy Richlin (2014), who paints a picture of Plautus as subversive, argues that we should understand the audience of Plautus as far more mixed than scholars thought previously. First and most obvious, most, if not all, of the actors were slaves: in one play, a character jokes that the actors who fail (to please the audience) will be beaten and those who do not fail will get a drink (Plautus, *The Casket Comedy* 785). Early Latin literary figures such as Terence, the other great Roman comic playwright, and Livius Andronicus were ex-slaves (see Chapter 6). According to one story, Plautus also came from the lower classes and worked his way up from being a stagehand (Aulus Gellius, *Attic Nights* 3.3.14). Second, Plautus and similar acting troupes needed to appeal to a mixed audience, both at major occasions in Rome and at their more usual venues in smaller cities of central Italy. Already Italian cities had begun to house the large populations of ex-slaves so amply attested later. Italy had suffered bitter warfare, including the fifteen years that Hannibal and the Carthaginian army was operating in the peninsula; members of the audience may have experienced slavery themselves or had relatives who had been enslaved. Not to mention actual slaves in the audience, a fact likely enough and confirmed by a reference in Plautus himself: Chrysalus, a slave character in *The Two Bacchises*, proclaims himself a fan of, and thus must have watched, another play, the *Epidicus* in fact (213–215).

In this reconstruction, substantial sections of the audience may have taken a simple and direct pleasure at seeing slaves get the better of their masters. This is all plausible enough, but a mixed audience at Rome also included slaveholders, who seem not to have been offended; for Plautine comedy was extremely popular from the beginning and remained so for centuries. Part of the explanation for this may lie in the capacity of audience members to decide what does and what does not apply to themselves: "These fictional Greek slave masters sure are stupid – and I admit some of my neighbors are too – but I'm in control of my slaves" or "That pimp is really nasty to his slaves, and I can't wait to see him get what he deserves, but I'm fair and generous, and I'm sure my slaves really love me." These possible reactions hint at one way to think about the conflict between the conservative and subversive readings of Plautus. Plautus was not interested in being consistent or in appealing just to one audience. Rather he just wanted to amuse every group more intensely or more often than he offended it. The best modern comparison may be the wide spectrum of strategies by which some Hollywood movies seem to engage with a controversial political issue but still manage to move, amuse, and entertain audience members of almost every viewpoint.

Paternalism

The Captives is another a play by Plautus. Its hero is again a slave, but a noble rather than a wily one.[13] This slave, Tyndarus, is captured in war along with his master. He changes identities with his master so that the latter can return home. As punishment, Tyndarus is loaded with chains and sent to work in a quarry with orders that he be treated even more harshly than the other workers (721–738). He endures this fate proudly in the knowledge that he is sacrificing himself for his master, who has treated him so well (682–688). According to one view, slaves were contemptible, inferior, and hostile; this justified their slavery. The other view, exemplified by Tyndarus, is that slaves and masters enjoyed a hierarchical, but mutually beneficial, affectionate, and familial relationship. This is the model of paternalism, the conception of slavery in terms of an analogy with the relation of a father and his children. Masters should benevolently rule their slaves, as a father treats his children; slaves should be loyal and obedient to their masters, as good children respect and obey their parents. The patriarchal family was a central institution in the classical world. And, if any outsiders deserved to be part of this family, it was those domestic slaves on terms of daily intimacy with the family. Ancient vocabulary illustrates this way of thinking in both Greece and Rome: *oiketēs*, member of the house (*oikos*), was one Greek word for slave; as we have seen the Roman *familia* could mean family in our sense, but it often referred only to the slaves of a household – and the related *famulus* meant slave. In both Greece and Rome – as in many slave systems – paternalism was a common and natural way that masters thought about slaves.

It is hard to judge how often ancient slave masters felt the need to justify slavery; in the United States South paternalism played a leading role in the defense of slavery in the generation before the Civil War (Dal Lago and Katsari 2008, 201). It was not unusual for a master to refer to "all my children, black and white" – a paternalistic sentiment, not a reference to children fathered on slave women! Not since the 1940s have any historians taken such claims seriously as a description of the relations between slaves and masters in any of the New World slave societies. Just as surely should we reject any notion that ancient slavery was accurately described by the analogy with the family: have you whipped or sold any family members recently? We'll investigate first how the paternal analogy sometimes and in some respects corresponded to the practice of slavery, but also the ways that it was a partial and distorted picture that primarily served the material and psychological needs of masters. Although paternalism is also easy to find in classical Greece – as in the Plato quotation at the start of this chapter – we will focus on the rich and varied Roman evidence.

Pliny the Younger was a wealthy senator and a kind and caring master to his slaves – according to himself, we need to add, since his letters are our only source of information. For example, he was upset when a beloved ex-slave got ill, and he spared no effort or

---

13 On *The Captives* I follow Thalmann (1996), who argues for a conservative interpretation of the play: "[it] stages a situation that implicitly raises questions about the bases of freedom and servitude, and in the end it resolves them reassuringly by sorting out who is 'properly' slave and who is free" (114).

expense to help him back to health – as did Cicero too when his slave secretary, Tiro, was sick.[14] Pliny considerately retired to a distant part of the house, so his work would not be disturbed by the loud partying during the Saturnalia nor the slaves by him (*Letters* 2.17.24). All this contributed to his view of himself as a father figure to his slaves: "Homer's expression – 'he was gentle as a father' – is always in my mind along with our own 'father of the household'" (Pliny, *Letters* 5.19.2).

This ideal was not just Pliny's; it was ubiquitous in Roman culture. We've seen that the full names of ex-slaves included their master's name in the place where a free-born son would put his father's name. Some noble Roman families granted the land for *columbaria* for their deceased slaves and freed persons; many Roman slaveholders took care of the burial and commemoration of individual slaves and ex-slaves. In both cases, they assuaged their slaves' and freedpersons' fear of ending up in the lime-pits by taking over a traditional familial duty. Born slaves were sometimes regarded as the lowest grade of slaves, but within a paternalistic framework slaves born within a household, *vernae*, could be regarded as the most tightly bound to the family (Tacitus, *Annals* 14.44; Statius, *Silvae* 2.1.72–78). Some epitaphs display particular affection for *vernae*: "Claudia Helpis [put this up] for Veneria, her own very dear *verna*, who lived ten years five months, and twenty-five days" (*CIL* 6.15459, second century CE). We already saw the gravestone of another *verna* in Figure 3.1. As you'll recall, she seems to have been murdered and, in the epitaph, her master called down a curse on the perpetrator. The duty of commemorating, the affections expressed, and the invocation of divine vengeance suggest familial ties between masters and slaves, especially those born in the house.

The Roman cult of the Lares, guardian spirits, also represented slaves as subordinate members of the family. At the Compitalia, the public neighborhood festival of the Lares, each household adorned a shrine with a puppet for each free member and with a little ball for each slave. Slaves were part of the household but symbolized without human features or gender (Edmondson 2011, 338). Sacrifice to the Lares within the house marked many important life events and transitions. It shows a similar pattern in terms of free and slaves. Many large houses had two sets of shrines to the Lares. A fancier *lararium* with actual bronze statuettes stood in the elegantly decorated areas of the house, inhabited by the *paterfamilias* and his family. A cheaper, cruder *lararium*, with figure painted on, was located in the service area of a house, often near the kitchen. Archaeologists suspect that the painted *lararium* was the place where slaves would worship the household gods. The slaves were symbolically included within the religious community and rites of the house. That their *lararium* was separate and merely painted marked the slave members of the household as on a different, lower plane than the head of the house and his family (Tybout 1996).

Romans like to think that their slaves regarded them as parents. They could bring to mind faithful slaves who returned their master's paternalistic care with the utmost devotion. Valerius Maximus devotes a short chapter of his book on *Memorable Doings and Sayings* to the "Fidelity of Slaves." Most of these stories come from the proscriptions, political executions, of the late Republic. In a typical example, a slave pretends to be his master and is killed so his master can escape (6.8.6). Another example shows devotion on both sides: slaves refuse to reveal their master's hiding place even under torture; he comes out to be killed to stop the suffering of such "faithful and exemplary" slaves (6.8.5).

---

14 Pliny, *Letters* 5.19; Cicero, *Letters to Friends* 40–44 (16.10, 16.13–15).

Figure 11.3 *Lararium* in the House of the Vettii. This house is located in the ancient Italian town of Pompeii, buried and largely preserved by the eruption of Mt. Vesuvius in 79 CE. The *lararium* was located in the kitchen and service area of the house and probably was intended for the use of the slaves – that archaeologists did not find another *lararium* for the master's family is puzzling. Its central panel depicts the house's Genius, closely associated with the head of the household (*paterfamilias*), who is preparing to pour a libation; he is flanked by two dancing Lares; the snake, which is typical, either represents prosperity or serves a protective function. *Source*: ©2016 Photo Scala, Florence. Courtesy of the Ministerio Beni e Att. Culturali.

Not every slave had a chance to save his master's life by sacrificing his own: a couple of comedies show an unexpected but more frequent duty of slaves within the framework of paternalism: household slaves were expected to give their masters gifts on special occasions such as weddings and birthdays.[15] Household slaves seem generally to have had their own money, a *peculium* at Rome. Some might willingly want to give a little something to a kind master on a special occasion. In comedy at least, slaves are pressured to cough up a "gift" for "a family member," whether they wanted to or not and even if they had acquired their little stash through extra work and self-deprivation and wanted eventually to buy their freedom with it.

---

15 Terence, *Phormio* 39–50 with McCarthy 2004, 108–109. An ancient commentator, Donatus, indicates that this scene was in the original Greek play, so we can't be sure whether it represents Greek or Roman practice – or both I suspect; cf. Plautus, *Pseudolus* 775–787.

When, at the Compitalia, a wealthy Roman with a household including more than a hundred slaves ordered balls to be put up for the slaves in his household, would he bother to be sure the numbers were exactly right? And what about all the slaves working in the fields on his many distant estates? The farmhouses could have *lararia*, but the actual slave owner was often absent and could not regularly participate in any familial rituals there. If there was any sense of family bond between slave and master that extended beyond a small circle of household slaves, it must have been weak. And the notion of slaves as members of the family in a paternalistic system competed with two other perspectives. First, Roman thinking often and sharply distinguished between the concern of a father for his children and the use a master made of his slaves. As Richard Saller points out "classical Roman authors, far from advocating the virtue of corporal punishment for children and slaves alike condemned the use of the whip on children precisely because it was important to differentiate children from slaves" (1994, 134, 151). Second, the same Romans who affected a paternal care for their slave children could also view slaves as hostile and kept in check by violence; the many counter-measures and precautions against flight, resistance, and rebellion attest amply to this suspicious attitude. This suggests that a more sinister consideration connected with intimacy also contributed to paternalism. Masters depended on their personal slaves and were probably aware that the slaves could hurt them, if they really wanted to – remember the slave mistress accused of poisoning in Chapter 7. Thinking of slaves as like family members and especially as like unthreatening children may have assuaged these fears somewhat.

We can sum up the limits and distortions of paternalism, just as we started, with Pliny the Younger, the self-styled gentle master and "father of his household." One historian estimates that Pliny owned at least six houses in four different areas of Italy. When he was able, he took an interest in the running of his farms, but his political career required that he spend most of his time in Rome; he was often an absentee owner. Pliny almost certainly owned at least 400 slaves, and he may have owned several times as many (Duncan-Jones 1965, 178, 182). We may well believe that he was a relatively mild slaveholder and that he cared sincerely about some of his closest slaves. But did his hundreds of slaves who rarely even laid eyes on the great master and took their orders from various overseers or tenant farmers have any reason to feel that Pliny, a very distant father figure, was caring for them?

For his part, Pliny's trust that his slaves reciprocated his paternal care like good children was shaky. When he describes the murder of Larcius Macedo by some of his slaves, he has no concern for Macedo's slaves, innocent as well as guilty, executed according to the *Senatus Consultum Silanianum* (see Chapter 9). Instead Pliny is indignant of behalf of masters subject to violence at the hands of ungrateful slaves: "There you see the dangers, outrages and insults to which we are exposed. No master can feel safe because he is kind and considerate; for it is their brutality, not their reasoning capacity, which leads slaves to murder masters" (Pliny, *Letters* 3.14.5, trans. Radice 1969). Even though he admits that Macedo was a cruel master, Pliny feels let down by the failure of slaves to live up to the paternalistic ideal. No doubt many slaves also felt let down by paternalism – far more often and with greater justice.

Conclusion

Some free people and masters saw slavery as exclusively a matter of bad luck, but many more thought it had a basis in some supposed inferiority of slaves: they were failed warriors, foreigners, childish, dishonest, cowardly, gluttonous, bibulous, or demeaned by the work they had to do. Slaves could be regarded as intrinsically hostile or, in contrast, as bound in pseudo-familial ties to their masters. All these notions were part of ancient ideologies of slavery: they were ways of describing or thinking about slavery that served an ulterior purpose, to make the institution seem just or natural or, at least, inevitable.

Historians possess their best evidence for the ideology of slaveholding males. Such men were the commissioners, audience, or actual producers of most of our evidence. We know almost nothing about the attitudes of the poor free or about whether women had distinct attitudes towards slavery. But what about what slaves themselves thought? Historians used to attribute great persuasive power to ruling-class ideology. According to this model, the ideologies that claimed that slaves were inferior somehow convinced slaves that they were inferior and that they ought to serve their masters well. In the case of paternalism, one scholar says that the inclusion of slaves in domestic religious cults – such as that of the Lares – was "an effective means of ensuring the servant's loyalty to the master and his house" (Tybout 1996, 370). I do not wish to dismiss the effects of ideology on subordinate classes altogether; for example, wealthy freedmen owned slaves themselves and, in other ways too, seem to have accepted many of their masters' values. Nevertheless, most historians today are deeply skeptical about the ability of ideology to win over the oppressed. The loyalty of slaves – from "wandering" slaves to Spartacus – was dubious at best; what obedience or diligence slaves displayed is usually better explained by concrete tools of social control, the rewards and punishments we have encountered repeatedly. And, as we saw last chapter, what historians have difficulty explaining is not that slaves were more passive and obedient than they could have been, but rather that they resisted and revolted even when an objective appraisal would have told them that they had little hope of success (Scott 1990, 79).

Suggested Reading

Hunt 2011 contains more detailed versions of the arguments I present about Greek literary representations of slaves above; Joshel 2011 provides a similar overview of the depiction of Roman slaves. Wrenhaven 2012 provides a recent survey of Greek representations of slaves. Fitzgerald 2000 is an important treatment of slavery and the metaphor of slavery in Roman literature. Alston, Hall, and Proffitt 2011 includes recent contributions on slaves in Greek and Roman literary genres as well as chapters on vase painting by Thalmann and Wrenhaven. Oakly 2000 also considers the representation of female attendants in Athenian art. On slaves in Roman comedy, I mainly used Parker 1989, Thalmann 1996, McCarthy 2000, and Richlin 2014 – see now also Richlin 2017 – but Segal 1968, 99–169, is already an insightful and engaging treatment. The representation of slaves in Greek comedy is also a fascinating topic, treated by Harsh 1955, Walin 2009, Sommerstein 2009, and the essays collected in Akrigg and Tordoff 2013. "A Funny Thing Happened on the Way to the Forum" is the movie version (1966) of a silly Broadway musical based on the plays of Plautus with Zero Mostel as Pseudolus, the lead role. Dal Lago and Katsari 2008 compare paternalistic models in ancient and modern slavery. Genovese 1976 provides a detailed and sophisticated portrayal of Southern slavery with particular emphasis on the ideology of paternalism.

12

Philosophy and Law

> *Others ... maintain that ... slavery is unjust, for it is based on force.*
> Aristotle, *Politics* 1.2, 1253b20–23, trans. Rackham 1932

> *Kindly remember that he whom you call your slave sprang from the same stock, is smiled upon by the same skies, and on equal terms with yourself breathes, lives, and dies.*
> Seneca, *Epistles* 47.10, trans. Gummere 1917

> *Slavery is an institution of the law of all peoples (ius gentium) whereby, contrary to nature, one person is subject to the control of another.*
> Justinian's Digest 1.5.4.1

Introduction

Rather than literary representations and popular notions about slaves and slavery, this chapter focuses on philosophy and law: early critics of slavery and Aristotle's response to them, the Stoics and Christians, and ameliorations of slavery in Roman law. Philosophy and law are systematic, abstract, and explicit, but they are not independent of popular sentiments: philosophers often systematize or react to common ideas in their societies; law derives in part from a society's moral sense. For example, Aristotle's notorious theory of natural slavery clarified and systematized the notion that slaves are inferior as part of his justification of slavery. And Aristotle's conclusion that foreigners are natural slaves drew on Greek ethnic chauvinism. Like some Greek tragedies, the Stoics, adherents of another school of philosophy, represented slavery as the result of bad luck. They rejected the idea that some people are radically different and inferior and thus natural slaves. They accepted slavery, however, as a natural part of a world shaped by divine reason. Christians shared the Stoic emphasis on the unity of humanity; they were no more inclined than the Stoics to overturn the hierarchies of this world. Last chapter, we considered the frequent descriptions of violence against slaves in Roman comedy; in addition to philosophical responses, this chapter surveys ancient legislation to limit such abuse. Inevitably these laws were narrow in their

Ancient Greek and Roman Slavery, First Edition. Peter Hunt.
© 2018 Peter Hunt. Published 2018 by John Wiley & Sons, Ltd.

scope: physical punishment played such a central role in slavery that the law could not proceed far without undermining the whole system – which Roman lawmakers were not inclined to do.

From the quotations at the start of this chapter, you might expect that there arose in antiquity widespread and fundamental criticisms of slavery, perhaps even an abolitionist movement hastening the decline of ancient slavery. The real story is more depressing. We hear no more than the single sentence quoted above about the "others," whose criticisms of slavery Aristotle tries to answer. At most times and places slavery does not seem even to have been controversial. Seneca, quoted above, aspired to be a good master. He did not want to end slavery nor even to free his own slaves, however much he thought of them as "brothers." Legal theorists may have found slavery contrary to nature. This conclusion did not prevent Roman law from regulating in minute detail virtually every legal consequence or controversy that resulted from treating some people as private property. Next chapter, we'll see that while slavery did decline with the disintegration of the Roman Empire, this was not because of moral objections or Christianity, and that some slavery continued. One recurring theme throughout this chapter will be the way that the conclusions of philosophers, Christians, and lawmakers were constrained by economic forces, especially the vested interest of the upper classes in the continuation of slavery. Other factors too contributed to the acceptance of slavery, not only by the average person – who may hardly have given this longstanding and ubiquitous institution a second thought – but also by philosophers and theologians, some of whom display exquisite moral sensibilities in other contexts and from whom one might have expected better.

Before turning to these topics, a few words about the use of slavery as a metaphor. Ancient Greeks and Romans thought more *with* slavery than *about* it (Weidemann 1997, 11). They used the metaphor or analogy of slavery as the basis (source domain) for thinking about many other areas of life (target domains). Humans often try to understand complicated or abstract objects or relations in terms of concrete and physical ones. Some examples are so ingrained in our thinking that we don't even notice them. *Up* is better and *down* is worse: the team playing at a *higher* level is likely to win the game as things go *downhill* for their opponents. It is telling that slavery provided the source domain for so many parts of the classical worldview; slavery was obviously a well-known, everyday, and concrete reality that could be used to think about more abstract relationships. Plato, for instance, insists repeatedly that the body needs to be the *slave* of the soul rather than have the soul the *slave* of the body (*Phaedo* 79e–80a, cf. 66d1; *Timaeus* 34c.4). The Stoics hold that most people are *enslaved* to things that are neither of vital importance nor under their control – food, money, health, ambition, sex, social status. Similarly, Christianity aims to liberate people from being *slaves* to sin (1 Cor. 7:22, Eph. 6:6, Rom. 6:22).

The analogy of slavery was often applied to other steep hierarchies in power or status, usually in a critical sense. For example, during the Peloponnesian War, the Spartan general Brasidas gave a speech at Acanthus, which Thucydides reports (4.86.1, 4.86.4): Brasidas wanted to *free* the city from Athens. He would not interfere in their internal politics, neither to *enslave* the many to the few (impose an oligarchy) nor to *enslave* the few to the many (impose a democracy). Both the active and passive sides of the slavery metaphor had negative associations: it was evil to try to impose

Figure 12.1 EID MAR Denarius, Roman silver coin (42 BCE). The Roman goddess Liberty had the staff, the *vindicta*, and the freedman's *pilleus* as her attributes. Brutus, one of the conspirators who killed Julius Caesar, famously minted coins with daggers, to symbolize the assassination, and the *pilleus*, to symbolize the freedom that this deed had restored. "Eid Mar," Ides of March (March 15th), refers to the date of the assassination. It is striking that elite Romans were willing to use symbols deriving from the emancipation of slaves. *Source*: Courtesy of John Nebel.

metaphorical slavery; it was cowardly or effeminate to endure it. These figurative uses of slavery remained just as important in Roman culture (as in Figure 8.1). And, for example, the emperor Tiberius would mutter, "men ready to be slaves," whenever he left a meeting of the Senate, whose obsequiousness exasperated him – a scathing putdown of Rome's wealthy and proud political elite (Tacitus, *Annals* 3.65). The use of the slavery metaphor was as common as the institution of chattel slavery was ubiquitous. Even the Western ideal of freedom had its origin as the opposite of this metaphorical slavery (Patterson 1991; Raaflaub 2004). But let's now turn from metaphor to our main subject, those relatively rare, but fascinating, ancient discussions of the justice or injustice of slavery.

The Anonymous Opponents of Slavery

The honor roll listing ancient critics of slavery is a short one. Near the top of the list stands a group known among historians today as the Anonymous Opponents of Slavery. The Greek philosopher Aristotle (384–322 BCE) summarized their critique on his way to developing his own theory of "natural slavery" near the beginning of his *Politics*.

Aristotle admits that there is controversy about the justice of slavery and summarizes the argument of the Anonymous Opponents:

> Others however maintain that for one man to be another man's master is contrary to nature, because it is only convention/law [*nomos,* plural: *nomoi*] that makes the one a slave and the other a freeman and there is no difference between them by nature [*phusis*], and that therefore it [slavery] is unjust, for it is based on force (*Politics* 1.2, 1253b20–23, all trans. Rackham 1932).[1]

The reference to convention/law (*nomos*) and nature *(phusis)* reflects a common type of argument, originally associated with the so-called Sophists, itinerant intellectuals of the fifth century BCE. Sophists would begin by showing that a certain social practice was conventional, in accord with *nomos*. By itself this was unobjectionable: especially if the *nomos* was widespread, one might assume there is a pretty good reason for its adoption. But a *nomos* is not an eternal law; it can be changed and ought to be changed when it is contrary to nature, against *phusis*. In some of Plato's dialogues, Sophists are represented as using this *nomos/phusis* argument to attack traditional rules that prevent the strong from doing and taking whatever they want. They argue that these *nomoi* are contrary to *phusis* and were merely the result of a conspiracy by the weak against the strong (e.g., *Gorgias* 482e–484a). In contrast to this, the dark, amoral use of the *nomos/phusis* distinction, the Anonymous Opponents use it to offer a moral argument against slavery as an institution originating from *nomos* but contrary to *phusis*.

The Anonymous Opponents added that the institution of slavery rests on violence. There are two ways to take this statement. No Greek could be unaware of the role in slavery of whipping and other violent punishments and threats. But Aristotle discusses a second role of violence in slavery: many slaves lost their freedom as the result of defeat in warfare (*Politics* 1.2, 1255a3–28). The Greeks considered it a *nomos* that the possessions of the defeated and the defeated themselves belonged to the victors in war (Xenophon, *Cyropaedia* 7.5.73). This *nomos* accorded with the high place accorded to military prowess in classical culture: defeat seemed to imply inferiority. Enslavement in war also provided some basis for a popular and longstanding, pseudo-contractual justification of slavery: slaves were permanently indebted to their captors, who had refrained from killing them. Accordingly, the Romans even believed that the word slave, *servus*, derived from the word, *servare*, "to save" (cf. Watson 1992, 1350–1353).

The Anonymous Opponents may overlap with another group – described by Aristotle as "many experts in law" – who object to this wartime *nomos* and argue that, "it is monstrous if the person powerful enough to use force, and superior in power, is to have the victim of his force as his slave and subject" (*Politics* 1.2, 1255a8–12). Aristotle concedes this point:

> Wars may be unjust in their origin and one would by no means admit that a man who does not deserve slavery can be really a slave – otherwise we shall have the result that persons reputed of the highest nobility are slaves and the descendants of slaves if they happen to be taken prisoners of war and sold. (*Politics* 1.2, 1255a25–29)

---

1 See also Euripides, *Ion* 854–856 and the scholiast on Aristotle, *Rhetoric* 1.13 1373b18 in Garnsey 1996, 75.

It may seem that Aristotle here accepts a strong argument against slavery as practiced, since wars and raids accounted for a large proportion of slaves in Greece either directly or indirectly. But, for Aristotle, non-Greeks were natural slaves anyway and wars against them just.[2] And while, like Plato, he condemns the enslavement of Greeks in war (*Politics* 1.2, 1255a29–32; Plato, *Republic* V 469b5–c1), they provided only a minority of slaves anyway – as we explored in Chapter 3.

Admittedly, Aristotle does concede that some slavery is by luck rather than by nature. Last chapter we interpreted the claim that slavery is a matter of bad luck as relatively benign; that is only true when compared to derogatory representations of slaves as inferior human beings. For masters to claim that it is just "bad luck" that their slaves are slaves is disingenuous. It is not bad luck but the master who whips the slaves, if they don't obey him, or who chains them up so they can't run away. The master bought slaves precisely for the work he could force them to do. When the Anonymous Opponents called slavery unjust, they went further than merely admitting that slaves and free people are not intrinsically different and then blaming their circumstances on luck.

Were the Anonymous Opponents abolitionists then? We simply don't know. Various rationalizations could have justified inaction despite their fundamental criticisms of slavery. They might have argued that slavery was unjust but necessary for some greater good, or that their individual action – for instance, freeing their own slaves – would make little difference to a ubiquitous institution. The Anonymous Opponents may have included intellectuals and teachers, who, like some Sophists, did not derive their income directly from slave labor. Nevertheless, their livelihood depended on their ability to attract students from elite families. These students, wealthy young men, may not have wanted to pay good money to hear the basis of their family wealth and lifestyle attacked. Sophists and philosophers did not shrink from controversy, but perhaps calling slavery unjust was quite enough without pressing for any concrete action.

Aristotle's Theory of Natural Slavery

Aristotle discusses the Anonymous Opponents in the context of his own, now notorious, theory of natural slavery. His reasoning is relatively simple, but the connection with the rest of his philosophy as well as the exact meaning of some passages can be complicated and obscure. Here I will merely organize some of his main arguments following a distinction made by Bernard Williams between Aristotle's "argument from above" and his "argument from below" (Williams 1993, 115). The argument from above is Aristotle's attempt to show that the institution of slavery is natural: great benefits derive from the hierarchy and specialization that slavery allows. This line of reasoning does not tell us whether there are people who are naturally slaves or masters and, if so, who they are. That is the function of Aristotle's argument from below: there actually exist people whose best function in life is to be slaves. To take a modern parallel, the conviction of economists that a society's wealth, health, and happiness depend on specialization is an argument from above. An argument from below, if somebody wanted to make it, would

---

2 See below and Aristotle, *Politics* 7.14, 1333b39–1334a3.

be that there are some people naturally suited to spend their lives as CEOs and others to spend their lives cutting up chickens in a poultry factory or digging ditches. Aristotle tries to show that slavery is natural in both senses, from above and from below.

Why did Aristotle think that the institution of slavery is natural, the argument from above? First of all, he conceives of the universe as deeply hierarchical: every composite has a ruling element and a ruled element. Within the household, a crucial composite and the building block of human society, masters rule slaves just as the soul should rule the body. The master thinks and the slave acts to carry out the master's orders with his body. Nature is not only hierarchical, but also purposeful. The purpose of human society can only be achieved in the city-state; the master of the house contributes to the city-state by using his intelligence and taking part in public life. Thus the hierarchy of slavery within the household allows for the accomplishment of the greatest human good. In reality, not all slaveholders were public-spirited philosophers: the time for politics and intellectual pursuits hardly constituted the only or main benefit the rich obtained through their slaves. Nevertheless, slavery makes sense within Aristotle's overall theory of a hierarchical universe and the goals he sets for humanity. That is his argument from above.

Aristotle moves from the argument from above to the argument from below when he tries to find the people who fit into this natural hierarchy of slavery:

> All men that differ as widely as the soul does from the body and the human being from the lower animal (and this is the condition of those whose function is the use of the body and from whom this is the best that is forthcoming) – these are by nature slaves, for whom to be governed by this kind of authority is advantageous. (*Politics* 1.2 1254b17–22)

But who are these people who are so inferior that they benefit from being slaves? Given the weight Aristotle puts on the slaves-are-like-bodies analogy and the priority he gives to intellectual activities, it is not surprising that he puts mental deficiency at the center of his definition of a natural slave: a person "who participates in reason so far as to apprehend it but not to possess it."[3]

Greek culture sometimes treated slaves as being almost mere bodies: one word for slave was simply *sōma*, "body." And a key distinction between free and slave at Athens was that slaves were subject to bodily punishment, whereas citizens were generally not (Demosthenes 22.55). For example, slaves could only give evidence in court under torture, a practice both cruel and puzzling.[4] Aristotle may be drawing on this common association of slaves with the body, but philosophically he has gotten himself into a tight spot. On the one side, slaves at Athens did a wide variety of intellectual jobs: some were bankers, bureaucrats, skilled craftsmen, or managed farms, household finances, or mines. These slaves showed no obvious sign of mental deficiency, so Aristotle seems to be insisting on a high standard for the possession of reason. He may mean that slaves do not possess the deliberative abilities needed for politics or philosophy. On the other side, the possession of reason cannot be something that only a few people display:

---

3 Aristotle, *Politics* 1.2 1254b23–24. Kraut 2002, 284–290 provides a charitable exploration of what Aristotle might have meant.

4 See Hunt 2016c, 146–150 for a brief discussion with bibliography.

otherwise non-philosophers – that is, most masters – would fail the test.[5] He can't set the bar too high either.

Aristotle's philosophical troubles are not yet over, since people's bodies should be suited for their natural tasks:

> The intention of nature therefore is to make the bodies also of freemen and of slaves different – the latter strong for necessary service, the former erect and unserviceable for such occupations, but serviceable for a life of citizenship. (*Politics* 1.2, 1254b28–32)

Unfortunately, as Aristotle admits, in this case nature *often* fails and "the very opposite comes about – slaves have the bodies of free men and free men the souls only" (*Politics* 1.2, 1254b33–34). This high failure rate is hard to reconcile with Aristotle's concept of nature, otherwise powerful and effective.

These issues may explain why Aristotle turned to a popular notion, the inferiority of non-Greeks, to save his thesis of natural slavery (*Politics* 1.2, 1255a29–32; see also 1252b6–10). There may be some people in slavery who are not slaves by nature – mainly captive Greeks – but non-Greeks were natural slaves. Even though there are examples throughout Greek culture of ambivalence or even admiration of non-Greeks, Aristotle turns to a particularly extreme and crude ethnic chauvinism to confirm his argument from below that some people were natural slaves.

The general notion that slaves were inferior people preceded Aristotle and continued after him throughout the classical world. His philosophical elaboration of this view did not make much of an impression upon later thinkers in the ancient world – though it was to have an important impact in the New World as we'll see. If we can trust a late source, Diogenes Laertius, an intriguing possibility arises: Aristotle was a hypocrite, albeit in a good sense (Diogenes Laertius, *Lives of Eminent Philosophers* 5.11–16). Nicomachus, to whom his *Nicomachean Ethics* is dedicated, was the son of Aristotle by his *pallakē* (see Chapter 7), his ex-slave, Herpyllis. In his will Aristotle gave immediate freedom to one slave and left orders that three others be given their freedom when his daughter married. The other slaves who took care of Aristotle were not to be sold – presumably so as not to break up families or other ties – and were to be given their freedom "at the appropriate age." It is difficult, but just possible, to reconcile manumission with Aristotle's theory, according to which natural slaves are better off in slavery (Kraut 2002, 297–298). In any case, from a modern point of view, Aristotle comes off far better from the instructions in this will than from his arguments for natural slavery in the *Politics*.

Stoicism and Christianity

Stoicism, the most influential of the Hellenistic schools of philosophy, was founded shortly after Aristotle's death by Zeno of Citium (ca. 344–262 BCE). Members of the Roman elite adopted and adapted Stoicism in the later Republic and early Empire. In

---

5 Aristotle, like many ancient philosophers, oversimplified and assumed that people are either slaves or masters. Presumably the audience or readership for philosophy consisted of wealthy slaveholders and not the free poor.

fact, the only complete works of Stoic philosophy to survive from antiquity were written under the Roman Empire. Two of these later Stoics, Seneca the Younger and Epictetus, will be the focus of my treatment, even though their outlook may diverge from the original and probably more radical theories of early Stoicism.[6] Many historians have linked Stoicism to more humane attitudes towards slaves and even to Roman laws protecting slaves. We'll first consider why the Stoics have enjoyed such a good reputation but also the basically conservative nature of their recommendations. Early Christian attitudes towards slavery show many parallels with the Stoics, some of which were the result of Stoic influence. That Rome was a slave society, and that its more affluent members depended economically on slavery, severely limited the changes that any philosopher or church father was willing to advocate.

Seneca was a rich senator, a famous intellectual, and a close advisor to the emperor Nero, by whom he was eventually executed. The contrast between his philosophical professions and his wealth and intimacy with Nero opened him up to criticism. Seneca may even have composed the unconvincing lies by which Nero tried to justify the murder of his mother (Tacitus, *Annals* 14.11). Nevertheless, his rejection of natural slavery and his pleas for the kind treatment of slaves constitute a famous and admired example of Stoic social critique. He devotes to the topic of slavery one of his series of letters designed to instruct a certain Lucilius – and posterity – in Stoic ethics (*Epistles* 47). Seneca begins by complimenting Lucilius on his easy familiarity with his slaves. He anticipates objections from people who look down on slaves as utterly different and inferior and eventually presents three Stoic arguments against drawing sharp distinctions between masters and slaves.

First, Seneca begins by recreating an imaginary debate with those who object to treating slaves on an equal footing:

> "They are slaves," people declare. No, they are men. "Slaves!" No, comrades. "Slaves!" No, they are lowly friends. "Slaves!" No, they are our fellow-slaves, if one reflects that Fortune has equal rights over slaves and free men alike." (*Epistles* 47.1, all trans. Gummere 1917, here modified)

Here Seneca repeatedly asserts the humanity of slaves. His last point, that they are "fellow-slaves" subject to fortune invokes an important Stoic doctrine, that the only thing that matters is inner calm and virtuous conduct. Everything else is an *indifferent* (Greek: *adiaphora*), because it does not make a difference to a person's true happiness.[7] Ignoring *indifferents*, however, is a tall order. As the modern meaning of the word *stoic* implies, ancient Stoics sought not to be affected by personal disasters such as illness, slavery, or the death of loved ones. So Zeno of Citium propounded a famous paradox in terms of the slave metaphor: only the (Stoic) sage is free; everybody else is a slave to *indifferents* that ought not to matter. Since there are few sages and lots of average Joes and Janes, no matter how rich and noble and self-confident you are, you are probably no better than a slave to things outside your control. Seneca here points out to his intended

---

6 See Brunt 1998 on slavery in the *Meditations* of Marcus Aurelius, a Roman emperor and the third of the famous Stoics of the imperial period.

7 The Stoics did admit that some *indifferents* were preferable to others, making for a more sensible, but less elegant philosophy. They mainly stressed the foolishness of worrying about *indifferents* at all.

readers (rich and educated Roman slaveholders) that they and actual slaves are equally dependent on *indifferents* and in this sense are "fellow-slaves." Conversely, slaves have the same (slim) chance as masters to attain wisdom and thus free themselves from *indifferents* (*On Benefits* 3.18.2, 3.28.1–2).

An example of fortune's power provides a second argument against natural slavery: you too could end up a slave. Seneca explains that, for example, many young and ambitious Roman nobles lost their freedom as the result of military disasters (*Epistles* 47.10). This point reminds us of the Greek tragedies, such as the *Trojan Women*, that also focus on nobles reduced to slavery. These changes in status can undermine a blanket theory of natural difference between slave or free, as Seneca stresses here. Nevertheless, we should not exaggerate this problem: remember that tragedy preserves a distinction between "born slaves" and the free and noble for whom slavery is a catastrophe; even Aristotle concedes these exceptional cases of nobles enslaved contrary to their nature, all the while insisting on natural slavery.

Seneca's third argument is that both slave and free are "sprung from the same stock" and have "the same origins" (*Epistles* 47.10; cf. *On Benefits* 3.28.1). This refers to the Stoic belief that the same divine spirit – *pneuma*, literally "breath" – constitutes the souls of all people (*Epistles* 31.11). All souls have this same origin and composition and all humans share a sort of kinship. Seneca's rejection of sharp intrinsic or natural differences between slave and free has roots in this Stoic cosmology.

From this fellowship of all humanity, Seneca infers that we have a duty to be kind to slaves. He occasionally invites slaves to join him at dinner – presumably served and cooked by his other slaves – even though he anticipates that some haughty readers will denounce this sort of familiarity as "debasing and disgraceful" (*Epistles* 47.13). He also condemns the usual harsh treatment of household slaves during dinner:

> All this time the poor slaves may not move their lips, even to speak. The slightest murmur is repressed by the rod; even a chance sound – a cough, a sneeze, or a hiccup – is visited with the lash. There is a grievous penalty for the slightest breach of silence. All night long they must stand about, hungry and mute. (*Epistles* 47.3)

He rejects the aphorism we encountered last chapter – "You have as many enemies as you have slaves" – with the rebuttal that slaves are not enemies until we make enemies of them (*Epistles* 47.5). He praises Lucilius for "lashing his slaves only with the tongue," and argues that only animals need physical punishment (*Epistles* 47.19). Such benign treatment of slaves in close contact with their masters – not as likely, I think, for slaves working under overseers on distant farms – may have been common well beyond the circle of Stoics (Griffin 1976, 256–285). For example, in another work Seneca mentions that "cruel masters" were scorned and hated throughout Rome (*On Mercy* 1.18.3). Still, Seneca and the Stoics look pretty good so far: they insist on the essential fellowship of slaves and masters and favor humane treatment.

A blind spot in the Stoics' moral outlook becomes apparent when we compare them with the Anonymous Opponents, who argue that slavery was contrary to nature, unjust, and violent. Since the Stoics find no essential distinction between masters and slaves, they reject Aristotle's argument from below and natural slavery. But there is also a profoundly conservative strain in Stoic thought. The Stoics believe that human society, including its hierarchies, is permeated with the divine reason (*logos*) and thus good and natural in some sense. Roman Stoics in particular did not aspire to change society but rather urged every individual to perform his or her given role virtuously (Garnsey 1996, 105). Seneca, for instance, sees his role as a father figure to his slaves, a paternalistic ideal (*Epistles* 47.14). He advises masters to act according to justice and mercy and to "treat your inferiors as you would be treated by your betters."[8] For slaves, performing their role well requires primarily that they do more for their masters than they are required to – including heroic self-sacrifice if needed – a view similar to that of Greek tragedy and not any more subversive (*On Benefits* 3.23–27).

Worldly wealth, including slaves, is a Stoic *indifferent* and attachment to it could hinder one's progress as a Stoic (e.g., *Epistles* 31.10). In fact, Zeno of Citium, the school's founder, reportedly did not possess a single slave (Seneca, *Consolation of Helvia* 12.4). Seneca also cites with approval a story about Diogenes of Sinope, the founder of Cynicism but also a Stoic hero, about his independence from material concerns. When Diogenes' single slave ran away, Diogenes did not pursue him: "It would be a disgrace if Diogenes is not able to live without Manes when Manes is able to live without Diogenes" (*On Tranquility of Mind* 8.7) – remember that Manes was a stereotypical slave name. Stoicism had become more conformist over the centuries and with its adoption by the Romans, so Diogenes and Zeno – like Christian monks in later centuries – became sources of inspiration rather than models for everybody's imitation. So Seneca ends his discussion of owning many slaves – which he represents as a source of aggravation, poor guy! – with the statement that we today do not have the "strength of character" of Diogenes and should merely try to limit the number of our slaves (*On Tranquility of Mind* 8.8–9).

Seneca's claim that master and slave were really fellow-slaves to fortune undermined the notion that some people were natural slaves. But diverting attention to metaphorical slavery – a common Stoic and later Christian ploy – tended to conceal the significance and possible injustice of actual, legal slavery. That the lifestyles and wealth of the rich required slavery goes a long way towards explaining this preference for talking about metaphorical slavery. Williams even argues that Aristotle's attempt to justify slavery was more honest than the Stoic avoidance of the topic: "Seneca and his various associates can let the social world be unjust, because they can, in accordance with one or another of their fantasies, suppose that one can get out of it" (Williams 1993, 116).

We might expect a more radical Stoic critique of slavery from Epictetus (ca. 55–135 CE), a Stoic philosopher from the opposite end of the social spectrum from Seneca. He was born a slave and transported to Rome. He won his freedom and eventually retired to teach Stoic philosophy in Greece. Epictetus was lame, according to one story, as the result of punishment or abuse he suffered as a slave. When it comes to his personal conduct, several stories indicate that he lived a simple life with little regard for property. It is entirely possible that, like Zeno, he did not own slaves.

In the *Discourses*, Epictetus sometimes seems to address the experiences of slaves rather than masters, Seneca's intended audience. For example, Epictetus argues that what is rational for a given person depends on what sort of person they are (*Discourses* 1.2.11). For one person, a slave, it is rational to hold a chamber pot for somebody else to avoid being deprived of food or whipped – remember Figure 9.1. But, Epictetus continues,

---

8 Seneca, *On Mercy* 1.18.1; Seneca, *Epistles* 47.11. Earlier Stoics propounded the same principle.

"Some other man feels that it is not merely unendurable to hold such a pot himself, but even to tolerate another's doing so" (*Discourses* 1.2.8–9, all trans. Oldfather 1925–1928). This second man, a better Stoic, does not care about being whipped or fed and will not submit to this indignity of slavery; he will not even allow others to be so treated. Perhaps we see here a flash of an ex-slave's deep-seated resentment of the humiliations of slavery. In another passage, Epictetus says that some birds starve themselves to death in captivity and constantly attempt to escape. He imagines an interchange with such a bird:

> "And what is wrong with you here in your cage?" "What a question! My nature is to fly where I please, to live in the open air, to sing when I please. You rob me of all this, and then ask, 'What is wrong with you?'" (*Discourses* 4.1.28)

Epictetus here vividly depicts how contrary to nature it is to deprive any creature of its freedom, as the institution of slavery does.

I would like to be able to represent Epictetus as one of the rare heroes in our story, but just after his subversive fable of the freedom-loving bird, Epictetus switches to the usual Stoic argument that "enslavement" to *indifferents* is worse than legal slavery and even uses the example of an actual slave. When a slave is freed, he imagines that he'll be happy and independent. But, if he lacks Stoic wisdom, he just suffers a succession of new slaveries to various people, ambitions, and vices as he ascends the social ladder (*Discourses* 4.1.33–38). This imaginary freed slave even reflects how good he had it in slavery, when somebody else was responsible for feeding and clothing him. Suddenly we are back to Seneca's complaint about slaves as a burden on their masters! Perhaps Arrian, the high-ranking senator who apparently wrote down and edited Epictetus' lectures to create the *Discourses*, distorted or softened some of Epictetus' more disturbing views. A process of self-censorship or deliberate ambiguity is also possible. Epictetus' career (to take a cynical perspective) or his ability to help his followers towards wisdom (on a more charitable view) depended on not alienating his wealthy students, who, we can assume, were all slaveholders. His predicament recalls for us a familiar constraint, succinctly summarized in a famous aphorism of the American socialist and novelist Upton Sinclair: "It is difficult to get a man to understand something, when his salary depends upon his not understanding it!" (1994 (originally 1935), 109).

You might not expect the same consideration to apply when it came to the early Christians, among whom every social class was represented. Jesus Christ was executed by crucifixion, a punishment reserved for slaves and non-citizens and called "the servile punishment." The *Gospels* contain several anti-elitist messages and early Christianity spread rapidly among diverse urban populations, containing many slaves and ex-slaves (e.g. Mark 10:25 (= Matt. 19:24, Luke 18:25); Meeks 2003, 9–73). Nevertheless, the Christianization of the Roman Empire and the conversion of the emperor Constantine – traditionally dated to 313 CE – did not result in the abolition of slavery or even contribute to its decline. The history of ancient Christian attitudes towards the institution of slavery is a long and complex one; the metaphor of slavery too played a large, but complicated, role in Christian theology. Here I'll merely highlight a couple of salient features, focusing mainly on the first century after Jesus.[9]

---

9 Important later developments include the critique of slavery by Gregory of Nyssa and Augustine's theology according to which slavery was somehow a punishment for original sin (Garnsey 1996, 80–86, 206–220).

One main stream of Christian thought, like Stoicism, denied essential differences between slave and free. Just as both possess the divine spirit according to Stoicism, so too are they equal in the eyes of Christ: "There is neither Jew nor Greek, there is neither slave nor free man, there is neither male nor female; for you are all one in Christ Jesus" (Gal. 3:28, all trans. *New American Standard Bible*; see Neutel 2015). Despite the spiritual unity of humanity, Christians no more intended in this world to get rid of social distinctions between slave and free than to eliminate those between male and female. Like the Stoics, Christians were more interested in playing their roles well than in any radical reformation of social structure. The apostle Paul (ca. 4–64 CE) recommended that people remain in the places in society – for example, slaves or free – that they occupied when called to the faith, although it was fine if a Christian slave won manumission (1 Cor. 7:20–24; cf. Philemon). Stoics adopted their conservative view on the ground that human society is natural and in accordance with the divine. Christian thinking was similar, but sometimes went further and viewed the relation of slave and master as parallel to man's relationship with God, an extremely unequal bond. Thus, a few notorious passages urge slaves to obey their masters: "Slaves, in all things obey those who are your masters on earth, not with external service, as those who merely please men, but with sincerity of heart, fearing the Lord."[10] These injunctions made the obedience of slaves a religious obligation and strongly condemned any sort of resistance, not to mention revolt. In a biblical passage from the generation after Paul, masters too were required also to keep God in mind (Eph. 6:9): "And masters, do the same things to them [slaves], and give up threatening, knowing that both their Master and yours is in heaven, and there is no partiality with Him." Christianity, like Stoicism, demanded virtuous behavior from those in power and, one hopes, this had some effect. Plentiful evidence, however, makes it clear that slave life was similar under Christian masters to what it had been before (Bradley 1994, 147; Harper 2011, 225–238). For example, Kyle Harper points out, "The ancient church, in all the voluminous material it has left behind, bequeathed to posterity not a single statement encouraging the protection of the slave family" (2011, 273).

Christian authors made just as much use of the metaphor of slavery as the Stoics: Jesus Christ was the great liberator of humanity (e.g., Gal. 4:1–10, 5:1, 5:13). In early Christian thought, however, there was a good as well as a bad metaphorical slavery: "One is either a slave to sin or a slave to God" (Garnsey 1996, 183). The Latin term *Dominus* is today translated "Lord," but it was originally a common way to refer to a master of slaves. That early Christians adopted *Dominus* as their word for God strongly implied an analogy with slavery. The negative implications of slavery to sin are easy to understand, but patristic scholars disagree about the exact reason that slavery to God was an appealing metaphor. Two aspects of slavery probably played a part: the slave was viewed as utterly subject and humble towards his master just as a pious person is to God; a slave was also closely connected with his or her master and derived prestige from the status of the master. So church leaders who claimed to be slaves of God were not only being modest – "I'm just like a slave compared to God" – but also asserting their close connection to God.

---

10 Col. 3:22, which may not be by Paul, but reflects early Christian attitudes; cf. Titus 2:9, 1 Tim. 6:1, Eph. 6:5, 1 Pet. 2:18.

Figure 12.2 Metal slave collar. Almost forty metal slave collars have been found. Their inscriptions often included "I am a runaway. Seize me," identified the master, and promised a reward for the return of the slave. All date to the late Empire and a number suggest Christian slaveholders. One plausible explanation for the late dates is that Christians considered it blasphemous to disfigure a person's face with a brand or tattoo, previously a common punishment and way to discourage flight (see Chapter 9). When this practice was outlawed under Constantine (*Theodosian Code* 9.40.2), good Christian slaveholders substituted slave collars which, unlike tattoos, can survive to be found by archaeologists. See Trimble 2016 for a fascinating discussion. *Source*: © 2016. Photo Scala, Florence. Courtesy of the Ministerio Beni e Att. Culturali.

The Amelioration of Slavery in Roman Law

Roman legal codes describe slavery as "an institution of the law of all peoples (*ius gentium*) whereby, contrary to nature, one person is subject to the control of another" (*Justinian's Digest* 1.5.4.1). This is the only case in Roman law where the *ius gentium* is said to be contrary to nature, and some historians suspect Stoic influence (Davis 1966, 83). In any case, the definition of slavery as contrary to nature did not undermine the validity of Roman laws about slaves or the determination of the Romans to enforce them.

Another legal principle, the *favor libertatis*, held that when the application of the law or facts of a case are uncertain, judges should rule so as to favor liberty (Brunt 1998, 144–146). For example, the child of a slave woman was by law a slave, but what if the mother's status changed during her pregnancy? By the *favor libertatis*, if the mother were free during any point in her pregnancy, the child would be free (*Pauli Sententiae* 2.24.3 in Watson 1987, 12). The *favor libertatis* again leans in the right direction, but most slaves were plainly slaves and not on any fuzzy border where they might hope for the benefit of the doubt. This thus provides our first example of a set of laws that show humane feelings but resulted only in amelioration around the edges of slavery rather than changing anything central to the institution.[11] A series of laws aiming to protect slaves from abusive treatment had similar and limited results.

To kill a slave was the most extreme measure a master could take.[12] Throughout Roman history, the law emphasized that masters had the power of life and death over their slaves (*Justinian's Institutes* 1.8.1). In reality, this right was gradually constrained. The earlier phases of this process are unclear, but by the reign of Claudius (41–54 CE) a master could be accused of murdering his own slave (Suetonius, *Claudius* 25.2). We learn more details from the second century CE, when an edict of the emperor Antoninus Pius made killing a slave "without cause" a capital offense (*Justinian's Institutes* 1.8.2; Watson 1987, 126). "Without cause" probably implied that a master needed to get the approval of a judge before having a slave executed. Other laws prevented masters from selling their slaves to the horrific animal fights – where gladiators fought wild animals or condemned criminals were simply eaten alive – or to the mines, also considered a capital punishment. But if the masters obtained approval from a judge, they could inflict these punishments on their slaves (*Justinian's Digest* 48.8.11.1).

One fourth-century CE legal response by the emperors Diocletian and Maximian to a soldier allows us to reconstruct a grim little story and illustrates one complication of trying to protect slaves even from murder:

> When you maintain that your slave died as a result of serious illness, your innocence – whose truth you maintain – does not permit the accusation of slander to be clearly seen, because of your immoderate punishment. (*Collatio Legum Mosaicarum et Romanarum* 3.4.1, trans. Watson 1987, 124)

A soldier claimed that his slave died of an illness, and the emperors' response neither contested nor accepted his version. The soldier also accused a third person of slander for saying, it seems, that he had murdered his slave. The emperors refuse to confirm this accusation of slander on the grounds that the soldier punished his slave so severely that it's not obvious whether the "slander" was true or not. We may imagine either that the

---

11 Three seemingly more substantial reforms turn out to be red herrings. A ruling of Constantine, eventually interpreted as a general law against breaking up slave families, condemned the practice, but only applied to the imperial estates in one province (Harper 2011, 271–273). The unreliable *Scriptores Historiae Augustae* reports that the emperor Hadrian banned the use of *ergastula* (private prisons) of slaves or of free people, an improbable story (Brunt 1998, 149; Eck 2006 on *Hadrian* 18.10). Romans could sell a slave woman on condition that she not be made a prostitute, but this did not affect slaves who were already prostitutes or those sold without such an agreement (McGinn 1998, 288–337).

12 In this section, I follow Watson 1987, 120–129, which also contains translations of most of the passages I cite.

solider deliberately inflicted a punishment so severe that the slave did not survive, or that he injured the slave in a violent rage and the slave eventually died. This was not an isolated case where the master's right to punish and the ban on killing a slave without official sanction made for a legal difficulty. The emperor Constantine promulgated two decrees to adjust previous policies regarding slaves who died as the result of punishment. He forbade killing slaves deliberately or in certain specific (horrible) ways, but his main goal was to reassure masters that there would be no investigations if their slaves died as the result of punishment: the interest of masters in "not destroying their own property" made for a presumption of innocence (*Codex Theodosianus* 9.12.1–2).

Slave eunuchs became more common over the course of the Roman Empire despite a series of increasingly harsh laws against the castration of slaves. These provide, unfortunately, a textbook case where repeated legislation against a practice provides evidence of its continued existence and not of its suppression (Suetonius, *Domitian* 7; *Justinian's Digest* 48.8.6, 48.8.4.2). The emperor Claudius tried to curb another callous practice: when sick slaves no longer seemed worth the trouble of caring for, some masters would just abandon them – for example, in the temple of Asclepius, a god of healing, on Tiber Island in Rome. In an edict Claudius ordered that, if such slaves recovered, they were to be free.[13] A kind thought and just deserts for the masters no doubt, but this measure only helped the small fraction of slaves who seemed sure to die and were abandoned, but pulled through. And the masters suffered no penalty other than the loss of a slave they had given up for dead in any case.

From the fifth century BCE, if not earlier, Greeks and then Romans permitted slaves to flee to temples to escape their master's ill treatment; in the Roman Empire statues of the emperor also served this function. As you may already suspect, neither the Greeks nor Romans were about to allow slaves to gain their freedom just because they were unhappy about their treatment and managed to get to a sanctuary. Rather a magistrate would investigate the slave's case and, if he determined that the abuse was indeed extreme, the slave would be auctioned to a new master. The abusive master would probably only get a low price – since a slave who'd gone to a sanctuary was suspect as damaged goods or as a trouble-maker – but he suffered no other punishment. The prospects were risky for the slave too, since likely buyers of cheap, possibly troublesome slaves included masters whose operations were based on brute violence and physical constraint. And, if the slave did not convince the magistrate, he or she would go back to his master, unlikely to be in a good mood. This whole procedure guaranteed that only the most cruelly abused slaves would decide to flee to a sanctuary.

One case, apparently involving a group of such slaves, made it all the way to the emperor Antoninus Pius, who, consulted by a governor, made the following decision: "So investigate the complaints of the slaves of Julius Sabinus who fled to the statue . . . Tell Sabinus that I will deal severely with him, if he tries to evade my decision" (*Justinian's Institutes* 1.8.2). It must have been reassuring to have this benevolent emperor taking a personal interest in your case. I suspect the deck was usually stacked the other way. Magistrates were slaveholders themselves, and they were likely to sympathize with other slaveholders about whether slaves suffered intolerable abuse or had just got what they deserved for their misbehavior and laziness – or whatever the master was claiming

---

13 Suetonius, *Claudius* 25.2; *Justinian's Digest* 40.8.2; *Justinian's Codex* 7.6.1.3.

in his own defense. And what if the master was a powerful man? In this case, why did a Roman governor need to check with the emperor about a longstanding practice? Was Julius Sabinus such a grand personage that even a governor didn't want to get into a quarrel with him without backup?

Another procedural difficulty affected all the laws curbing abuse: slaves were rarely permitted to bring accusations against their masters; as witnesses, they typically gave evidence under torture (Watson 1987, 81–80). Thus, Constantine ordered that slaves who brought charges against their masters or freedmen against their patrons were not to be given a hearing at all but were to be crucified instead for their "atrocious audacity" (*Codex Theodosianus* 9.5.1.1). Admittedly, these laws were complicated and changed over time, but generally a third party, a free citizen, would have to bring charges against a master on the slave's behalf. No doubt some citizens wanted to do the right thing or used an opportunity to harass an enemy: the "slanderer" of the soldier we mentioned above might fit into either category. How often would such a third party both know and care enough to institute legal proceedings against a fellow slaveholder?

With all these protective laws, the state intruded into the areas of private property and the rule of the *paterfamilias* over the household, interventions that Roman law was usually hesitant to encourage (Manning 1989, 1540). Our sources give two justifications. First, such interventions prevented the destruction of familial property, that is, slaves. They are parallel to laws protecting family fortunes from being wasted by spendthrifts (*Gaius's Institutes* 1.53). Second, Emperor Antoninus Pius argued that, "it is in the interest of masters that help against savagery or hunger or intolerable injury should not be denied to those who rightly entreat for it" (*Justinian's Institutes* 1.8.2, trans. Watson 1987, 120). Historians interpret this as suggesting that egregious abuses by individual masters threatened the interests of the slaveholding class as a whole. Recall that the first Sicilian revolt reportedly began with the slaves of a particularly abusive master. The motivations of reformers were admittedly mixed, but to stress only the selfish and prudential ones is too simplistic (Griffin 1976, 274). It is also redundant: these reforms did not threaten the stability of slavery or the wealth and lifestyle of slaveholders. Slaveholders could afford to indulge humane feelings when it came to a few outrageously mistreated slaves.

Whether or not these humane feelings derived from any philosophy or religion is hard to gauge. We've noted that Seneca was not necessarily much ahead of some of his non-Stoic contemporaries among Roman slaveholders. And no clear pattern connects Stoic statesmen like Seneca with more benign legislation about slaves and freedmen (Manning 1989, 1536). The satirist Juvenal even mocks a slaveholder who proclaims that the souls and bodies of slaves are the same as "our own" – a reference to Stoic doctrine – but terrifies his own slaves and delights in having them tortured if they ruin a few towels (*Satires* 14.16–22). The possibility of such hypocrisy is worth keeping in mind, but Juvenal's portrayal of Roman morals and practices is notoriously negative and hostile. A more balanced approach is not only to imagine occasional positive impacts of philosophy and religion, but also to allow for humane feelings among the un-philosophical and irreligious. Occasional kind feelings, however, were not of central importance as long as slavery survived and continued, inevitably, to depend on violence. Most telling for the whole story of legal amelioration is the *Senatus Consultum Silanianum*, which required the torture and execution of all slaves in the house of a master killed by a slave (see Chapter 9). This remained the law of the land, repeatedly revised and refined, into the sixth century CE, an indication of how little the violent institution of slavery had changed.

Conclusion: Why no Abolitionists?

This survey of philosophical treatments and legal amelioration of slavery has revealed only a few good guys, no clear abolitionists, and plenty of villains and equivocators. And, with the exception of Aristotle's reference to the Anonymous Opponents, we rarely get the sense that theories of slavery were defensive, that they were reacting to criticisms of the institution. For instance, the Stoic belief that human society, including slavery, was in accord with nature derived from their cosmology; they were not trying to counter calls for abolition. Indeed, Seneca defends himself from attacks on the other side, from people who didn't think slaves are equally human and should be treated kindly. One might contrast the justifications of slavery in the United States South before the Civil War, which were obviously and vehemently reacting to abolitionist attacks on the institution. In the classical world, abolitionism was not an organized body of opinion that required refutation.

We have noted repeatedly that the most obvious factor that precluded the development of abolitionist tendencies was the almost universal ownership of slaves among the upper classes, who dominate our extant literary evidence just as they dominated their own society. We don't know what criticisms of slavery individual slaves or ex-slaves might have developed in conversations with friends for example. And we have scarcely an inkling about what free people too poor to own slaves thought. A wide range of individual opinions may have existed without leaving evidence. But the texts that discuss the justice or injustice of slavery were almost all written by, or at least for, people likely to own at least a couple of slaves – or those who aspired to, a group that included many ex-slaves. So our surviving evidence is slanted in a pro-slavery direction. The acceptance – in various guises – of slavery and the general lack of interest in the subject is still striking. Other factors beyond the vested interest of the elite and literate probably contributed.

One theory points to the weakness or absence of a concept of human rights in the classical world (Bradley 2010, 627). On this view, classical culture did not acknowledge that people had rights as the result simply of being human; they had rights only within their own community or state. Outside his or her homeland, a person was already on a slippery slope towards the "natal alienation" of slavery. To take a Greek example, "enslaving" – to abduct citizens in order to sell them as slaves – was a capital crime in Athens, but the many non-Athenian slaves there were perfectly legal. This viewpoint helps to explain why slavery seemed natural and unobjectionable but can't be the whole story. To resume our example, Athens was a major center of trade and accorded strong legal rights to foreigners for practical, economic reasons (Cohen 1973); we are far from "open season" on foreigners on the streets of Athens. And this chapter is about philosophers: the Stoics, for example, were cosmopolitan in rejecting distinctions between different nationalities. Ethnic chauvinism and the strong distinction between citizens and outsiders must have made slavery seem less like criminal abduction to most people, but it provides less insight into the complicity of intellectuals.

In a vicious circle, the fact that slavery was ubiquitous contributed to its acceptance: widespread practices can seem natural and slavery was practiced in virtually every ancient society around the Mediterranean and on Rome's frontiers.[14] And, as far as classical Greeks and Romans were concerned, slavery was an eternal institution with its origins lost in the mists

---

14 Two possible exceptions are the Essenes, perhaps the community that produced the Dead Sea Scrolls, and the "Therapeutae" (Philo in Garnsey 1996, 78).

of time (Vidal-Naquet 1986). So, for example, after they gained their own freedom, affluent ex-slaves typically bought slaves themselves. Nobody thought this was remarkable: owning slaves was just part of being successful and rich. But this approach too may be more successful in helping to understand popular rather than philosophical views. Classical philosophers questioned all sorts of seemingly natural and universal institutions. Most famously, Plato's *Republic* envisages a ruling class without the family or private property, but most scholars believe that the *Republic* nonetheless includes slaves.[15] The acceptance of slavery among ancient philosophers remains something of an oddity, since in other cases they happily presented radical critiques of their society and suggested alternative social arrangements.

In sum, our sources may under represent the full span of ancient opinions about slavery, but the lack of moral concern for outsiders, the ubiquity of slavery in ancient societies, and, most of all, the economic and social dependence on slavery help explain why the institution was rarely, if ever, subject to sustained critique. Indeed, scholars of modern abolitionism tend to argue in the opposite direction (e.g., Davis 1966, 90; Davis 1984): what special circumstances made slavery an urgent moral issue after millennia of acceptance?

Suggested Reading

Peter Garnsey's *Ideas of Slavery from Aristotle to Augustine* (1996) covers justifications, criticisms, and ameliorations of slavery through most of classical antiquity with extensive translations of original sources and concise and perceptive discussions. The bibliography on Aristotle's theory of natural slavery and on his Anonymous Opponents is immense and grows each year. Cambiano's reconstruction of the basis and context of the opinions of the Anonymous Opponents (1987) provides an excellent introduction. Williams 1993 provides an insightful reading and suggests the division into the argument from above and from below, which I follow above. Kraut 2002 provides a clear and thorough treatment of the whole theory in the context of Aristotle's general political philosophy; he tends to present a charitable view of Aristotle's thinking. Millett 2007 considers Aristotle's theory in the context of the practice of slavery at Athens. In the chapter "Freedom, Stoicism, and the Roman Mind," Patterson (1991) discusses slavery in Roman Stoic thought and particularly in Epictetus and Marcus Aurelius, the former slave and the emperor, respectively. Manning 1989 provides clear and judicious discussion of Stoic views on slavery and the possibility that they influenced Roman law. Griffin's biography of Seneca (1976) includes a clear and important chapter arguing mainly that his views on slavery were not particularly ahead of their time. Brunt 1998 considers in its historical context the treatment of slavery in the *Meditations* of Marcus Aurelius, a Roman emperor and the third of the famous Stoics of the imperial period. G. E. M. de Ste. Croix, a Marxist historian, provides a critical and trenchant approach to Christian attitudes (Ste. Croix 1975). Balch and Osiek 2003 includes several chapters on slavery within early Christian households and Powery 2013, a recent "special forum" section of *Biblical Interpretation*, includes diverse articles by distinguished scholars of early Christianity and a reply by Keith Bradley. Lenski 2012 presents a positive view of the impact of Christianity and particularly Constantine on the law and practice of slavery. Watson 1983 and 1987, 115–133, takes a skeptical view of the theory that reforms in Roman law improved the life of most slaves.

---

15 Vlastos 1973; *contra* Gonda 2016. In Plato's *Laws*, slaves and ex-slaves are subject to harsher regulations than in contemporary Athens (Morrow 1939) – which is hard to explain if Plato were a closet critic of slavery.

13

Decline and Legacy

> *Finally, when did ancient slavery end? At the end of Roman Antiquity and at the time of the invasions, reply, with one voice, the Marxists, all remarkably faithful on this point to the letter of the writings of Marx. In the eleventh century, according to Georges Duby. At some indeterminate date between the fifth and the eleventh centuries, say, lastly, with some embarrassment (if they say anything at all), most others.*
> Pierre Bonnassie, "The survival and extinction of the slave system in the early medieval West (fourth to eleventh centuries)" (1991), 14

> *The competitive system [capitalism] is a system of antagonism and war; ours of peace and fraternity. The first is the system of free society; the other that of slave society. The Greek, the Roman, Judaistic, Egyptian, and all ancient polities were founded on our theory.*
> George Fitzhugh, *Sociology for the South, or The Failure of Free Society* (1854), 26

Introduction

Last chapter's explorations of philosophical and legal justifications, criticisms, and ameliorations of slavery concluded our treatment of slavery in the classical world. This postscript answers two sets of questions about what came afterwards. How, when, and why did classical slavery end? What were and what continue to be its legacies in the modern world? Looking for answers to these questions will highlight continuities as well as differences between ancient and New World slavery.

It is not possible to put a date on the end of classical slavery. None of the successor states to the Roman Empire was a slave society; the importance of agricultural slavery in particular diminished drastically in the centuries after the Empire's dissolution. Yet all these societies contained some slaves centuries after the fall of the western Roman Empire. Even when, much later in the Middle Ages, slavery died out entirely in some central areas of Europe, it survived in others. For example, wars and hostility between Islamic and Christian states provided the context for slavery to thrive around the medieval Mediterranean.

These conflicts added the element of religious difference to the conception and the institution of slavery, something rarely seen in the classical world. The later racist

Ancient Greek and Roman Slavery, First Edition. Peter Hunt.
© 2018 Peter Hunt. Published 2018 by John Wiley & Sons, Ltd.

justification of the enslavement of black Africans was also something new. Greek ethnocentrism – as in Aristotle's insistence that non-Greeks are natural slaves – provides an analogy, but modern racism was more comprehensive, systematic, and even pseudo-scientific (Isaac 2004, 1–6). And the importance that racist ideology placed on skin color made it much harder for ex-slaves to assimilate or climb socially. Despite these differences, that a continuous history of slavery stretched from antiquity to the New World is one factor that explains why the institution is so easily recognizable from archaic Greece through the Roman Empire to the New World.

This thread of historical continuity and the prestige of classical civilization were preconditions for the powerful legacy of ancient slavery in the New World. Spanish intellectuals and Dominican monks debated the enslavement of Native Americans in Aristotelian terms. Apologists for slavery in the antebellum South sought antecedents in classical culture for their racist and paternalistic justifications of slavery. The legal systems of many European states were based on Roman law. Some of these states enacted law codes governing slavery just as if New World slavery were like Roman slavery and were not based on race.

The Decline of Classical Slavery

Starting in the late third century CE, the eastern and western halves of the Roman Empire became increasingly independent of each other. At times, they even had different emperors. In the late fourth century CE, the history of the two sections diverged dramatically. In 378 CE, the Goths defeated a Roman army at the battle of Hadrianopolis in Thrace. The Empire did not bounce back as it had after similar disasters and invasions in the past. Instead the Goths turned west, ravaging and plundering, and eventually sacked Rome itself in 410 CE. By this time, other Germanic tribes had also invaded the Empire. Although some historians emphasize "transformation" rather than Edward Gibbon's "Decline and Fall," the fifth century CE was disastrous (Gibbon 1914, orig. 1776–1789). By its end, kingdoms of Ostrogoths, Visigoths, Franks, Vandals, Burgundians, Anglo-Saxons, and others had replaced Roman government in the West. The Greek-speaking eastern half of the Empire – which historians call the Byzantine Empire even though its people still referred to themselves as Romans – fared better. In the sixth century CE, the Byzantine Empire even succeeded in retaking parts of Italy, Spain, and North Africa. The Byzantines eventually had to abandon those territories, and they lost Syria and Egypt to Muslim invaders in the mid-seventh century CE. For the rest of its long history, until 1452 CE, the Byzantine Empire comprised territories mainly in the Balkan Peninsula and modern Turkey.

The centuries from 400 to 700 CE also saw a fundamental decline in the importance of slavery. The dozen or more smaller states that ruled what had once been the western Roman Empire were *societies with slaves* but not *slave societies* (Harper 2011, 509). The Byzantine Empire too became less dependent on slaves; in particular, their role in agriculture faded (Harper 2010a; *contra* Rotman 2009, 107–116). In the eighth century, slaves could be found throughout the area of the former Roman Empire, but they were mainly domestic slaves serving the elite, a pattern common in many societies with slaves. It is difficult to be any more precise than this, both because of the probable complexity of the process and because of the scarcity of good evidence.

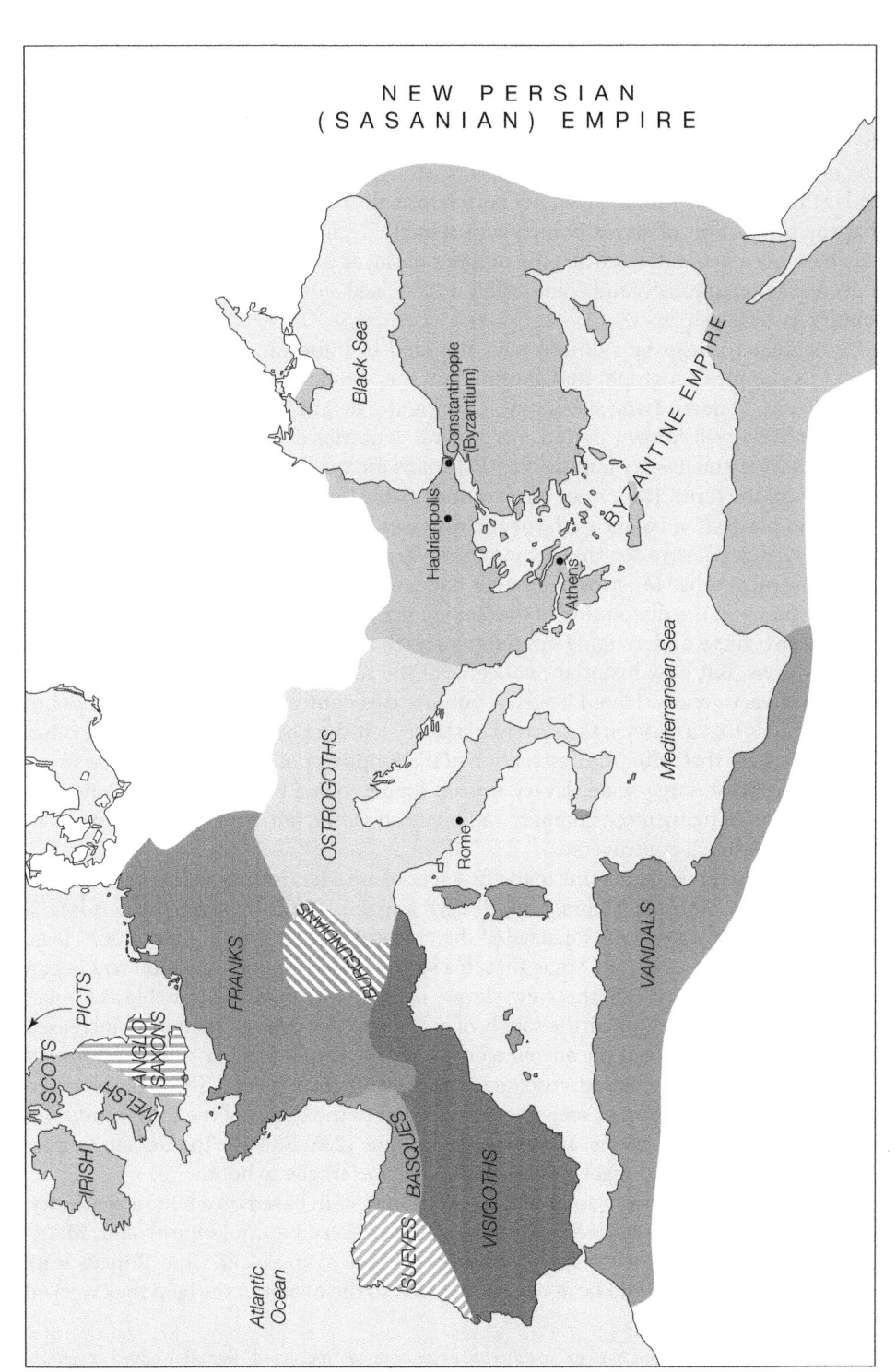

Map 6 After the disintegration of the Roman Empire: Europe and the Mediterranean in 530 CE. *Source:* Courtesy of Stephanie Krause.

There may not even be a single answer for when slavery declined. In some contexts, one can speak about slavery in the Roman Empire as a whole. But, especially when the topic is something like the importance of slavery, it is important to be more specific. In Egypt? In Britain? In the city of Rome itself or in the countryside of southern Italy? After the fall of the western Empire, geographic variation became even more pronounced. The practice and extent of slavery in rural North Africa under the Vandals and in Syria under the Byzantine Empire need not correlate at all. There is also no reason to assume that the proportion of slaves politely and steadily declined from 400 to 700 CE: there may have been generations when the number of slaves remained the same, some when it declined precipitously, and some when it increased – for example, in the early fifth century as we'll see.

Unfortunately, historians do not have the kind of information they would need to trace this complex geography and chronology. This should not be too surprising. Recall the difficulty of quantifying slavery even during the height of the Empire (see Chapter 3), a relatively well-known period. For several centuries after the fall of the western Empire, such estimates are impossible. Historians today tend to avoid the negative connotations of the term "Dark Age," but it is undeniable that our evidence is thin for many times and places. On balance, I favor the necessarily imprecise position that the sixth century CE was decisive for the decline of slavery in many places. But that argument makes the most sense in terms of another issue, which we need to tackle first: the relationship between the dissolution of the Roman state and the decay of slavery.

These two huge and roughly contemporary changes must have been intertwined in many ways. But how historians conceive of the relationship and what aspects they emphasize vary greatly. Here I'll sketch out just two contrasting views. One school of thought holds that a crisis in the system of slavery left the Empire vulnerable. The other side emphasizes that, after the destruction of the Empire's political and economic structures in the West, large-scale slavery was no longer viable there. This dichotomy is a simplification of many more complex and nuanced views, but it gets to the heart of an important historical controversy.

The most prominent adherents of the first school are Marxist historians committed to the primacy of economic factors. They discern a major shift from slavery to serfdom: a "feudal mode of production" superseded the classical "slave mode of production" (e.g., Anderson 1974, 18–19). They argue that this social and economic transition had begun by the second century CE. On this view, slavery became less and less profitable as Roman conquests slowed and stopped: the supply of new slaves thinned and their price increased (compare Chapter 3). Even the encouragement of slave reproduction – one response to a decreased supply – involved costs and concessions for masters. These problems in the economic base of Roman society eventually led to the "crisis of the third century," a period of civil wars, invasions, and economic decline (235–284 CE). The Roman Empire recovered, but it was no longer a slave society and was fragile to boot.

In this model, once widely accepted, an agrarian system based on a bound peasantry, essentially serfs, had largely replaced agricultural slavery by the Empire's end. Marxist historians find support in fourth-century references to *coloni*.[1] The Roman state assigned some peasants and farm workers, *coloni*, to the owner of the land they worked

---

1 *Colonus* originally just meant "farmer," so *adscripti or adscripticii*, "registered," was often added or can be assumed. See Grey 2012a and 2012b on *coloni*.

and deprived them of their right to move. This policy was probably originally intended just to assure the effective collection of taxes, but by 332 CE a law refers to *coloni* who were "under the legal power" of one landowner or another; it threatens runaway *coloni* with chains and enslavement (*Theodosian Code* 5.17.1). All of this suggests that some peasants were losing their independence and becoming more like medieval serfs than Roman citizens. And, from the opposite direction, some slaves and ex-slaves were "hutted up": instead of closely supervising their slaves, masters settled them on their land and exacted a rent, often in kind and labor. Thus, slaves too were becoming serf-like. Marxists see all these developments as part of an overall transition to serfdom well before the Empire fell.

Marxist historians connect this shift in the mode of production with the vulnerability of the Roman Empire that led to its fall. The treatment of G. E. M. de Ste. Croix provides an example.[2] Rather than depending on slaves, the elite turned more and more intensely to the exploitation of the peasantry, who constituted a large majority of the population and were the traditional source of Roman military manpower. Of course, the peasants resented this. Signs of their discontent, resistance, and even revolts dot the history of the late Empire. The peasants had little stake in resisting the barbarian invasions and even joined them on occasion. In sum, de Ste. Croix argues that a problem with the economic base, slavery, led to political consequences, the most important of which was the conquest of much of the Empire by foreign tribes.

This whole picture – which I have admittedly simplified – is liable to several lines of criticism (Wickham 2005, 259–265). First, the Marxist model has just one trend in ancient slavery, downward, and one trend in serfdom, upward. Most historians today prefer a more complicated timeline. Evidence attests to large-scale slavery in the fourth and fifth centuries CE: for example, a fourth-century tax record lists over 150 slaves on a single farm on the Greek island of Thera; other sources refer to rich men and women like Melania the Younger possessing thousands of slaves (Harper 2011, 167–168, 192–195). Some historians infer that slavery never declined and that reproduction entirely filled the gap when the pace of conquest slowed. But the evidence does not allow us to rule out more complicated scenarios: slavery may have declined in the first and second centuries CE when Rome stopped expanding. The late Empire, however, witnessed a growing concentration of wealth as well as increased warfare and lawlessness. These two circumstances could provide both a cheap supply of and continued demand for slaves. For example, from a letter of Augustine of Hippo, historians learn that slave raids had become endemic in Roman Africa in the early fifth century and that the people enslaved were being sold in other parts of the empire (Augustine, *Letter 10* [Divjak] in Eno 1989; Harper 2011, 92–94).

However common bound *coloni* may have been in the late Empire, medieval serfdom did not directly replace slavery. For example, Chris Wickham presents a radically different picture of early medieval social structure. He argues for a period marked in many places by a "peasant mode of production": relatively unburdened peasants dominated the countryside in much of what had been the western Empire and the aristocracy endured a period of reduced power and wealth.[3] This is a controversial thesis, but

---

[2] Ste. Croix 1983, 452–503. McKeown 2007, 52–76, provides a lively appraisal of the work of the Russian Marxist scholars Shtaerman and Trofimova.

[3] Wickham 2005, 303–306, 153–258, 519–588; criticized by Collins 2009, 662–665 and Banaji 2009, 71–78.

medieval historians agree that the large-scale reduction of peasants to serfdom was a much later development. The popular notion that serfs replaced slaves is false (e.g., Bonnassie 1991, 58; cf. Davies 1996).

Finally, the organization of labor in the countryside was almost always mixed, including slaves, tenant farmers, sharecroppers, and bound peasants of various sorts. Even at its peak, slave labor only dominated agricultural production in some areas of the Roman Empire (e.g., Lenski 2017). And few medieval historians today believe that serfs ever constituted the majority of the rural population in western Europe. Even in the high Middle Ages (1000–1300 CE), most peasants were not subject to the full obligations of serfdom (Freedman 1991, 1–17, 214). A more complicated rural social structure also undermines the idea that slavery varies inversely with serf-like status. In the late fourth century CE, for example, there may have been many slaves and many serf-like *coloni*; two centuries after the sack of Rome, there may have been few of either.

In addition to these criticisms, a second paradigm reverses Marxist economic determinism. On this view, the political and military catastrophes of the fifth century led to the decline of slavery. The economic complexity that had made the large-scale use of slave labor profitable did not survive the fall of the western Roman state and the associated wars and chaos (Harper 2011, 497–506). The dissolution of the Roman Empire greatly reduced trade. Cities too had shrunk: the population of Rome in the seventh century CE was only about one-tenth its former size. Trade and cities had provided the markets for produce that made agricultural slavery profitable. The overall movement away from market agriculture made slaves, who require closer supervision, a less attractive labor force than peasants or serfs, who can provide labor and rents without requiring much attention.

This model implies a later date for slavery's decline: after the political catastrophes rather than before them. Kyle Harper has recently argued that the sixth century CE was probably the pivotal era in many regions. One of his arguments rests on the price differential between male and female slaves (Harper 2010b; cf. Saller 2003). In the fourth century CE, male slaves typically commanded higher prices than female slaves. This is consistent with Harper's view that slavery was still thriving in the late Empire, for male slaves generally outnumber females in slave societies and command higher prices – despite the reproductive capacity of female slaves. In contrast, in the vast majority of societies with slaves, females outnumber males and are priced higher. They are valued in terms of their contribution to their master's lifestyle and prestige not only in terms of the products of their labor. By the eighth century, female slaves cost more, the pattern for the rest of the medieval era and up to the reinstitution of plantation slavery. Harper concludes that the transition from the one big slave society of the Roman Empire to the many societies with slaves of the medieval world was essentially complete by 700 CE. And in the medieval period, slaves were more expensive, suggesting a luxury item rather than a productive investment.

The atrophy of the slave trade provides additional evidence for a decline of slavery after the fall of the western Empire. In the late sixth century CE, Gregory the Great, then a bishop in Rome, still possessed slaves. But on two occasions he had to request somebody to buy slaves elsewhere and to bring them to him (Harper 2011, 498). Such a scanty slave trade is almost inconceivable in a slave society such as Rome in the late Republic or early Empire. The direction of the early medieval slave trade was also significant: slaves went east to the Byzantine Empire – and later to the Muslim world (Harper 2010b, 237). The East was richer and western kingdoms had little other than slaves to trade anymore, another dramatic reversal from the centuries when Rome was the center of a vast slave trade.

The picture in the Byzantine Empire was different and closer to the Marxist model in some ways. The eastern Mediterranean remained prosperous, with large urban markets still thriving in late antiquity. Nevertheless, slavery and especially agricultural slavery withered (Harper 2010a, 949; 2011, 505). Slavery may have declined because other sources of labor became easier to obtain. Wage labor had always been more common in the East, and, backed by a strong state, rich Byzantine landowners subjected the peasantry more and more tightly (Banaji 2009, 78–86). The terms of peasant oppression varied, but many peasants ended up in a position little different from serfdom. Here peasant vulnerability to exploitation may have contributed to the decline of slavery – a reversal of the dynamic that linked the growth of citizen rights and of slavery in classical Greece and the Roman Republic (see Chapter 5).

In some places, slavery merely declined, but in large areas of Europe it almost disappeared by the high Middle Ages. Marc Bloch makes a pointed contrast:

> Under Charlemagne [reigned 768–814 CE] and under Philip Augustus [reigned 1180–1223 CE], there lived and labored on the soil of France men who in both reigns were designated in Latin as *servi*, men who in both reigns were considered to be deprived of that juridical characteristic known as freedom, but what a contrast between their actual conditions. (Bloch 1975, 34)

In the time of Charlemagne, France was a society with slaves. There may have been far fewer of them than in the fourth century, but the Latin word *servus* (plural: *servi*) still denoted a chattel slave. By the end of the twelfth century, slavery was so marginal an institution and a certain type of un-free peasants was so common that *servus* was applied to the latter. Historians translate this use of *servus* as "serf," to distinguish these bound peasants from the chattel slaves for whom *servus* was earlier used. An entirely new word denoted chattel slaves: many medieval slaves came from the Slavic peoples on the eastern frontier of Europe and this led to the use of their ethnic name to designate slaves, a usage that began in the ninth century (*Oxford English Dictionary*, "Slave."). Hence the English word *slave* – and variants of slave in other modern European languages.

Slavery may have almost died out in the heartland of Europe, but it continued on its periphery. Most obviously, the wars between Christians and Muslims in Spain and across the Mediterranean gave medieval slavery a religious aspect. In theory, Christians only enslaved Muslims and vice versa, but the reality was more complicated. Medieval Italian city-states, such as Genoa and Venice, played a large role in this trade, which in turn contributed to their wealth and power. For the Mediterranean, now divided along religious lines, continued to provide a conduit for an active slave trade as it had in classical times. And, as we mentioned, the eastern land frontier of Europe was a source of Slavic slaves for centuries; these often ended up in Muslim territory. I can do no more here than mention these places where slavery persisted, but one point is important. Although slaves became rare in the core of Europe, slavery persisted. Areas such as Spain and Portugal had continuous experience of slavery from the fall of Rome to the establishment of Indian and then African slavery in their colonies. The religious conflict that provided the basis of much medieval slavery and the racist basis of New World slavery were essentially post-classical developments, but in other ways New World slave systems were direct, if distant, descendants of classical slavery.

The Legacy of Ancient Slavery

Slavery was intrinsic to daily life in the classical world; it was also apparent in many aspects of the enduring legacy of Greek and Roman civilization. So, wherever admiration for classical culture thrived, slavery was a familiar institution, often from the books people read, if not in their daily lives. In some eras and places, modern slavery even gained a specious respectability through its association with classical Greece and Rome. This connection was often vague and implicit, but before the American Civil War, advocates for the South and for slavery regularly pointed out that classical civilization was based on slavery. In their opinion, the same institution of slavery lay behind the accomplishments of Greece and Rome and behind their own culture (DuBois 2009, 72–74). In some cases, it was not classical culture in general, but a particular legacy of Greek and Roman slavery that had the greatest impact on New World slavery. Two influential aspects of ancient slavery were the Aristotelian theory of natural slavery and the Roman law of slavery.

Aristotle in the New World

As we saw, Aristotle's theory of natural slavery drew upon prejudices against slaves and against foreigners. Aristotelian philosophy in general came to dominate medieval thought in western Europe after his works were translated into Latin in the late eleventh century and twelfth century. For example, Thomas Aquinas, the most important philosopher and theologian of the medieval period, reconciled Aristotelian philosophy with Christian dogma in the thirteenth century. His Aristotelian views have remained central to Catholic theology through to the present day; they were particularly dominant among the Dominican order. Aristotle's high status among Catholics provided the background for a fascinating and consequential debate in sixteenth-century Spain about the treatment of those New World peoples whom the Spanish had conquered or planned to conquer.

This debate featured a Dominican Friar, Bartholome de Las Casas, on one side, and Juan Gines de Sepúlveda, a famous intellectual and translator of Aristotle's *Politics* on the other. There were several issues at play including the American Indians' supposed sins against nature and the need to convert them to Christianity and to protect the weak among them from oppression by the strong.[4] The main debate, however, revolved around whether they were natural slaves according to Aristotle's ancient definition. Not only would this determine their treatment after the Spanish conquest, but Aristotle had also identified the reduction of natural slaves to slavery as legitimate grounds of war (*Politics* 7 1333b39–1334a3). If the Indians were natural slaves, Spain need not worry about the justice of any wars they started against them – at least as far as Aristotelian theory was concerned.

This debate, turning on the application of a philosophical theory almost two millennia old, had profound and concrete results. The early Spanish conquests in Mexico and South America were relentless and brutal, but the horribly oppressed natives had found sympathetic allies, especially among the Dominicans. For example, when he was bishop

---

4 I follow the account of Hanke 1959 in this section; see also Pagden 1982, 109–145.

in Chiapa in southern Mexico, Las Casas had refused confession to Spaniards holding Indians in servitude. Some of these powerful and wealthy Spaniards had endured for years the state of being unconfessed and thus liable to purgatory or perhaps damnation. They were enraged and retaliated in whatever ways they could. In Peru, the local conquistadors actually killed a viceroy who tried to enforce laws protecting the Indians – and they carried his head around on a string as a display of their defiance (Hanke 1959, 34).

In 1550, Charles V, the Holy Roman Emperor and King of Spain, ordered all Spanish conquests to cease (!) until it was determined whether the enslavement of the Indians was just. The king appointed judges to make this decision. Before them, Sepúlveda argued that the Indians ought to be enslaved, "On account of the rudeness of their natures, which obliged them to serve persons having a more refined nature, such as the Spaniards" (Hanke 1959, 41). Although earlier in his career Las Casas had pictured Aristotle burning in hell, by 1550/1551 he accepted that the debate had to be conducted in terms of Aristotle's theory. Las Casas had served the church for almost fifty years in the New World and provided copious evidence that the American Indians were not natural slaves. He claimed that they were in many respects superior even to the ancient Greeks and Romans. Although the debate was inconclusive and the judges did not return a decision, the tide was turning Las Casas' direction. Eventually, the Spanish "basic law of 1573" governing the treatment of Indians included many of the reforms Las Casas had fought for (Hanke 1959, 86–87). This was far from the end of the oppression of Indians, but the "basic law" was superior to earlier rules and encouraged treatment less harsh than before.

Some advocates for slavery in the United States South adopted a version of Aristotle's theory in the nineteenth century. For example, George Fitzhugh, an outspoken apologist for slavery before the Civil War, explained that when he read Aristotle, he had realized with great pleasure that their views were identical (1857, xxi). He went on to appeal to Aristotle's authority at least a dozen times in his two books. In one place, Fitzhugh attempted to rebut the Declaration of Independence with a crude paraphrase of the Aristotelian view of slaves:

> [Men are not] born entitled to equal rights! It would be far nearer the truth to say, that some were born with saddles on their backs, and others booted and spurred to ride them, – and the riding does them good. They need the reins, the bit and the spur. (Fitzhugh 1854, 179)

In other words, slavery was in the interest both of natural slaves and of masters. In the ancient world, Aristotle was not influential with intellectuals, who tended to prefer some variant of the Stoic attitude. Antebellum racist ideology found his most ambitious claims plausible. Most Southern racists did not, of course, treat *non-Greeks* as natural slaves, as Aristotle did; rather they justified the enslavement of black Africans on the grounds of their supposed inferiority.

Fitzhugh often appealed to the prestigious, slave-based civilizations of Greece and Rome to highlight what he saw as the failures of the capitalist, free-market Northern states; he sometimes even found common cause with socialism. His main argument was an extreme and eccentric version of paternalism, a way of thinking too common to attribute to classical antecedents. One of his favorite tactics was to contrast the supposed familial affection and mutual care of slaves and masters in the South to the capitalist North, where unabashed competition meant that nobody cared for the workers – as in the passage at the start of the chapter denouncing "free society." His views occasionally went even beyond racism: he believed that poor white laborers would also benefit from slavery.

In defending slavery, Fitzhugh had to justify the ownership of people, which does not seem the most organic or familial of institutions. He was undismayed and claimed that ownership is the key to affection and benevolent treatment. He repeated a description of an English farm:

> The cattle, the horses and the sheep are fat, plentifully fed and warmly housed . . . two freezing, shivering, half-clad boys, who have to work on the Sabbath, are the slaves [metaphorically] to these animals . . . if the boys had belonged to the owner of the farm, they too would have been well-treated, happy and contented. (Fitzhugh 1854, 46–47)

Fitzhugh's criticisms of the early period of unregulated capitalism were not always wrong. But historians in recent decades have emphasized the extent to which Southern plantations too resembled capitalist enterprises much more than extended families (e.g., Fogel and Engerman 1974). Ownership was obviously no guarantee of good treatment. Fitzhugh's paternalistic justification of slavery was obviously tendentious, and vulnerable to all sorts of objections and rebuttals, which abolitionists naturally made. His arguments were thus more transparently self-serving than those of ancient paternalists, like Seneca and Pliny, who did not have to anticipate an audience likely to question their professions of fatherly care for their slaves.

The Roman Law of Slavery and Modern Slave Codes

In the sixteenth century, Roman law constituted the basis of most continental legal systems, a circumstance that would persist until the early nineteenth century. Consequently, the Roman law of slavery played a large role in the law codes of Spanish, French, and Portuguese slave societies in Latin America and the Caribbean. In contrast to most of continental Europe, Great Britain retained its common law even as Roman law gained influence after the twelfth century. The influence of Roman law on British law and thus on the United States was much less, though not negligible.

France instituted the first version of the *Code Noir*, "Black Code," for Caribbean islands like Saint-Domingue (Haiti) in 1685 and later for Louisiana, still a French possession. Alan Watson argues that the *Code Noir* incorporated the Roman law of slavery wherever applicable (Watson 1997; *contra* Palmer 1995/1996). For example, it preserved the Roman legal procedure of noxal surrender: if Marc's slave ruined Jean's property, Marc could either pay damages or surrender his slave to Jean. Despite its name and its topic, slavery, the *Code Noir* was rarely racist. In particular, manumitted slaves became colonial subjects of France with similar rights to what whites possessed. This policy was out of line with prevalent racism, but French jurists followed Roman laws, originally designed to regulate a non-racist and more open system of slavery.

Slave law in the southern United States was less subject to Roman influence. It tended to be more racist and to reflect more precisely the experiences and needs of Southern slaveholders, who dominated the region. How strong a dichotomy we should draw between the institution of slavery in Latin America and the United States is a complex and controversial topic. And the large role that Watson attributes to the Roman antecedents of the *Code Noir* is also contested (Schwarz 1991 on Watson 1989). That it had some influence is clear.

Conclusion

The legacy of ancient slavery paradoxically includes the image of its most bitter enemy, Spartacus, who remains today a symbol of heroic opposition to oppression. Communist admiration for Spartacus is the most conspicuous and well-known case. Already Marx admired Spartacus, and a group of German communists after World War I called themselves the Spartacists. In the United States, the Spartacist League still publishes the *Workers Vanguard*, a socialist newspaper. The classic movie *Spartacus* (1960) was directed by Stanley Kubrick and starred Kirk Douglas. It won four-academy awards, clear evidence of Spartacus' appeal beyond the far left. The historian Art Eckstein sums up:

> The screenplay [of *Spartacus*] was written by the blacklisted Communist Party writer Dalton Trumbo (his name appeared as a credit for the first time in almost ten years); the pamphlet handed out at the film's gala premier was red. Spartacus, then, served as a signpost to the rebellious 1960s. But Spartacus the person was also a hero to Voltaire, to Garibaldi, to Ze'ev Jabotinsky, one of the founders of Zionism, and even to Ronald Reagan, who, speaking to the British parliament in 1982, employed Spartacus as a symbol of sacrifice in the struggle of freedom against totalitarianism. (Eckstein 2010, 1)

Indeed, President John Kennedy ignored a hostile demonstration by the American Legion to watch the movie Spartacus (*New York Times*, February 5, 1961). His action symbolized the end of the 1950s era of persecution of communists, suspected communists, and their sympathizers, most notoriously by Senator Joseph McCarthy. In one of the movie's last and most famous scenes, the defeated slaves are offered their lives in return for turning in Spartacus. None of the slaves points out Spartacus; nobody "names names" as people had before the House Un-American Activities Committee in the 1950s. Rather, one after another the slaves claim to be him. They say "I'm Spartacus" and go bravely to their deaths.

This is, of course, the Hollywood version, not a happy ending but a heroic one. Actual events and people are messier. The aim of this book has been an intellectual one: to understand, as far as possible, classical slavery in all its messiness and complexity. But this does not mean that history has no ethical side or that I have never ventured judgments of persons, practices, policies, and ideas. Nonetheless, I do not pretend that to condemn the slaveholders of antiquity requires any courage today. Nor does it do ancient slaves any good. Our understanding may have the past as its object, but our moral and political aims need to be present ones.

The world would be a better place if, in one way or another, we all said "I'm Spartacus," more often. One obvious way to do this is to oppose slavery today. Although slavery is illegal everywhere in the world, the anti-slavery organization, Free the Slaves, estimates that something between twenty and forty million people live in slavery today. Despite the high total and the immense human misery involved, the proportion of slaves in the whole population is probably the lowest in history.[5] Free the Slaves defines slavery in terms of coerced work for another's profit. So major categories of slavery include debt bondage (especially among migrant workers), involuntary prostitution, domestic servitude, and forced child labor. Not all these forms of slavery today fit the historian's definition of slavery in terms of property or natal alienation. Many do and, in any case, all are wretched and oppressive conditions for any person to endure; there do not seem to be modern equivalents to, say, the Athenian slave bankers.

Modern slavery is far from the only injustice in our world worth bravely fighting. Yet opposing injustice is not really the main purpose of a book on ancient slavery. The varied and complicated aspects of ancient slavery we have tried to understand, often from poor evidence, have made this an ambitious enough undertaking in any case: our topics have ranged from economics to politics, from daily resistance to bloody rebellion, from family life and sex to manumission, from slaves in drama to philosophy and law – and throughout the alternation of Greek and Roman cases with parallels and contrasts between them. No single intellectual approach is appropriate for this large and motley range of subjects involving slavery. Nonetheless, whenever possible I have tried to imagine actual slaves and masters and picture their lives and interactions rather than formulating theories in abstract terms. Such an effort of imagination is critical for all students of history, but it is just as important not to mistake what you imagine for what you know.

Suggested Reading

Finley 1998 (originally 1980) is a classic book about how twentieth-century political tensions have influenced historians' treatment of ancient slavery. It also includes a chapter on the decline of ancient slavery, dated but still insightful. Based on a wide variety of evidence, some of it new, Harper 2011 argues that Rome remained a slave society in the "long fourth century," in contrast to previous scholarship, which posited an earlier decline in slavery. Wickham 2005, an immense and influential book on the centuries of and after the disintegration of the Roman Empire, is clear, lively, and well written. At almost a thousand pages, most readers will prefer to consult it on issues of interest rather than read it through. Phillips 1985 surveys the persistence of some slavery in and around Europe between the late Roman Empire and the establishment of the New World slave systems. Davis 1966, a Pulitzer Prize winning book, analyzes Western responses to "the intrinsic contradiction of slavery" (ix) – that the slave is both a thing and a person. He eventually focuses mainly on the roots of modern abolitionist sentiment, but sets the scene by arguing for important modern continuities from the classical and early Christian reactions to slavery. Sinha 2016 is a recent reappraisal of abolitionism, which places more weight on the role of slave resistance and black abolitionists. Richard 2009 contains a fascinating treatment of the role Classics and classical slavery played in antebellum debates about Southern slavery and abolition (181–203). The deployment of the examples of Greece and Rome in the defense of slavery is obvious, but Malamud 2016 explores the opposite tendency: the way African-Americans used their classical knowledge in the struggle for abolition and for civil rights. Bales 2012 is a fascinating but horrifying treatment of modern slavery in five countries by a leading expert and activist.

---

5 For this paragraph, I depend on the Free the Slaves website: http://www.freetheslaves.net/about-slavery/slavery-today/.

References

Akrigg, Ben, and Rob Tordoff, eds. 2013. *Slaves and Slavery in Ancient Greek Comic Drama*. Cambridge: Cambridge University Press.

Alford, Terry. 2007. *Prince Among Slaves: The True Story of an African Prince Sold into Slavery in the American South*. 30th Anniversary Edition. Oxford: Oxford University Press.

Alston, Richard, Edith Hall, and Laura Proffitt, eds. 2011. *Reading Ancient Slavery*. London: Bristol Classical Press.

Anderson, Perry. 1974. *Passages from Antiquity to Feudalism*. London and New York: New Left Books.

Andreau, Jean, and Raymond Descat. 2011. *The Slave in Greece and Rome*. Translated by Marion Leopold. Madison: University of Wisconsin Press.

Aubert, Jean-Jacques. 1994. *Business Managers in Ancient Rome: A Social and Economic Study of Institores, 200 BC-AD 250*. Vol. 21, Columbia Studies in the Classical Tradition. Leiden: E. J. Brill.

Bagnall, Roger S. 2011. *Everyday Writing in the Graeco-Roman East*. Sather Classical Lectures 69. Berkeley: University of California Press.

Bagnall, Roger S., and Bruce W. Frier. 1994. *The Demography of Roman Egypt*. Cambridge: Cambridge University Press.

Balch, David, and Carolyn Osiek, eds. 2003. *Early Christian Families in Context: An Indisciplinary Dialogue*. Grand Rapids, Michigan and Cambridge: William B. Eerdmans.

Bales, Kevin. 2012. *Disposable People: New Slavery in the Global Economy*, 3rd ed. Berkeley and Los Angeles: University of California Press.

Banaji, Jairus. 2009. "Aristocracies, peasantries, and the framing of the early Middle Ages." *Journal of Agrarian Change* 9:59–91.

Bennett, Emmett L. 1955. *The Pylos Tablets: Texts of the Inscriptions Found 1939–1954*. Princeton, NJ: Princeton University Press for the University of Cincinnati.

Bloch, Marc. 1975. "Personal liberty and servitude in the Middle Ages, particularly in France. Contribution to a class study." In *Slavery and Serfdom in the Middle Ages: Selected Essays by Marc Bloch*, 33–92. Berkeley: University of California Press.

Blok, Josine H., and André P. M. H. Lardinois, eds. 2006. *Solon of Athens: New Historical and Philological Approaches*. Leiden: Brill.

Boatwright, Mary T., Daniel J. Gargola, Noel Lenski, and Richard J. A. Talbert. 2013. *A Brief History of the Romans*, 2nd ed. Oxford: Oxford University Press.

Bodel, John. 1994. *Graveyards and Groves. A Study of the Lex Lucerina*. Vol. 11, American Journal of Ancient History. Cambridge, MA: Harvard University Press.

Bodel, John. 2005. "Caveat emptor: Towards a study of Roman slave traders." *Journal of Roman Archaeology* 18:181–195.

Bonnassie, Pierre. 1991. "The survival and extinction of the slave system in the early medieval West (fourth to eleventh centuries)." In *From Slavery to Feudalism in South-Western Europe*, 1–59. Cambridge: Cambridge University Press.

Borbonus, Dorian. 2014. *Columbarium Tombs and Collective Identity in Augustan Rome*. Cambridge: Cambridge University Press.

Bradley, Keith. 1978. "The Age at Time of Sale of Female Slaves." *Arethusa* 11:243–252.

Bradley, Keith. 1987. *Slaves and Masters in the Roman Empire: A Study in Social Control*. Oxford: Oxford University Press.

Bradley, Keith. 1989. *Slavery and Rebellion in the Roman World, 140 BC–70 BC* Bloomington: University of Indiana Press.

Bradley, Keith. 1990. "Servus onerosus: Roman law and the troublesome slave." *Slavery and Abolition* 11:135–157.

Bradley, Keith. 1994. *Slavery and Society at Rome*. Cambridge: Cambridge University Press.

Bradley, Keith. 2010. "Freedom and slavery." In *The Oxford Handbook of Roman Studies*, edited by Alessandro Barchiesi and Walter Scheidel, 624–635. Oxford: Oxford University Press.

Braund, David. 2011. "The slave supply in classical Greece." In *Cambridge World History of Slavery. Volume I: The Ancient Mediterranean World*, edited by Keith Bradley and Paul Cartledge, 112–133. Cambridge: Cambridge University Press.

Braund, David, and Gocha Tsetskhladze. 1989. "The export of slaves from Colchis." *Classical Quarterly* 39:114–125.

Brown, Vincent. 2010. "Social death and political life in the study of slavery." *American Historical Review* 114 (5):1231–1249.

Brunt, P. A. 1975. "Two Great Roman Landowners." *Latomus* 34:619–635.

Brunt, P. A. 1988. "The army and the land in the Roman revolution." In *The Fall of the Roman Republic and Related Essays*, 240–275. Oxford: Clarendon Press.

Brunt, P. A. 1998. "Marcus Aurelius and slavery." In *Modus Operandi: Essays in Honour of Geoffrey Rickman*, edited by Michel Austin, Jill Harries and Christopher Smith, 139–150. London: Institute of Classical Studies, University of London.

Bruun, Christer. 2013. "Greek or Latin? The owner's choice of names for *vernae* in Rome." In *Roman Slavery and Roman Material Culture*, edited by Michele George, 19–42. Toronto: University of Toronto Press.

Büllow-Jacobsen, Adam. 2012. "Private letters." In *Didymoi. Une garnison romain dans le désert Oriental d'Égypte*, edited by Hélène Cuvigny, 234–399. Cairo: Institute Français d'archéologie orientale.

Cambiano, Giuseppe. 1987. "Aristotle and the anonymous opponents of slavery." In *Classical Slavery*, edited by M. I. Finley, 28–52. London: F. Cass.

Cameron, Catherine M. 2011. "Captives and cultural change: Implications for archaeology." *Current Anthropology* 52 (2):169–209.

Cartledge, Paul. 2002. *Sparta and Lakonia: A Regional History 1300 to 362 BC*, 2nd ed. London: Routledge.

Cartledge, Paul. 2003. "Rebels and sambos in classical Greece: A comparative view." In *Spartan Reflections*, 127–152. London: Duckworth.

Chadwick, John, and Michael Ventris. 1973. *Documents in Mycenaean Greek*, 2nd ed. Cambridge: Cambridge University Press.

Childs, Matt. 2011. "Slave culture." In *The Routledge History of Slavery*, edited by Gad Heuman and Trevor Burnard, 170–186. Oxford and New York: Routledge.

Cohen, Edward. 1973. *Ancient Athenian Maritime Courts*. Princeton, NJ: Princeton University Press.

Cohen, Edward. 2000. *The Athenian Nation*. Princeton, NJ: Princeton University Press.

Cohen, Edward. 2003. "Athenian prostitution as a liberal profession." In *Gestures. Essays in Ancient History, Literature, and Philosophy Presented to Alan L. Boegehold*, edited by Geoffrey Bakewell and James Sickinger, 214–236. Oxford: Oxbow Books.

Collins, Roger. 2009. "Review: Making sense of the early Middle Ages." *English Historical Review* 124:641–665.

Conlin, Diane. 1997. *The Artists of the Ara Pacis: The Process of Hellenization in Roman Relief Sculpture*. Chapel Hill: University of North Carolina Press.

Crawford, Michael. 1977. "Republican denarii in Romania: The suppression of piracy and the slave-trade." *Journal of Roman Studies* 67:117–124.

Crawford, Michael. 1985. *Coinage and Money under the Roman Republic: Italy and the Mediterranean Economy*. Berkeley and Los Angeles: University of California Press.

Dal Lago, Enrico, and Constantina Katsari. 2008. "Ideal models of slave management in the Roman world and in the ante-bellum American South." In *Slave Systems: Ancient and Modern*, edited by Enrico Dal Lago and Constantina Katsari, 187–213. Cambridge: Cambridge University Press.

Daly, Lloyd W., trans. 1961. *Aesop without Morals*. New York: Thomas Yoseloff.

Daube, David. 1952. "Slave catching." *Juridical Review* 64:12–28.

Daux, G. et al., eds. 1909–1954. *Fouilles de Delphes*, Vol. 3. Paris: École française d'Athènes.

Davidson, James. 1997. *Courtesans and Fishcakes: The Consuming Passions of Classical Athens*. London: Harper Collins.

Davies, Wendy. 1996. "On servile status in the early Middle Ages." In *Serfdom and Slavery: Studies in Legal Bondage*, edited by Michael Bush, 225–246. New York: Longman.

Davis, David Brion. 1966. *The Problem of Slavery in Western Culture*. Ithaca, NY: Cornell University Press.

Davis, David Brion. 1984. *Slavery and Human Progress*. Oxford and New York: Oxford University Press.

De Ligt, Luuk. 2012. *Peasants, Citizens and Soldiers: Studies in the Demographic History of Roman Italy 225 BC–AD 100*. Cambridge: Cambridge University Press.

de Melo, Wolfgang, trans. 2012. *The Little Carthaginian. Pseudolus. The Rope*. Loeb Classical Library 260. Cambridge, MA: Harvard University Press.

Dew, Charles B. 1994. *Bond of Iron: Master and Slave at Buffalo Forge*. New York: W. W. Norton.

Dillon, M. P. J. 1995. "Payments to the disabled at Athens: Social justice or fear of aristocratic patronage?" *Ancient Society* 26:27–57.

duBois, Page. 2009. *Slavery: Antiquity and Its Legacy*. Oxford: Oxford University Press.

Duff, A. M. 1928. *Freedmen in the Early Roman Empire*. Oxford: Oxford University Press.

Duhoux, Yves. 2008. "Mycenaean Anthology." In *A Companion to Linear B: Mycenaean Greek Texts and Their World*, edited by Yves Duhoux and Anna Morpurgo Davies, 243–393. Leuven: Peeters.

Duncan-Jones, Richard. 1965. "The finances of the Younger Pliny." *Papers of the British School at Rome* 33:177–188.

Eck, Werner. 2006. "Ergastulum." In *Brill's New Pauly Online*, edited by Hubert Cancik and Helmuth Schneider. DOI: 10.1163/1574-9347_bnp_e401310.

Eckstein, Arthur M. 2010. "Review of Barry Strauss, *The Spartacus War*." *Michigan War Studies Review* 2010.02.04:1–4.

Edmondson, Jonathan. 2011. "Slavery and the Roman family." In *Cambridge World History of Slavery. Volume I: The Ancient Mediterranean World*, edited by Keith Bradley and Paul Cartledge, 337–361. Cambridge: Cambridge University Press.

Ehrenberg, Victor. 1974. *The People of Aristophanes*, 3rd ed. New York: Barnes and Noble.

Eidinow, Esther. 2012. "What will happen to me if I leave? Ancient Greek oracles, slaves and slave owners." In *Slaves and Religions in Graeco-Roman Antiquity and Modern Brazil*, edited by Stephen Hodkinson and Dick Geary, 244–278. Newcastle upon Tyne: Cambridge Scholars Publishing.

Eno, Robert B., ed. 1989. *St. Augustine, Letters VI, 1–29*. Vol. 81, *Fathers of the Church*. Washington, DC: Catholic University of America Press.

Fenoaltea, Stephano. 1984. "Slavery and supervision in comparative perspective: A model." *Journal of Economic History* 44:635–668.

Finley, M. I. 1977. "Aulus Kapreilius Timotheos, slave trader." In *Aspects of Antiquity*, 162–176. Harmondsworth: Penguin.

Finley, M. I. 1982a. "Was Greek civilisation based on slave labour?" In *Economy and Society in Ancient Greece*, edited by Brent Shaw and Richard Saller, 97–115. New York: Viking Press.

Finley, M. I. 1982b. "Between slavery and freedom." In *Economy and Society in Ancient Greece*, edited by Brent Shaw and Richard Saller, 116–132. New York: Viking.

Finley, M. I. 1998. *Ancient Slavery and Modern Ideology*. Edited by Brent Shaw. Expanded ed. Princeton, NJ: Markus Wiener.

Fisher, N. R. E. 1993. *Slavery in Classical Greece*. Classical World Series. London: Bristol Classical Press.

Fitzgerald, William. 2000. *Slavery and the Roman Literary Imagination*. Cambridge: Cambridge University Press.

Fitzhugh, George. 1854. *Sociology for the South, or, The Failure of Free Society*. Richmond: C. H. Wynne.

Fitzhugh, George. 1857. *Cannibals All! Slaves without Masters*. Richmond, VA: A. Morris.

Fogel, Robert William, and Stanley Engerman. 1974. *Time on the Cross*. Boston: Little, Brown and Co.

Follett, Richard. 2011. "The demography of slavery." In *The Routledge History of Slavery*, edited by Gad Heuman and Trevor Burnard, 119–137. Oxford and New York: Routledge.

Forsdyke, Sara. 2012. *Slaves Tell Tales: And Other Episodes in the Politics of Popular Culture in Ancient Greece*. Princeton, NJ: Princeton University Press.

Frank, Tenney. 1916. "Race mixture in the Roman Empire." *American Historical Review* 21:689–708.

Freedman, Paul. 1991. *The Origins of Peasant Servitude in Medieval Catalonia*. Cambridge Iberian and Latin American Studies. Cambridge: Cambridge University Press.

Garlan, Yvon. 1988. *Slavery in Ancient Greece*. Translated by Janet Lloyd. Ithaca, NY: Cornell University Press.

Garlan, Yvon. 1999. "War, piracy, and slavery in the Greek world." In *Classical Slavery*, edited by M. I. Finley, 7–21. London: Frank Cass.

Garnsey, Peter. 1996. *Ideas of Slavery from Aristotle to Augustine*. Cambridge: Cambridge University Press.

Garrigus, John 2011. "Free Coloureds." In *The Routledge History of Slavery*, edited by Gad Heuman and Trevor Burnard, 234–247. Oxford and New York: Routledge.

Gaspar, David Barry. 1985. *Bondmen and Rebels: A Study of Master–Slave Relations in Antigua*. Durham, NC: Duke University Press.

Genovese, Eugene. 1976. *Roll, Jordan, Roll: The World the Slaves Made*. New York: Vintage Books.

Genovese, Eugene. 1979. *From Rebellion to Revolution*. Baton Rouge: Louisiana State University Press.

George, Michele. 2011. "Slavery and Roman material culture." In *Cambridge World History of Slavery*. Volume I: *The Ancient Mediterranean World*, edited by Keith Bradley and Paul Cartledge, 385–413. Cambridge: Cambridge University Press.

Gerber, Douglas, trans. 1999. *Greek Elegiac Poetry: From the Seventh to the Fifth Centuries BC*. Loeb Classical Library 258. Cambridge, MA: Harvard University Press.

Gibbon, Edward. 1914. *The History of the Decline and Fall of the Roman Empire*. Edited with Introduction, Notes and Appendices by J. B. Bury. New York: MacMillan.

Gillen, Kieron, Ryan Kelly, and Jordie Bellair. 2014. *Three*. Vol. 1. Portland: Image Comics.

Glazebrook, Allison, ed. 2015. *Beyond Courtesans and Whores: Sex and Labour in the Greco-Roman World*. *Helios* (special issue) 42 (1).

Glazebrook, Allison, and Madeleine M. Henry. 2011. "Introduction: Why prostitutes? Why Greek? Why now?" In *Greek Prostitutes in the Ancient Mediterranean, 800 BCE–200 CE*, edited by Allison Glazebrook and Madeleine Henry, 3–13. Madison: University of Wisconsin Press.

Golden, Mark. 2011. "Slavery and the Greek family." In *Cambridge World History of Slavery*. Volume I: *The Ancient Mediterranean World*, edited by Keith Bradley and Paul Cartledge, 134–152. Cambridge: Cambridge University Press.

Gonda, Joseph. 2016. "An argument against slavery in the *Republic*." *Dialogue* 55 (2):219–244.

Graham, Sandra Lauderdale. 2002. *Caetana Says No: Women's Stories from a Brazilian Slave Society*. New Approaches to the Americas. Cambridge: Cambridge University Press.

Green, Peter, trans. 1999. *Juvenal: The Sixteen Satires*, 3rd ed. London: Penguin Books.

Grey, Cam. 2012a. "Colonate." In *The Encyclopedia of Ancient History* (on-line). Malden, MA: Wiley-Blackwell.

Grey, Cam. 2012b. "Coloni Adscripti." In *The Encyclopedia of Ancient History* (on-line). Malden, MA: Wiley-Blackwell.

Griffin, Miriam. 1976. *Seneca: A Philosopher in Politics*. Oxford: Clarendon Press.

Gruen, Erich. 1974. *The Last Generation of the Roman Republic*. Berkeley and Los Angeles: University of California Press.

Gruen, Erich. 1992. *Culture and National Identity in Republic Rome*. Ithaca, NY: Cornell University Press.

Guite, Harold. 1962. "Cicero's attitude to the Greeks." *Greece and Rome* 9:142–159.
Gummere, Richard, trans. 1917. *Seneca. Epistles*, Volume 1: *Epistles 1–65*. Loeb Classical Library 75. Cambridge, MA: Harvard University Press.
Gutman, Herbert. 1976. *The Black Family in Slavery and Freedom, 1750–1925*. New York: Vintage.
Hall, Edith. 1989. "The archer scene in Aristophanes' *Thesmophoriazusae*." *Philologus* 133:38–54.
Hall, Edith. 1997. "The sociology of Athenian tragedy." In *Cambridge Companion to Greek Tragedy*, edited by P. E. Easterling, 93–126. Cambridge: Cambridge University Press.
Hamel, Debra. 2003. *Trying Neaira: The True Story of a Courtesan's Scandalous Life in Ancient Greece*. New Haven, CT: Yale University Press.
Hanke, Lewis. 1959. *Aristotle and the American Indians*. Chicago: Henry Regnery Company.
Hanson, J. W. 2016. *An Urban Geography of the Roman World, 100 BC to AD 300*. Oxford: Archaeopress.
Harper, Kyle. 2010a. "Review of Youval Rotman, *Byzantine Slavery and the Mediterranean World*." *Comparative Studies in Society and History* 52 (4):948–950.
Harper, Kyle. 2010b. "Slave prices in late antiquity (and in the very long term)." *Historia* 59 (2):206–238.
Harper, Kyle. 2011. *Slavery in the Late Roman World AD 275–425*. Cambridge Cambridge University Press.
Harris, Edward. 2002. "Did Solon abolish debt bondage?" *Classical Quarterly* n.s., 52:415–430.
Harris, Edward. 2004. "Notes on a lead letter from the Athenian agora." *Harvard Studies in Classical Philology* 102:157–170.
Harris, Edward. 2012. "Homer, Hesiod and the 'origins' of Greek slavery." *Revue des études anciennes* 114:345–366.
Harris, William V. 1980. "Towards a study of the Roman slave trade." *Memoirs of the American Academy in Rome* 36:117–140.
Harris, William V. 1999. "Geography and the sources of Roman slaves." *Journal of Roman Studies* 89:62–75.
Harsh, Philip Whaley. 1955. "The intriguing slave in Greek comedy." *Transactions of the American Philological Association* 86:135–142.
Harvey, David. 2004. "The clandestine massacre of the Helots (Thucydides 4.80)." In *Spartan Society*, edited by Thomas J. Figueira, 199–217. Swansea: The Classical Press of Wales.
Hasegawa, Kinuko. 2005. *The Familia Urbana During the Early Empire, A Study of the Columbaria Inscriptions*. BAR International Series 1440. Oxford: Archaeopress.
Hawthorne, Walter. 2010. *From Africa to Brazil: Culture, Identity, and an Atlantic Slave Trade, 1600–1830*. Cambridge: Cambridge University Press.
Heseltine, Michael, trans. 1987. "Petronius." In *Petronius, Senneca. Satyricon. Apocolocyntosis*. Loeb Classical Library 15. Cambridge, MA: Harvard University Press.
Hin, Saskia. 2013. *The Demography of Roman Italy: Population Dynamics in an Ancient Conquest Society 201 BCE–14 CE*. Cambridge: Cambridge University Press.
Hodkinson, Stephen. 2008. "Spartiates, helots and the direction of the agrarian economy: Towards an understanding of helotage in comparative perspective." In *Slave Systems: Ancient and Modern*, edited by Enrico Dal Lago and Constantina Katsari, 285–320. Cambridge: Cambridge University Press.

Hodkinson, Stephen, and Dick Geary, eds. 2012. *Slaves and Religions in Graeco-Roman Antiquity and Modern Brazil*. Newcastle upon Tyne: Cambridge Scholars Publishing.

Hopkins, Keith. 1978a. "Conquerors and slaves: The impact of conquering an empire on the political economy of Italy." In *Conquerors and Slaves: Sociological Studies in Roman History I*, 1–98. Cambridge: Cambridge University Press.

Hopkins, Keith. 1978b. "The political power of eunuchs." In *Conquerors and Slaves: Sociological Studies in Roman History I*, 172–196. Cambridge: Cambridge University Press.

Hopkins, Keith. 1993. "Novel evidence for Roman slavery." *Past and Present* 138:3–27.

Hopkins, Keith, and P. J. Roscoe. 1978. "Between slavery and freedom: On freeing slaves at Delphi." In *Conquerors and Slaves: Sociological Studies in Roman History I*, 134–171. Cambridge: Cambridge University Press.

Horsfall, Nicholas. 2003. *The Culture of the Roman Plebs*. London: Duckworth.

Hunt, Peter. 1997. "The Helots at the Battle of Plataea." *Historia* 46 (2):129–144.

Hunt, Peter. 1998. *Slaves, Warfare, and Ideology in the Greek Historians*. Cambridge: Cambridge University Press.

Hunt, Peter. 2001. "The Slaves and the Generals of Arginusae." *American Journal of Philology* 122.3:359–380.

Hunt, Peter. 2006. "Arming slaves and Helots in classical Greece." In *Arming Slaves: From Classical Times to the Modern Age*, edited by Christopher Leslie Brown and Phillip D. Morgan, 14–39. New Haven, CT: Yale University Press.

Hunt, Peter. 2011. "Slaves in Greek literary culture." In *The Cambridge World History of Slavery*, Volume I: *The Ancient Near East and Mediterranean World to AD 500*, edited by Keith Bradley and Paul Cartledge, 22–47. Cambridge: Cambridge University Press.

Hunt, Peter. 2015. "Trojan slaves in classical Athens: Ethnic identity among Athenian slaves." In *Communities and Networks in the Greek World*, edited by Claire Taylor and Kostas Vlassopoulos, 128–154. Oxford: Oxford University Press.

Hunt, Peter. 2016a. "Review of *Démocratie contre les experts: Les esclaves publics en Grèce ancienne*, by Paulin Ismard." *Sehepunkte* 16 (3 [15.03.2016]).

Hunt, Peter. 2016b. "Slaves or serfs? Patterson on the Thetes and Helots of ancient Greece." In *On Human Bondage: After Slavery and Social Death*, edited by John Bodel and Waler Scheidel, 55–80. Malden, MA: Wiley-Blackwell.

Hunt, Peter. 2016c. "Violence against slaves in classical Greece." In *The Topography of Violence in the Greco-Roman World*, edited by Werner Riess and Garrett Fagan, 136–161. Ann Arbor: University of Michigan Press.

Hunt, Peter. 2017. "Slaves as active subjects: individual strategies." In *Oxford Handbook of Greek and Roman Slaveries*, edited by Stephen Hodkinson, Marc Kleijwegt, and Kostas Vlassopoulos. Oxford: Oxford University Press. Oxford Handbooks Online. Online at: [text to come].

Hunter, Virginia. 1994. "Slaves in the household: Was privacy possible?" In *Policing Athens: Social Control in the Attic Lawsuits, 420–320 BC*, 70–96. Princeton, NJ: Princeton University Press. I added a reference to this in a caption to Fig. 9.1.

Isaac, Benjamin. 2004. *The Invention of Racism in Classical Antiquity*. Princeton, NJ: Princeton University Press.

Ismard, Paulin 2017. *Democracy's Slaves: A Political History of Ancient Greece*, translated by Jane Marie Todd. Cambridge, MA: Harvard University Press.

Jacobs, Harriet A. 1987. *Incidents in the Life of a Slave Girl: Written by Herself*. Edited by Jean Fagan Yellin. Cambridge, MA: Harvard University Press.

Jameson, Michael. 1992. "Agricultural Labor in Ancient Greece." In *Agriculture in Ancient Greece*, edited by Berit Wells, 135–146. Stockholm: Paul Å. Forlag.

Johnson, Walter. 2003. "On agency." *Journal of Social History* 37 (1):113–124.

Jones, Christopher. 2008. "Hyperides and the sale of slave families." *Zeitschrift für Papyrologie und Epigraphik* 164:19–20.

Jongman, Willem. 2003. "Slavery and the growth of Rome. The transformation of Italy in the second and first centuries BCE." In *Rome the Cosmopolis*, edited by Catherine Edwards and Greg Woolf, 100–122. Cambridge: Cambridge University Press.

Jordan, D. R. 1985. "A survey of Greek defixiones not included in the Special Corpora." *Greek Roman and Byzantine Studies* 26 (2):151–197.

Jordan, David R. 2000. "A personal letter found in the Athenian agora." *Hesperia* 69:91–103.

Joshel, Sandra R. 1992. *Work, Identity, and Legal Status at Rome*. Oklahoma Series in Classical Culture. Norman and London: University of Oklahoma Press.

Joshel, Sandra R. 2010. *Slavery in the Roman World*. Cambridge: Cambridge University Press.

Joshel, Sandra R. 2011. "Slavery and Roman literary culture." In *Cambridge World History of Slavery. Volume I: The Ancient Mediterranean World*, edited by Keith Bradley and Paul Cartledge, 214–240. Cambridge: Cambridge University Press.

Joshel, Sandra R., and Lauren Hackworth Petersen. 2014. *The Material Life of Roman Slaves*. Cambridge: Cambridge University Press.

Kajanto, Iiro. 1970. "Tacitus on the slaves: An interpretation of the *Annals*, XIV.42–45." *Arctos* 6:43–60.

Kamen, Deborah. 2010. "A corpus of inscriptions: Representing slave marks in antiquity." *Memoirs of the American Academy in Rome* 60:95–110.

Kamen, Deborah. 2011. "Reconsidering the status of khōris oikountes." *Dike* 14:43–53.

Kamen, Deborah. 2013. *Status in Classical Athens*. Princeton, NJ: Princeton University Press.

Kassel, Rudolf, and Colin Austin, eds. 1983–. *Poetae Comici Graecae*. Berlin: Berolini.

Keaveney, Arthur. 2007. *The Army in the Roman Revolution*. London and New York: Routledge.

Kennel, Nigel. 2010. *Spartans: A New History*. Malden, MA: Wiley-Blackwell.

Kennedy, Rebecca Futo. 2014. *Immigrant Women in Athens: Gender, Ethnicity, and Citizenship in the Classical City. Routledge Studies in Ancient History*. New York and London: Routledge.

Knigge, Ursula, and Wilfried Kovacsovics. 1981. "Kerameikos: Tätigkeitsbericht 1979." *Archäologischer Anzeiger*:385–391.

Kock, Theodor, ed. 1880–1888. *Comicorum Atticorum Fragmenta*. 2 vols. Leipzig: Teubner.

Kolchin, Peter. 1993. *American Slavery, 1619–1877*. New York: Hill and Wang.

Kolendo, Jerzy. 1979. "Elements pour une énquête sur l'iconographie des esclaves dans l'art hellénistique et romain." In *Schiavitù, manomissione e classi dipendenti nel mondo antico*, edited by Capozza Maria, 161–174. Rome: L'Erma di Bretschneider.

Konstan, David. 1998. "Reciprocity and friendship." In *Reciprocity in Ancient Greece*, edited by Christopher Gill, Norman Postlethwaite, and Richard Seaford, 279–301. Oxford: Oxford University Press.

Kraut, Richard. 2002. *Aristotle: Political Philosophy. Founders of Modern Political and Social Thought*. Oxford: Oxford University Press.
Kühn, Karl G., ed. 1821–1833. *Claudii Galeni Opera Omnia*. 20 vols. Leipzig: C. Cnobloch.
Lape, Susan. 2010. *Race and Citizen Identity in the Classical Athenian Democracy*. Cambridge: Cambridge University Press.
Lattimore, Richmond, trans. 1967. *The Odyssey of Homer*. New York: Harper and Row.
Lattimore, Richmond, trans. 2013. *The Trojan Women. In The Complete Greek Tragedies: Euripides III*, 3rd ed., edited by Mark Griffith and Glenn Most. Chicago: University of Chicago Press.
Lauffer, Siegfried. 1979. *Die Bergwerkssklaven von Laureion*, 2nd ed. Wiesbaden: Steiner.
Launaro, Alessandro. 2011. *Peasants and Slaves. The Rural Population of Roman Italy*. Cambridge Classical Studies. Cambridge: Cambridge University Press.
Lenski, Noel. 2012. "Constantine and Slavery: Libertas and the Fusion of Roman and Christian Values." In *Atti dell'Accademia Romanistica Costantiniana XVIII*, edited by Stefano Giglio, 235–260. Perugia: Aracne.
Lenski, Noel. 2017. "Peasant and slave in late antique North Africa, c. 100-600 CE." In *Late Antiquity in Contemporary Debate*, edited by Rita Lizzi Testa, 113–156. Newcastle upon Tyne: Cambridge Scholars Publishing.
Lenski, Noel, and Catherine M. Cameron, eds. 2018. *What Is a Slave Society? The Practice of Slavery in Global Perspective*. Cambridge: Cambridge University Press.
Lewis, David M. 2016. "Orlando Patterson, property, and ancient slavery: The definitional problem revisited." In *On Human Bondage: After Slavery and Social Death*, edited by John Bodel and Walter Scheidel, 31–54. Malden, MA: Wiley-Blackwell.
Lewis, David. Forthcoming. *Greek Slave Systems and Their Eastern Neighbors: A Comparative Study*. Oxford: Oxford University Press.
Lewis, Sian. 1998–1999. "Slaves as viewers and users of Athenian pottery." *Hephaistos* 16–17:71–90.
Llewelyn, Stephen. 1997. "P. Harris I 62 and the pursuit of fugitive slaves." *Zeitschrift für Papyrologie und Epigraphik*:245–250.
Lockyear, Kris. 2004. "The late iron age background to Roman Dacia." In *Roman Dacia: The Making of a Provincial Society*. Journal of Roman Archaeology Supplementary Series 56, edited by W. P. Hanson and I. P. Haynes, 33–74. Portsmouth, RI: Journal of Roman Archaeology.
Loomis, William T. 1998. *Wages, Welfare Costs and Inflation in Classical Athens*. Ann Arbor: University of Michigan Press.
Lovejoy, Paul E. 2012. *Transformations in Slavery: A History of Slavery in Africa*, 3rd ed. Cambridge: Cambridge University Press.
Luraghi, Nino. 2002. "Helotic slavery reconsidered." In *Sparta: Beyond the Mirage*, edited by Anton Powell and Stephen Hodkinson, 227–248. Swansea: Classical Press of Wales.
Malamud, Margaret. 2016. *African Americans and the Classics: Antiquity, Abolition and Activism*. London: I. B. Tauris.
Mandelbaum, Allen, trans. 1971. *The Aeneid of Virgil*, new ed. Berkeley and Los Angeles: University of California Press.
Manning, Charles E. 1989. "Stoicism and slavery in the Roman Empire." *Aufstieg und Niedergang der romischen Welt II*.36.3:1518–1543.
Marx, Karl, and Friedrich Engels. 1955. *The Communist Manifesto*. Arlington Heights, IL: Harlan Davidson.

Mattoso, Katia M. de Queirós. 1991. *To Be a Slave in Brazil: 1550–1888*. Translated by Arthur Goldhammer. New Brunswick, NJ: Rutgers University Press.

McCarthy, Kathleen. 2000. *Slaves, Masters, and the Art of Authority in Plautine Comedy*. Princeton, NJ: Princeton University Press.

McCarthy, Kathleen. 2004. "The joker in the pack: Slaves in Terence." *Ramus* 33:100–119.

McGinn, Thomas A. J. 1998. *Prostitution, Sexuality, and Law in Ancient Rome*. Oxford: Oxford University Press.

McGinn, Thomas A. J. 2004. *The Economy of Prostitution in the Roman World: A Study of Social History and the Brothel*. Ann Arbor: University of Michigan Press.

McKeown, Niall. 2007. *The Invention of Ancient Slavery*. Duckworth Classical Essays. London: Bristol Classical Press.

McKeown, Niall. 2011. "Resistance among chattel slaves in the classical Greek world." In *Cambridge World History of Slavery*. Volume I: *The Ancient Mediterranean World*, edited by Keith Bradley and Paul Cartledge, 153–175. Cambridge: Cambridge University Press.

Meeks, Wayne A. 2003. *The First Urban Christians: The Social World of the Apostle Paul*, 2nd ed. New Haven, CT: Yale University Press.

Meyer, Elizabeth A. 2010. *Metics and the Athenian Phialai-Inscriptions: A Study in Athenian Epigraphy and Law*. Volume 208, *Historia Einzelschriften*. Stuttgart: Franz Steiner Verlag.

Middleton, David. 1982. "Thrasyboulos' thracian support." *Classical Quarterly* 32:298–303.

Miller, Norma, trans. 1987. *Menander: Plays and Fragments*. Harmondsworth: Penguin.

Millett, Paul. 1989. "Patronage and its avoidance in classical Athens." In *Patronage in Ancient Society*, edited by Andrew Wallace-Hadrill, 15–47. London: Routledge.

Millett, Paul. 2007. "Aristotle and slavery in Athens." *Greece and Rome* 54 (2):187–209.

Moore, John, trans. 1969. *Ajax*. In *Sophocles. The Complete Greek Tragedies 2*, 2nd ed. Chicago: University of Chicago Press.

Morris, Ian. 1998. "Remaining invisible: The archaeology of the excluded in classical Athens." In *Differential Equations: Woman and Slaves in Greco-Roman Culture*, edited by Sandra Joshel and Sheila Murnaghan, 193–220. London: Routledge.

Morris, Ian. 2011. "Archaeology and Greek slavery." In *Cambridge World History of Slavery*. Volume I: *The Ancient Mediterranean World*, edited by Keith Bradley and Paul Cartledge, 176–193. Cambridge: Cambridge University Press.

Morrow, Glenn R. 1939. "Plato and Greek slavery." *Mind* 48:186–201.

Mouritsen, Henrik. 2005. "Freedmen and decurians: Epitaphs and social history in imperial Italy." *Journal of Roman Studies* 95:38–63.

Mouritsen, Henrik. 2011. *The Freedman in the Roman World*. Cambridge: Cambridge University Press.

Mouritsen, Henrik. 2013. "Slavery and manumission in the Roman elite: A study of the columbaria of the Volusii Saturnini and the Statilii Tauri." In *Roman Slavery and Roman Material Culture*, edited by Michele George, 43–68. Toronto: University of Toronto Press.

Murray, A. T., trans. 1939. *Demosthenes. Orations*, Volume V: *Orations 41–49*. Loeb Classical Library 346. Cambridge, MA: Harvard University Press.

Nauck, Augustus. 1889. *Tragicorum Graecorum Fragmenta*. Leipzig: Teubner.

Neutel, Karin B. 2015. *A Cosmopolitan Ideal: Paul's Declaration 'Neither Jew Nor Greek, Neither Slave Nor Free, Nor Male and Female' in the Context of First Century Thought*. Library of New Testament Studies 513. London: Bloomsbury.

Nieboer, Herman Jeremias. 2010 (orig. 1900). *Slavery as an Industrial System: Ethnological Researches*. Cambridge Library Collection. Cambridge: Cambridge University Press.

Nietzsche, Friedrich 1994 (orig. 1887). *On The Genealogy of Morals*. Translated by Carol Diethe. Cambridge: Cambridge University Press.

Noussia-Fantuzzi, Maria. 2010. *Solon the Athenian, the Poetic Fragments. Mnemosyne Supplement 326*. Leiden and Boston: Brill.

Oakley, John H. 2000. "Some 'other' members of the Athenian household: Maids and their mistresses in fifth-century Athenian art." In *Not the Classical Ideal: Athens and the Construction of the Other in Greek Art*, edited by Beth Cohen, 227–247. Leiden: Brill.

Ogden, Daniel. 2004. *Aristomenes of Messene: Legends of Sparta's Nemesis*. Swansea: The Classical Press of Wales.

Oldenziel, Ruth. 1987. "The Historiography of Infanticide in Antiquity: A Literature Stillborn." In *Sexual Asymmetry: Studies in Ancient Society*, edited by Josine Blok and Peter Mason, 87–107. Amsterdam: J. C. Gieben.

Oldfather, W. A., trans. 1925–1928. *Epictetus*. Loeb Classical Library 131 and 218. Cambridge, MA: Harvard University Press.

Pagden, Anthony. 1982. *The Fall of Natural Man: The American Indian and the Origins of Comparative Ethnology*. Cambridge: Cambridge University Press.

Palmer, Vernon V. 1995/1996. "The origins and authors of the Code Noir." *Louisiana Law Review* 56 (2):363–408.

Papadopoulos, John, and Sarah Morris. 2005. "Greek towers and slaves: An archaeology of exploitation." *American Journal of Archaeology* 109:155–225.

Paradiso, Annalisa. 2004. "The logic of terror: Thucydides, Spartan duplicity and an improbable massacre." In *Spartan Society*, edited by Thomas J. Figueira, 179–198. Swansea: The Classical Press of Wales.

Parker, Holt. 1989. "Crucially funny or Tranio on the couch: The *servus callidus* and jokes about torture." *Transactions of the American Philological Association* 119:233–246.

Parker, Robert. 1996. *Athenian Religion: A History*. Oxford: Clarendon Press.

Patterson, Orlando. 1971. "Quashee." In *The Debate over Slavery: Stanley Elkins and His Critics*, edited by A. J. Lane, 210–217. Chicago: University of Illinois Press.

Patterson, Orlando. 1982. *Slavery and Social Death: A Comparative Study*. Cambridge, MA: Harvard University Press.

Patterson, Orlando. 1991. *Freedom in the Making of Western Culture*. Vol. 1. New York: Basic Books.

Penner, Linsay Rae. 2013. "The Epigraphic Habits of the Slaves and Freed Slaves of the Julio-Claudian Households." Ph.D. diss., University of Calgary.

Perry, Matthew. 2014. *Gender, Manumission, and the Roman Freedwoman*. Cambridge: Cambridge University Press.

Petersen, Lauren Hackworth. 2006. *The Freedman in Roman Art and Art History*. Cambridge: Cambridge University Press.

Phillips, William D. 1985. *Slavery from Roman Times to the Early Transatlantic Trade*. Minneapolis: University of Minnesota Press.

Pollitt, J. J. 1978. "The impact of Greek art on Rome." *Transactions of the American Philological Association* 108:155–174.

Pomeroy, Sarah, Stanley Burstein, Walter Donlan, and Jennifer Roberts. 2013. *A Brief History of Ancient Greece: Politics, Society, and Culture*, 3rd ed. Oxford and New York: Oxford University Press.

Powery, Emerson B. 2013. "Special forum: Roman slavery and the New Testament: Engaging the work of Keith Bradley." *Biblical Interpretation* 21 (4–5):495–546.

Pritchett, W. Kendrick. 1953. "The Attic Stelai, Part I." *Hesperia* 22:225–299.

Pritchett, W. Kendrick. 1961. "Five new fragments of the Attic Stelai." *Hesperia* 30:23–29.

Pritchett, W. Kendrick, and Anne Pippin. 1956. "The Attic Stelai, Part II." *Hesperia* 25:178–317.

Raaflaub, Kurt. 2004. *The Discovery of Freedom in Ancient Greece*, 2nd ed. Translated by Renate Franciscono. Chicago: University of Chicago Press.

Rackham, Horace, trans. 1932. *Aristotle. Politics.* Loeb Classical Library 264. Cambridge, MA: Harvard University Press.

Radice, Betty, trans. 1969. *Pliny: Letters.* Volume II: *Books 8–10. Panegyricus.* Loeb Classical Library 59. Cambridge, MA: Harvard University Press.

Ramsay, John T., trans. 2015. *Sallust: Fragments of the Histories. Letters to Caesar.* Loeb Classical Library 522. Cambridge, MA: Harvard University Press.

Rauh, Nick. 1993. *The Sacred Bonds of Commerce: Religion, Economy, and Trade Society at Hellenistic Roman Delos, 166–87 BC.* Leiden: Brill Academic.

Rawson, Beryl. 1966. "Family life among the lower classes at Rome in the first two centuries of the empire." *Classical Philology* 61:71–83.

Reeve, C. D. C. 1998. *Aristotle: Politics.* Indianapolis, IN: Hackett Publishing Company.

Richard, Carl. 2009. *The Golden Age of the Classics in America: Greece, Rome, and the Antebellum United States.* Cambridge, MA: Harvard University Press.

Richlin, Amy. 2014. "Talking to slaves in the Plautine audience." *Classical Antiquity* 33 (1):174–226.

Richlin, Amy. 2017. *Slave Theater in the Roman Republic: Plautus and Popular Comedy.* Cambridge: Cambridge University Press.

Richter, Gisela M. A. 1951. "Who made the Roman portrait statues – Greeks or Romans?" *Proceedings of the American Philosophical Society* 95 (2):184–208.

Ringrose, Kathryn M. 2003. *The Perfect Servant: Eunuchs and the Social Construction of Gender in Byzantium.* Chicago and London: University of Chicago Press.

Robertson, Bruce. 2008. "The slave names of IG I³ 1032 and the ideology of slavery at Athens." In *Epigraphy and the Greek Historian*, edited by Craig Cooper, 79–116. Toronto: University of Toronto Press.

Robinson, E. S. G. 1920. "Antiochus, King of the Slaves." *Numismatic Chronicle* 20:175–176.

Roediger, David. 1999. *The Wages of Whiteness: Race and the Making of the American Working Class*, rev. ed. London and New York: Verso.

Rosenstein, Nathan. 2004. *Rome at War: Farms, Families, and Death in the Middle Republic.* Chapel Hill and London: University of North Carolina Press.

Rosivach, Vincent J. 1989. "Talasiourgoi and Paidia in IG 2 2 1553–78: A note on Athenian social history." *Historia* 38:365–370.

Rosivach, Vincent J. 1999. "Enslaving *Barbaroi* and the Athenian ideology of slavery." *Historia* 48:129–157.

Roth, Ulrike. 2007. *Thinking Tools: Agricultural Slavery Between Evidence and Models.* Bulletin of the Institute of Classical Studies Supplement 92. London: Institute of Classical Studies.

Roth, Ulrike. 2010. "Review of Monika Trümper, *Graeco-Roman Slave Markets: Fact or Fiction?*" *Bryn Mawr Classical Review* 2010.12.20.

Rotman, Youval. 2009. *Byzantine Slavery and the Mediterranean World.* Translated by Jane Marie Todd. Cambridge, MA: Harvard University Press.

Saller, Richard. 1994. *Patriarchy, Property and Death in the Roman Family*. Cambridge: Cambridge University Press.
Saller, Richard. 2003. "Women, slaves, and the economy of the Roman household." In *Early Christian Families in Context: An Indisciplinary Dialogue*, edited by David Balch and Carolyn Osiek, 185–204. Grand Rapids, MI and Cambridge: William B. Eerdmans.
Saller, Richard, and Brent Shaw. 1984. "Tombstones and Roman family relations in the Principate: Civilians, soldiers and slaves." *Journal of Roman Studies* 74:124–156.
Sandbach, F. H., ed. 1972. *Menandri Reliquiae Selectae*. Oxford: Clarendon Press.
Scheidel, Walter. 1997. "Quantifying the sources of slaves in the early Roman Empire." *Journal of Roman Studies* 87:156–169.
Scheidel, Walter. 2003. "Helot numbers: A simplified model." In *Helots and Their Masters in Laconia and Messenia: Histories, Ideologies, Structures*, edited by Nino Luraghi and Susan E. Alcock, 240–247. Cambridge, MA: Harvard University Press.
Scheidel, Walter. 2005a. "Human mobility in Roman Italy II: The slave population." *Journal of Roman Studies* 95: 64–79.
Scheidel, Walter. 2005b. "Real slave prices and the relative cost of slave labour in the Greco-Roman world." *Ancient Society* 35:1–17.
Scheidel, Walter. 2008. "The comparative economics of slavery in the Greco-Roman world." In *Slave Systems: Ancient and Modern*, edited by Enrico Dal Lago and Constantina Katsari, 105–126. Cambridge: Cambridge University Press.
Scheidel, Walter. 2011. "The Roman slave supply." In *Cambridge World History of Slavery*. Volume I: *The Ancient Mediterranean World*, edited by Keith Bradley and Paul Cartledge, 287–310. Cambridge: Cambridge University Press.
Scheidel, Walter. 2013. "Italian manpower: Review article on Luuk De Ligt, *Peasants, Citizens and Soldiers. Studies in the Demographic History of Roman Italy 225 BC–AD 100* and Alessandro Launaro, *Peasants and Slaves. The Rural Population of Roman Italy (200 BC to AD 100)*." *Journal of Roman Archaeology* 26:678–687.
Scholl, Reinhold, ed. 1990. *Corpus der Ptolemäischen Sklaventexte*. 3 vols. Stuttgart: F. Steiner.
Schwartz, Stuart B. 1985. *Sugar Plantations in the Formation of Brazilian Society: Bahia, 1550–1835*. Cambridge Latin American Studies 52. Cambridge: Cambridge University Press.
Schwarz, Philip J. 1991. "Review of Alan Watson, *Slave Law in the Americas*." *Journal of the Early Republic* 11 (1):136–137.
Scott, James C. 1985. *Weapons of the Weak: Everyday Forms of Peasant Resistance*. New Haven, CT: Yale University Press.
Scott, James C. 1990. *Domination and the Arts of Resistance: Hidden Transcripts*. New Haven, CT: Yale University Press.
Segal, Erich. 1968. *Roman Laughter: The Comedy of Plautus*. Harvard Studies in Comparative Literature 29. Cambridge, MA: Harvard University Press.
Shaw, Brent. 1998. "'A wolf by the ears': M. I. Finley's *Ancient Slavery and Modern Ideology* in Historical Context." Introduction to *Ancient Slavery and Modern Ideology* by M. I. Finley, 3–74. Princeton, NJ: Markus Wiener.
Shaw, Brent. 2001. *Spartacus and the Slave Wars. A Brief History with Documents*. Bedford Series in History and Culture. Boston and New York: Bedford/St. Martin's.
Shelmerdine, Cynthia W. 2008. "Mycenaean Society." In *A Companion to Linear B: Mycenaean Greek Texts and Their World*, edited by Y. Duhoux and Anna M. Davies, 115–158. Louvain-La Neuve: Peeters.

Shrimpton, Gordon S. 1991. *Theopompus the Historian*. Montreal: McGill-Queen's University Press.

Sinclair, Upton. 1994 (orig. 1935). *I, Candidate for Governor: And How I Got Licked*. Berkeley: University of California Press.

Sinha, Manisha. 2016. *The Slave's Cause. A History of Abolition*. New Haven, CT: Yale University Press.

Skocpol, Theda, and Margaret Somers. 1980. "The uses of comparative history in macrosocial inquiry." *Comparative Studies in Society and History* 22 (2):174–197.

Smith, Adam. 1937 (orig. 1776). *An Inquiry into the Nature and Causes of the Wealth of Nations*. New York: Random House.

Sommerstein, Alan. 2009. "Slave and citizen in Aristophanic comedy." In *Talking about Laughter and Other Studies in Greek Comedy*, 136–154. Oxford: Oxford University Press.

Sosin, Joshua. 2015. "Manumission with Paramone: Conditional freedom?" *Transactions of the Philological Association* 145:325–381.

Stampp, Kenneth. 1956. *The Peculiar Institution: Slavery in the Ante-Bellum South*. New York: Vintage Books.

Ste. Croix, G. E. M. de. 1975. "Early Christian attitudes to property and slavery." *Studies in Church History* 12:1–38.

Ste. Croix, G. E. M. de. 1983. *The Class Struggle in the Ancient Greek World: From the Archaic Age to the Arab Conquests*. Paperback reprint edition with corrections. Ithaca, NY: Cornell University Press.

Stevenson, Walter. 1995. "The rise of eunuchs in Greco-Roman antiquity." *Journal of the History of Sexuality* 5:495–511.

Stewart, Peter. 2008. *The Social History of Roman Art*. Cambridge: Cambridge University Press.

Stewart, Roberta. 2008. "Who's tricked? Models of slave behavior in Plautus's 'Pseudolus.'" *Memoirs of the American Academy in Rome Supplement* 7:69–96.

Straus, Jean A. 2004. *L'achat et la vente des esclaves dans l'Egypte romaine: contribution papyrologique à l'étude de l'esclavage dans une province orientale de l'Empire romain*. Munich and Leipzig: Saur.

Taylor, Lily Ross. 1961. "Freedmen and freeborn in the epitaphs of imperial Rome." *American Journal of Philology* 82:113–132.

Thalmann, William. 1996. "Two versions of slavery in the Captivi of Plautus." *Ramus* 25.2:112–145.

Thalmann, William. 2011. "Some ancient Greek images of slavery." In *Reading Ancient Slavery*, edited by Richard Alston, Edith Hall, and Laura Proffitt, 72–96. London: Bloomsbury Academic.

Thompson, F. Hugh. 1993. "Iron age and Roman shackles." *Archaeological Journal* 150:57–168.

Thompson, F. Hugh. 2003. *The Archaeology of Greek and Roman Slavery*. London: Bristol Classical Press.

Tougher, Shaun. 2008. *The Eunuch in Byzantine History and Society*. London and New York: Routledge.

Treggiari, Susan. 1969. *Roman Freedmen During the Late Republic*. Oxford: Clarendon Press.

Treggiari, Susan. 1975a. "Jobs in the household of Livia." *Papers British School at Rome* 43:48–77.

Treggiari, Susan. 1975b. "Family life among the staff of the Volusii." *Transactions of the American Philological Association* 105: 393–401.

Treggiari, Susan. 1979. "Questions on women domestics in the Roman West." In *Schiavitù, manomissione e classi dipendenti nel mondo antico*, 185–201. Rome: L'Erma di Bretschneider.

Treggiari, Susan. 1991. *Roman Marriage: Iusti Coniuges from the Time of Cicero to the Time of Ulpian*. Oxford: Clarendon Press.

Trevett, Jeremy. 1992. *Apollodorus, the Son of Pasion*. Oxford: Oxford University Press.

Trimble, Jennifer. 2016. "The Zoninus collar and the archaeology of Roman slavery." *American Journal of Archaeology* 120 (3):447–472.

Tucker, C. Wayne. 1982. "Women in the manumission inscriptions at Delphi." *Transactions of the American Philological Association* 112:225–236.

Turley, David. 2000. *Slavery. New Perspectives on the Past*. Oxford: Blackwell.

Tybout, R. A. 1996. "Domestic shrines and 'popular painting': Style and social context." *Journal of Roman Archaeology* 9:358–374.

Urbainczyk, Theresa. 2004. *Spartacus, Ancients in Action*: Duckworth Publishers.

Urbainczyk, Theresa. 2008. *Slave Revolts in Antiquity*. Berkeley and Los Angeles: University of California Press.

Versnel, Hendrik S. 1999. "Κόλασαι τοὺς ἡμᾶς τοιούτους ἡδέως βλέποντες 'Punish those who rejoice in our misery': On curse texts and Schadenfreude." In *The World of Ancient Magic*, edited by David R. Jordan, Hugo Montgomery, and Einar Thomassen, 125–162. Bergen: Norwegian Institute at Athens.

Vidal-Naquet, Pierre. 1986. "Slavery and the rule of women in tradition, myth, and utopia." In *The Black Hunter: Forms of Thought and Forms of Society in the Greek World*, 205–223. Baltimore: Johns Hopkins University Press.

Vlassopoulos, Kostas. 2010. "Athenian slave names and Athenian social history." *Zeitschrift für Papyrologie und Epigraphik* 175:113–144.

Vlassopoulos, Kostas. 2011a. "Greek slavery: From domination to property and back again." *Journal of Hellenic Studies* 131:115–130.

Vlassopoulos, Kostas. 2011b. Review of *Metics and the Athenian Phialai-Inscriptions: A Study in Athenian Epigraphy and Law*, by Elizabeth Meyer. *Bryn Mawr Classical Review* 2011.02.48.

Vlassopoulos, Kostas. 2016a. "Finley's slavery." In *M. I. Finley: An Ancient Historian and His Impact*, edited by Daniel Jew, Robin Osborne, and Michael Scott, 76–99. Cambridge: Cambridge University Press.

Vlassopoulos, Kostas. 2016b. "Does slavery have a history? The consequences of a global approach." *Journal of Global Slavery* 1:5–27.

Vlastos, Gregory. 1973. "Does slavery exist in Plato's *Republic*?" In *Platonic Studies*, 140–146. Princeton, NJ: Princeton University Press.

Walin, Daniel. 2009. "An Aristophanic slave: *Peace* 819–1126." *Classical Journal* 59:30–45.

Wallace-Hadrill, Andrew. 1994. *Houses and Society in Pompeii and Herculaneum*. Princeton, NJ: Princeton University Press.

Wallace-Hadrill, Andrew. 2008. *Rome's Cultural Revolultion*. Cambridge: Cambridge University Press.

Walsh, P. G., trans. 1994. *Apuleius: The Golden Ass*. Oxford: Oxford University Press.

Walton, Francis R., trans. 1967. *Library of History*, Volume XII: *Fragments of Books 33–40*. Loeb Classical Library 423. Cambridge, MA: Harvard University Press.

Waltzing, J. P. 1904. "Oralavum vicus. Ses inscriptions, ses monuments et son histoire." *Le Musée Belge: Revue de Philologique Classique* 8:296–303.

Walvin, James. 1994. *Black Ivory: A History of British Slavery*. Washington, DC: Howard University Press.

Warner, Rex, trans. 1958. *Fall of the Roman Republic: Six Lives By Plutarch*. Harmondsworth: Penguin.

Watson, Alan. 1983. "Roman slave law and Romanist ideology." *Phoenix* 37:53–65.

Watson, Alan. 1987. *Roman Slave Law*. Baltimore: The Johns Hopkins University Press.

Watson, Alan. 1989. *Slave Law in the Americas*. Athens: University of Georgia Press.

Watson, Alan. 1992. "Seventeenth-century jurists, Roman law, and the law of slavery." *Chicago-Kent Law Review* 68:1343–1354.

Watson, Alan. 1997. "The origins of the Code Noir revisited." *Tulane Law Review* 71 (4):1041–1072.

Watson, James L. 1980. "Slavery as an institution, open and closed systems." In *Asian and African Systems of Slavery*, edited by James L. Watson, 1–15. Berkeley and Los Angeles: University of California Press.

Weaver, P. R. C. 1972. *Familia Caesaris: A Social Study of the Emperor's Freedmen and Slaves*. Cambridge: Cambridge University Press.

Webster, Jane. 2005. "Archaeologies of slavery and servitude: bringing 'New World' perspectives to Roman Britain." *Journal of Roman Archaeology* 18:161–79.

Webster, Jane. 2008. "Less beloved. Roman archaeology, slavery and the failure to compare." *Archaeological Dialogues* 15:103–123.

West, David, trans. 2008. *Horace. The Complete Odes and Epodes*. Oxford: Oxford University Press.

White, Horace. 1913. *Appian's Roman History*. Loeb Clasical Library 4 and 5. Cambridge, MA: Harvard University Press.

Wickham, Chris. 2005. *Framing the Early Middle Ages: Europe and the Mediterranean*. Oxford: Oxford University Press.

Wiedemann, Thomas. 1985. "The regularity of manumission at Rome." *Classical Quarterly* 35 (1):162–175.

Wiedemann, Thomas, ed. 1988. *Greek and Roman Slavery*, reprint ed. London: Routledge.

Wiedemann, Thomas. 1997. *Slavery. Greece and Rome: New Surveys in the Classics 19*. Reprint with additions. Oxford: Clarendon Press.

Wiles, David. 1988. "Greek theatre and the legitimation of slavery." In *Slavery and Other Forms of Unfree Labour*, edited by L. J. Archer, 53–67. London: Routledge.

Williams, Bernard. 1993. *Shame and Necessity*. Berkeley: University of California Press.

Williams, Eric. 1964. *Capitalism and Slavery*. London: André Deutsch.

Williams, Kathryn. 2006. "Pliny and the Murder of Larcius Macedo." *Classical Journal* 101:409–424.

Wrenhaven, Kelly. 2009. "The identity of the 'wool-workers' in the Attic manumissions." *Hesperia* 78:367–386.

Wrenhaven, Kelly. 2011. "Greek representations of the slave body: A conflict of ideas?" In *Reading Ancient Slavery*, edited by Richard Alston, Edith Hall, and Laura Proffitt, 97–120. London: Bloomsbury Academic.

Wrenhaven, Kelly. 2012. *Reconstructing the Slave: The Image of the Slave in Ancient Greece*. London: Bloomsbury Academic.

Wrenhaven, Kelly. 2013. "Barbarians at the gate: Foreign slaves in Greek city-states." *Electryone* 1 (1):1–17.
Zelnick-Abramovitz, Rachel. 2000. "Did patronage exist in classical Athens?" *L'antiquity classique* 69:65–80.
Zelnick-Abramovitz, Rachel. 2005. *Not Wholly Free: The Concept of Manumission and the Status of Manumitted Slaves in the Ancient Greek World*. Mnemosyne Supplementa 266. Leiden: Brill.
Zelnick-Abramovitz, Rachel. 2013. *Taxing Freedom in Thessalian Manumission Inscriptions*. Mnemosyne Supplementa 361. Leiden: Brill.

Index

Page numbers in italic indicate figures, page numbers in bold indicate tables

a

a libellis, a rationibus, ab epistulis   78–80
abolition
    of enslavement of Greeks   177
    modern   28
    no ancient   191–2, 195, 207–8
    see also inferiority of slaves, denied; anonymous opponents of Aristotle
absentee owners of farms   22, 55, 84, 141, 145, 147, 170, 189
accountant, *see* work, slave
Aesop, *see Life of Aesop*; fables
African slaves in ancient world   32, 55, 179
agency   137–40
Agesilaus   63
agriculture, slaves in
    conditions of life   42, 53, 62, 84, 111, 113, 138, 141, 145–7, 189, 199
    economics   51, 54, 57, 59, 68, 210, 214
    and Greek democracy   68–72
    resistance among   142–3, 148
    role of   13, 24, 43, 52, 65, 169, 214
    and Roman expansion   55–9
    see also Columella; manager, farm; peasants, versus agricultural slavery; Varro; Xenophon
Alexander the Great   7
Alföldy, Géza   119
amorous relations between master and slave   109–11; *see also* rape and coerced sex
Anaxandrides   117, 123
Andronicus, Livius   94–5, 185
anonymous opponents of Aristotle   193–5
Antiochus (leader of slave revolt), *see* Eunus
Antiphon   104, 152–3
Antisthenes   21
    Apollodorus (Athenian litigant and son of the ex-slave, Pasion, ca. 394–340 BCE)   88–9, 103–4, 106, 124–8, 135

Appian (Greek writer of Roman history, ca. 95–165 BCE)   58, 165, 171
Apuleius (Roman novelist, 2nd century CE)   122, 137, 150, 151
Aquillius, Manius   165
Aquinas, Thomas   216
archaeology
    of Roman countryside   51, 58–9
    of slavery   9, 24, 36, 57, 84, 85–6, 100, 106, 144, 182, 187–8, 203; *see also* chains; Eurysaces; grave reliefs and monuments
    survey   24, 58–9, 65
    For artifacts with texts, see coinage; collars, slave; epitaphs; inscriptions; papyrus, evidence on
Archippe   125, 126
Aristophanes (Athenian writer of comic dramas, ca. 446–386)   23, 63, 90, 144, 148, 150, 177, 180
Aristotle (Greek philosopher, ca. 384–322 BCE)   2, 17, 18, 105, 127, 141, 160, 179, 191, 192, 199, 200, 207, 208, 210
    in the New World   216–18
    personal life   197
    theory of natural slavery   23, 195–7
    see also anonymous opponents of Aristotle
army, slaves in, *see* military service of slaves
art, freedmen's   128
asylum, *see* sanctuary
Athenian Empire   6
Athenion   165, 167
Attic Stelai   35–6, 59
attitudes towards slaves   173–5; *see also* inferiority of slaves, supposed, and inferiority of slaves, denied
Augustales, seviri   131–2
Augustine (theologian, ca. 354–430)   201n, 208, 213

Augustus (first Roman emperor, 63 BCE–14 CE) 12, 26, 40, 41, 46, 75–6, 110
Aurelius, Marcus (Roman emperor, 121–180 CE) 198n, 208

b
bad luck, slavery as 99, 174, 175, 176, 189, 191, 195, 199
Ballio 181, 184
bandits 46, 108, 146, 169
banker, *see* work, slave
barber, *see* work, slave
bias
  modern 28–9
  see also men, wealthy; evidence, problems with
Bendis 87, 90
birth culture, *see* ethnic identity and enslavement, geography
Bithynia 93
Black Sea 31
Bloch, Marc 215
body, slaves associated with 196–7
Bonnassie, Pierre 209
"boy" for slaves 178–9
branding, *see* tattoos
Brazil, slavery in 20, 27, 29, 34–5, 64, 90, 98, 113, 169
breeding, slave, *see* children; family, slave; home-born slaves
brigands, *see* bandits
Building Z 87, 103
burial, *see* epitaphs; grave reliefs and monuments
Byzantine Empire 3, 4, 7, 11, 13, 80–2, 145, 210, 212, 214–15

c
Caesar, Julius (Roman senator, general, and dictator, 100–44 BCE) 46, 47, 119, 167, 175, 181, *193*
captives, enslavement of, *see* enslavement, war
Caribbean, slavery in the 45, 50, 157, 169
Casianus 112
Cassius, Gaius 83, 153
castration 80; *see also* eunuchs
Catholicism 216–17
Cato (the Elder, Roman senator and writer on agriculture, 234–149 BCE) 41, 142, 143, 148
Cestius, Gaius 133
chains 24, 58, 62, 64, 132, 137, 138, 145, 146–7, 149, 151, 170, 185, 186, 195, 213

chamber pot *144*, 177, 200–1
Charlemagne 215
Charles V of Spain 217
children 18, 42, 56, 63, 81, 94, 105, 120, 163, 175, 183
  of ex-slaves 28, 120, 124–8
  slave 3, 31, 36–7, 39, 41, 43, 45, 52, 64, 77, 80, 84, 99, 100, 105, 107–16 *passim*, 120, 133, 134, 143, 149, 170, 176, 178, 179, 187, 189, 220
  status of 19, 33, 77–8, 112, 204
  see also exposure
Chios 71, 157, 172
choris oikountes 19
Christianity 2, 13, 28, 191, 192, 198, 200, 201–3, *203*, 208, 209, 215, 216–17, 220
Cicero (Roman statesman, orator, and intellectual, 106–43 BCE) 35, 94n, 96, 97, 119, 122, 124, 133, 149–50, 165, 173, 187
Cinadon 160
citizenship
  Greek 11–12, 14, 39, 60, 67, 69–74 *passim*, 82, 104, 111, 117, 126, 135, 159–60, 196, 197, 207, 215
  Roman 11–12, 14, 46, 57, 71, 77, 112n, 126, 129, 135, 213, 215
  see also open versus closed slave systems
city-state, Greek 5, 37
Claudius (Roman emperor, ruled 41–54 CE) 9, 62, 67, 78, 79, 204, 205
Cleon 167
clever slave 23, 180–6
closed slave system, *see* open versus closed slave systems
clothing, *see* work, slave, weaving
Code Noir 218–19
coerced sex, *see* rape and coerced sex
coinage 55n, 71, 73, 105, 148
  Antiochus (Eunus) coin *168*
  EID MAR denarius *193*
  Manius Aquillius denarius *165*
collaboration with masters 139–40
collars, slave 150, *203*
collegia 130
coloni 13, 20, 212–14
columbaria *131*, 187
Columella (prolific writer including works on agriculture, published about 50 CE) 41, 111, 120, 142, 143, 146, 147, 170n
comedy
  Greek 23, 31, 36, 37, 87, 108, 146, 180, 181; *see also* Aristophanes; Menander
  Roman 180–6; *see also* Plautus; Terence

common sense   26–7
comparative history   27–8
Compitalia   189
concubine, *see hetaira*
conservative reading of Roman
   comedy   182–6
Constantine (first Christian Roman emperor,
   272–337 CE)   13, 201, 203, 204, 205,
   206, 208
construction, *see* work, slave
contemporary slavery, *see* modern slavery
   contrasts between Greek and Roman
      slavery   14–15, 51–2, 59–61, 97–8,
      123–4, 134–5, 161, 171, 175, 180
contubernium   112–13
cook, *see* work, slave
Corinth   51, 103–4, 123
cowardice, *see* inferiority of slaves, supposed
craftsman, *see* work, slave
Crassus, Marcus Licinius   161, 164–5
Crisis of the Third Century   11, 13, 212
crucifixion   140, 147, 155, 165, 201, 206
culture, slave   83–5; *see also* ethnic identity;
   Greek slaves at Rome
curse tablets   150–1

d

Dacia   47, 61
de Las Casas, Bartholome   216–17
de Supúlveda, Juan Gines   216
debt bondage   11, 19, 32–3, 39, 61, 70–1, 220
decline and fall of Roman Empire, *see*
   disintegration of the Western Roman
   Empire
decline of classical slavery   210–15
definitions of slavery   17–20, 220
Delian League   6
Delphi, manumission records at   1, 22, 26,
   55, 106–107, 114, 116, 118, 124, 135
Demeter   168
Demetrous   112
democracy, Athenian   6, 60–1, 68–75;
   see also citizenship, Greek
demography   41–7, 120
Demosthenes (Athenian orator, ca.
   384–322 BCE)   2, 36, 73, 97, 104, 106,
   125, 126, 127, 196
dichotomy
   between slave and free   14, 23, 69–70, 73,
      74, 135, 177
   between slaves and masters   73, 197n
   see also the Other, slaves as
Diocletian   204

Diodorus Siculus (Greek writer of history,
   mid-first century BCE)   163, 164, 168
Dionysus   167
dishonesty, attributed to slaves   97, 141–2
   see also embezzlement; malingering; theft
disintegration of the Western Roman
   Empire   13, 210, 214
displacement of Italian peasants, *see*
   peasants
Dodona, oracle of Zeus at   148
domestic work, *see* household slaves
Dominicans   216–17
doorkeeper, *see* work, slave
double standard, in sex   101, 106
doulos   3, 4, 161
drama, *see* tragedy; comedy
Drimakos   157

e

economics   52–4
   in Athens versus Roman Empire   59–61
   in Rome's expansion   54–9
Egyptian slaves   3
   in Athens   31, 87, 91
   Hellenistic   7, 32, 148–9, 150
   Roman   43, 52, 59–60, 63, *105*, 112, 114,
      143, 148–9, 150
EID MAR denarius   193
Eisias   106–7
elite self-definition   132–3
embezzlement   142, 143, 152
enslavement   31–48
   Athens   35–40, 60
   effect on whole system of slavery   33–5
   geography   31–2
   Rome   40–7, 60
   in war   33–41 *passim*, 46, 47–8, 174,
      176–7, 194–5, 199
   see also debt bondage; exposure
Epaphroditus   151
ephors   159
Epictetus (ex-slave Stoic philosopher, ca.
   55–135 CE)   22, 198, 200–1, 208
epigraphy, *see* inscriptions
Epirus   46, 62
epitaphs   22, 27, *34*, 36, 43, 45, 64–5, 77, 82,
   84, 86, 88, 89, 90, 96, 100, 110, 113–14,
   115, 116, 118, 119, 120, 130–1,133, 134,
   135, 159, 178, 179, 187
Erechtheion work records   121, 123
ergastula   204n; *see also* chains
escape, *see* fugitive slaves
Essenes   207n

ethnic identity
  and resistance   91–2
  retention of   89–91
  of slaves at Athens   85–9
  see also Greek slaves at Rome
ethnocentrism, *see* inferiority of slaves, supposed
etymology of words for slave   186, 194, 215
eunuchs   80–2, 204
Eunus   163, 164, 167, *168*, 169
Euripides (Athenian playwright, ca. 480–406 BCE)   1, 140, 175–7
Eurysaces   133
evidence, problems with   20–4
ex-slaves   117–18, 124–35
  elite resentment of   79–80, 81, 126–8, 132–3
  Greek versus Roman   134–5
  relations with former masters   124–5, 128–30
  as slaveholders   64, 94–5, 208
  wealth and status   125–8, 130–4
  see also epitaphs; manumission
exposure   33, 47

f

Fabius Pictor   93
fables   84–5, 141
faithful slaves, *see* loyalty, of slaves
fall of the Roman Empire, *see* disintegration of the Western Roman Empire
fall of the Roman Republic   75–6
familia   76, 119, 186; *see also* paternalism
familia Caesaris   75–80, 82, 119
family, slave   26, 100, 111–15, 143, 204n; *see also* children, slave; marriage
famulus   186
farming, *see* agriculture, slaves in
fasces   163
favor libertatis   204
female slaves, *see* women slaves
Fenoaltea, Stephano   53
fetters, *see* chains
filiation   129, 134, 165
Finley, M. I.   67, 68–72
Fitzhugh, George   2, 209, 217–18
flute player, *see* work, slave
food, of slaves   122, 146
foreign, slaves as, *see* ethnic identity; inferiority of slaves, supposed, ethnocentrism; sources of slaves, geography
fortune, slavery to   198–200
foundlings, *see* exposure

Free the Slaves   219
free versus slave labor   52–4, 59–61
freedmen and freedwomen, *see* ex-slaves; imperial slaves, *see familia Caesaris*
fugitivarius, see slave catchers
fugitive slaves   44, 141, 145, 147–51, 156; *see also* slave catchers

g

Galen (medical writer, ca. 129–216 CE)   142, 146
Gaul, Gallic   9, 47, 93, 161, 163, 164, 170, 175, 181
gender studies   81; *see also* marriage; prostitution; rape and coerced sex; sex ratio; women slaves
Genovese, Eugene   89, 143n, 155, 169, 170, 172, 190
German   13, 46, 152, 168, 219
Getae   86
gladiators   97, 147, 151–2, 155, 163, 204
gossip   92, 143–4, *182*
Gracchus, Tiberius (Roman populist statesman, ca. 165–133 BCE)   57–8, 169
Grand Chamberlain   80–1
grave reliefs and monuments   62, 64, 65, 113, 118, 130, 132, 133, 149, 177–8; *see also* epitaphs
Greco-Roman culture   2–3, 92–8, 180
Greek
  history (outline)   3–7
  influence on Roman culture   92–7
Greek slaves at Rome   92–7
Gregory of Nyssa   201n
Gregory the Great (Pope from 590–604 CE)   214
groom, *see* work, slave

h

Hammurabi, code of   5
Hannibal   10, 161, 185
Hecuba   175, 176
Hegeso, grave relief of   *178*
hektemoroi   71
Hellenistic Kingdoms
  formation of   7, 93
  slavery in   15, 32, 148–50
  see also Egypt, Hellenistic; *paramonē*; Delphi
Helots   51, 74–5, 172
  in Messenia   60, 71, 157–9, 171, 172
  rebellious   156, 157–60, 171
  serfs or slaves   18, 19–20, 51, 71, 160–1

herdsman, *see* work, slave
Hermeros   134
Herodotus (Greek historian of Persian Wars, ca. 484–425 BCE)   39
Hesiod (Greek poet, ca. 700 BCE?)   72
hetaira (-ai)   100, 101, 102, 103–5, 109, 115, 121
Hippocrates   177
home-born slaves   34, 36, 187; *see also* family, slave; children, slave
Homer (epic poet, ca. 700 BCE?)   2, 5, 6, 18, 31, 36, 72, 88, 94, 95, 176, 187
homoioi   159
honor   17, 19, 72–3
Hopkins, Keith   55–9, 65, 81, 82, 114, 135,
Horace (Roman poet, 65–8 BCE)   92, 101n, 132, 155n
horses   24–5
household slaves
  attitudes towards   141, 186, 189; *see also* paternalism
  conditions of life   1, 27, 89, 90, 95, 107, 115, 122, 140, 142, 147, 180, 188, 199
  extent of use   7, 15, 23, 43, 51–2, 89, 175, 210, 220
  sex ratio   37, 45
Hunt, Peter   74–5, 82, 86, 154, 160
hybridity   85, 88, 89, 92, 95
Hyperides (Athenian statesman and author of law court speeches, ca. 390–322 BCE)   63, 127

i

imperial bureaucracy, slaves and ex-slaves in   75–80; *see also* eunuchs; *familia Caesaris*
incentives, for slaves   52–3, 74, 121–2, 113, 120, 139, 140, 145, 146, 170
inferiority of slaves, denied   175–6, 191, 198–9; *see also* loyalty
inferiority of slaves, supposed
  the body   196–7
  cowardice   74, 97, 174, 176–7
  ethnocentrism   6, 73, 83, 87, 97, 126, 153, 174, 177, 179–80, *182*, 191, 195, 197, 207, 210, 216
  food, drink, and sex   182–3
  militarism   63, 176–7, 194–5
  work   179
  see also body, slaves associated with; natural slavery, Aristotle's theory of
inheritance   105, 107, 111, 113, 124, 125, 129, 145

inscriptions
  manumission   22, 26, 55, 100–1, 106–7, 114, 116, 118, 135,
  other   4, 36, 37–*38*, 59, 79, 87–8, 90, 109, 120, 133, 147, 159, 203
  see also epitaphs
intellectual, *see* work, slave
Ismard, Paulin   73–4
Ithome   158
ius gentium   77, 191, 203

j

Jacobs, Harriet   141
Jamaica   157
jeweler, *see* work, slave
Johnson, Samuel   168
Julian (Roman Emperor, 331–363 CE)   81
Justinian (Byzantine emperor who oversaw collections of Roman laws, ca. 482–565)   80, 191
Juvenal (Roman satirist, early second century CE)   83, 93, 96, 206

k

Kennedy, President John F.   219
kidnapping   46
Kleomantis   106–7

l

Laconia   71, 157–8, 160; *see also* Sparta
Laertius, Diogenes (writer of biographies of philosophers, ca. 3rd century CE)   197
language of slaves   91–2
Lares, Lararium   187, *188*, 189
Laurion   86, 88, 156; *see also* mining
laws about slaves   22, 33, 40, 46–7, 73, 77–8, 100, 106, 107n, 109–10, 113, 115, 121, 122, 125, 128–9, 130, 132, 142, 148, 150, 151, 153, 191–2, 198, 208, 213
  amelioration of slavery   203–6
  early   5, 9
  indirect interpretations   106, 148, 150, 151, 191–2
  lack of legal standing   206; *see also* torture
  legacy   2, 210, 218–19
  slaves as property   17–18, 25, 64, 100, 112, 121, 133, 143
legacy of classical slavery, *see* Code Noir; New World slavery; South, antebellum United States
Lesis   137–8
Leuctra   159
liberti ingrati (ungrateful ex-slaves)   129

libertination   129, 134
libertus (*-i*)   *see* ex-slave
lictor   122, 167
life expectancy   42
Life of Aesop (fictional biography of the slave Aesop, author of fables)   62, 106, 112, 141–2
linear B tablets, slaves in   4
literacy   21
litter bearers, *see* work, slave
loyalty, of slaves   173, 176, 180, 187–9, 190
luxury
  condemnation of   200
  slaves as   10, 55, 145, 200, 214
Lysias (metic at Athens and writer of law court speeches, ca. 450–380 BCE)   103–4, 123, 147

m

Macedo, Larcius   152, 189
Macedonia   2, 4, 5, 7, 8, 10, 51, 93, 96, 97, 127
Macrones   83
malingering   142
Malthus, Thomas   54
manacles, *see* chains
managers
  farm (*vilicus, -a*)   141, 142, 145, 146, 147, 148, 170
  slaves as   46–7, 76, 88, 113, 125
manumission   9, 43–4, 95–96, 118–24
  consequences   123–4
  for marriage   109–10
  process and ritual   122
  purchase   121–2
  rate   118–20
  reasons   120–2
  Roman versus Greek   134
  testamentary   122
  see also ex-slaves; *paramonē*
manumissio per vindictam   122
Marius, Gaius   96
markets
  for products of slave labor   57, 59, 72, 214
  slave   33, 62–3
maroon   156–7, 172
marriage   86
  between slaves   111–15 passim
  of *familia Caesaris*   77–8
  see also manumission, for marriage
Marx, Karl and Marxist history   2, 48, 50–1, 68, 208, 209, 212–15, 219
mask, comic slave   *182*
masseur/masseuse, *see* work, slave

material evidence, *see* archaeology
Maximian   204
Maximus, Valerius   187
McCarthy, Senator Joseph   219
meat carver, *see* work, slave
Melania the Younger   213
Melos   36
Menander (Athenian writer of comic dramas, ca. 344–291 BCE)   86, 108, 109, 146n, 180
messenger, *see* work, slave
Messenia, *see* Helots
metalwork, *see* work, slave
Metaneira   104
metaphor of slavery   2, 192–3
metic   14, 121, 123, 124, 134
militarism, *see* inferiority of slaves, supposed
military service of slaves   10, 74–5, 160
mines, mining   29, 36, 53, 61, 85, 89, 90, 117, 156, 163
mirror holder, *see* work, slave
mistress, slave or ex-slave   104–5; *see also hetaira*
modern slavery   219–20
Morris, Ian   38, 85–6, 98
Moschion   143
Mouritsen, Henrik   119–20, 128, 130, 135
mule driver, *see* work, slave
murder
  of masters   152–3
  of slaves   204–5
Muslim   210, 214, 215
Mycenaean Civilization   3–4

n

names   31, 86, 88–9, 94, 129, 133–4, 179–80
natal alienation   17, 19, 81, 100, 112, 113–14, 123, 161, 207, 220
natural reproduction, *see* reproduction
natural slavery, theory of, *see* Aristotle
Naupactus   158
navy, slaves in, *see* military service of slaves
Neaira   103–5, 115, 116, 127
negotiations, versus conflict   140
Nero (Roman emperor, 37–68 CE)   3, 78, 79, 128, 153, 198
New Testament, *see* Christianity
New World   20, 28, 31, 34, 35, 39, 41, 48, 53–6 passim, 64, 89, 90, 91, 92n, 139, 149, 151, 160, 165n, 172, 174, 186, 215
  legacy of classical slavery   2, 210, 215, 216–18
  see also Brazil; Caribbean; South, antebellum United States
Nicomedes, king of Bithynia   93

Nietzsche, Friedrich   2
Nikarete   103–4
Nike statue   159
nomenclator, see work, slave
nomos versus *phusis*   194
novel
   Greek romance   108, 109, 179
   see also Apuleius; Petronius
noxal surrender   218
numbers of slaves, *see* population, slave
nurses, *see* work, slave

O
Oiketēs   186
Oinokles Painter   *144*
old slaveholders   143
oligarchy, Greek   71–2
Olympiodorus   104
open versus closed slave systems   9–10, 123–4
the Other, slaves as   67–8, 73, 174, 177; *see also* dichotomy

P
Paeonius   159
Pallas   78, 79, 80, 117
papyrus (-i), evidence on   3, 7, 21, 22, 43, 59–60, 63, 108, 112, 114, 143, 148–9, 150
paramonē   20, 106–7, 116, 124, 135
Parker, Holt   183
Pasicles **125**
Pasion   88, 124–6, 135
pastoral slaves, *see* herdsmen
paterfamilias   183, 187, 188, 189, 206
paternalism   63–4, 129, 175, 180, 186–9, 190, 217
patronage
   of ex-slaves   128–30
   little at Athens   70
   at Rome   124
Patterson, Orlando (sociologist of slavery; b. 1940)   29, 62, 133, 172
   definition of slavery   17–19, 123, 161; *see also* natal alienation
   materialistic freedmen?   133
   slave stereotype   97
   slavery and honor   72–3
   Western ideal of freedom   193
Pausanias   159
peasants   91, 160–1
   definition   68–9
   dependent or bound   40, 212–13, 215
   displacement of Italian   56–9
   mode of production   213–14
   versus agricultural slavery   7, 14, 15, 43, 51–2, 54, 60–1, 65, 68–9, 70–1, 169, 214
   see also coloni; debt bondage; displacement of Italian peasants; *hektemoroi*; serfs
peculium, see property of slaves
Peel, Mr.   54
Peloponnesian War   4, 7, 75, 148, 157, 158–9, 192
periods
   of Greek history   **4**
   of Roman History   **11**
Persian Wars   6, 37, 74, 160, 177
Petronius (Roman senator and author of the Satyricon, dies in 66 CE)   64, 108–9, 117, 128–34, 144
Phaedo of Ellis   101
Phaedrus (writer of fables)   141
philosophy   191, 193–201
   see also anonymous opponents of Aristotle; Aristotle; Epictetus; Plato; Seneca; Stoicism
Phoenicia   5, 9, 84, 88–9, 161, 184
Phormio   125–7
Phrygia   38, 86, 90, 99, 180
pilleus   122, 184, *193*
piracy   46
Piraeus   85, 87, 126, 127
Pius, Antoninus (Roman emperor, 86–161 CE)   204, 205, 206
Plataea   160
Plato (Athenian philosopher, ca. 429–347)   101, *102*, 126, 147, 157, 173, 176, 177, 186, 192, 194, 195, 208
Plautus (Roman writer of comic dramas produced between ca. 205–184)   93, 174, 180
   The Captives   112n
   Casket Comedy   185
   Epidicus   183, 185
   The Ghost   110
   Pseudolus   181–6, 188n, 190
   Two Bacchises   185
Pliny (Roman senator and intellectual, ca. 61–112 CE)
   indignant at honors for ex-slave   79
   on the murder of a master   152–4
   paternalistic   186–7, 189
Plutarch (Roman biographer and intellectual, ca. 46–120 CE)   58, 163, 164
pneuma   199
poison   104
police   74
polis (*poleis*), *see* city-state, Greek
Polybius (imperial freedman)   78–9
Pompeii   100–1, 109, 116, 120, *188*

Pompey 46, 164
population, slave
  Athens 60
  Italy 59
  Roman Empire 43
pornē (*pornai*) 103; *see also* prostitution
prejudice, *see* inferiority of slaves, supposed
prices, of slaves 21–2, 55, 59–61, 104, 106–7, 214
property, belonging to slaves 19, 102, 121–2, 145, 150, 188
property, slaves as, *see* laws about slaves
prostatēs, of an ex-slave 124
prostitution 87, 100–5, 108, 110, 115, 116, 128, 149, 181, 182, 184, 204n, 220
Ptolemaic Egypt, *see* Egypt
public slaves
  at Athens 73–4
  see also familia Caesaris
Punic War, Second 10, 93, 161
punishments 146–7, 150, 183–5; *see also* chains; shaved head; torture; violence; whipping
Pylos 3, 4, 158

q
quarters, slave 24, 58, 89, 102, 144, 175

r
racism 28, 35, 53, 73, 98, 174, 177, 209–10, 215, 217–18; *see also* ethnocentrism inferiority of slaves, supposed
ransom, for captives instead of enslavement 6, 37, 46, 176
rape and coerced sex 106–9, 115, 155
Reagan, President Ronald 219
rebellion, *see* revolts
religion 167, 168, 206, 215
  pagan 26–7
  of slaves 87–8, 90, 91, 98
  see also Christianity
rental, of slaves 101, 102, 104, *105*, 138
reproduction, of slaves 33–5, 40, 44–6
resistance, slave 12, 15, 85, 91–2, 121, 137–54, 169n, 170, 189, 220
  every day 140–4
  extent 145
  theoretical issues 137–40
  see also embezzlement; fugitive slaves; gossip; malingering; murder of masters; theft; wandering
revolts 155–72
  factors 168–71
  Greece 156–7
  Helot 157–61
  New World 155, 157, 163, 165n, 169, 172
  Roman Italy and Sicily 161–72, 184–5, 206
rewards
  for return of fugitive slaves 3, 148, *203*
  for slaves, *see* incentives, for slaves
rich men, *see* wealthy men
Richlin, Amy 184
ring, right of gold 132
Roman army 56, 76, 166, 168
Roman comedy 180–6; *see also* Plautus; Terence
Roman law, *see* laws about slaves
Rome
  ambivalence towards Greece 96–7
  expansion of 9–10
  government of 11, 12–13
  Republic to Empire 12
  see also disintegration of the Western Roman Empire
runaway slaves, *see* fugitive slaves

s
sabotage 25, 53, 143
sale of slaves 19, 21, 104, 161, 175
  apart or as punishment 63, 99, 100, 107, 109, 112–16 *passim*, 147, 175, 204n
  to gladiatorial schools, animal shows, or mines 204
  see also enslavement; markets, slave; prices, of slaves; self-sale; trade, slave
Sallust (Roman historian and senator, ca. 86–35 BCE) 162–3, 166
sanctuaries, slave 205–6
Saturnalia 184, 187
Scheidel, Walter 42–7, 53, 59–61
Scythian archers 74
Secundus, Pedanius 153
self-sale into slavery 46–7
senate, Roman 10, 11, 12, 13, 77, 79, 94, 153, 164, 193
Senatus Consultum Silanianum 153, 189, 206
Seneca (Roman senator, advisor to Nero, and philosopher, ca. 4 BCE–65 CE) 3, 145, 173, 201, 207
  attitudes towards imperial freedmen 78–9
  on gladiator's suicide 152
  Stoic views on slavery 191, 192, 198–200, 206
serfs
  similar classes in classical world 14, 18, 51, 60, 61, 69, 71, 74, 160–1, 171

212, 213, 214, 215; *see also* helots
transition to medieval? 2, 13, 20, 40, 212–15
sex life of slaves 101–2, 111–12; *see also* marriage; rape and coerced sex
sex ratio 34–5, 37, 44–5, 101–2
sexual abuse of slaves, *see* rape and coerced sex
shackles, *see* chains
sharecroppers 43, 54, 56, 61, 70–1, 161, 214
shaved head 150
shepherds, *see* herdsmen
Sicily, slave revolts in Roman 161–72
sick slaves 205; *see also* malingering
silentarius, *see* work, slave
Sinclair, Upton 201
slave catchers 150, 164
slave society 13, 20, 50–2, 210
slaveholder tactics 145–7
Smith, Adam (economist and philosopher, 1723–1790 CE) 49, 52
social death, *see* Patterson, Orlando
Solon (Athenian legal and social reformer, archon in 594/3 BCE) 11, 39, 70–2, 82
Sophocles (Athenian writer of tragedies, ca. 495–405 BCE) 99, 175, 176
Sounion 117, 123, 156
sources of slaves, *see* enslavement
South, antebellum United States
  legacy of classical slavery 2, 28, 209, 216, 217–18, 220
  as slave society 1, 20, 50
  slavery in 26, 35, 45, 52, 53, 63, 73, 82, 89, 90, 95, 100, 114, 120, 143, 155, 169, 179, 185, 186, 190, 207
Sparta 7, 63 *see also* Helots
Spartacus 2, 52, 152, 154, 155, 156, 161–72, 190, 219
Statius (Roman poet, ca. 45–96 CE) 78
status symbols, slaves as 55
Ste. Croix, G. E. M. de 50–1, 213
stealing, *see* theft, by slaves
Stephanos 104–5
stereotypes of slaves 97, 174–80; *see also* inferiority of slaves, supposed
Stoicism 3, 93, 152, 191, 192, 197–201, 202, 203, 206, 207, 208, 217
Straus, Jean 114
subversive reading of Roman comedy 182–6
suicide, by slaves 64, 151–2
supply, slave, *see* enslavement
Swan River Colony 54
Symmachus 151–2

Symposium 101, *102*, 103
Syracuse, revolt at 156
Syria 31, 83, 92, 210, 212
"Syrians" 164, 167, 169, 170

t

Tacitus (Roman historian, ca. 56–118 CE) 2, 67, 83, 85, 91, 129, 153, 155, 169, 187
tattoos 150, 179
taxes 21–2
teacher, *see* work, slave
tenant farmers 51, 58, 69, 189, 214
Terence (Roman comic playwright, 195–159 BCE) 22, 93, 180n, 185, 188n
Thalmann, William 179, 186n, 190
Thebes 159, 160
theft, by slaves 140, 142–3, 148
Theognis 179
Theophrastus (Greek philosopher, ca. 372–286 BCE) 109, 142, 148, 151
Theopompus (Greek historian, ca. 378–319 BCE) 6, 38
Thera 213
Thrace 31, 36, 37, 39, 84, 86–7, 88, 91, 164, 170, 179
Thucydides (Athenian historian of the Peloponnesian War, ca. 460–400 BCE) 7
time off, for slaves 90
Timothea 34
Tiro (freedman of Cicero, 1st century BCE) 119, 173, 187
tombs and tombstones, of ex-slaves, *see* grave reliefs and monuments; epitaphs; Eurysaces
torture of slaves 97, 104, 143, 147, 153, 155, 165, 185, 187, 196, 206
trade, slave 39, 61–5, 214–15
tragedy, Greek 175–7; *see also* Euripides; Sophocles
Trajan 47, column of 61
Treggiari, Susan 94, 98, 110, 111, 116
trickster 84–5
Trimalchio 128–34
Troy, Trojan 36, 86–8, 93, 175–6, 199
Trumbo, Dalton 219
Turner, Nat 155, 163, 185
tutor, *see* teachers
Twelve Tables 9
Tyndarus 186
typicality, problem of 25–6
Tyrtaeus 158

u

urbanization 50, 57

V

Varro (agricultural and architectural writer, 116–27 BCE) 41, 45n, 52, 143, 145, 169
vase paintings of slaves 93, *102*, 102–3, *144*, 177–9, 190
Vedius Pollio (wealthy Roman, 1st century BCE) 26
Vegetius (Roman writer on military matters and veterinary medicine, 4th or 5th century CE) 24–5
verna (-ae), *see* home-born slaves
vilicus or *-a*, *see* manager, farm
villa, Roman 58–9
violence of slavery 19, 63–4, 108, 140, 145–7, 170, 183–4, 189, 194–5, 205, 206; *see also* murder, of slaves
Virgil (Roman poet, 70–19 BCE) 95, 96–7
volones 10
Voltaire 172, 219

W

wages and wage labor 52, 54, 59–61, 68, 75, 121, 215
wandering slave 64, 142, 145, 147, 151, 190
wanted posters 148–9, *149*
war
  see enslavement
  see also militarism; inferiority of slaves, supposed
Watson, Alan 218–19
wealthy men
  acquiesce in Athenian democracy 69, 72
  depend on slave labor 15, 20, 50–2, 56–8, 61, 72, 195, 201, 206, 207, 213
  writers and readers of most classical literature 22–3, 141, 197, 201
"weapons of the weak" 141–2
Weaver, P. R. C. 77, 82
weaving, *see* work, slave
whipping 18, 53, 132, 141, 146, 147, 150, 184, 194; *see also* punishment
Wickham, Chris 213, 220
Wiles, David 182, 183
wills, *see* inheritance
Williams, Bernard 195–6, 200, 208
women slaves 2, 3, 4, *5*, 33, *34*, 35, 36, 37, 43, 44–5, 57, 64, 77–8, 86, 87, 99–116 *passim*, 118, 120, 122–3, 135, 148–9, 171, 175–6, 177, 178, 179, 190, 214; *see also* family; marriage; prostitution; rape and coerced sex; sex ratio

woodworking, *see* work, slave
work, slave 85, 121–2, 128, 130–1, 145, 196
  accountant 76, 77, 78, 133
  banker 84, 118, 124, 126, 196, 220
  barber 131
  bureaucrat 196; *see also familia Caesaris*; public slaves at Athens Caesaris
  construction 53, 59, 121
  cook 109, 141, 151, 199
  craftsman 51, 53, 61, 85, 126, 157, 179, 196
  doorkeeper 90, 121, 131
  flute player 102
  groom 24–5, 53, 143
  hairdresser 55, 121
  herdsman 58, 120, 165, 168–9, 171
  intellectual 84, 92–4, 98
  jeweler 53, 55
  litter bearers 55, 121
  masseur/masseuse 55, 131
  meat carver 130, 131
  messenger 121, 122, 131
  metalwork 137–8
  mirror holder 128
  mule driver 131
  nomenclator 55, 128
  nurses 112, 114, 122, 175
  silentarius 145
  skilled 53, 85, 157, 196–7
  teacher 18, 94, 98
  weaving 45, 57, 177
  woodworking 100–1, 102–3
  see also agriculture, slaves in; *hetaira*; household slaves; managers, farm; managers, slaves as; mines, mining; prostitution

X

Xenocles 138
Xenophon (Athenian mercenary officer and intellectual, ca. 430–354 BCE)
  on abandoning children 63, 111
  and Macronian ex-slave 83
  on managing slaves 51, 102, 142, 145, 146, 147
  on resentment towards Spartans 160
  on slaving raid 39
  (pseudo-)Xenophon 177

Z

Zeno of Citium 197, 198, 200